FOCUS

ON COLLEGE AND CAREER SUCCESS

Constance Staley
University of Colorado, Colorado Springs

Steve Staley
Colorado Technical University

WADSWORTH
CENGAGE Learning™

Australia • Brazil • Japan • Korea • Mexico • Singapore • Spain • United Kingdom • United States

WADSWORTH
CENGAGE Learning™

FOCUS on College and Career Success
Constance Staley and Steve Staley

Senior Publisher: Lyn Uhl

Director of College Success and Developmental
English: Annie Todd

Development Editor: Marita Sermolins

Assistant Editor: Melanie Opacki

Media Editor: Amy Gibbons

Senior Marketing Manager: Kirsten Stoller

Marketing Coordinator: Ryan Ahern

Marketing Communications Manager:
Courtney Morris

Content Project Manager: Jessica Rasile

Senior Art Director: Pam Galbreath

Print Buyer: Julio Esperas

Senior Rights Acquisition Account Manager—
Images: Jennifer Meyer Dare

Senior Rights Acquisition Account Manager—
Text: Katie Huha

Production Service: Lachina Publishing Services

Text Designer: Susan Gilday

Photo Researcher: Josh Brown/Pre-PressPMG

Cover Designer: George Restrepo

Compositor: Lachina Publishing Services

Cover images, from left to right:
 Business man: © Andresr/Shutterstock.com
 Chef: © George Doyle & Ciaran Griffin/
   PhotoLibrary
 IT guy: © Purestock/Alamy
 Fashion Designer: © Radius Images/Alamy
 Kia Washington/Charmaine: Larry Harwood
   Photography
 Architect: © Edyta Pawlowska/Shutterstock
   .com
 Police officer: © BlueMoon Stock/Alamy

Library of Congress Control Number: 2010940900

ISBN-13: 978-1-4390-8390-1

ISBN-10: 1-4390-8390-8

Wadsworth
20 Channel Center Street
Boston, MA 02210
USA

Cengage Learning is a leading provider of customized learning solutions
with office locations around the globe, including Singapore, the United
Kingdom, Australia, Mexico, Brazil and Japan. Locate your local office at
international.cengage.com/region

Cengage Learning products are represented in Canada by Nelson Education, Ltd.

For your course and learning solutions, visit **www.cengage.com**

Purchase any of our products at your local college store or at our preferred
online store **www.cengagebrain.com**.

Printed in the United States of America
2 3 4 5 6 7 14 13 12 11

Brief Contents

Contents

chapter 1

Getting the Right Start   1

chapter 2

Building Dreams, Setting Goals   25

chapter 3 — Learning about Learning — 47

chapter 4 — Managing Your Time, Energy, and Money — 73

chapter 5 — Thinking Critically and Creatively — 103

chapter 6 — Developing Technology, Research, and Information Literacy Skills — 127

chapter 7 — Engaging, Listening, and Note-Taking in Class — 155

chapter 8 Developing Your Memory   185

chapter 9 Reading and Studying   207

chapter 10 Taking Tests 235

chapter 11 Building Relationships, Valuing Diversity 263

chapter 12   Assessing Your College Major and Career   295

chapter 13   Creating Your Future   313

Acknowledgments

It's been said that "Achievement is a *we* thing, not a *me* thing, always the product of many heads and hands." Certainly that's true of the monumental effort involved in writing a first edition textbook. There are so many people to thank that this acknowledgments section could be as long as a chapter of *FOCUS on College and Career Success*! However, here we'll at least mention those who have contributed the most, including all the students and colleagues over the last 30-plus years who have taught us more than we've ever taught them.

Family   Let us start at the center of our lives. Our daughters Shannon and Stephanie helped bring some much-needed balance to our lives. And aside from being the most adorable children on the planet, our grandtwins Aidan and Ailie have been a living learning laboratory for us. As children mastering one new thing after another, they truly have taught us about of the pure joy of learning. And to our beautiful 80-something mothers, Elizabeth and Evelyn, who lovingly alternated between urging us to "slow down and relax" and "hurry up and finish," heartfelt thanks to you both for all your motherly love.

Reviewers   The list of reviewers who have contributed their insights and expertise to *FOCUS on College and Career Success* is long. Starting any new edition from scratch requires substantial input. And our heartfelt thanks to the reviewers who provided valuable input to help shape this book: Craig Baranovic, Remington College; Virginia Ann Berent, Gallipolis Career College; James Booker, Remington College; Jennifer Cooper, The Art Institute of Pittsburgh Online Division; Angelina Dale, Goodwin College; Annette Davis, Madison College; Mominka Fileva, Davenport University; Andrea Goldstein, South University; Evelyn Hyde, Brown Mackie College-Salina; Laura Ristrom Goodman, Pima Medical Institute; Kevin Kelly, Andover College; Forrest Marston, Sanford Brown Institute Tampa; Gurmeet Mohem, Heald College; Kelley Montford, Colorado Technical University; Katrina Neckuty-Fodness, Globe University; Debra Olsen, Madison Area Technical College; Vickie Saling, Heald College; John Smith, Corinthian Colleges, Inc; Kristen Smith, Hallmark College; Camilla Swain-LeDoux, Ivy Tech Community College, Evansville; Cynthia Vessel, Northwestern College; Pamela Walker, Northwestern College; Pamela White, Springfield Technical Community College.

The Wadsworth Team   No book, of course, gets very far without a publisher, and *FOCUS* has had the best publishing team imaginable: the dynamic, highly people-skilled Annie Todd, Director of College Success; the meticulous, multi-talented Marita Sermolins, Development Editor; the energetic, industrious Kirsten Stoller, Marketing Manager; a true professional who combed the first pages and probably did more than we'll ever know, Jessica Rasile, Content Project Manager; and the staff at Lachina Publishing Services. We'd like to especially thank Larry Harwood, the master photographer who spent a long, hard weekend clicking photos of the *FOCUS* cast on the University of Colorado at Colorado Springs campus. And heartfelt thanks to Wadsworth's Annie Mitchell and Sean Wakely, who believed in this project from the very start; Sylvia Shepherd, whose creative vision shaped much of this book, and Lauren Larsen, whose wit and wisdom formed the basis for several of the early chapters.

Other Contributors   We'd also particularly like to thank the "*FOCUS* All-Stars," as we call them, who modeled for the photo shoots and starred in the "Inside the *FOCUS* Studio" videos. They followed artistic direction like pros, and they make this book unique. We also can't go without thanking the many authors who granted us permission to use their work and three essential scholars who allowed us to use, apply, and extend their instruments throughout the book: Neil Fleming, Brian French, and John Bransford. And thanks to our expert student research assistants; to John Cowles and Ric Undershile, our expert Instructor's Resource Manual co-authors; and to Aren Moore, who worked with us to create the "props" for each chapter's opening case study, and the dynamic, ground-breaking, multimedia FOCUSpoints for each chapter. And finally, we'd like to thank Matt McClain, the comedy writer who brought his innovative humor to the learning process through podcast summaries of the chapters and television scripts for the website TV shows. He took the "big ideas" from *FOCUS* chapters and made them memorable to students by using their own best-loved media.

Above all, *FOCUS* has taught us truly to focus. Writing a book takes the same kind of endurance and determination that it takes to get a college degree. Our empathy level for our students has, if anything, increased—and we are thankful for all we've learned while writing. It has been a cathartic experience to see what has filled each computer screen as we've tapped, tapped, tapped away. Ultimately, what we have chosen to put into each chapter has told us a great deal about who we are, what we know (and don't), and what we value. There's no doubt: we are better teachers for having written this book. May all our readers grow through their *FOCUS* experience, too.

Meet the Cast

©Larry Harwood Photography. Property of Cengage Learning.

Chapter 1: Darnell Williams / Calil

Hometown: Colorado Springs, Colorado

Major: History with a secondary education emphasis

Lessons Learned: Calil noticed many similarities between himself and the FOCUS Challenge Case character he portrayed, besides playing football and watching movies. Calil, too, had problems with the transition from high school to college. He admits he was a student who "coasted" through his senior year of high school, which made his first year of college more difficult.

Toughest First-Year Class: English, like Darnell, because he wasn't fully aware of the instructor's expectations.

Advice to New Students: "Determination is the key to success. If you are determined, there is nothing in the world that can stop you."

©Larry Harwood Photography. Property of Cengage Learning.

Chapter 2: Gloria Gonzales / Debbie

Hometown: Saguache, Colorado

Major: Business with a minor in Communication

Lessons Learned: Debbie learned through her first-year seminar course that it takes time and effort to establish great relationships. She got involved in intramural sports, which helped her meet new people and make friends. Although she's doing well now, she wishes she'd studied more her first term.

Toughest First-Year Class: Microeconomics because it was an entirely new subject for her.

Advice to New Students: "Get your priorities straight; college is a great place to be, so get a great start by setting good study habits, and I HIGHLY recommend a planner because you will be surprised at how fast your time can become occupied."

Chapter 10: Joe Cloud / Alvin

Hometown: Ganado, Arizona (Navajo Nation)

Major: Business

Toughest First-Year Course: Spanish because he comes from a place where no other languages are ever spoken.

Lessons Learned: President of the American Indian Science and Engineering Society on campus, Alvin identifies closely with his *FOCUS* Challenge Case character. He, too, is one of a minority of Native Americans in higher education, so a lot of people in his hometown are carefully watching his academic success. Alvin admits his biggest mistake in his first term was not opening up to people—he came to school for class and left without trying to meet new people. But he learned from his mistakes and eventually came to value meeting all sorts of different people through activities on campus.

Advice to New Students: "Learn from *my* mistakes: Be open to try new things, get out of your comfort zone, and be free to be silly—everyone is at some point. You meet a lot of new people that way and it makes your first year the experience of a lifetime."

Chapter 11: Kia Washington / Charmaine

Hometown: Colorado Springs, Colorado

Major: Psychology and Sociology

Toughest First-Year Course: General psychology because there was so much to learn in such a short period of time.

Lessons Learned: Charmaine learned how to manage her time more effectively, as well as the necessity of keeping yourself healthy in mind, body, and spirit, something she felt her *FOCUS* Challenge Case character could have benefited from.

Advice to New Students: "Remember to have fun in everything that you do, both academically and otherwise. Take care of yourself first and don't feel as though you have to do everything all the time; sometimes the best parts of life come during moments of down time. This is where you are able to truly reflect on what it is you're doing and remember why you're doing it in the first place!"

Chapter 3: Tammy Ko / Jessica

Hometown: Manitou Springs, Colorado

Major: Marketing

Lessons Learned: Juggling a part-time job while in school, Jessica loved meeting new people, but she regretted not talking to other students about which instructors and courses to take towards her marketing major. In order to succeed, she says, you've "gotta give it all you've got!"

Toughest First-Year Class: Microeconomics because it wasn't like high school courses that just required memorizing a lot of facts.

Advice to New Students: "Talk to other students to learn about the best instructors, and make sure you are studying something that you are interested in."

Chapter 4: Derek Johnson / Derrick

Hometown: Colorado Springs, Colorado

Major: Communications/Recording Arts

Lessons Learned: Even though he's not married and has no children, Derrick and his case study character have much in common—too much to do and too little time! Derrick felt his biggest mistake in college was not asking enough questions in class. He knows now he should ask for clarity on content or assignments he doesn't understand.

Toughest First-Year Class: English because he and his instructor had differing opinions, but they communicated through the tough spots and earned an "A".

Advice to New Students: "Surround yourself with positive people. As the saying goes, 'you are the company you keep.' I've seen many of my friends drop out because the people they called friends were holding them back from their full potential."

Free Time: composing music and producing films

Chapter 5: Desiree Moore / Regina

Hometown: Colorado Springs, Colorado

Major: M.A. Communication

Lessons Learned: Organization, time management, study groups, and note cards.

Toughest First-Year Course: Psychology because in this class I had to be very organized to keep my notes in order. There were only two exams in this class during the entire semester. I did not organize my notes or my time very well.

Advice to New Students: "Get to know your professors, ask questions, and have a study buddy."

Free Time: In my free time, I work out at the gym. I also spend quality time with my son.

Chapter 6: Dario Jones / Orlando

Hometown: Fountain, Colorado

Major: MA, Communication

Lessons Learned: Start strong, work hard, and finish strong

Toughest First-Year Course: Math 099

Advice to New Students: "Get to know your instructors and fellow classmates. Ask questions in class when you're not sure about something."

Free Time: What free time? To relax, I listen to jazz or classical music, or I'll channel surf until I find something interesting to watch.

Chapter 7: Rachel White / Shannon

Hometown: Denver, Colorado

Major: Philosophy

Lessons Learned: Go to class!

Toughest First-Year Course: Intro to Geography (it might have been easier if I'd gone to class)

Advice to New Students: "Balance fun and schoolwork, so you don't get burned out on either one!"

Free Time: Acting and improv

Chapter 8: Kevin Baxter / Dave

Hometown: St. Paul, Minnesota

Background: Portraying a student returning to school after fif[...] in the working world, Dave is currently a professor of chemist[...] of Colorado at Colorado Springs.

College Memories: Dave remembers how much he liked the dif[...] environment college provided after graduating from high schoo[...]

Toughest First-Year Course: English Composition since writing [...] his forte.

Advice to New Students: "Study hard, and use your time wisely."

Free Time: woodworking, hiking, and climbing

Chapter 9: Katie Alexander / Chris[...]

Hometown: Colorado Springs, Colorado. Since she went to college [...] hometown, Christina really enjoyed the opportunity college provid[...] new people.

Major: Nursing

Lessons Learned: Spending her free time with her friends watching [...] going bowling or dancing, and just hanging out, Christina found tha[...] FOCUS Challenge Case character, she, too, would make up excuses [...] of studying and doing her homework. She quickly learned the impor[...] reading and taking notes. "As weird as it may sound, reading cuts yo[...] study time by more than half. Reading the material ahead of time hel[...] understand everything so much better."

Advice to New Students: "Stay motivated. College is going to FLY by! [...] stay motivated and get good grades, it really will be over before you k[...]

Chapter 12: Ethan Cole / Josh

Hometown: Fort Morgan, Colorado

Major: Sociology

Lessons Learned: Like his *FOCUS* Challenge Case character, Josh noticed that he, too, didn't always push himself to reach his potential. But he learned through his first-year seminar course that he is responsible for himself and that instructors aren't like high school teachers. They will let you fail a class if you don't do what you need to. It's up to you.

Advice to New Students: "Not only did getting involved on campus help me have more fun in school, but it has also helped me academically. It has taught me how to manage my time and has made it so much easier for me to participate with confidence in class. Just make sure you get what you need to do done, and you will enjoy your college experience so much more."

Free Time: "Free time? What's that?! I'm too busy to have free time!" (But he secretly admits he snowboards, plays guitar, draws, and spends time with friends.)

Chapter 13: Anthony Lopez / Luis

Hometown: Aguascalientes, Mexico

Major: Spanish with an emphasis on secondary education

Lessons Learned: Luis is extremely involved on campus and within his community—he is President of the Association of Future Teachers, sings with his church choir, plays intramural soccer, and works for the Air Force on weekends. Luis thinks one mistake he made in his first term was that he procrastinated with homework because his new freedom let him think he could have fun first and study later, but he quickly learned he was wrong.

Advice to New Students: "Be smart and be involved, but always do your homework first. If you are involved on campus, you will meet people that will help make your college experience easier and more fun."

MEET THE AUTHOR: Constance Staley

Hometown: Pittsburgh, Pennsylvania (although she never actually lived there. Instead, she lived all over the world and went to ten schools in twelve years.)

Background: Connie has taught at the University of Colorado at Colorado Springs for more than 30 years after getting a bachelor's degree in education, a master's degree in linguistics, and a Ph.D. in communication.

College Memories: Connie remembers loving her public speaking class as a first-year student and having tons of friends, but being extremely homesick for her family.

Advice to New Students: "Earning a college degree is hard work, takes a long time, and requires a substantial investment of your time, energy, and resources. But it's the best investment you can make in your own future—one you'll never regret."

Free Time: Spending time with her husband, her two daughters, and her boy-girl grandtwins; relaxing at her cabin in the mountains; and traveling around the country to speak to other instructors who also care about their first-year students and their success.

MEET THE AUTHOR: Steve Staley

Hometowns: Watford City, North Dakota; then Seattle, Washington, for twelve school years; finally Colorado Springs, Colorado, off and on for the last 45 years.

Background: Following several years as an Air Force instructor pilot, Steve worked for a year in Thailand, and was an English professor at the Air Force Academy, a professor of strategy and policy at the Naval War College, a research fellow at the United Nations Peace Academy, and a Fulbright Fellow teaching in Kyrgyzstan.

College Memories: Steve remembers trying to balance studying and relaxing on busy weekends, attending football and basketball games, playing lacrosse, singing in the chorale, and being inspired by his favorite professors in psychology, history, and physics.

Advice to New Students: "Take it one day at a time—but plan ahead as you do. Work your calendar, but don't stress out over things coming up weeks and months ahead. Plan your work, and work your plan. Bottom line? Enjoy college. You'll look back on your classes, friendships, and instructors as some of the best memories you've built."

Free Time: Spending time reading, traveling with his wife, enjoying good times with his daughters and grandkids, fly-fishing in a wonderful little stream below his Rocky Mountain cabin, and talking about what makes great teaching and effective learning with college colleagues around the world.

Introduction to Students

Dear Reader,

This book is different. It won't coerce, coddle, caution, or coax you. Instead, it will give *you* the tools you need to coach yourself. Ultimately, this book is about you, your college career, and your career beyond college. It's about the future you will create for yourself.

FOCUS on College and Career Success stars a cast of my own students (several colleagues, and one of my daughters), like a stage play. One student "actor" is featured in each chapter's opening case study. All thirteen cast members reappear throughout the book, so that you'll get to know them as you read. I've been teaching for more than 30 years now and worked with thousands of students. Each case study is about a real student (with a fictitious name) that I've worked with or a mixture of several students. You may find you have some things in common with them. But whether you do or not, I hope they will make this book come to life for you. You'll also be able to meet these "actors" electronically in *FOCUS TV* videos on the book's CourseMate website.

I love what I do, and I care deeply about students. I hope that comes through to you as a reader. You'll see that I've inserted some of my personality, had a bit of fun at times, and tried to create a new kind of textbook for you. In my view, learning should be engaging, personal, memorable, challenging, and fun.

Most importantly, I know that these next few years hold the key to unlock much of what you want from your life. And from all my years of experience and research, I can tell you straightforwardly that what you read in this book works. It gets results. It can turn you into a better, faster learner. *Really?* you ask. Really! The only thing you have to do is put all the words in this book into action. That's where the challenge comes in.

Becoming an educated person takes time, energy, resources, and focus. At times, it may mean shutting down the six windows you have open on your computer, and directing all your attention to one thing in laser-like fashion. It may mean disciplining yourself to dig in and stick with something until you've nailed it. Can you do it? I'm betting you can, or I wouldn't have written this book. Invest yourself fully in what you read here, and then decide to incorporate it into your life. If there's one secret to college success, that's it.

So, you're off! You're about to begin one of the most fascinating, liberating, challenging, and adventure-filled times of your life. I may not be able to meet each one of you personally, but I *can* wish you well, wherever you are. I hope this book helps you on your journey.

Constance Staley

Answers to the back cover questions are 1) b; 2) d; 3) b; 4) a; 5) a.

Take a look at this poem, written by Jason Gaulden. He wrote this poem as he finished his associate's degree, and now he has an important job in an organization that provides scholarships, grants, and funding that make a difference in people's lives.

Passion in Action

By Jason Gaulden

There's no such thing as an answer
to a question that is not asked.
And there's no way to find yourself
until you take off the mask.
And get rid of all of those thoughts
about chasing your dreams.
And start having some thoughts
of catching every one of those things.

There's a world of opportunity
that is waiting for you.
But it's passion in action
that makes dreams come true.

It is by grace,
and by faith,
and by fate
that at this time,
at this place,
we've crossed paths.
This fork in the road is great
because this intersection
is a marketplace for life lessons.
You've seen things on your path
that I didn't see on mine.
I've seen things on my path
that you didn't see on yours.
These are my expressions of pain
and pleasure, risk and reward.
This is the formula that made me.
Just like your experiences made you.

Now, we're all on a journey
and we've all come a long way
but today is that day
that marks in a significant way
that what is behind you
is behind you.
In some ways that bind you
into a state of reminiscence and reflection.

A state of introspection.
That's a good place to visit
but you do not want to stay there.

For what is before you is before you
and I implore you
to experience the magnitude of this moment.
Today is the link between potential and promise.

This moment is yours for the making.
Success is yours for the taking.
And the future is yours for the shaping.

The world is yours.
If these things seem too much for you,
realize that today is the bridge between dreams
and dreams come true.

I don't know how you define success,
but it has something to do with moving
from where you are
to where you want to be.
So let's be about the business
of transforming dreams into reality.

To accept or reject the mission
you have to choose between the two,
but it's passion in action
that makes dreams come true.

There are countless complexities
for you to get through,
but it's passion in action
that makes dreams come true.

To the bottom or to the top,
it's all up to you,
but it's passion in action
that makes dreams come true.

There's absolutely nothing wrong
with having something to prove,
but it's passion in action
that makes dreams come true.

So believe in yourself
and know that the determination within you
is greater than the past that is chasing you.
Greater than the obstacles in front of you.
Greater than the pressures that surround you.

They are no match
for who you are destined to be.
They are no match
for what you are destined to do.
Because it's passion in action that makes dreams come true.
Put your passion in action
and make your dreams come true.

FOCUS Entrance Interview

Although you may not have experienced life as a new college student for long, we're interested in how you expect to spend your time, what challenges you think you'll face, and your general views of what you think college will be like. Please answer thoughtfully.

INFORMATION ABOUT YOU

Name _____

Student Number _____ Course/Section _____

Instructor _____

Gender _____ Age _____

1. **Ethnic Identification (check all that apply):**
   ___ American Indian or Alaska Native   ___ Native Hawaiian or Other Pacific Islander
   ___ Asian   ___ Hispanic/Latino
   ___ Black or African American   ___ White   ___ Prefer not to answer

2. **Is English your first (native) language?**
   ___ yes   ___ no

3. **Where are you living this term?**
   ___ with my immediate family   ___ on my own
   ___ with a relative other than my immediate family ___ other (please explain)_____

4. **Did your parents graduate from college?**
   ___ yes, both   ___ neither
   ___ yes, father only ___ not sure
   ___ yes, mother only

5. **How many credit hours are you taking this term?**
   ___ 6 or fewer   ___ 15-16
   ___ 7-11   ___ 17 or more
   ___ 12-14

6. **Did you start college elsewhere before attending this school?**
   ___ yes   ___ no

7. **In addition to going to college, do you expect to work for pay at a job (or jobs) this term?**
   ___ yes   ___ no

8. **If so, how many hours per week do you expect to work?**
   ___ 1-10   ___ 31-40
   ___ 11-20   ___ 40+
   ___ 21-30

9. **Which of the following describes why you are working for pay this term? (Mark all that apply.)**
   ___ to pay for college tuition   ___ to pay for child care
   ___ to pay for basic expenses that I need (rent, housing, food, etc.) ___ to pay for textbooks
   ___ to pay for extra expenses that I want (clothes,   ___ to save money for the future
       entertainment, etc.)   ___ to see how much I can make
   ___ to buy a car   ___ other (please explain)
   ___ to support a family   _____

10. How will you pay for your college expenses? (Check all that apply.)

___ my own earnings   ___ scholarships and grants

___ my parents' contributions   ___ loans

___ my spouse or partner's contributions   ___ other (please explain)_____

___ my employer's contributions

11. If you plan to work for pay, where will you work?

___ on campus   ___ off campus   ___ at more than one job

12. If you are entering college soon after completing high school, how many total hours per week (on average) did you spend studying outside of class in high school?

___ 0-5   ___ 26-30

___ 6-10   ___ 31-35

___ 11-15   ___ 36-40

___ 16-20   ___ 40+

___ 21-25   ___ I am a returning student and attended high school some time ago.

13. What was your high school grade point average?

___ A+   ___ C+

___ A   ___ C

___ A−   ___ C−

___ B+   ___ D or lower

___ B   ___ I don't remember.

___ B−

INFORMATION ABOUT YOUR COLLEGE EXPECTATIONS

14. How do you expect to learn best in college? (Check all that apply.)

___ by looking at charts, maps, graphs   ___ by reading books

___ by looking at color-coded information   ___ by writing papers

___ by looking at symbols and graphics   ___ by taking notes

___ by listening to instructors' lectures   ___ by going on field trips

___ by listening to other students during an in-class discussion   ___ by engaging in activities

___ by talking about course content with friends or roommates   ___ by actually doing things

15. For each of the following pairs of descriptors, which set sounds most like you? (Please choose between the two options on each line and place a checkmark by your choice.)

___ Extraverted and outgoing   or   ___ Introverted and quiet

___ Detail-oriented and practical   or   ___ Big-picture and future-oriented

___ Rational and truthful   or   ___ People-oriented and tactful

___ Organized and self-disciplined   or   ___ Spontaneous and flexible

16. *FOCUS* is about 13 different aspects of college life. Which are you most interested in? Which may contain information you expect to find most challenging to apply in your own life? (Check all that apply.)

Most interested in	Most challenging to apply to myself	Most interested in	Most challenging to apply to myself
___	___ Getting the right start	___	___ Engaging, listening, and note-taking in class
___	___ Building dreams, setting goals	___	___ Developing your memory
___	___ Learning to learn	___	___ Reading and studying
___	___ Managing time, energy, and money	___	___ Taking tests
___	___ Thinking critically and creatively	___	___ Building relationships, valuing diversity
___	___ Developing technology, research, and information literacy skills	___	___ Assessing your major and career
		___	___ Creating your future

17. Which one of your current classes do you expect to find most challenging this term and why?

Which class? (course title *or* department and course number) _____

Why? _____

Do you expect to succeed in this course? ___ yes ___ no

Perhaps (please explain): _____

18. **How many total hours per week do you expect to spend outside of class studying for your college courses this term?**

    ___ 0-5   ___ 16-20   ___ 31-35
    ___ 6-10   ___ 21-25   ___ 36-40
    ___ 11-15   ___ 26-30   ___ 40+

19. **Which of the following on-campus resources do you plan to use once or more this term? (Please check all that apply.)**

    ___ library
    ___ campus learning centers (whatever is available on your campus, such as a Writing Center, Math Learning Center, etc.)
    ___ computer labs
    ___ the Student Success Center or New Student Center, if one is available
    ___ the Counseling Center, if one is available
    ___ instructors' office hours for individual meetings/conferences/help
    ___ student clubs or organizations
    ___ none

20. **For the following sets of opposite descriptive phrases, put a checkmark on the line between the two that best represent your response.**

    I expect my first term of college to:

challenge me academically	___ ___ ___ ___ ___	be easy
be very different from high school	___ ___ ___ ___ ___	be a lot like high school
be very different from previous college	___ ___ ___ ___ ___	be a lot like previous college
be exciting	___ ___ ___ ___ ___	be dull
be interesting	___ ___ ___ ___ ___	be uninteresting
motivate me to continue	___ ___ ___ ___ ___	discourage me
be fun	___ ___ ___ ___ ___	be boring
help me feel a part of this campus	___ ___ ___ ___ ___	make me feel alienated

21. **Please mark your *top three areas of concern* relating to your first term of college by placing 1, 2, and 3 next to the items you choose.**

    ___ I might not fit in.
    ___ I might have difficulty making friends.
    ___ I might not be academically successful.
    ___ My performance might disappoint my family.
    ___ My personal life might interfere with my studies.
    ___ My studies might interfere with my personal life.
    ___ I might have financial difficulties.
    ___ My job might interfere with my studies.
    ___ My studies might interfere with my job.
    ___ My social life might interfere with my studies.
    ___ My studies might interfere with my social life.
    ___ My instructors might not care about me as an individual.
    ___ I might not finish my degree.
    ___ I might not manage my time well.
    ___ I might be bored in my classes.
    ___ I might feel intimidated by my instructors.
    ___ I might feel overwhelmed by all I have to do.
    ___ other (please explain)_____

22. **Broadly speaking, which area do you expect to major in?**

    ___ A bachelor's degree in _____.
    ___ An associate's degree in _____.
    ___ A certificate in _____.
    ___ Other (please explain) _____

23. **How certain are you now of a chosen major? (1 = totally sure, 5 = totally unsure)** ___

24. **How certain are you now that you will complete your degree or certificate? (1 = totally sure, 5 = totally unsure)** ___

25. **How certain are you now that you will complete your degree or certificate at this school? (1 = totally sure, 5 = totally unsure)** ___

26. **How certain are you now of your intended career choice? (1 = totally sure, 5 = totally unsure)** ___

27. **How certain are you now about whether you'll transfer to another school? (1 = totally sure, 5 = totally unsure)** ___

28. **What do you expect your grade point average to be at the end of your first term of college?**

    ___ A+   ___ B+   ___ C+   ___ D or lower
    ___ A   ___ B   ___ C
    ___ A−   ___ B−   ___ C−

29. **All college students develop expectations of what college will be like from various sources. How did you develop your expectations of what college might be like? (Mark your top three information sources with 1, 2, and 3.)**

____ TV and movies   ____ talks with my family

____ friends/family who have already gone to college   ____ talks with my friends who are also now starting college

____ discussions with teachers/counselors in high school   ____ the Internet

____ information I received from colleges in the mail   ____ other (please explain) _____

30. **How confident are you in yourself in each of the following areas? (1 = very confident, 5 = not at all confident)**

____ overall academic ability   ____ technology skills

____ mathematical skills   ____ physical well being

____ leadership ability   ____ writing skills

____ reading skills   ____ social skills

____ public speaking skills   ____ emotional well being

____ study skills   ____ teamwork skills

31. **Why did you take the course for which you are using this textbook? (Mark your top three reasons with 1, 2, and 3.)**

____ It was required.   ____ My advisor recommended it.

____ It sounded interesting.   ____ A teacher/counselor recommended it.

____ I thought it would help make my transition to college easier.   ____ The information I received in campus mailings convinced me.

____ I thought it would help me learn about the campus.   ____ The materials I received at freshman orientation convinced me.

____ I thought it would help me make friends.   ____ A friend/sibling who'd taken this course recommended it.

____ I thought it would help me academically.   ____ other (please explain) _____

____ My parent(s) or other family member(s) thought it was a good idea.

32. **What is the most important reason you decided to attend this school? (Check one)**

____ Recommendation of friend(s) who attended here   ____ Financial aid I was offered

____ Reasonable cost   ____ Recommendation of teachers/counselors

____ Reputation of the school   ____ Campus website

____ Location of the school   ____ Flexibility of course offerings and times

____ Availability of academic programs I'm interested in   ____ other (please explain) _____

____ Flexibility of course offerings and times

33. **Was this school your first choice among the colleges you considered?** ____ yes ____ no

34. **Why did you decide to go to college? (Check all that apply)** ____ Because it was expected of me.

____ Because I want to build a better life for myself.   ____ Because of active duty military or VA assistance.

____ Because I want to build a better life for my family.   ____ Because the career I am pursuing requires a degree.

____ Because I want to be very well off financially in the future.   ____ Because I was unsure of what I might do instead.

____ Because I need a college education to achieve my goals.   ____ other (please explain) _____

____ Because my friends were going to college.

____ Because my family encouraged me to go.

35. **Looking ahead, how satisfied do you expect to be with your decision to attend this school?**

____ very satisfied   ____ somewhat dissatisfied

____ satisfied   ____ very dissatisfied

____ not sure

36. **What are you most looking forward to in college?** _____

37. **How would you describe the best outcomes you hope for at the end of this term? Why are they important to you?** _____

38. **Do you expect to achieve these outcomes? Why or why not?** _____

Getting the Right Start

YOU'RE ABOUT to DISCOVER...

✔ Who goes to career colleges and why

✔ How to be a professional student

✔ What different types of degrees are available

✔ How to master a syllabus

✔ Why fundamental skills courses are important

✔ Why college success courses work

© Larry Harwood Photography. Property of Cengage Learning.

What do you **Know?**

Before beginning this chapter, take a moment to answer these questions. Your answers will help you assess how ready you are to focus.

1 = not very/not much/very little/low   5 = very/a lot/very much/high

How much do you *already* know?

Rate your current level of knowledge about topics covered in this chapter.

The characteristics of students who go to career or technical colleges

1 2 ③ 4 5

The differences among certificates, associate's degrees, and bachelor's degrees

1 2 3 4 ⑤

The expectations of college instructors

1 2 3 4 ⑤

The success rates of college success courses

1 2 ③ 4 5

How motivated are you to learn *more*?

In general, how motivated are you to learn the material in this chapter?

1 2 3 ④ 5

How much do you think this information might affect your college success?

1 2 ③ 4 5

How much do you think this information might affect your career success after college?

1 2 ③ 4 5

How ready are you to read *now*?

How ready are you to focus on this chapter—physically, intellectually, and emotionally? Which of these three areas is most challenging for you right now? Circle a number to represent it.

1 2 3 ④ 5

If any of your answers is below a 3, consider addressing the issue before reading. Then, read the chapter carefully, while looking for ways to improve your focus.

Finally, how long do you think it will take you to complete this chapter? If you start and stop, keep track of the overall time.

_____ Hour(s) _____ Minutes

DARNELL WILLIAMS

Quite honestly, Darnell Williams hadn't found high school all that challenging. Playing football his last two years had made it bearable. But at his school, if you showed up and had a pulse, you could count on passing your courses. There wasn't anything in particular he really wanted to do after high school, so he didn't do much of anything except hang out with friends, watch movies, and play an occasional game of football. But that got boring fast, and after a year had gone by, his friends started getting jobs and had less time to hang out with him. So Darnell decided to take some courses at the career college in his hometown. Maybe something there would appeal to him—perhaps from the list of online courses he found in the catalog.

But after two weeks, Darnell admitted that he didn't find his classes all that engaging. Although he was strong physically from working out for football, he knew he was out of shape academically. He didn't do any homework in high school, but how much would he have to do here? Since Darnell had no idea which classes to take, he figured he'd just get some required courses out of the way during his first term. He'd always heard people say, "College is about your communication skills, like writing and speaking. If your basic skills are good, and you're willing to work hard, you'll do fine." Based on that advice, he'd enrolled in two courses: English Composition and Public Speaking.

Earlier that morning, Darnell had received an e-mail from his best friend, Curtis, at the large state university two hours from home. It read like this:

Man, I hope I can make it here! The competition is stiff, and I wish I'd taken more college prep courses. Remember how we had lots of tests in our high school classes—every couple of weeks? If we just memorized a few things, like math formulas, even if we didn't understand them, we could do well on tests. And since there were so many tests, one low grade didn't matter. Here, there's a midterm and a final exam. If I blow one of those, I'm in big trouble. How long B4 midterms 4 you? AFAIK, I'm already off to a rough start. I gotta just T+. GTG 8 :-) Curtis

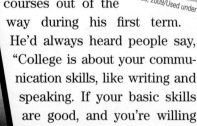

CINEMA
Good Only Date Sold
ADMIT ONE
048107

Fall Football Schedule

DATE	OPPONENT	TIME
...ember 6	Colorado State	7:00 PM ET
...ember 11	at Toledo	9:00 PM ET
...tember 19	Wyoming	3:30 PM ET
...tober 1	at West Virginia	7:30 PM ET
...tober 10	at Texas	7:00 PM ET
...tober 17	Kansas	9:00 PM ET
October 24	at Kansas State	3:30 PM ET
October 31	Missouri	9:00 PM ET
November 7	Texas A&M	3:30 PM ET
November 14	at Iowa State	9:00 PM ET
	at Oklahoma State	7:30 PM ET
		3:30 PM ET

Course Schedule
Main Campus
FALL SEMESTER
Williams, Darnell

Course Title	Hrs	Days	Meeting Times	Bldg	Room	Meeting Dates
ENGLISH COMPOSITION						

Toward the end of the message, Darnell noticed that Curtis had slipped into the usual e-mail abbreviations like T+ for "think positively" and AFAIK for "as far as I know." *I wish I could write like that in my composition class,* Darnell thought. *In e-mails, texts, and IMs, you can be informal, and no one worries about it. That's an easier way to write.* But he knew that kind of informality wouldn't fly with his teacher, Professor Monroe. But one particular aspect of the e-mail caught Darnell's attention. Even though they were at different schools, both he and Curtis noticed a big difference between high school and college. Looking back, high school seemed like a piece of cake. In college, you actually had to work for your grades by getting assignments done on time and paying attention to the instructor's high standards.

Darnell wondered if he'd be more motivated in college if he could have found some courses he'd actually been interested in, like Sports in Society or Modern American Cinema. Sports and movies were two of his favorite things. At the moment, Darnell had absolutely no idea what to major in. He was—as his college put it—an "undecided" student.

Professor Monroe had already begun when Darnell walked into class, and she shot a scowl in his direction. As he sat down at his computer station in the writing lab and pulled up the course website, his mind went totally blank. In high school, he hadn't been required to write anything longer than a few paragraphs. *I'm going to blame this stress on my senior-year English teacher, Mr. Forester. This is his fault. He should have done a better job of preparing us for college*, Darnell decided.

Just then, Professor Monroe was reminding the students that they'd get back their first graded essays today. "I have to be honest with you, class," she'd warned, "I expected more from you, and frankly, I'm disappointed in your work. We have a lot of work to do this term!" *Ouch!* Darnell thought to himself. *I hope she's not talking about me!*

Darnell held his breath as he looked at the paper she handed him, and then he saw it. At the top there was no grade at all—nothing but the teacher's note that said, "See me." What could that possibly mean? *This college thing is going to be more challenging than I thought*, he said to himself. One thing was clear to him: If he wanted to do well, he'd probably have to cut back on movies and sports now that he was in college.

Jeremy Edwards/ iStockphoto.com & Sergiy Zavgorodny, 2010; Andresr, 2010; bikeriderlondon, 2010; Lorelyn Medina, 2010. Used under license from Shutterstock.com.

© Cengage Learning

EAST HIGH SCHOOL
OFFICIAL TRANSCRIPT

STUDENT INFORMATION

NAME: Darnell Williams

ENTS/GUARDIAN: Michael and Joan Williams

ACADEMIC RECORD

OL YEAR: 2005–2006   GRADE LEVEL: 9th   SCHOOL YEAR: 2006–2007   GRA

Title	Credit Earned	Final Grade	Course Title
lsh I	1.0	B	English II
ematics I	1.0	C	Mathematics II
gy w/lab	1.0		

1. Do you have anything in common with Darnell? If so, what steps are you taking to help make sure you're successful?
2. Why do you think the instructor didn't give Darnell a grade? Would a teacher's note on a paper that says "See me" always indicate a problem?
3. In your experience, what are some of the main **academic** differences between high school and college? How did you read and study in high school, and how do you think that will change in college?

academic having to do with education

You're in College Now

Congratulations! You're in college. You've just started a new chapter of your life! As the saying goes, "The first step toward getting somewhere is to decide that you are not going to stay where you are." In choosing to go to college, that's what you've decided. You're *not* going to stay where you are. Your journey has begun. This chapter will launch you on your journey by covering the basics. You may already know much of this information, but not everyone does. So, let's start at the beginning.

Why do people go to a professional, career, or technical college? Generally, people go to college to improve their skills or gain completely new ones. Often students are aiming at specific careers, and choose the school and their academic majors in order to get a good start in that career. Many students who attend a school like yours differ from traditional college students in ways like these: they attend school part-time, support themselves, work full-time, are married or are single parents, waited to go on to college, or got their high school degrees in nonstandard ways.

> **Reason 1: Transitioning from High School to College.** If you finished high school recently or even some years ago, you may see college as the obvious next step. Like Darnell, you'll find college to be a very different game. Think of it this way: Darnell arrived at college, playing what he thought was a decent game of checkers. But he quickly discovered that his instructors expected him

> "
> **First say to yourself what you would be; and then do what you have to do.**
>
> *Epictetus, Greek philosopher, 55–135 a.d.*

The road to success is lined with many tempting parking spaces.

Traditional proverb

to play chess. He'd been successful in high school, and to the inexperienced eye, college looked like the same game board. After all, school is school, right? Wrong! Darnell quickly discovered that college is a new game with different rules!

Other students you know may have gone off to college somewhere else. But you considered things like cost and convenience and chose a college in your own community, one that offered the convenience of online courses as well as personal support from faculty, advising, and financial aid. A career college is a *real* college—a **marketplace of ideas**, where you can try out all kinds of new things. A career college that focuses on teaching—and on you—can be a good place to be.

marketplace of ideas a place where many ideas are exchanged freely

A career or technical college can also be a great place to test the waters. You may want to see if college is right for you at this point in your life. After you get into the rhythm of your classes, you may decide you've made a good decision. Or you may decide to wait until your life is less complicated or your head is in the right place. (That's okay, but your instructor hopes you'll decide to follow through and prove that you can be successful—and you can if you follow this book's advice!)

> **Reason 2: Going Back to School after a Break.** Perhaps you graduated from high school years ago. Or perhaps you've tried college before and quit. But now you've decided to get back on the road to career success. Maybe you're absolutely committed to making it this time, so you're more motivated. Something may have changed in your life, or you worked to save up for college for a while, or you've been a stay-at-home mom, or you have an employer now who will help foot your tuition bill.

One of the most interesting things about career and technical colleges is the amazing mix of students from all walks of life. You're just as likely to be sitting beside a grandmother who's decided it's her turn now, a soldier who's just come back from overseas, or a businessman gaining credentials for a promotion. College classrooms like yours are rich learning environments because different types of people are gathered in one place to discuss the same ideas. Adult college students are practical, self-directed learners who want to build on their past experiences and apply what they learn to their everyday lives. Does that describe you?

WOW! REALLY? TYPO.

Or perhaps you're returning to school to gear up with a select course or two. For example, maybe you have a new job that requires giving presentations, and the thought of it terrifies you. So you take a course to help you overcome your fear of public speaking. You don't necessarily want a degree; you just want to take a course or two. There's probably no better place than a career or technical college to meet those kinds of focused needs.[1]

EXERCISE 1.1

We'd Like to Get to Know You...

Take a few minutes to finish the following statements. Think about what each sentence says about you. Use your responses to introduce yourself to the class or form pairs, talk over your responses together, and use your partner's answers to introduce him or her to the class.

1. I'm happiest when _I'M IN A RELAXED STATE. DOIN WHAT I LOVE_.
2. If I had an extra $100, I'd _PRIORITIESZE IT. $40 -SAVE $20- GAS, $20-FOOD._
3. The thing I'm most proud of is _____.
4. Once people get to know me, they're probably surprised to find I'm _HILARIOUS_.
5. I've been known to consume large quantities of _WATER_.
6. I'd rather be _RADICAL_ than _ORIGINAL_.
7. My best quality is _EDUCATIONAL FLEXIBILITY._
8. My worst quality is _SOMETIMES IDLE._
9. The academic skill I'd most like to develop is _FOCUS IN STUDY._
10. One thing I'd like to figure out about myself is _How FAR CAN I COMMIT_.

People go to a college like yours at a particular point in their lives for a variety of reasons. As you discuss this exercise in class, explore these additional questions: What is your background and why are you here?

Choosing a Four-Year Degree? A Two-Year Degree? A Certificate Program?

If you're in college to earn a degree, you may consider whether you'd be better aiming for a four-year bachelor's degree or a two-year associate's degree. An associate's degree will prepare you to go one of two ways in a relatively short amount of time: (1) into a career or (2) on to further education. If you want a career-oriented associate's degree, in two years you can train for one of the fastest-growing jobs in the economy by taking approximately twenty classes. The best jobs for the future requiring a two-year degree include becoming a nurse, environmental technician, paralegal, fashion designer, dental hygienist, occupational therapist, or radiologic technologist.[2] If you prefer hands-on coursework and a career like one of these is your goal, a career college is exactly the right place for you. (It's also quite possible that you couldn't prepare for some of these specific degrees in a four-year program.)

Instead of a career-oriented associate's degree, you may want to earn a fairly general two-year degree to apply toward a bachelor's degree, perhaps even at another institution. Part of the coursework you'll complete to get an associate's degree will consist of core requirements or general education courses, like writing and speaking, that apply to any career field. If those are your plans, you'll graduate from your college with transferable courses when the time comes.[3]

Perhaps instead of a two-year associate's degree, you want to specialize even further, and finish your coursework sooner, so instead, you opt for a certificate. Certificates generally require fifteen to as many as fifty credits, and you'll most likely only take courses that apply specifically to the career field you're preparing for. You set your sights on a target and finish your certificate program in as little as one year, sometimes less.[4]

One of the biggest differences between an associate's degree and a certificate is that the courses you take for an associate's degree usually carry over to a four-year program and include core requirements, general courses like speaking, writing, and math.[5] That may not be true of certificate programs. So if you think you may want to earn a bachelor's degree at some point, choose an associate's degree. It's up to you. How soon do you need a job? What interests you? How hands-on do you want your course of study to be?[6]

How College Works: Being "In the Know"

This chapter is about the advice that the Greek philosopher Epictetus offered centuries ago: "Do what you have to do." But exactly what are those things?

One of the first ways to demonstrate you're "in the know," is to understand that your college instructors will expect you to be a professional

> **If everyone is moving forward together, then success takes care of itself.**
>
> *Henry Ford, American industrialist (1863–1947)*

student. Here is a list of ten suggestions that are important to them, and therefore to you:

1. **Don't just pile on.** If you want to be successful in college, you may have to give something up to give it all you've got. Some people hope they'll be able just to add college to an already-long list of obligations. But when they add one more thing, the entire stack crumbles. Something in your life will need adjusting to make room for coursework. You may need to reduce your hours at work temporarily, or tell your aunt that you can't watch her kids on Thursday nights so she can go to class, because you have to go to class, too.

priority something considered to be particularly important

2. **Reserve class time as a top priority.** Let's face it: Life is complicated. Your boss wants a piece of you, your kids (if you have any) disturb your attempts to study, your friend wants to go to the movies the night before your midterm exam, the bills keep mounting, and on and on. Because some students see college as just one more commitment, they decide to miss class for less important tasks: to pick up a relative at the airport or shop with a friend who's in town, for example. Sometimes true emergencies in your personal life will interfere with your academic life. But your instructors will expect you to plan nonemergencies around your already scheduled (and paid-for!) classes. Many things in your life are important—it's true—but while you're in school, coming to class and doing your coursework should be at the top of your list. Unfortunately, many college students sabotage themselves within the first few weeks of classes by skipping class (25 percent), turning in an assignment late (33 percent), or not turning an assignment in at all (24 percent). Don't allow yourself to become one of these statistics![7]

conscientiously responsibly paying attention to detail

3. **Complete your assignments conscientiously and on time.** In high school, your teachers may have cut you some slack. Remember that teacher who dropped your lowest quiz grade, forgave a homework assignment that didn't get done, and curved the test if the whole class didn't do well? Your college instructors aren't likely to do that. This is college, and college is the big leagues. Your instructors are preparing you, not only for a job, but for life, and they have your long-term, best interests in mind.

4. **Don't come late and don't leave early.** One thing instructors dislike is getting a sense from students that school isn't a top priority. When you breeze in late or sneak out early, you're communicating that you don't value school, your instructor, and your classmates, whether you realize it or not.

5. **Dress like a professional student.** Dress like you're a serious student who's there to learn. Leave the muscle tanks and halter tops for truly informal occasions. You're not in college to score fashion points, draw attention to your tattoos, or define your personality with your baseball cap. That doesn't mean you can't be yourself, but it does mean that you should use good judgment. Always remember why you're there: To learn.

> **"** If you don't know where you are going, you might wind up someplace else. **"**
>
> *Yogi Berra, major league baseball player and manager*

6. **Ask questions if things are unclear.** Even though you may be afraid to speak up or not want to admit that you're fuzzy about something, your instructors will rely on *you* to let them know that. They aren't mind readers.

7. **Come prepared.** Get ready for class beforehand, and then jump in once you're there. Bring your books, notebook, and pen, and sit up straight, too, just like mom always used to say. College isn't a place to just slide by or wing it. It's a place to put your best foot forward.

8. **Learn to work in groups.** Your instructors know the value of teamwork later in your career, so they'll expect you to work with your classmates in class, outside of class, or online. They may even think it's important enough to assign points for group projects in the course syllabus. Even though you may prefer to work alone, teamwork skills are highly valued in today's workplace, and you'll learn things from other students that you might not learn from your instructor.[8]

9. **Take charge.** Sometimes new students don't realize that *they're* supposed to be in charge. They wait to be told what to do, and if no one tells them, they don't do whatever needs to get done. If you want to know how to study for a test, ask your instructor. If you're unclear about the homework directions, ask your instructor. It's much better to take responsibility than it is to hope for the best. As the advertising slogan goes, "Just do it."

10. **Engage!** Students who soak up all they can enjoy college most. When they're in class, they're tuned in. Sure, Professor Whoever may not be quite as entertaining as your favorite TV star, and going to class isn't as much fun as going to the movies. But college is about becoming an *educated* person, not an *entertained* one.

Any time you start something new, there's a **learning curve** involved. The best thing to do is to admit it, decide what to do, and start climbing! Beyond conducting yourself as a professional student, what other things will help you be in the know? Here's a basic list of essentials.

learning curve a measure of how long it takes you to learn something and how hard it is

CAREER OUTLOOK: *Be Noticeable*

 You never get a second chance to make a first impression.
ANONYMOUS

Start strong. When you show up for an advisor appointment, a first class, or a job interview, you want to create a positive first impression. This valuable truth goes far beyond just that first interaction, however. Each day on the job shows your professional colleagues who you are in small but important ways, and these interactions add up. For example, if you're late turning in your first project on the new job, and if you show up for work with unkempt hair, dirty fingernails, and body-odor problems, you start out in a hole—and it may be hard to dig your way out. When someone is late, we tend to think he'll be unreliable. When someone takes good care of the way she dresses, we tend to believe she'll also take good care of details on the job. Those who dress thoughtfully, who cultivate habits of personal hygiene, who keep their work area neat, and whose work is always correct, organized, and punctual—these are the people who end up on the "A-list."

How **FULL** is your plate?

> *There is one thing we can do, and the happiest people are those who can do it to the limit of their ability. We can be completely present. We can be all here. We can . . . give all our attention to the opportunity before us.*
>
> —MARK VAN DOREN, PULITZER PRIZE–WINNING POET (1894–1972)

One reason many of us are overwhelmed by all we have to do is because we do the right things, but we do them at the wrong times. We aren't truly present. If you're a morning person, and math is your toughest course, study math in the mornings! The same goes for night owls. In order to be completely present for challenging tasks, ready to give all our attention, we must know ourselves and our own natural rhythms.

Stefan Glebowski, 2010/Used under license from Shutterstock.com

TRY IT!

Along the side of a piece of paper, vertically, write down your waking hours: 8 A.M., 9 A.M., 10 A.M., etc. Put a circle around your peak energy times. Now go back to your list of times, and put a checkmark by your regular study times. Do they match up? Are you studying when you're most effective? If not, can you rearrange things so that you are?

Develop a Degree Plan and Plan Your Coursework

In some ways, college is like a journey with parts of the itinerary planned for you. You can't just hitchhike wherever you like. It's more like a guided tour planned by experts in the areas you'd like to explore. You can choose to go left or right at particular moments, but much of the trip is planned in advance.[9] If you'd like to become a nurse, for example, your coursework will be prescribed for you. However, everyone appreciates the focused knowledge of nurses when they need one!

concentration focused effort; specialization

core basic

Some courses will count toward your major or area of **concentration**, and some will satisfy **core** requirements. Core requirements often make students wonder: "I'm never going to be another Stephen King. Why do I have to suffer through writing courses I'll never use?" The key words in that last sentence are *never use*. You'll speak and write and think and solve problems in any career. Even though you're in college to prepare for a career, becoming a more knowledgeable person in general should be a big part of your mission.

Most colleges will ask you to fill out a degree plan up front. You'll plan your coursework for each semester or quarter from now until you've finished. Not only do you end up taking the right courses, but you can watch your progress as you go.

If you are transferring credits from a previous college, or planning to transfer later to another institution, work closely with your current college advisors. But realize that while your advisors will be knowledgeable about requirements at your school, they probably won't know everything about the other institution you're dealing with. Do some digging on your own by calling an advisor at that school for information that will help you with your planning now. And remember that there's a difference between whether a course will **transfer** (for general credit) or **count** (toward a specific degree).

Why Do I Have to Take This Class?

Here is a road map, or a sample degree plan, for Darnell, assuming he decides to get a general Associate of Arts Degree. (The requirements at your college will be different from this example.)

GREAT BLUFFS TECHNICAL COLLEGE

DEGREE TRACKING WORKSHEET ◄—

> Many colleges, yours included, use a worksheet or degree plan, like this one of Darnell's, to help you stay on course and track your progress as you earn your degree. Check with an advisor to see what aids like this your campus provides.

NAME___Darnell Williams_____   EMAIL ADDRESS___dwilliams@gbtc.edu____

STUDENT NUMBER___123-45-6789_____   PHONE_____555-9876_____

GENERAL STUDIES

Associate of Arts Degree

> In the "Notes" column, Darnell can keep track of his thoughts about each course and things to keep in mind when registering for the next term.

Program Course #	Course Title	Term (to be) Taken	Term Hours	Grade A = 4 B = 3 C = 2 D = 1 F = 0	Notes
ENGL 111	English Composition I	Fall 2011	3	?	
HIST 103	United States History I		3		
	Foreign Language		5		
GBTC 100	College Success		3		
SPE 115	Public Speaking	Fall 2011	3	?	
ENGL 112	English Composition II		3		
HIST 104	United States History II		3		
	Foreign Language (must be the same language)		5		
	Humanities		3		
PSC 205	United States Government		3		
	Literature		3		
	Visual and Performing Arts		3		
SOC 103	Introduction to Sociology		3		
	Mathematics		3		
	Humanities		3		
PSC 206	State and Local Government		3		
	Natural Science I		3–4		
	Natural Science II		3–4		
	Unrestricted Elective		3		
	Unrestricted Elective		3		

> The courses with department abbreviations and numbers listed are required for Darnell's degree plan. The open categories are places where he can choose from a list of possible courses. His advisor will help him know his options.

(Adapted from Austin Community College website. Available at www3.austincc.edu/deggens01.rtf; and Colorado Technical University catalog. Available at http://catalog.careered.com/catalogs/80/catalog.pdf)

To complete this activity, visit your academic advisor to get a completion plan for the degree or certificate program you're most interested in now. (You may change your mind later.) Fill it in with the help of your advisor, looking ahead to which courses you'll take, term by term. Use this plan as a working document as you progress through your program.

Be Advised! Advising Mistakes Students Make

One of the most important relationships you'll have as a college student is the one you build with your academic advisor. In your college this person may be an advisor, a counselor, or a faculty member who can steer you toward courses you can handle and instructors you can learn best from. An advisor can keep you from taking classes that bog you down academically or unnecessary ones that take you extra time to earn your degree. Here's a list of advising mistakes students make from real advisors who work with college students every day.

1. **Not using the campus advising office or your faculty advisor.** If you don't get regular advice from an advisor, counselor, or a designated faculty member who's serving as your advisor, your degree may take longer and cost more money. It's that simple. It's your college career, after all, and it's important that you and your advisor work as partners.

2. **Not planning ahead.** Some students walk into the advising office or e-mail an advisor and expect help right away, and sometimes that works. However, planning ahead is a better option. Planning ahead includes making an appointment, looking through the course offerings, making a list of questions to ask, and thinking in advance about which days you can attend classes based on your work schedule, how many classes you can take, and on which days of the week. And, if you're leaving your advisor a voice-mail, remember to include all of this important information. What's wrong with this message? "Hi, this is Tony. I have a question about my schedule. Please call me back, OK?" Tony who? And what's his phone number? Or how about an e-mail like this from hotchick13@email.com? "Do I need to take English 090? Please let me know." Exactly who is "hotchick13"?

3. **Procrastinating.** It's important not to put off advising appointments. To drop a class, you may need to meet a deadline. Or you may need help from an advisor to solve a problem with a faculty member, but by the time you get around to it, the instructor has already left campus for the summer. If you deal with problems right away, while they're small, they may be reversible. (And it's always a good idea to discuss dropping a class with the instructor first.)

prerequisites courses that you need to take before advancing on to other ones

4. **Skipping prerequisites.** Some students want to skip the required **prerequisites**. They think they can handle the work. They think prereqs are a waste of time and money when, actually, they're in place because hundreds of students before you have proven that these classes help you succeed. And in some cases, students who haven't taken a prereq are actually disenrolled from the course that requires it.

5. **Choosing the wrong major.** Sometimes students lock on to a major because someone else thinks it's a good idea or because a particular career field pays well, not because they enjoy the subject and are suited for it. Staying motivated is hard when you're not interested in something. Advisors can help you figure out which major is right for you.

6. **Taking too many credits or too few.** Some students are overly optimistic and think they can handle a heavier course load than the other factors in

their lives will permit. Other students may underestimate the number of courses they should take, which increases the time it takes them to finish school. An advisor can help you stay on target.

7. **Ignoring problems.** If you run into difficulty and end up on academic probation, for example, an advisor or college official will work with you to get you back on track. But you must agree to that bargain and accept the help, possibly by signing a contract of steps you must take to reverse the situation.

8. **Being afraid to drop a course.** Sometimes, when you've tried everything (for example, tutoring, extra help sessions, and the campus learning center), but you're still not succeeding in a course, the best thing to do may be to drop the course by filling out a drop form (online or on paper) and submitting it. Then retake the course later. That option is better than just not going to class and assuming by not coming, you've dropped the course. Colleges require deliberate action from you. It's always best to know your school's rules and talk with your instructor first. *And beware that dropping a course may affect your financial aid.*[10]

Make the Grade: Computing Your GPA

One of the most important things to learn as a new college student—and fast—is what grade point averages (GPAs) are and how they work. Your GPA is an indication of how well you're doing, and you keep track of it over time, term by term. Your academic record will follow you for the rest of your life! Some students don't realize how grade points add up. They end up on academic probation, even if they only have one failing grade. Let's say you're taking four courses this term, and you earn the following grades:

GPA an average of all your grades for a single semester or a running average across all your coursework

Course	Credits	Final Grade	Grade Point Value
English Composition	3 credits	C (2 points)	6
College Algebra	3 credits	F (0 points)	0
College Success	3 credits	B (3 points)	9
Public Speaking	3 credits	D (1 point)	3
TOTAL	**12 credits**		**18 grade points**

You may look at this record and think, *Not bad. I passed three of my four courses.* But divide that Grade Point Value column total (18) by the total number of credits (12), and you get 1.5.

GPA = Grade Point Value ÷ Total Number of Credits

At most schools, a 1.5 GPA puts you on academic probation, and eventually, you may be facing suspension. That can be a discouraging way to start, and digging yourself out of a GPA hole once you're there takes a very long time, like paying off credit card debt.

Not only is it important to keep track of your grades over the whole term, but it's also important to keep track of your grade in each course. If you stop going to your math class because it's too hard or because you don't like the teacher, your grade will suffer. If an assignment is worth 25 percent of your grade, and you don't turn it in, the highest grade you can possibly earn, even if you do everything else perfectly, is a 75 percent or "C." You may think, *but it's only one assignment*. It is only one assignment, but it counts as one-quarter of your grade. In college, everything counts. The typical grading scale in college is:

A = 90–100%   B = 80–89%   C = 70–79%   D = 60–69%   F = 59% and below

Realize the Value of Remediation

Many career and technical colleges have what's called an open-door admissions policy. That means that anyone who wants to get an education is invited in. You don't have to get a certain score on the SAT or ACT standardized national tests, and you don't have to have a particular GPA in high school to be admitted. That's a good thing. As a nation, we are opening the doors of education to everyone, and our society as a whole benefits in many ways. Education improves the quality of life.[11]

developmental designed to develop or improve a skill

But when restrictions are removed, more variety is a natural result, right? Think of it this way: If every student at your college had to be over six feet tall to be admitted, then you and all your classmates would tower over the general public. But if anyone of any height could attend, you'd see a range from very short to very tall. Some people would need steps to reach high places, and others would have to duck under low ceilings. But variety presents challenges. Career colleges are characterized by variety, and they've devised ways to make it work. Here's how.

New career college students bring standardized test scores or take placement tests that help schools know where to *place* them. If you're "short" on some necessary skills for success, like reading, writing, or math, they may place you in a **developmental** (sometimes called *remedial*) class to help you catch up fast. Some students see these courses negatively, thinking they're a waste of time or money. Not so! Don't get discouraged if you're in one or more of these classes. They're insurance that you'll grow into the skills you'll need.

If you're enrolled in a developmental class, you're in good company. In one study of 35 colleges that are

Photoservice/iStockphoto.com

> **Problems are only opportunities in work clothes.**
>
> *Henry J. Kaiser, American industrialist (1882–1967)*

Your current safe boundaries were once unknown frontiers.

Anonymous

all part of a proposal to increase student success, 37 percent of incoming students required one remedial course, 26 percent required two courses, and 22 percent required three courses—for a total of 85 percent. And note this piece of good news: In a related study, students who earned a C or better in a developmental course during their first semester were, from that point forward, more likely to stay in school and succeed than students who weren't required to take a developmental course in the first place![12] In another study, students who took a developmental writing course earned higher English grades in later courses and higher GPAs overall than students who did not.[13] If you're enrolled in a developmental class, perhaps you're beginning to see its value *now*. If you don't see the value yet, chances are you'll greatly appreciate what it did for you *later*.

Master the Syllabus

You'll get a syllabus (or course schedule) for most all of the college classes you'll take. If the syllabi (plural of syllabus) for your courses are available online, check them often to keep up with any changes in the schedule or new assignments. If you have a hard copy, keep it handy and refer to it often. Think of a syllabus as:

> a preview of what to expect during every class

> a road map for where the course will take you

> a contract between you and your instructor

> a summary of all the assignments and how much they count toward your grade

> a tool that lists reading and homework to help you prepare for class

> evidence of an instructor's standards, grading system, and values

BOX 1.1 # Analyzing a Syllabus

Take a look at this example syllabus and see what you think. What is this professor like? Do you get a sense of his standards and values from his syllabus? Will this be a challenging course? Take a close look at a syllabus from one of your current classes. Analyze it, just as this one has been analyzed, and make a list of things you learn about specific aspects of the syllabus that can help you be successful.

> Some colleges have a syllabus template or standard format, so that your syllabus for each class will look basically the same and contain similar kinds of information.

> Send the instructor an e-mail the first week of class, introducing yourself and discussing your thoughts about how this class will help you. Remember, however, that in college, you must use good grammar and correct spelling in ALL your writing, including e-mails.

GREAT BLUFFS TECHNICAL COLLEGE
COURSE SYLLABUS

Course ID: SPE 115
Term: Fall 2011
Instructor: Steve Staley
Office: Vail Hall 501
Office Hours: MW 10:00–11:00 a.m., TR 2:00–3:00 p.m., by appointment only

> It's appropriate to ask the instructor what he prefers to be called: Steve, Mr. Staley, Professor Staley, etc.

Course Title: Professional Speaking
Credit Hours: 3
E-mail Address: steve.staley@gbtc.edu
Office Phone: 555-1234

> Pay attention to the course description. It's a summary of what you can expect.

Course Description: This course covers the essentials of business and professional presentations, including **introduction, impromptu, demonstration, briefing,** and **persuasive** presentations. It applies information on word choices, organization, audience analysis, and PowerPoint skills to several evaluated experiences in speech preparation and presentation. We also stress both theoretical understanding and practical experience. The concepts and skills we'll study and practice are adaptable to platform speaking, boardroom discussions, class interactions, and personal conversations.

> You can buy the textbook from your college bookstore or order it online. But often textbooks are "customized" with portions inserted from different books or material that pertains to your own campus. You must buy those books from your campus bookstore. Even though textbooks cost money, they are a critical investment. Trying to get by without one puts you at a disadvantage right from the start.

Prerequisites/Co-Requisites: ENG 090, REA 090

Course Textbook: *Speak Out! A Public Speaker's Guide to Success,* 2011.

Professional Conduct in Class: Students are responsible for knowing and abiding by the "Standards of Conduct" listed in the 2011–2012 GBTC Catalog (beginning on page 10). Your cell phone or pager should be turned off, set to vibrate only, or left at home. Eating, sleeping, social discussions, or doing reading or homework for other classes are distracting behaviors and communicate indifference and disrespect for this learning environment and subject matter. Children should not be brought to class. Getting up and coming in and out during class (unless you are sick, of course) is distracting to your classmates. These activities are unacceptable in academic environments and qualify as examples of inappropriate conduct in class, which may result in your academic withdrawal from the class.

> The instructor has devoted a substantial portion of the syllabus to this topic, and he has spelled out his expectations in detail. Professional conduct must be important to him.

Online Course Management System (CMS): e-CC (pronounced EASY). All students have access to the materials posted on the CMS website through the Internet from a campus computer lab or from home.

Attendance: If you must miss a class for an emergency, you must still submit assigned work by the due date. Please provide documentation to indicate that the absence was due to a situation beyond your control. There are no excused absences without documentation. In order to receive credit for attendance, you must attend the ENTIRE class period. IF YOU MISS A CLASS, IT IS YOUR RESPONSIBILITY TO CONTACT A CLASSMATE FOR NOTES AND ASSIGNMENTS. NO MAKEUP WORK IS ALLOWED.

Grading: Assignments must be turned in on time and speeches must be presented on schedule. Grades for makeup speeches are automatically reduced by 20 percent. Only one makeup day will be scheduled for speeches missed due to emergencies! THERE ARE NO MAKEUP EXAMS OR WRITTEN ASSIGNMENTS.

Americans with Disabilities Act (ADA): Any student eligible for academic accommodations because of a learning or physical disability should speak with the instructor during the first week of class and contact the Office of Support Services.

> This syllabus actually continues on for several more pages and includes three other things: 1) a campus statement about academic honesty and plagiarism, 2) due dates for each assignment, and 3) specific information on how speeches will be graded.

Speeches: You will be required to give a minimum of four speeches.
· SP 1: Informative 5 mins. (Process description, "how to.") Prep and speaking outline required.
· SP 2: Career (Impromptu) Speaking on the spot!
· SP 3: Business Briefing 5 mins. Informative, typical business or professional subject matter, may include persuasive component.
· SP 4: Persuasive 7 mins. (+ or −1 min.) (2 visual aids and 2 sources) Prep and speaking outline required.

Source: Steve Staley, Colorado Technical University.

Avoid the PCP Syndrome:
Use Campus Resources

The convenience of a career college can also be a drawback. Since you're not living in a dorm on a traditional campus, it's easy to develop a drive-through mentality. You show up for classes and then hightail it for work or home right away. Some experts describe this phenomenon as the "PCP Syndrome: Parking Lot, Class, Parking Lot." What's wrong with that? you ask. When you've finished grocery shopping, you get back in your car and go home, right? You don't cruise the aisles and hang around.

But going to college is very different from shopping for groceries. Your campus has many things available for you to take advantage of: student clubs, special presentations, and learning resource centers, for example. You may never find out about these "free samples" if you're not there. You won't make new friends or get to know your instructors. The danger is that when the going gets rough, which can happen during exam time, you may be tempted to retreat to what you're most familiar with—your life before college—and abandon your efforts. Whatever the problem, there's a place to go for help on campus. Even if your campus doesn't have every possible kind of support center right there, your advisors or instructors can always direct you to services off campus.

Remember that "HELP" is not a four-letter word. Getting help when you need it isn't a stigma; it's smart. Take this example: In 1979, Diana Nyad achieved the record for open-water swimming over a distance of 102.5 miles. But it took 51 other people to help her reach her goal (guides to check winds and currents, divers to look for sharks, and NASA nutrition experts to keep her from losing more than the 29 pounds she lost during that one swim).[14] Your campus has all kinds of resources available for the taking, but you must take them. They won't come to you. Here are some of the FAQs new college students often ask:

> **How can I meet other students?** Take advantage of favorite gathering spots on campus. If you're finding it hard to meet people, could it be because you're not around? To meet people, it helps to be where they are.

> **What if I need help with a challenging course?** Many campuses have support centers: a science learning center or a math learning center, for example. Or particular courses may offer what's called supplemental instruction, extra help beyond class sessions with basic course materials or homework assignments. You may be able to work with a tutor, too—a student who's extra-good at math, for example. Check out whatever options are available to you, and use them, rather than struggle on your own if you're not getting results.

> **I'm thinking of dropping a class. How do I do it?** The Office of the Registrar, Academic Support, or Office of Admissions and Records is where to go. They also help with things like transferring credits and getting transcripts if you've attended college somewhere before or plan to transfer. Think through the results of dropping a class, however. Will doing so change your financial aid status, for example?

> **What if I need a counselor?** College is a time of change. Your relationships may be affected or you may suffer from symptoms of stress. If your

campus has a counseling center and you need to use its services, do so. And if you find yourself in the middle of a real crisis, call the campus hotline for immediate help.

> **How can I find out if I have a learning disability?** Check to see if your campus has a learning center or a special office that helps with learning disabilities. You can work with a specialist there who can help. If you've been diagnosed with a learning disability before, bring your documentation to that office for their records and let your instructors know. They can help, too.

> **What if I have a technology crisis?** Your campus probably has a computer help desk, where techies can often solve what sounds like a complicated problem with simple advice. Also, use the campus computer labs. They may have better computers than yours at home, and you can make good use of blocks of time between classes.

> **What do I want to be when I grow up?** Thinking ahead to a career when you finish college is sometimes hard when so much is going on at the moment. What do you like to do? What people skills do you have? Visit your campus's career center. Experts there can help you discover a major and career that will work for you.

> **Is child care available?** Some campuses have inexpensive child care available. Being able to drop off a child in the morning right on campus and pick her up after your classes are over can be a real help.

> **Where can I buy my books?** Textbooks are a big investment these days, and it's important to buy the right editions for your classes. Should you buy them from your campus bookstore or order online? Buying books online may save you money, although you'll have to wait for shipment. The bookstore is a much quicker option, and it's a good idea to find out where it is, no matter where you buy your books. You'll most likely need it for other school supplies. Renting your books or buying an e-book that you can read online may be an option, too.

waliik/iStockphoto.com

66

One hundred percent of the shots you don't take don't go in.

Wayne Gretzky, called the greatest ice hockey player of all time

99

> **Where can I get other pieces of information I may need?** Try your campus website, the school bulletin or catalog, the student handbook, and the school newspaper.

> **What if I need the help of Campus Security?** If you feel unsafe walking to your car late at night or you need information about parking permits on campus, check with the Campus Security or Public Safety Office. They're there for your protection.

What's the bottom line? Get to know your campus and its full range of offerings—and take advantage of everything that's in place to help you be as academically successful as possible.

EXERCISE 1.3

Top Ten Resources Your Campus Offers

Make a list of ten resources your campus offers that can help you succeed in your coursework. For example, does your campus have a career center, a day care center, or a learning center? Visit each location, and identify specific ways you will use each office or service.

Name of office/service	Contact information	How will I use this resource?
1. JOHN DELLO RUSSO		QUESTIONS
2. EDUCATION DIRECTOR WILL SMITH	WILL SMITH@ LINCOLN TECH.COM	ISSUE WITH CAMPUS IN GENERAL
3. STUDENT SERVICES DIANE CARBO.		
4. LIBRARY.		
5. COMMUTER LOUNGE.		
6. CAREER SERVE TRICIA DANAHOE		CREATE A RESUME.
7.		
8.		
9.		
10.		

Toughing It Out: What College Takes

What does it mean to succeed? Actually, success is difficult to define, and different people define success differently. Right now in college, you may think of success in terms of the money you'll make after you finish. But is success just about money? Is it about fame? Status? According to motivational author Robert Collier, "Success is the sum of small efforts, repeated day in and day out." Perhaps to you, success is somewhere off in the distant future, and it happens more or less suddenly, like winning the lottery.

Actually, success begins right now. You should be the one to define what success will look like in your life, but generally, success is *setting out to do something that means something to you, and then being fully engaged while doing it*. It's that simple. And it applies to your college experience as well. It starts now.

In order to understand your own definition of success in college, first you need to ask yourself why you're here. Why *did* you come—or return—to college, anyway? Do you want to develop into a more interesting, well-rounded, educated human being? Are you working toward a degree that leads to a specific career? Do you have children and want an education in order to give them a better life? This book will provide you with an honest look at what that takes, including plenty of opportunities to ask yourself questions about these things. It will also offer you tools you can use throughout your college courses and in your life beyond college.

Some students think going to college is like any other financial transaction: buying a gallon of milk, for example. You pay the cashier the money, and the milk now belongs to you. They think if they pay tuition, the college credits should be theirs. Not so. There's much more to it than that. A college education requires more than a financial commitment. It requires you to invest your ability, your intellect, your drive, your effort—and yourself. College has to do with more than the brain matter found between your ears.

The Good News and the Bad News (Benefits and Obstacles)

What's the good news about going to college? The benefits are wide-reaching and long-lasting. Think about how this list applies to you.

1. **Higher earning potential.** College increases your potential to earn money. It's that simple. On average, people with associate's degrees earn 20 to 30 percent more than those with a high school diploma only, while those with a bachelor's degree earn about twice as much as high school grads. Experts say that one-third of new job growth from 2008 until 2018 will require some education after high school.[15] And there's some evidence that jobs requiring certificates or associate's degrees will grow at an even faster rate than jobs requiring a four-year degree.[16] Sixty percent of jobs right now are held by people with post–high school education or training.[17]

2. **Lower unemployment rates.** College decreases your risk of unemployment. This is especially helpful when the economy takes a downturn.

> **Always bear in mind that your own resolution to succeed is more important than any one thing.**
>
> *Abraham Lincoln, 16th President of the United States (1809–1875)*

3. **Wisdom.** College gives you opportunities to gain understanding about many things—politics, people, and current affairs to name a few. Beyond theories, facts, and dates, well-educated people know how to think critically, contribute to society, and manage their lives.

4. **Insight.** College students have the opportunity to understand themselves better as they learn different ways of doing things.

5. **Lifelong learning.** College students are prepared to become lifelong learners. It's not just about grades. It's about becoming the best student-learner you can be—inside or outside of the classroom. This one benefit will stay with you through the rest of your life.

What's the bad news? What obstacles may stand in your path? Darnell Williams isn't quite sure why he's in college. Will he be successful? It depends, doesn't it? Here's some evidence on what "it" consists of.

Some studies show that only around half of college students reach their educational goals.[18] But who goes, who finishes later, and who transfers to another school are hard things to track. The risk factors for dropping out of college include working more than thirty hours per week, going to school part-time, being a single parent or having children at home, and being a first-generation college student.[19] It's true that going to college is "A Whole 'Nother World," as one major report's title says. Juggling a job, family, friends, transportation, tuition, and all the things that are impacted by the energy and effort it takes to go to college can be overwhelming. If you're a first-generation college student, you may not have a role model at home that can help you, because your parents didn't go to college. (That's why it's important to make connections with your classmates, instructors, and advisors who can guide you.)[20] Even though college may be more challenging for first-generation students, you can still be highly successful. Perhaps the most famous current example is Michelle Obama, who went from first-generation college student to First Lady.[21]

The important thing to keep in mind as you think about risk factors is that they alone cannot determine your ultimate level of success. Don't throw in the towel now if you had a child at age sixteen or are working thirty-five hours per week. These factors are presented merely as information to assist you on your journey. They are simply **predictors**—not *determiners*. Your effort, attitude, and willingness to get any help you need to succeed are vital. Only you can determine your outcomes in life, and that includes college.

predictors something that indicates something in the future may happen

Luis Pedrosa/iStockphoto.com

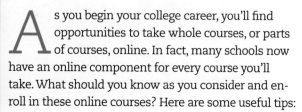

ONLINE **TechKnow**

Improve Your Grade
Online Flashcards
Glossary

As you begin your college career, you'll find opportunities to take whole courses, or parts of courses, online. In fact, many schools now have an online component for every course you'll take. What should you know as you consider and en-roll in these online courses? Here are some useful tips:

- Pay close attention to your school's CMS, or Course Management System—the online system your school uses to deliver and manage your course materials. Learn how to use everything your online course offers, like discussion boards, chat rooms, online assign-ments, and other course resources.

- Create a VPN (Virtual Private Network) account to access library data bases from home. Your library will help you set up and use that connection.

- Turn to your school's IT help desk when you have questions or when things don't work the way you think they should.

- Use this self-evaluation checklist as you prepare for online learning:

  Rarely – 1   Sometimes – 2
  Most of the Time – 3   All of the Time – 4

A. I am able to easily access the Internet as needed for my studies.

B. I am willing to communicate actively with my class-mates and instructors electronically.

C. I am willing to set aside an amount of time each week to effectively engage in online study.

D. I believe that online learning can be as effective as traditional classroom learning.

E. When it comes to learning and studying, I am a self-directed person.

F. I am able to manage my study time effectively and easily complete online assignments on time.

G. I am the one responsible for my learning—even when I work online without a teacher in my presence.

Be especially aware of those questions where you answered "Rarely." Ask for help and look for ways to improve in those areas yourself. For example, if you answered "Rarely" to question 2, look for ways to build learning communities, form online study groups, or join in when you're assigned virtual group projects.[22]

This Course Has a Proven Track Record

If you're reading this book, there's a good chance you're enrolled in a college success course, called something like First-Year Seminar, First-Year Experi-ence, College Success, Learning Community, or any of a host of other names. These courses are designed to introduce you to college life, familiarize you with your own campus, and help you improve your academic skills. Do they work? According to experts, the answer is yes![23] Of course, you have to keep your part of the bargain, but in general, college students who complete college success courses are much more successful. Take a look at the results of one major study in Figure 1.1.

Students who completed a college success course were more likely to stay in school and succeed academically. And students who completed a college success course and also needed to take developmental courses in one to three subject areas were even more likely to achieve these results! That's what this course is about: your success. Your instructor and your classmates are rooting for you. Now it's up to you!

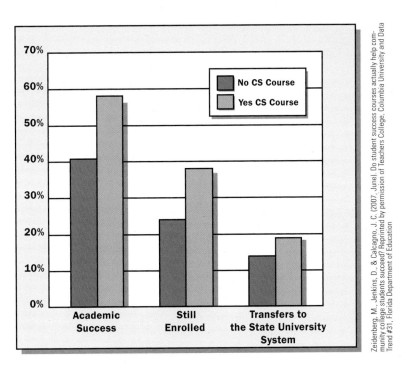

Zeidenberg, M., Jenkins, D. & Calcagno, J. C. (2007, June). Do student success courses actually help community college students succeed? Reprinted by permission of Teachers College, Columbia University and Data Trend #31, Florida Department of Education

FIGURE 1.1

Outcomes of College Students Completing a College Success Course and Those Who Did Not (1999–2000 through 2003–2004)

How Do I Want to Be Different When I'm Done?

One thing is sure: College will change you. Most every high-intensity experience full of opportunities does. Take advantage, meet new people, and stretch yourself. You may notice that as a result of your college experience, your old relationships may "fit" differently. Your romantic partner may brag about you or secretly envy you. Your family may praise your efforts or hardly notice. But you will. If you finish what you've begun, you will watch yourself become a more sophisticated, more knowledgeable, more confident person. You can't help but be. Ask yourself now, at the beginning of your college experience, just how you'd like to change, and make it happen.

I am only one,
But still I am one.
I cannot do everything,
But still I can do something;
And because I cannot do everything
I will not refuse to do the something that I can do.

Edward Everett Hale, American author
(1822–1909)

INSIGHT *Now* What Do You Think?

At the beginning of this chapter, Darnell Williams faced a series of challenges as a new college student. Now after learning from this chapter, would you respond differently to any of the questions you answered about the "FOCUS Challenge Case"? Using what you learned in the chapter, write a paragraph ending Darnell's case study. What are some of the possible outcomes for Darnell?

ACTION Your Plans for Change

1. Identify one new thing you learned in reading this chapter. Why did you select the one you've selected? How will it affect what you do in your college classes?
2. Why are you going to college? How do you see your college experience impacting your future?
3. How do you want college to change you? Why?

REALITY CHECK | What did you **Learn?**

On a scale of 1 to 5, answer these questions now that you've completed this chapter.

1 = not very/not much/very little/low   5 = very/a lot/very much/high

How much do you know *now*?

Now rate your current level of knowledge about topics covered in this chapter.

The characteristics of students who go to career or technical colleges

1   2   3   4   (5)

The differences among certificates, associate's degrees, and bachelor's degrees

1   2   3   4   (5)

The expectations of college instructors

1   2   3   4   (5)

The success rates of college success courses

1   2   3   (4)   5

How useful might the information in this chapter be to you?

How much do you think this information might affect your college success?

1   2   3   4   (5)

How much do you think this information might affect your career success after college?

1   2   3   4   (5)

How long did it actually take you to complete this chapter (both the reading and writing tasks)?

___3___ Hour(s) __30__ Minutes

 Challenge Yourself Online Quiz. To find out how much you've learned, access the CourseMate via www.cengagebrain.com/shop/ISBN/1439083908 to take the Challenge Yourself Online Quiz.

Compare these answers with your answers from the "Readiness Check" at the beginning of this chapter. How might the gaps between what you thought before starting the chapter and what you now think affect how you approach the next chapter?

chapter 2

Building Dreams, Setting Goals

You're About to Discover...

- ✔ How this book will help you learn
- ✔ What motivates you
- ✔ How your attitude can sabotage you
- ✔ Why you should distinguish between dreams and goals
- ✔ How to develop goals that work

© Larry Harwood Photography.
Property of Cengage Learning.

READINESS CHECK | What do you **Know?**

Before beginning this chapter, take a moment to answer these questions. Your answers will help you assess how ready you are to focus.

1 = not very/not much/very little/low   5 = very/a lot/very much/high

How much do you *already* know?

Rate your current level of knowledge about topics covered in this chapter.

How people learn

    1 2 3 4 ⑤

Intrinsic versus extrinsic motivation

    1 2 3 4 ⑤

Dreams versus goals

    1 2 3 4 ⑤

FOCUSed goal-setting

    1 2 ③ 4 5

How motivated are you to learn *more*?

In general, how motivated are you to learn the material in this chapter?

    1 2 3 ④ 5

How much do you think this information might affect your college success?

    1 2 3 ④ 5

How much do you think this information might affect your career success after college?

    1 2 3 ④ 5

How ready are you to read *now*?

How ready are you to focus on this chapter—physically, intellectually, and emotionally? Which of these three areas is most challenging for you right now? Circle a number to represent it.

    1 2 3 ④ 5

If any of your answers is below a 3, consider addressing the issue before reading. Then, read the chapter carefully, while looking for ways to improve your focus.

Finally, how long do you think it will take you to complete this chapter? If you start and stop, keep track of the overall time.

_3_ Hour(s) _15_ Minutes

Gloria Gonzales

© Larry Harwood Photography. Property of Cengage Learning.

I t was her first day of college. As Gloria Gonzales walked from the parking lot to her first class, "College Success," she had mixed feelings: excitement, anticipation, anxiety, and apprehension. She wondered if she'd meet any interesting people, if she'd like her instructor, and if she'd learn anything important in this class. After all, she'd gotten good grades in high school without even trying. If she just put in some effort, she thought, she'd be successful in college, too. *How can you study something like "College Success" for a whole term?* she asked herself.

Mom & Dad - last summer

Andresr, 2009/Used under license from Shutterstock.com

To be honest, Gloria thought she probably already knew most of what there was to learn in this course, and if she didn't, so what? She knew what she had to do to get good grades—everyone does—but she didn't always choose to do it, that's all. School was part of her life, but it wasn't always her top priority. At least this course would probably be easier than her math course or her developmental writing course.

Gloria wasn't the first person in her family to go to college. Her sister had tried it, but she'd dropped out after her first term and gotten a job. "College, who needs it?" she'd exclaimed. "I want to start earning good money right away, not years from now!" There were times when Gloria thought her sister might be right. She certainly seemed able to afford some of the things Gloria had always wanted herself. Was college really going to be worth all the time, effort, and expense? But everyone she knew was going to college; it was the right thing to do after high school, and everyone expected it of her.

Gloria's family didn't have much money. They were sacrificing to help finance her college education. She'd better perform, they'd said. They'd told her point-blank that her sister had set a bad example, and that her first-term grades had better not include anything lower than a B. Frankly, Gloria was beginning to feel a twinge of performance pressure. Of all the children in her family, her sister had always been considered the smart one, and she'd given up after only one term. If

Google, Inc.

her sister couldn't do it, how could Gloria? If she were to succeed, exactly what would it take?

Despite her worries as she walked down the hallway toward the classroom, Gloria was sure of one thing: She looked good today—really good. Her sister's skirt fit perfectly, the new red shirt was definitely her color, and thankfully it was a good hair day. Gloria had always been able to make heads turn. Beneath it all, Gloria knew what she wanted, anyway. She was going to get a certificate in fashion merchandising at the career college she'd chosen, and eventually go into the fashion industry. She'd dreamed of that since she was ten years old and loved to watch fashion design TV shows. She was hooked, but wasn't sure exactly what she'd need to do to make it. Luckily, she'd worked in a clothing store at the mall all through high school and she was good at it. In fact, the store kept trying to give her more hours because she had such amazing customer service skills. She thought she'd probably just work her college courses around her forty-five hours a week there. But she sensed that fitting everything in could be tough.

Gloria's parents wanted her to go to a four-year university and get a "real" degree in business, instead. They were always clipping articles about good jobs in business from the newspaper and giving them to her, but she kept telling them she had no interest. "There'll always be good jobs waiting for you, if you play your cards right," they said. She'd heard it so many times that her usual response now was "Yeah, whatever. . . ." Gloria knew her parents meant well, but they had never gone to college, and frankly, sometimes they interfered a little too much. Did they want to live her life *for* her? While they talked of jobs in big companies, she dreamed of becoming a famous fashion designer with her own line of clothing. She was going to call it "Gloria." Her parents had named her after their favorite rock-and-roll song of all time, "G-L-O-R-I-A." Imagine—her own clothing label with her name on it!

As she reached for the classroom doorknob, Gloria couldn't help wondering about the two questions at the forefront of her mind: "Will I be successful?" and "How long will it take me to finish?" She took a deep breath as she opened the classroom door. *This is it*, she thought. Somehow, she felt as if she were outside herself, watching on the big screen—with Panavision and DTS sound. *This is real; this is me, starring in my own movie*, she said to herself. And even though it felt good, Gloria had to wonder about the ending. All she could do was hope for the best.

SDV 101: Academic Fi...
Focus on College Suc...

CHECK IT OUT!

"Excellence is achieved by the mastery of fundamentals"
Vince Lombardi

Contacts:
Constance Staley

In this require...

- Empower yourself
- Navigate School resources
- Network with professors and...

Classified

JOBS in BUSINESS!
ACME Business Professionals, Inc. is a rising company in North America that employs a wide range of business professionals. Currently seeking professionals ready to launch a career in business (marketing, finance, and sales).

JOB TITLE: Sales Associate, Midwestern Region

RESPONSIBILITIES:
- Assess current status of all existing business
- Provide current level of service or improve service to all clients
- Formulate plan to develop all new business
- Work with local interns to develop future staffing opportunities
- Select and train new associates
- Develop regional hiring/training opportunities
- Expand regional potential

SALARY: commensurate with experience and qualifications Acme Business Professionals, Inc. is known for its commitment to quality, diversity, and exceptional service.

TO APPLY: Send a current resume, along with a cover letter, to our Human Resources Department at Dana.Horner@acmepro.com.

A distributor of office and computer products is in

Course Schedule
Main Campus

FALL SEMESTER

GBTC

Student: Gonzales, Glori...		Meeting	Status
Course ID	Course Title		
Psych 100	INTRO TO PSYCH		
ENGL 099	DEV ENGLISH		
SDV 101	COLLEGE SUCCE...		
	Credit Load...		

Work Schedule   Week # 46

Chique Street South

	Sunday	Monday	Tuesday	Wednesday	Thursday	Friday	Satu...
Abel, Nora	8-5	2-CL			8-5	9-6	8
Collins, Becky	2-CL		9-6	2-CL		2-CL	9-
Gonzales, Gloria		8-5	2-CL		9-6	8-5	

1. Do you have anything in common with Gloria? If so, how are you managing the situation so that you can be successful?
2. Is Gloria a *learner* or a *performer*? Does she think college is mostly about *effort* or *ability*? What do you think?
3. Is Gloria's vision of becoming a fashion designer a goal or a dream? Why?
4. Identify three things (attitudes, beliefs, fears, and so on) that do not show focus and might cause Gloria to make poor life management choices.
5. Identify three things that do show focus and might help Gloria make good life management choices.

Who Are You? And What Do You Want?

Imagine this voicemail greeting: "Hi. At the tone, please answer two of life's most important questions. Who are you? And what do you want?" Beep. Can you answer these questions right now? How much do you really know about yourself and what you want from this life of yours?

Don't worry. These aren't trick questions and there are no wrong answers. But there are some answers that are more right for you than others. College is a great time to think about who you are and what you want. In addition to learning about mathematics or computers or business, college will be a time to learn about yourself: your motivation, values, dreams, and goals. You may make some of the most important choices of your life. Which major will you choose? Which career will you aim for? From this point on, it's up to you. Have you ever heard this phrase with ten two-letter words: "If it is to be, it is up to me"? It's true.

Think about it: a college education is one of the best investments you can make. Once you've earned a college degree, it's yours forever. Someone can steal your car or walk away with your cell phone, but once you've earned a college degree, no one can ever take it from you. Your choice to go to college will pay off in many ways. So even if you aren't sure exactly how you want to spend the rest of your life right now, you can't go wrong by investing in your future.

This book starts with the big picture: managing your life. Notice the phrase is "managing your life"—not controlling your life. Let's face it: Many things in life are beyond our control. But you can manage your life by making smart choices, setting goals you can work toward, paying attention to your time and energy, and motivating yourself. As the title of this book states boldly, it's about focus.

For many of us, focusing is a challenge. We work too many hours, crowd our lives with obligations, and rush from one thing to the next. We think we're good at **multitasking**. We can surf the Internet, text our friends, watch a DVD, and read this chapter—all at the same time! The truth is multitasking causes us to sacrifice some of the

> " What is important is to keep learning, to enjoy challenge, and to tolerate ambiguity. In the end there are no certain answers. "
>
> *Martina Horner, former President of Radcliffe College*

Left: FogStock LLC/Index Open. Right: PhotoObjects.net/Jupiter Images

multitasking doing many different things at once

self-discipline we need to focus and study. Multitasking may make us *feel* highly productive, but learning to focus is what most college students need.[1]

Of course, some people achieve success without a college degree, but by and large, they're the exception. Even Steven Spielberg, self-made billionaire in the film industry and winner of Academy Awards for *Schindler's List* and *Saving Private Ryan*, felt the need to finish the college degree he had started more than thirty years before. "I wanted to accomplish this for many years as a 'thank you' to my parents for giving me the opportunity for an education and a career, and as a personal note for my own family—and young people everywhere—about the importance of achieving their college education goals," he said. "But I hope they get there quicker than I did. Completing the requirements for my degree 33 years after finishing my principal education marks my longest post-production schedule."[2]

If you read this book carefully and follow its advice, it will help you become the best student you can possibly be. It will give you practical tools to help you manage your life. It will take you into your next level of education or into your career. And most of all, it will encourage you to become a true learner. That is this book's challenge to you as you begin your college experience.

Spending Time "in the System"

Spending time "in the system"? No, being in college isn't like being in jail—far from it. "The system" is the approach used in this book to help you learn: the Challenge → Reaction → Insight → Action system. It is based on the work of Dr. John Bransford and his colleagues, who together wrote an influential book called *How People Learn* (2000).

Bransford believes learning is a chain reaction that might look something like this:

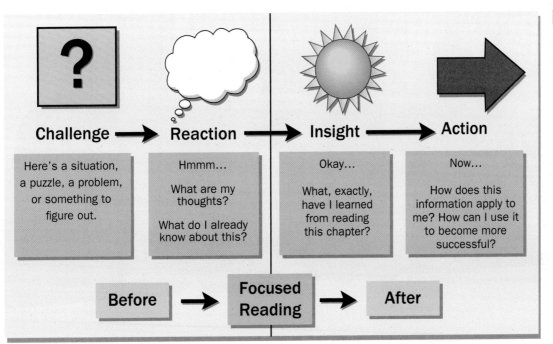

FIGURE 2.1

CRIA System: How People Learn

Source: Based on J. Bransford, et al. (2000). *How People Learn: Brain, Mind, Experience, and School.* Washington, DC: National Academy Press.

This Challenge → Reaction → Insight → Action learning chain reaction is integrated into *FOCUS* to help you learn. Each chapter takes you through "the system" by walking you through four steps:

STEP 1: Challenge. Every time you study a new subject or take a new course, you are challenged, right? Within each chapter of this book, you'll be presented with challenges, beginning with a case study about a college student—perhaps someone like you or a friend—who is experiencing something new and difficult. Research shows that people generally learn more from examples of things going wrong than they can from examples of things going right. As you continue to read, you'll be presented with additional challenges related to the chapter's content to pique your curiosity, motivate you to keep reading, and start a learning chain reaction. Don't skip over this step; it's an important part of the learning process. Challenge yourself!

STEP 2: Reaction. After you read the case study, you are asked for your reaction by answering a few questions about it. What is the student in the case study doing wrong or right? What should the student do differently? Your instructor may ask you to discuss your reaction in class or answer the questions in writing. This step of the learning process shows you how much you already know—before you begin reading. It also shows you what you don't know and what you can learn by reading. The goal of this book is help you become

Surround yourself with people who take their work seriously, but not themselves, those who work hard and play hard.

Colin Powell, former
U.S. Secretary of State

a **deep learner**, as opposed to someone who skims the surface and simply rushes on to the next assignment and the next course. It will ask you to pause, **take stock**, focus, and think.

deep learner someone who learns everything they can about a topic

take stock evaluate your progress

STEP 3: Insight. At the end of each chapter, you'll be asked to revisit the "Reality Check's" same knowledge questions you were asked about in the chapter's opening "Readiness Check." Comparing your responses on the two sets will help you gauge how much you've learned. You'll also be asked to revisit the chapter's opening case study. For example, when Gloria Gonzales and her challenge of turning her dreams into goals may have seemed simple, but after reading about it in the chapter, you might decide that you really hadn't thought about it very deeply and hadn't thought much at all about setting your own goals. The difference between Step 2 (your immediate reaction) and Step 3 (the new insights you've gained from reading) demonstrates that you've learned!

STEP 4: Action. The final step in this learning chain reaction is about action. What have you learned that will change how you face similar challenges? Learning takes place when it relates to you personally, and insights have no impact unless they lead to change. The bottom line is: You must use your insights to take action. Think of this comparison. One day you feel tired, you notice that your clothes are tight, and you are suddenly aware that you're out of shape. You realize that you must eat healthier food and exercise more. But if you don't take action, it won't happen. To become real, new knowledge must lead to personal insights that result in action. What you learned by reading relates to you, and you must use it!

If you follow the system built into this book and use it as you read all your textbooks, the learning chain reaction will become automatic for you.

EXERCISE 2.1

How Do You "Spend" Your Time?[3]

Add up the cost of going to college for an entire term: tuition for one semester/trimester/quarter, the total estimated cost of all the gas you will use to get to and from class for the term, books and supplies, a computer you may have bought, and childcare, or any other expenses related to your going to school. Put down everything you can think of. Divide that grand total by the number of hours you are in school (number of weeks class is session multiplied by the number of hours you are scheduled to be in class). For example, if you are taking two, three-hour classes for a 16 week semester, the number you divide your grand total by will be 96 (= 6 hours × 16 weeks). Completing this exercise will show you how much money each class session costs you—and the cost of missing class! Compare your "hourly rate" with that of your classmates and discuss the results as a group.

How Motivated *Are* You
and *How* Are You Motivated?

Academic Intrinsic Motivation Self-Assessment

*How intrinsically motivated are you? Read each of the following statements and circle
the number beside each statement that most accurately represents your views about yourself.*

	Completely Not True	Somwewhat Not True	Neutral	Somewhat True	Completely True
1. I have academic goals.	1	2	3	4	(5)
2. I am confident I can complete my degree.	1	2	3	4	(5)
3. I determine my career goals.	1	2	3	4	(5)
4. I enjoy solving difficult problems.	1	2	3	(4)	5
5. I work on an assignment until I understand it.	1	2	3	4	(5)
6. I am confident I will finish a degree or certificate.	1	2	3	4	(5)
7. I determine the quality of my academic work.	1	2	3	4	(5)
8. I am pursuing college because I value education.	1	2	3	4	(5)
9. I feel good knowing that I determine how my academic career develops.	1	2	3	4	(5)
10. I have high standards for academic work.	1	2	3	4	(5)
11. Staying in college is my decision.	1	2	3	4	(5)
12. I study because I like to learn new things.	1	2	3	4	(5) ✓
13. I enjoy doing outside readings in connection to my future coursework.	1	2	3	4	(5) ✓
14. I am intrigued by the different topics introduced in my courses.	1	2	3	4	(5)
15. I study because I am curious.	1	2	3	4	(5)
16. I look forward to going to class.	1	2	3	4	(5)
17. I am excited to take more courses within my major.	1	2	3	4	(5)
18. I enjoy learning more within my field of study.	1	2	3	4	(5)
19. I like to find answers to questions about material I am learning.	1	2	3	4	(5)
20. I enjoy studying.	1	2	(3)	4	5
21. I have pictured myself in a career after college.	1	2	3	4	(5)
22. I am excited about the job opportunities I will have later.	1	2	3	4	(5)
23. I have pictured myself being successful in my chosen career.	1	2	3	4	(5)

	Completely Not True	Somewhat Not True	Neutral	Somewhat True	Completely True
24. I believe I will make a substantial contribution to my chosen profession.	1	2	3	4	(5)
25. I feel good knowing I will be a member of the professional community in my area of study.	1	2	3	(4)	5

Total each column, then add your scores across. ___ + ___ + *1* + *2* + *22* =

_ *25* _____ OVERALL SCORE

Continue reading to find out what your overall score means.

French, B. F., & Oakes, W. (2003). Measuring academic intrinsic motivation in the first year of college: Reliability and validity evidence for a new instrument. *Journal of the First Year Experience 15*(1), 83–102.

When it comes to getting a college education, where does motivation come into the picture? In general, motivation is your desire to put forth effort, even when the going gets rough. The word *motivation* comes from Medieval Latin, *motivus*, meaning "moving." What moves you to learn? There are many ways to define motivation, and different people are motivated by different things.

How motivated would you be to learn something difficult, like a new language, one you'd never studied before? Let's say that you were offered a chance to learn Finnish, a challenging language that is not related to English. For example, in Finnish *Kiitoksia oikein paljon* means "thank you very much." Finnish would be a challenge to learn. To determine your level of motivation, it would help to know your attitude toward Finland and Finnish people, whether you needed to learn Finnish for some reason, how you felt about learning it, if you thought you could learn it successfully, if you were rewarded in some way for learning it, and just how stimulating you found the learning process to be.[4] In other words, your motivation depends on many factors, right?

You'd probably be more motivated to learn Finnish if these sorts of things were part of the picture: (a) you were going to visit relatives in Finland and were excited about it, (b) you'd always been good at learning foreign languages and you expected to learn this one easily, (c) your boss was planning to transfer you to Helsinki as part of a big promotion, or (d) you enjoyed your Finnish language class, thought the instructor was a gifted teacher, and found the other students to be as motivated as you were. So, whose job is it to motivate you? Your instructor's? This book's? Yours? *Can* anyone else besides you motivate you? This book will ask you: how motivated *are* you to succeed in college? And *how* are you motivated?

To assess your own motivation, it's important to understand the difference between *extrinsic* and *intrinsic* motivation. People who are **extrinsically**, or externally, motivated learn in order to get a grade, earn credits, or complete a requirement, for example. They are motivated by things outside themselves. You could be motivated

extrinsically outside yourself

You are never given a wish without the power to make it come true. You may have to work for it, however.

Richard Bach, from Illusions

intrinsically inside yourself

to learn Finnish to earn three credits or to get an A. People who are **intrinsically**, or internally, motivated learn because they're curious, fascinated, challenged, or because they truly want to master a subject. They are motivated from within. You could be motivated to learn Finnish for the challenge, because you're curious about it, or because you find it fascinating. Let's be realistic, however. Extrinsic motivation is real and important. You need to earn college credits, and you'd rather get A's than F's. But how intrinsically motivated you are in college will have a great deal to do with just how successful you are. The motivation to become truly educated must come from within you.

FIGURE 2.2

Extrinsic versus Intrinsic Motivation

Extrinsic Motivation

Intrinsic Motivation

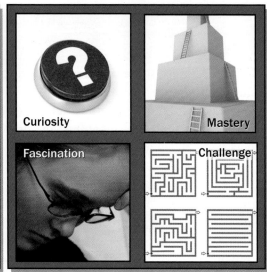

(clockwise from top left): Christopher Hall, 2009/Used under license from Shutterstock.com; Yari, 2009/Used under license from Shutterstock.com; Palto, 2009/Used under license from Shutterstock.com; Pling, 2009/Used under license from Shutterstock.com; Vasilius, 2009/Used under license from Shutterstock.com; Yuri Arcurs, 2009/Used under license from Shutterstock.com; Andresr, 2009. Used under license from Shutterstock.com; Scott Maxwell/LuMaxArt, 2009/Used under license from Shutterstock.com.

CAREER OUTLOOK: *Be Observant*

> **You have to learn the rules of the game. And then you have to play better than anyone else.**
> ALBERT EINSTEIN

Learn the rules of the game. In school—and throughout your life—you'll be learning what's sometimes called "The Hidden Curriculum." These are things everyone knows, more or less, but never learned formally. For example, most people know that it's not polite to tell off-color jokes to people you've just met or smack your gum while giving a speech. In the same way, the "grapevine" or informal network on the job is important to understand. To be successful, you must be tuned in. Observe your colleagues and supervisors. How do they act, how do they talk, what are their values and boundaries, what lines do they just not cross? When you have questions about these things, talk about them with people who seem to be "in the know." Understand the culture of the organization you work for. What does it value? Who holds the power? Where do you fit in, and what can you contribute?

You completed the Academic Intrinsic Motivation Scale (AIMS) in Exercise 2.2, which is designed to measure your intrinsic, or internal, motivation to succeed in college in terms of these four C-Factors:

1. **Curiosity.** Do you want to learn new things? Are you truly interested in what you're learning? Are you curious? Do you ask questions?

2. Control. Do you think working hard in your academic courses will pay off? Do you believe you can control how successful you'll be?

3. Career outlook. Are you goal oriented? Are you future oriented? Can you imagine yourself using what you learn in college to help you get a job you want?

4. Challenge. Does your college coursework challenge you? It is important that the level of challenge is right for you. Too much challenge can cause you to become frustrated and give up. Not enough challenge can cause you to lose interest.[5]

Think about it this way: If your overall score on the AIMS was 100–125, you're intrinsically motivated at a high level. If you scored between 75 and 99, you're intrinsically motivated at a moderate level, but increasing your intrinsic motivation may help you achieve more. If you scored below 75, a lack of intrinsic motivation could interfere with your college success. If you're intrinsically motivated, you'll use all the learning tools offered to you in FOCUS.

Like the Challenge → Reaction → Insight → Action system, the Academic Intrinsic Motivation Scale's C-Factors reappear throughout the book to boost your intrinsic motivation:

 Curiosity: Each chapter includes a short article on something that's related to college success. You'll read cutting-edge information that may make you curious to read more about it somewhere else.

 Control: You are encouraged throughout this book to apply what you are learning to your most challenging task this term. You can apply the information to your toughest class or to a challenging part of your job outside school.

 Career: Each chapter includes a unique feature designed to connect your academic experiences, your coursework, and your college learning, with the world of professional and career success. For example, when the text emphasizes the importance of good communication skills in college, the Career Outlook feature will also stress how effective writing, speaking, and listening skills can be crucial to on-the-job success. In each chapter, college success skills are extended and underscored as career skills.

 Challenge: In general, if a course is too challenging, you may be tempted to give up. If it's too easy, you may lose interest. Adjusting the level of challenge to what's right for you is key to keeping yourself motivated to learn. Online quizzes for each chapter will challenge you so that you can work at your best. For more practice online, access the CourseMate via www.cengagebrain.com/shop/ISBN/1439083908 to take the Challenge Yourself Online Quiz.

The Ideal Student

Create your own personal top-ten list of the characteristics (attitudes and actions) of an ideal student. Bring your completed list to your next class session so that everyone can read their lists and create a master list that everyone can agree on. Put your initials next to each of the ten items on the master list that you promise to do throughout the term. Your personal top-ten list, which your instructor may discuss with you individually at a later time, will become your own list of goals for the course.

Give Yourself an Attitude Adjustment

attitude state of mind or mental position

aptitude natural ability

There's a difference of opinion on the subject of **attitude**. Some people say attitude is not all that important. Attitude-schmattitude, they say. Others say that *attitude* is more important than **aptitude**. What do you think?

In research studies conducted by Rick Snyder at the University of Kansas, students who scored high on a measure of hope got higher grades. Snyder explained that students with high hopes set themselves higher goals and know how to work hard to attain them.

Quick quiz. How many times a day do you catch yourself saying "Whatever . . . ," and rolling your eyes? Whatever-ness—an attitude of boredom and impatience—takes a lot less effort than staying positive. Whether you realize it or not, whatevers chip away at your motivation, and they can cause you to give up on your dreams and goals. When it comes to your college education, one good thing you can do for yourself is to delete the word *whatever* from your vocabulary. Your education is much too important for whatevers—and so are you.

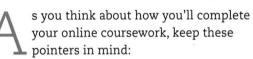ONLINE **TechKnow**

 **Improve Your Grade**
Online Flashcards
Glossary

As you think about how you'll complete your online coursework, keep these pointers in mind:

- **Be detailed in setting your goals.** Include *what* you will achieve, *where* (at home or in a lab on campus), and *when* (Thursday afternoon from 5–7 p.m. after I get off work). For example, "I will do online research for my next assignment for two hours every weeknight with no interruptions until the due date."

- **Make sure your goals are realistic.** Don't say you'll work in the evening for two hours on online homework, two hours on tasks from your job, two hours on answering emails, and spend two hours with your family. There's not enough time in the evening to do all that—so prioritize and cut back in your goals

- **State your goals positively.** It's better to say, "I will work on my online assignments for one hour before checking my emails," than "I won't check email until I complete my online studies."

- **Approach your goals with a positive attitude.** Respond to online assignments with spirit, enjoyment, and enthusiasm. You'll be much more productive and proud of what you accomplish.[6]

> **You must motivate yourself EVERY DAY!**
>
> *Matthew Stasior, motivational speaker*

Six Ways to Adjust Your Attitude

The good thing about attitude is that you can change it yourself. As you think about benefits of fine-tuning your attitude, keep these six recommendations in mind:

1. **Know that you always have choices.** Regardless of circumstances—your income, your background, or your academic experiences—you always have a choice, even if it's limited to how you choose to view your current situation.

2. **Take responsibility for your own outcomes.** Coach Vince Lombardi used to have his players look in a mirror before every game and ask themselves, "Am I looking at the person who is helping me win or the one who is holding me back?" Blaming others simply weakens your own power to work toward **constructive responses** to challenges.

   constructive responses
   statements or actions that promote improvement

3. **Choose your words carefully.** "Can't" and "won't" are two of the biggest obstacles to a healthy attitude. Also pay attention to how you describe things. Is the cup half empty or half full? State things in the positive rather than the negative (for example, "stay healthy" rather than "don't get sick"). Language is a reflection of attitude.

4. **Fill your mind with messages about the attitude you want to have.** The old saying, "garbage in, garbage out," applies to attitudes as well. There are plenty of books, CDs, and films that offer positive, motivating messages. Paying attention to role models whose traits you admire is also a great way to boost your outlook.

5. **Turn learning points into turning points.** Have you ever watched someone do something so badly that you've said to yourself, "I'm never going to do that! I'm going to do it differently!"? You can also choose to learn from your own mistakes and setbacks. They all offer some sort of lesson, even if it takes a bit of distance from the event to see what you can learn.

6. **Acknowledge your blessings.** Taking time at the end of each day to recognize and feel gratitude for the blessings in your life—no matter how large or small—is a great way to develop a positive attitude.

BOX **2.1**

Statements That Ought to Be Outlawed in College . . . and Why

Since words reflect attitudes (and help shape them), listen for statements like these escaping from your mouth. They can negatively affect your attitude and therefore your learning:

- **"I thought college classes would be more interesting than they are."** Interesting is in the mind of the beholder.

- **"I didn't learn a thing in that class."** Actively search for what you can take away from a class, even if it didn't quite meet your expectations.

- **"The textbook is really dull. Why bother reading it?"** Reading may not be your favorite pastime, but

you may learn more from a textbook than you can predict.

- **"The professor is soooo-o-o boring."** In life, we all interact with all types of personalities, so begin to appreciate differences in communication styles.

- **"Why do I have to take this required course? What's the point?"** The point is to broaden your horizons, expand your skills as a critical thinker, and become a lifelong learner.

Care enough to give yourself every opportunity to do your best. And, yes, every class, every situation in life, is an opportunity. You're worth it.[7]

Your Academic Autobiography

Write a three-paragraph academic autobiography describing your preparation for college. Describe the quality of your primary, middle, and high school learning experiences, and your work experiences as well. Did they prepare you for what you're experiencing now in college? What do you think will be your strengths and weaknesses as a college student? Look back at your academic self throughout your schooling and look ahead to the kind of student you're planning to be in college, then write your academic autobiography. Or as an alternative, create a presentation answering these questions for your classmates.

Ability versus Effort: What's More Important?

Successful people have several things in common: They love learning, seek challenges, value effort, and persevere even when things become difficult.[8] They demonstrate both ability and effort. These two things are the basic requirements for success. College is about both.

Think about some of the possible combinations of ability and effort. If you have high ability and exert great effort, you'll most likely succeed. If you have high ability and exert little effort, and still succeed, you've just proved how smart you must be! But if you have high ability and exert little effort and fail, you can always claim you didn't have the time to invest or you didn't care, right? You can always say that you could have done well if you'd tried harder: "I could have written those Harry Potter books; I'm a great writer." If you had really tried for that kind of success, you wouldn't have been able to say that. Such rationalizing can be a dangerous strategy, one that's called **"self-handicapping."**[9] Some college students consciously or unconsciously

self-handicapping hurting your own chances to succeed

apply this strategy. They exert little effort, perhaps because they have no confidence in themselves or because they fear failure, and then they rationalize when they don't do well.

EXERCISE 2.5

Theories of Intelligence Scale

What is intelligence? Are people born with a certain amount? Or can it be cultivated through learning? Using the following scale, write in the number that corresponds to your opinion in the space next to each statement. There are no right or wrong answers.

1	2	3	4	5	6
Strongly Agree	Mostly Agree	Agree	Disagree	Mostly Disagree	Strongly Disagree

___6___ 1. You have a certain amount of intelligence, and you can't really do much to change it.

___6___ 2. You can learn new things, but you can't really change your basic intelligence.

___1___ 3. You can always substantially change how intelligent you are.

___5___ 4. No matter how much intelligence you have, you can always change it quite a bit.

Research shows that what you *believe* about your own intelligence—your *mindset*—can make a difference in how successful you'll be in college. At first glance this statement seems absurd. After all, you're either smart or you're not, right? Wrong.

The scaled questions demonstrate that there are two basic ways to define intelligence. Some of us are **performers**, who agree with statements 1 and 2, while others of us are **learners**, who agree more with statements 3 and 4. *Performers* believe that intelligence is a fixed trait that cannot be changed. From the moment you're born, you have a certain amount of intelligence that belongs to you, and that's that. *Learners*, on the other hand, believe you can grow your intelligence if you capitalize on opportunities to learn. Whenever you tackle a tough challenge, you learn from it. The more you learn, the more intelligent you can become. Understanding which view of intelligence you believe in will make a difference in how you approach your college classes, and how successful you'll be.

Students who are taught the value of a learning mindset over a performance mindset can actually achieve more than students who don't.[10] In one study, college students' views of intelligence predicted the goals students valued in college. *Performers* were more likely to want to give up in challenging situations; learners wanted to try harder.[11] In one study that measured the electrical activity in college students'

performers someone who is driven to appear smart

learners someone who is driven to learn, even by making mistakes

© Larry Harwood Photography. Property of Cengage Learning.

"The greatest mistake you can make in life is to be continually fearing you will make one.

Elbert Hubbard, American writer, artist, and philosopher, 1856–1915

In Class: Think about the courses you're enrolled in this term. Which one will be the toughest? Use the following chart to analyze your C-Factors for this course. Describe this course in terms of its challenge level, your curiosity about the subject, how much control you believe you have to succeed, and the way each class impacts your career outlook. Once you've determined the levels of challenge, curiosity, control, and career outlook, remember that it's your responsibility to adjust them.

- What is the relationship between the four C-Factors and your intrinsic motivation to learn? For example, if you don't feel you have much control over how well you do, how can you change that?

- What can you do to increase your intrinsic motivation and become more successful?

Look at Gloria's entry as a model.

On the Job: If you prefer, think about your toughest task on the job. Perhaps you've been assigned a new project, and you're not sure where to start. Use the bottom to analyze the level of challenge, how much curiosity you have about figuring it out, how much control you think you have over how successful you'll be at it, and how learning from this experience might affect your targeted career. Finally, what can you do to adjust these factors, if you need to?

Course Title	Challenge	Curiosity	Control	Career Outlook	Adjustments Required
Composition	Very High: never been good at writing	Very Low: had a discouraging teacher in H.S.	Moderate: probably higher than it feels to me	Will need to know how to write in any job	Need to spend more time pre-writing and going to the campus Writing Center for help

Job Task	Challenge	Curiosity	Control	Career Outlook	Adjustments Required

brains as they performed a difficult task, brain activity showed that *performers* cared most about whether their answers were right or wrong, while *learners* were interested in follow-up information they could learn from.[12] Yet another study showed that *learners* are more likely to buckle down academically, even when they feel depressed.[13] It's clear: Believing you're a *learner* provides advantages in motivation, achievement, enjoyment, and commitment.

Regardless of what you believe about your precise intelligence level, the fact is this: *Intelligence can be cultivated through learning.* And people's theories about their intelligence levels can be shifted.

> Ability is what you're capable of doing. Motivation determines what you do. Attitude determines how well you do it.
>
> *Lou Holtz, former college football coach and ESPN sports analyst*

What Drives You? Values, Dreams, and Goals

EXERCISE 2.6

Core Values Self-Assessment

What are your core values? What's most important to you—deep down inside? Review the following list and check off the items that you value. Don't spend too much time thinking about each one; just go with your initial gut reaction. For each item, ask yourself "Is this something that's important to me?"

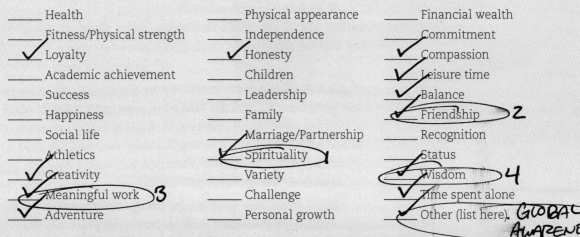

_____ Health	_____ Physical appearance	_____ Financial wealth
_____ Fitness/Physical strength	_____ Independence	✓ Commitment
✓ Loyalty	✓ Honesty	✓ Compassion
_____ Academic achievement	_____ Children	✓ Leisure time
_____ Success	_____ Leadership	✓ Balance
_____ Happiness	_____ Family	✓ Friendship 2
_____ Social life	_____ Marriage/Partnership	_____ Recognition
_____ Athletics	_____ Spirituality	_____ Status
✓ Creativity	_____ Variety	✓ Wisdom 4
✓ Meaningful work 3	_____ Challenge	✓ Time spent alone
✓ Adventure	_____ Personal growth	_____ Other (list here) GLOBAL AWARENESS 5

Now review all of the items you checked off and circle the five that are most important to you at this point in your life. Then rank them by putting a number next to each of the five circled values with number one as your top priority. Finally, take stock. Is this the person you want to be? Is there anything about your values that you would like to change? If so, what's keeping you from making this change?

Before tackling the big questions about what you want to create with your life, it's important to first take a close look in the mirror. Who are you? What makes you tick? What do you **value**? What are your **goals**? Where will your **dreams** take you?

value something you think is important

goals something you make specific plans to achieve

dreams something you wish for

Values at the Core

What do you value in life? By taking time to examine your personal values, managing your life will become easier and make more sense. Values can be things you can't exactly see or touch, like love or respect, or things that are visible and real, like family or money. Understanding how they motivate you isn't as simple as it might seem. Values can change as you go through life. For example, if you're single now, you may value the freedom to meet a variety of potential romantic partners. Later, however, you may want a committed relationship because you want stability in your life. For this reason, it's important to look at your values from time to time and rethink them.

Another complicating factor is that values can conflict with one another. Suppose that you value honesty and

> **Knowing others is intelligence; knowing yourself is true wisdom. Mastering others is strength; mastering yourself is true power.**
>
> *Lao Tzu, Taoist philosopher*

© Patrick Giardino/Corbis

Self-knowledge is far more important than self-confidence.

Simon Cowell, American Idol *judge,*
from I Don't Mean to Be Rude, But . . .

kindness, and you are at a party and a friend asks you what you think of her new hair color. You honestly think it's hideous, but telling her so would hurt her feelings, thus violating your value of being kind. How do you respond? That would depend on which value is a higher priority for you. You have to make an on-the-spot decision about which value to use. Once you define your values, however, they can help you make everyday choices, as well as big decisions, like which major to pursue in college. For example, if academic achievement is one of your top values, the next time you have the urge to cut class, consider what that choice says about your value system. There is a great inner satisfaction that comes from living a life tied to core values.

Dreams versus Goals

Do you agree or disagree with this statement: "I can be anything I want to be"? You've probably heard this statement over and over. Your family and teachers all want you to have positive self-esteem, and certainly there are many career options available today. But is it true? Can you be *anything* you want to be? What's the difference between a dream and a goal?

As a student, you may dream of being a famous doctor or a famous athlete or just plain famous. That's the beauty of dreams—you can imagine yourself doing anything. When you're dreaming, you don't even have to play by the rules of reality. Dreams are fantasy-based—*you* in a perfect world. But when it's time to come back to reality, you discover that there are rules, after all. You may have dreamed of becoming a top-earning NBA player or a top fashion model when you were a child, but you have grown up to be the same height as Uncle Al or Aunt Sue—and that's not tall enough.

Dreams alone are not enough when it comes to creating your future. As professional life coach Diana Robinson says, "A dream is a goal without legs." And without legs, that goal is going nowhere. Dreaming is the first step to creating the future you want, but making dreams come true requires planning and hard work. Gloria Gonzales wanted to become a fashion merchandiser because she liked clothes and people always told her she looked good. As she continues through college, however, she will come to understand the nuts and bolts of the fashion business. The fashion industry might be challenging to break into, but that doesn't mean she should abandon her dream. She must find a realistic way to help her turn her dreams into goals. Just dreaming isn't enough.

CURIOSITY: *KNOW THYSELF! HOW HARD CAN THAT BE?*

Knowing yourself doesn't sound like much of a challenge, does it? After all, you've lived with yourself for a long time. You know every freckle, every dimple, every quirk. Or do you?

Socrates advised many centuries ago, "Know thyself." But David Dunning, professor of psychology at Cornell University and author of *Self-Insight: Roadblocks and Detours on the Path to Knowing Thyself,* says that most of us really don't know ourselves as well as we think we do. In fact, when we're asked to predict how well we'll do at something, and that prediction is compared to how well we actually did, most of us are off base. In one study, college students were given a pop quiz after they finished a task, like memorizing a list of words or figuring out a problem. Then they were asked how well they thought they did.

Dunning and his research colleague, Justin Kruger, split the test-takers into four quarters: students who actually did the worst, those that did a little better, those that did pretty well, and those who did best.

In general, students who thought they did well sometimes performed in the bottom quarter, and students with the highest scores sometimes underestimated their performance. Take a look at Figure 2.3, which summarizes the typical pattern uncovered in Dunning's research to date. In particular, compare participants in the bottom quarter with those in the top one, and you'll see that the participants who did the worst were extremely optimistic!

Why is this so? Why aren't we all right on the mark? Specifically, why can't people tell when they're not doing a good job? One reason Dunning offers is that people can't be expected to always know when they're not doing well. Because they don't know how to do what they're doing (and therefore they

aren't doing it well), they're simply not in a position to know how they actually did. The skills they need in order to do a good job are the exact same skills they need to recognize whether they are doing a good job. So they hope for the best. And while optimism isn't a bad thing—in fact, it's generally a good thing—realism is critical, too, in college and in life.

That's why it's important to seek input from your instructors about the quality of your work. Grading it and giving you feedback is their job! Work with other students so that you can see their skill levels compared with your own. Learn from the self-assessments in this book. Use your classes as an opportunity to gather all the self-knowledge you can. Rather than simply hoping for the best, do all you can to get to know yourself better and give college your best shot.

FIGURE 2.3

Typical Relationship Found between Perceived and Actual Performance

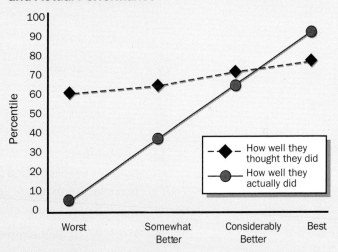

Source: D. Dunning. (2005). *Self-Insight: Roadblocks and Detours on the Path to Knowing Thyself.* New York: Psychology Press, p. 18.

Dreams are exciting; you can let your imagination run wild. Goals are real; you must work out how to actually achieve your dreams. Goal setting is an important part of the life management skills this book will help you develop. Your goals may not seem at all clear to you right now, but the important thing is to learn that there's a right way and a wrong way to set your

What you get by achieving your goals is not as important as what you become by achieving your goals.

Zig Ziglar, Motivational speaker, writer, and trainer

goals. The best way to ensure that the goals you set will serve you well is to make sure you *FOCUS*. Here's a brief overview of what that means.

F **Fit.** Your goal must fit your values, your character, and who you are as a person. Goals that conflict with any of these things will not only be difficult to accomplish, but they just won't work. If your goal is to become a writer for a travel magazine because you love adventure, but flying in planes terrifies you, you're in trouble.

O **Ownership.** Own your goals: See it, taste it, want it! It must be your goal, not someone else's goal for you. Ask yourself: Does the thought of achieving this goal get me fired up? Do I genuinely own this goal or do I feel I ought to have this goal because it sounds good or makes someone else happy?

C **Concreteness.** For any goal to be effective, it must be real. In other words, you must be able to describe your goal in detail: "To run a mile in less than six minutes by March 4th" is much more concrete than "to eventually run faster." The more concrete, the better.

U **Usefulness.** Goals must be useful. They must serve a purpose, and that purpose should be tied to your long-term vision of the person you want to become. For example, if you want to work for an international hotel some day, it would be useful to begin studying a foreign language now.

S **Stretch.** In the business world, people talk about stretch goals. These are goals that require employees to stretch beyond their usual limits to achieve something more challenging. Goals must be based in reality, but also offer you a chance to grow beyond the person you currently are.

Your goals should include both short- and long-term goals. Once your long-term goals are set (though they may shift over time as *you* shift over time), you will then want to set some short-term goals, which act as in-between steps to achieving your long-term goals.

| Long-Term Goals | Short-Term Goals |
What do I want to accomplish...	What do I want to accomplish...
In my lifetime?	This year?
In the next twenty years?	This month?
In the next ten years?	This week?
In the next three to five years?	Today?

How FULL is your plate?

"This constant, unproductive preoccupation with all the things we have to do is the single largest consumer of time and energy."

—KERRY GLEESON, TIME MANAGEMENT EXPERT

How much time do you spend worrying about how much is on your plate—as opposed to removing things one at a time in a systematic way? Sometimes the biggest enemy of time management is worry. We're stopped by our worries and fears. How true is that statement for you?

-A3K-/iStockphoto.com

TRY IT!

List the three items you worry about getting done most, and for each one, list three suggestions you should follow to improve your time management skills and your life.

step 3 INSIGHT *Now* What Do You Think?

At the beginning of this chapter, Gloria Gonzales faced a series of challenges as a new college student. Now after learning from this chapter, would you respond differently to any of the questions you answered about the "FOCUS Challenge Case"? Using what you learned in the chapter, write a paragraph ending to Gloria's case study. What are some of the possible outcomes for her?

step 4 ACTION Your Plans for Change

1. Identify one new thing you learned in reading this chapter. Why did you select the one you've selected? How will it affect what you do in your college classes?
2. Do you have some of the same questions Gloria does about your own level of motivation to achieve in college? How could you increase your motivation? How important might that be?
3. How do your own goals and dreams differ? How do you plan to turn your dreams into goals?

On a scale of 1 to 5, answer these questions now that you've completed this chapter.

1 = not very/not much/very little/low   5 = very/a lot/very much/high

How much do you know *now*?

Now rate your current level of knowledge about topics covered in this chapter.

How people learn

1   2   3   4   ⑤

Intrinsic versus extrinsic motivation

1   2   3   4   ⑤

Dreams versus goals

1   2   3   4   ⑤

FOCUSed goal-setting

1   2   3   4   ⑤

How useful might the information in this chapter be to you?

How much do you think this information might affect your college success?

1   2   3   4   ⑤

How much do you think this information might affect your career success after college?

1   2   3   4   ⑤

How long did it actually take you to complete this chapter (both the reading and writing tasks)?

___4___ Hour(s) ___15___ Minutes

 Challenge Yourself Online Quiz. To find out how much you've learned, access the CourseMate via www.cengagebrain.com/shop/ISBN/1439083908 to take the Challenge Yourself Online Quiz.

Compare these answers with your answers from the "Readiness Check" at the beginning of this chapter. How might the gaps between what you thought before starting the chapter and what you now think affect how you approach the next chapter?

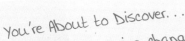

chapter 3 Learning about Learning

You're About to Discover. . .

✔ How learning changes your brain
✔ How people are intelligent in different ways
✔ How you learn through your senses
✔ How to become a more efficient and effective learner
✔ How your personality type can affect your learning style

READINESS CHECK | What do you **Know?**

Before beginning this chapter, take a moment to answer these questions. Your answers will help you assess how ready you are to focus.

1 = not very/not much/very little/low   5 = very/a lot/very much/high

How much do you *already* know?

Rate your current level of knowledge about topics covered in this chapter.

Learning and the human brain
1   2   3   4 ⑤

Multiple intelligences
1   2   3 ④ 5

Sensory preferences for learning
1   2 ③ 4   5

Becoming a better learner
1   2   3   4 ⑤

How motivated are you to learn *more*?

In general, how motivated are you to learn the material in this chapter?
1 ② 3   4   5

How much do you think this information might affect your college success?
1   2   3 ④ 5

How much do you think this information might affect your career success after college?
1   2 ③ 4   5

How ready are you to read *now*?

How ready are you to focus on this chapter—physically, intellectually, and emotionally? Which of these three areas is most challenging for you right now? Circle a number to represent it.
1   2 ③ 4   5

If any of your answers is below a 3, consider addressing the issue before reading. Then, read the chapter carefully, while looking for ways to improve your focus.

Finally, how long do you think it will take you to complete this chapter? If you start and stop, keep track of the overall time.

_____ Hour(s) _____ Minutes

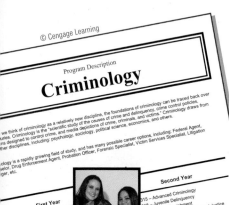

Tammy Ko

How depressing!" Tammy Ko whispered under her breath as she walked out of her "Introduction to Criminology" class on a dark, rainy Thursday afternoon. *What's with him, anyway?* she asked herself about the instructor.

Program Description

Criminology

we think of criminology as a relatively new discipline, the foundations of criminology can be traced back over uries. Criminology is the "scientific study of the causes of crime and delinquency, crime control policies, ms designed to control crime, and media depictions of crime, criminals, and victims." Criminology draws from ther disciplines, including: psychology, sociology, political science, economics, and others.

ology is a rapidly growing field of study, and has many possible career options, including: Federal Agent, elor, Drug Enforcement Agent, Probation Officer, Forensic Specialist, Victim Services Specialist, Litigation ger, etc.

First Year

CRIM 103 – Introduction to Criminolo
CRIM 105 – Research Methods for S
ENGL 130 – Scientific Writing
CHEM 106 – General Chemistry I
CHEM 108 – General Chemistry II
MATH 135 – Calculus I
MATH 136 – Calculus II
Elective – 3 credits

ELECTIVES
- CSI: Fact or Fantasy?
- Interview and Interroga
- Professionalism and E
- Investigation of Injury
- Crime Scene & Crime
- Psychosociology of C
- Legal Aspects of Crim

Second Year

315 – Advanced Criminology
318 – Juvenile Delinquency
320 – Capital Punishment
300 – Ethical Dilemmas in Criminal Justice
M 350 – The Correctional System
M 360 – The Judicial System
YC 310 – Abnormal Psychology
ectives – 6 credits

Tammy was a first-semester student at the booming career college in the city where she grew up. Even though she found college life hectic because of all the hours she had to work to pay her own tuition, Tammy was excited about working on her associate's degree in criminal justice. She wanted to get into her state's police academy and specialize in forensics, and she knew a degree would help her chances. The crime shows on TV were her favorites. She watched them all each week. She rationalized how much time it took by thinking of it as career development. The fun was picturing herself as an investigator solving headline cases: "Man Slain, Found in City Park" or "Modern Day 'Jack the Ripper' Terrorizes Las Vegas." She could envision herself hunched over laboratory equipment, testing for fibers or DNA, and actually breaking the case.

When she registered for classes, her academic advisor had told her that taking an "Introduction to Criminology" course would be the right place to start. "It'll teach you how to think," he'd said, "and it'll give you the background you need to understand the criminal mind. At the end of this class," he said, "you'll know if you really want to pursue a career in law enforcement." *Maybe it would teach me how to think*, Tammy thought to herself now that the term was underway, *if only I could understand the instructor. Forget understanding the criminal mind—I'd just like a glimpse into his!*

Mr. Caldwell was quiet and reserved, and he seemed a bit out of touch. He dressed as if he hadn't bought a new piece of clothing in twenty years. In class, he organized all his papers neatly on his desk and covered each day's material carefully, point by point. Tammy wished

POLICE LINE DO NOT CROSS

he'd depart from his notes occasionally to explore other interesting things. Tammy had always preferred teachers who created exciting things to do in class over teachers who went completely by the book. Tammy's biggest complaint about Mr. Caldwell was that he only talked about *theories* of criminology. When was he ever going to get to the hands-on part of the course? She couldn't help thinking, *When will we stop talking about theories and start working on real cases—like the ones on all those TV shows?*

To make matters worse, learning from lectures was not Tammy's strong suit. She hadn't done well on the first exam because she'd had to just memorize things that didn't make much sense to her, and her D grade showed it.

The entire exam consisted of one question: "Compare and contrast two theories of criminology discussed in class thus far." Tammy hated essay tests. She was at her best on tests with right or wrong answers, like true-false or multiple-choice questions. Making sense out of spoken words that go by very quickly during a lecture and trying to figure out what instructors wanted on essay tests were usually challenges for her.

But her "Introduction to Criminology" class was far from hands-on. In fact, Tammy had noticed that many of her teachers preferred *talking* about things to *doing* things. They seemed to take more interest in theories than in the real world. *Too bad,* she thought, *the real world is where exciting things happen.* Although she hated to admit it, sometimes Tammy couldn't wait for college to be over so that she could begin her career in the real world.

A few of Tammy's friends had taken Mr. Caldwell's classes, too. Her friends' advice was "Just try and memorize the stuff; that's all you can do." Regardless of what they happened to be talking about, somehow the conversation always came around to Mr. Caldwell and how impossible it was to learn in his classes.

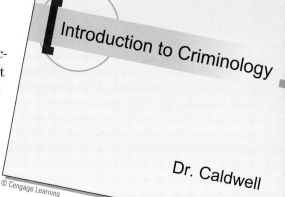

Introduction to Criminology

Dr. Caldwell

© Cengage Learning

Michael J. Thompson, 2009/Shutterstock.com

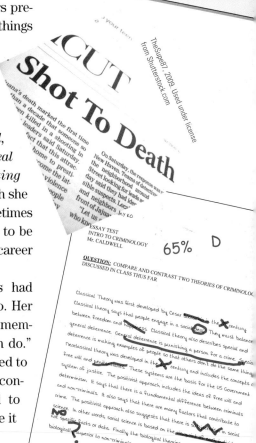

Shot To Death

TheSupe87, 2009. from Shutterstock.com. Used under license

© Cengage Learning

NORTH RIVERVIEW POLICE
Requirements for Applicants

Prospective North Riverview Police Officers must meet all of the following minimum requirements. Requirements are determined by the City of North Riverview and the State Government.

QUICK CHECKLIST:

Be 19 years of age or older as outlined above.

Possess a high school diploma or GED.

Be a citizen of the United States.

Be free from convictions of disqualifying offenses.

Be personally examined by a State licensed physician.

Be personally examined by a State licensed psychologist.

Be subject to a thorough background investigation.

Successfully complete a basic police training course given at a commissioned, certified school.

CANDIDATES MUST HAVE A WORKING KNOWLEDGE OF:

• the laws controlling, and the procedures, practices, and techniques necessary to police patrol operations

© Cengage Learning

Dusan Po, 2010. Used under copyright from Shutterstock.com.

1. Do you have anything in common with Tammy? If so, how are you managing the situation so that you can be successful?
2. Is Tammy smart? If so, in what ways? What is she particularly good at?
3. What sensory modality does Tammy prefer for taking in information? Does she learn best by viewing information through charts and graphs, for example, by talking and listening, by reading and writing, or by actually doing things?
4. What are the differences between Mr. Caldwell's teaching style and Tammy's learning style? How do these differences affect Tammy's learning?
5. What should Tammy do to become a better learner in Mr. Caldwell's class?

Go to the Head of the Class: Learning and the Brain

EXERCISE 3.1

What Is Learning?

*The following statements represent common student views on learning. Think about each statement, and mark it **true** or **false** based on your honest opinion.*

F 1. Learning is often hard work and really not all that enjoyable.

T 2. Memorization and learning are basically the same thing.

F 3. The learning done in school is often gone in a few weeks or months.

T 4. In college, most learning takes place in class.

F 5. Learning is usually the result of listening to an instructor lecture or reading a textbook.

F 6. The best way to learn is by working alone.

T 7. Most students know intuitively how they learn best.

F 8. Teachers control what students learn.

F 9. Learning only deals with subjects taught in school.

F 10. The learning pace is controlled by the slowest learner in the class.

You probably noticed that many of these statements attempt to put learning in a negative light. How many did you mark true? This chapter will help you understand more about learning as a process and about yourself as a learner. As you read, your goal should be to use the insights you gain to become a better learner.

Let's start our exploration of the learning process close to home—in our own heads. What's going on up there, anyway? While your hands are busy manipulating test tubes in chemistry lab, or your eyes are watching your psychology instructor's PowerPoint presentation, what's your brain up to? The answer? Plenty.

Use It or Lose It

The human brain consists of a complex web of connections between neurons or nerve cells. This web grows in complexity as it incorporates new knowledge.

But if the connections are not reinforced frequently, you lose them. As you learn new things, you work to hardwire these connections, making them less likely to deteriorate. When your instructors repeat portions of the previous week's lecture or assign homework so you can practice material covered in class, they're helping you to form connections in your brain by using and reusing them—or, in other words, to learn. Repetition is vital to learning. You must use and reuse information in order to hardwire it.

American humorist Will Rogers once said, "You know, you've got to exercise your *brain* just like your muscles." He was right. Giving your brain the exercise it needs—now and in your years after college—will help you form connections between neurons that, if you keep using them, will last a lifetime. From a biological point of view, that's what being a lifelong learner means. The age-old advice "use it or lose it" is true when it comes to learning.

Ask Questions and Hardwire Your Connections

Your instructors have been studying their disciplines for years, perhaps decades. They have developed extensive hardwired connections between their brain neurons. They are *experts*.

By contrast, you are a *novice* or newcomer to whatever discipline you're studying. You've not yet developed the brain wiring that your instructors have developed. That can lead to a potential problem. Sometimes instructors are so familiar with what they already know from years of traveling the same pathways in their brains that what you're learning for the first time seems obvious to them. Without even realizing it, they can expect what is *familiar* to them to be *obvious* to you. Think of how challenging it is when you try to teach something that you understand thoroughly to another person who doesn't, like teaching someone who has never used a computer before how to upload an assignment.

Since you're a novice, you may not understand everything your instructors say. Ask questions, check, clarify, probe, and persist until you do understand. Sometimes your confusion is not due to a lack of knowledge, but a lack of the *correct* knowledge. For example, you may study for a test by doing only one thing—reading and rereading the textbook. Actually, it's important to be familiar with many different ways to study and then choose the ones that work best for you.

Think of it this way. Some of the brain wiring you brought with you to college is positive and useful, and some actually hurts more than it helps. When you learn, you not only add new connections, but you rewire some old connections. While you're in college, you're under construction![1]

Take Charge and Create the Best Conditions for Learning

Throughout this discussion, we've been talking about processes inside your brain. *Your* brain, not anyone else's. The bottom line is this: Learning must be *internally initiated*—by you. It can only be *externally encouraged*—by someone else. You're in charge of your own learning. Learning changes your brain.

Colin Anderson/Blend Images/Corbis

When we come to know something, we have performed an act that is as biological as when we digest something.

Henry Plotkin, Darwin Machines and the Nature of Knowledge *(1994)*

prerequisite something that must be completed before something else

Let's look at food as an analogy: If learning is a process that is as biological as digestion, then no one can learn for you, in the same way that no one can eat for you. The food in the refrigerator doesn't do you a bit of good unless you walk over, open the door, remove it, and start eating. It's there for the taking, but you must make that happen. To carry the analogy further, you eat on a daily basis, right? "No thanks, I ate last week" is a silly statement. Learning does for your brain what food does for your body. Nourish yourself!

Brain researchers tell us the best state for learning has ten conditions.

1. **You're intrinsically motivated (from within yourself) to learn material that is appropriately challenging.**

   > **Examine where your motivation to learn comes from.** Are you internally motivated because you're curious about the subject and want to learn about it or externally motivated to get an A or avoid an F? Can you generate your own internal motivation? This book has built-in reminders to boost your intrinsic motivation. Use them to your advantage as a learner.

   > **Adjust the level of challenge yourself.** If you're too challenged in a class, you become nervous. Make sure you're keeping up with the workload and that you've completed the **prerequisites**. In many classes, you must know the fundamentals before tackling more advanced concepts. If you're not challenged enough, you can become bored and tune out. Your instructor will provide one level of challenge for everyone in the class. But it's up to you to fine-tune that challenge for yourself. Get extra help if you aren't quite up to the task or bump up the challenge a notch or two if you're ahead of the game so that you're continually motivated to learn.

2. **You're appropriately stressed, but generally relaxed.**

   > **Assess your stress.** According to researchers, you learn best in a state of relaxed alertness, a state of high challenge and low threat.[2] While relaxed alertness may sound impossible, it can be achieved. No stress at all is what you'd find in a no-brainer course. Some stress is useful; it helps you learn. Stress can heighten your alertness and help you focus. How stressed are you—and why—when you get to class? Are you overstressed because you've rushed from your last class, you're late because you missed your bus, or because you haven't done the reading and hope you won't be called on? Prepare for class so that you're ready to jump in. Or instead of too much stress, are you understressed because you don't value the course material? Consider how the information can be useful to you—perhaps in ways you've never even thought of. Here's the vital question to ask yourself: How much stress do I need in order to trigger my best effort?

   > **Pay attention to your overall physical state.** Are you taking care of your physical needs so that you can stay alert, keep up with the lecture, and participate in the discussion?

Stressed Out?

" **Movement is a medicine for creating change in a person's physical, emotional, and mental states.** "

—CAROL WELCH

Research shows that just twenty minutes of exercise can help calm you for as long as twenty-four hours. Vigorous exercise helps you get rid of excess adrenaline and pumps in endorphins that block pain and anxiety.[3] Not only does exercise help you burn off cheeseburgers, recent brain-imaging and neurochemical studies indicate that "sweating makes you smart." Physical exercise helps reinforce existing connections and create new ones between brain wiring via a protein called BDNF (brain-derived neurotrophic factor). Brain wiring helps you process and store information: "Learning is taking signals that come in from your senses and embedding them into brain anatomy," according to Dr. Vassilis Koliatsos, a psychiatrist at Johns Hopkins University. BDNF affects memory and mood; it literally helps rewire your brain.[4]

TRY IT!

Keep an exercise log for a week. On a daily basis, record the type of physical activity, the length of time you do it, and the level of workout (mild, medium, or high exertion). Using an online exercise calculator, record the number of calories you burned. Finally, monitor your stress level to see if exercise helps lower it (1 = low, 10 = high).

Devon Stephens/iStockphoto.com

	Sunday	Monday	Tuesday	Wednesday	Thursday	Friday	Saturday	TOTAL
Activity								
Time								
Exertion Level								
Calories Burned								
Overall stress level for the day (1 = low; 10 = high)								

3. **You enter into a state researchers call "flow" when you're so totally absorbed in what you're doing that you lose track of everything else.[5]**

   > **Identify the kinds of learning situations that help you "flow."** Do you get fully engaged by hands-on activities? Do you find that certain courses naturally capture your attention so much so that you're surprised when it's time for class to end? Understanding your own preferences and style as a learner are key here.

   > **Think about what you can do as a learner to get yourself there.** Not all classes or subjects will naturally induce a flow state in you. Nevertheless, ask yourself what you can do to focus on learning and exclude distractions. How can you become more engrossed in what you're learning?

Take Charge and Create the Best Conditions for Learning   53

4. **You're curious about what you're learning, and you look forward to learning it.**

> **Get ready to learn by looking back and by looking ahead.** When you're about to cross the street, you must look both ways, right? Keep that image in mind because that's what you should do before each class. What did class consist of last time? Can you predict what it will consist of next time?

> **Focus on substance, not style.** Part of Tammy's bias against Mr. Caldwell focused on his appearance. Despite society's obsession with attractiveness, grooming, and fashion, a student's job is to ask: What can I learn from this person? Deciding an instructor isn't worth paying attention to because he doesn't dress well or because his hair style is outdated is just an excuse not to learn.

5. **You're slightly confused, but only for a short time.**[6]

> **Use confusion as a motivator.** You may not be getting the lecture's main points because you don't understand new terms used along the way. Look them up early on in the learning process. Ask yourself what background information would help things click—and find out the answers to those questions.

> **Ask questions!** To your professor, questions indicate interest, not idiocy. Don't be afraid to probe more deeply into the material. As they say, "The only stupid question is the one you don't ask."

6. **You search for personal meaning and patterns.**

> **Ask yourself: What's in it for me?** Why is knowing this important? How can I use this information in the future? Instead of dismissing material that appears unrelated to your life, try figuring out how it could relate. You may be surprised!

> **Think about how courses relate to one another.** How does this new knowledge relate to things you're learning in other courses? Does sociology have anything to do with history? Psychology with economics?

7. **Your emotions are involved, not just your mind.**

> **Evaluate your attitudes and feelings.** Do you like the subject matter? Do you admire the teacher? Remember your high school teacher, Mr. Brown, whose class you just couldn't stand? Not every class will be your favorite. That's natural. But if a class turns you off as a learner, instead of allowing your emotions to take over, ask why and whether your feelings are in your best interest.

> **Make a deliberate decision to change negative feelings.** Fortunately, feelings can be changed. Hating a course or disliking a professor can only build resentment and threaten your success. It's possible to do a one-eighty and transform your negative emotions into positive energy.

> It is not the answer that enlightens, but the question.

Eugene Ionesco, Romanian and French playwright (1909–1994)

© Larry Harwood Photography. Property of Cengage Learning.

8. **You realize that as a learner you use what you already know in constructing new knowledge.**[7]

> **Remember that passive learning is impossible.** When it comes to learning, you are the construction foreman, building on what you already know to construct new knowledge. You're not just memorizing facts someone else wants you to learn. You're a full partner in the learning process!

> **Remind yourself that constructing knowledge takes work.** No one ever built a house by simply sitting back or just hanging out. Builders work hard, but in the end, they have something to show for their efforts. In your college courses, identify what you already know and blend new knowledge into the framework you've built in your mind. By constructing new knowledge, you are building yourself into a more sophisticated, more polished, and most certainly, a more educated person.

It is what we think we know already that often prevents us from learning.

Claude Bernard, French physiologist (1813–1878)

9. **You understand that learning is both conscious and unconscious.**

> **Watch where your mind goes when it's off duty.** Does learning take place when you're not deliberately trying to learn? Some of what you learn will be immediately obvious to you, and some will dawn on you after class is over, while you're in the shower, or eating lunch, or falling asleep at night, for example. Pay attention to your *indirect* learning and move it into your line of vision.

> **Remember that both kinds of learning are important.** Both conscious learning and unconscious learning count. There are no rules about when and where learning can occur. Capitalize on both.

10. **You're given a degree of choice in terms of what you learn, how you do it, and feedback on how you're doing.**

> **Make the most of the choices you're given.** College isn't a free-for-all in which you can take any classes you like toward earning a degree. However, which electives you choose will be up to you. Or in a particular course, if your instructor allows you to write a paper or shoot a video, choose the option that will be more motivating for you. When you receive an assignment, select a topic that fires you up. It's easier to generate energy to put toward choices you've made yourself.

> **Use feedback to improve, and if feedback is not given, ask for it.** It's possible to get really good at doing something the wrong way. Take a golf swing or a swimming stroke, for example. Without someone intervening to give you feedback, it may be difficult to know how to improve. Your instructors will most likely write comments on your assignments to explain their grades. Evaluating your work is their job; it's what they must do to help you improve. Take their suggestions to heart and try them out.

All of us are already good learners in some situations. Let's say you're drawn to technology, for example. You're totally engrossed in computers and eagerly learn everything you can from books, classes, and online sources—and you sometimes totally lose yourself in a flow state as you're learning. No one has to force you to practice your technology skills or pick up an issue of *Wired* or *PC World*. You do it because you want to. In this case, you're self-motivated and therefore learning is easy. This chapter provides several different tools to help you understand your own personal profile as a learner so that you can try to learn at your best in *all* situations.

CONTROL: *YOUR TOP-TEN LIST*

Reflect on yourself as a learner in your toughest class this term. How optimal are the conditions for learning? Put a check mark in the box if any of the following conditions are present. If not, beside each item, write in a suggestion to help create the condition and improve your own learning.

Ten Conditions for Optimal Learning   Course Title: _____

1. You're intrinsically motivated to learn material that is appropriately challenging. ✓

2. You're appropriately stressed, but generally relaxed. ✓

3. You enter into a state researchers call flow. ✓ I GUESS

4. You're curious about what you're learning, and you look forward to learning it. ✓ ABSOLUTELY

5. You're slightly confused, but only for a short time. ✗ NOPE

6. You search for personal meaning and patterns. ✓ YES.

7. Your emotions are involved, not just your mind. ✓ YES

8. You realize that as a learner you use what you already know in constructing new knowledge. ✓

9. You understand that learning is both conscious and unconscious. ✓

10. You're given a degree of choice in terms of what you learn, how you do it, and feedback on how you're doing. ✓

Multiple Intelligences: *How Are You Smart?*

EXERCISE 3.2

Multiple Intelligences Self-Assessment

Are people smart in different ways? How so? On each line, put check marks next to all the statements that best describe you.

Linguistic Intelligence: The capacity to use language to express what's on your mind and understand others ("word smart")

- ✓ I'm a good storyteller.
- ✗ I enjoy word games, puns, and tongue twisters.
- ✓ I'd rather listen to the radio than watch TV.
- ✗ I've recently written something I'm proud of.
- ✓ I can hear words in my head before I say or write them.
- ✗ When riding in the car, I sometimes pay more attention to words on billboards than I do to the scenery.
- ✱ ✓ In high school, I did better in English, history, or social studies than I did in math and science.
- ✱ ✓ I enjoy reading.
- 5 / ✗ TOTAL check marks

Logical-Mathematical Intelligence: The capacity to understand cause/effect relationships and to manipulate numbers ("number/reasoning smart")

- I can easily do math in my head.
- ✓ I enjoy brainteasers or puzzles.
- ✓ I like it when things can be counted or analyzed.
- ✓ I can easily find logical flaws in what others do or say.
- ✓ I think most things have rational explanations.
- Math and science were my favorite subjects in high school.
- ✓ I like to put things into categories.
- ✓ I'm interested in new scientific advances.
- 6 TOTAL check marks

Spatial Intelligence: The capacity to represent the world visually or graphically ("picture smart")

- I like to take pictures of what I see around me.
- ✓ I'm sensitive to colors.
- ✓ My dreams at night are vivid.
- ✓ I like to doodle or draw.
- ✓ I'm good at navigating with a map.
- ✓ I can picture what something will look like before it's finished.
- ✓ In school, I preferred geometry to algebra.
- I often make my point by drawing a picture or diagram.
- 6 TOTAL check marks

— SO TRUE ABOUT ME

(continued)

Bodily-Kinesthetic Intelligence: **The capacity to use your whole body or parts of it to solve a problem, make something, or put on a production ("body smart")**

_____ I regularly engage in sports or physical activities.

✓ I get fidgety (tap my foot, etc.) when asked to sit for long periods of time.

_____ I get some of my best ideas while I'm engaged in a physical activity.

_____ I need to practice a skill in order to learn it, rather than just reading or watching a video about it.

_____ I enjoy being a daredevil.

✓ I'm a well-coordinated person.

✓ I like to think through things while I'm doing something else like running or walking.

_____ I like to spend my free time outdoors.

_____ TOTAL check marks

Musical Intelligence: **The capacity to think in music, hear patterns and recognize, remember, and perhaps manipulate them ("music smart")**

_____ I can tell when a musical note is flat or sharp.

✓ I play a musical instrument.

✓ I often hear music playing in my head.

✓ I can listen to a piece of music once or twice, and then sing it back accurately.

✓ I often sing or hum while working.

✓ I like music playing while I'm doing things.

✓ I'm good at keeping time to a piece of music.

✓ I consider music an important part of my life.

5 TOTAL check marks

Interpersonal Intelligence: **The capacity to understand other people ("people smart")**

✓ I prefer group activities to solo activities.

✓ Others think of me as a leader.

✓ I enjoy the challenge of teaching others something I like to do.

✓ I like to get involved in social activities at school, church, or work.

_____ If I have a problem, I'm more likely to get help than tough it out alone.

✓ I feel comfortable in a crowd of people.

✓ I have several close friends.

✓ I'm the sort of person others come to for advice about their problems.

7 TOTAL check marks

Intrapersonal Intelligence: **The capacity to understand yourself, who you are, and what you can do ("self-smart")**

✓ I like to spend time alone thinking about important questions in life.

✓ I have invested time in learning more about myself.

✓ I consider myself to be independent minded.

_____ I keep a journal of my inner thoughts.

_____ I'd rather spend a weekend alone than at a place with a lot of other people around.

✓ I've thought seriously about starting a business of my own.

✓ I'm realistic about my own strengths and weaknesses.

✓ I have goals for my life that I'm working on.

6 TOTAL check marks

Naturalistic Intelligence: **The capacity to discriminate between living things and show sensitivity toward the natural world ("nature smart")**

- ✓ Environmental problems bother me.
- ✓ In school, I always enjoyed field trips to places in nature or away from class.
- ✓ I enjoy studying nature, plants, or animals.
- ___ I've always done well on projects involving living systems.
- ✓ I enjoy pets.
- ✓ I notice signs of wildlife when I'm on a walk or hike.
- ___ I can recognize types of plants, trees, rocks, birds, and so on.
- ✓ I enjoy learning about environmental issues.
- _6_ TOTAL check marks

Which intelligences have the most check marks? Write in the three intelligences in which you had the most number of check marks.

INTERPERSONAL   SPATIAL   LOGICAL.

Although this is an informal instrument, it can help you think about the concept of multiple intelligences, or MI. How are you smart?

Based on Armstrong, T. (1994). *Multiple intelligences in the classroom.* Alexandria, VA: Association for Supervision and Curriculum Development, pp. 18–20.

Have you ever noticed that people are smart in different ways? Consider the musical genius of Mozart, who published his first piano pieces at the age of five. Olympic Gold Medalist Lindsey Vonn started skiing whe she was two years old. Not many of us are as musically gifted as Mozart or as physically gifted as Lindsey Vonn, but we all have strengths. You may earn top grades in math, and not-so-top grades in English, and your best friend's grades may be just the opposite.

According to Harvard psychologist Howard Gardner, people can be smart in the eight different categories you saw in Exercise 3.2. Most schools focus on particular types of intelligence, linguistic and logical-mathematical intelligence, reflecting the three R's: reading, writing, and 'rithmetic. But Gardner claims there are many different types of intelligence. It can't be measured by traditional one-dimensional standardized IQ tests and represented by a three-digit number: 100 (average), 130+ (gifted), or 150+ (genius). Gardner defines intelligence as "the ability to find and solve problems and create products of value in one or more cultural setting."[8]

So instead of asking the traditional question "How smart are you?" a better question is "How are you smart?" The idea is to find out *how*, and then apply this understanding of yourself to your academic work in order to achieve your best results.

Translate Content into Your Own Intelligences

Do you sometimes wonder why you can't remember things for exams? Some learning experts believe that memory is intelligence-specific. You may have a good memory for people's faces but a bad memory for their names. You may be able to remember the words of a country-western hit but not the dance steps that go with it. The Theory of Multiple Intelligences may explain why.[9]

Examine your own behaviors in class. If your instructors use their linguistic intelligence to teach, as many do, and your intelligences lie elsewhere, do you get frustrated? Instead of zeroing in on the lecture, do you fidget (bodily-kinesthetic), doodle (spatial), or socialize (interpersonal)? You may need to translate the information into your own personal intelligences, just as you would if your instructor speaks French and you speak English. This strategy might have worked for Tammy Ko from the "FOCUS Challenge Case." Mr. Caldwell's most developed intelligence is linguistic, whereas Tammy's are bodily-kinesthetic (manipulating test tubes) and interpersonal (interacting with people). Tammy's learning problems are partially due to a case of mismatched intelligences between Mr. Caldwell and herself.

Let's say one of your courses this term is "Introduction to Economics," and the current course topic is the Law of Supply and Demand. Basically, "the theory of supply and demand describes how prices vary as a result of a balance between product availability at each price (supply) and the desires of those with purchasing power at each price (demand)."[10] To understand this law, you could:

- read the textbook (linguistic)
- study mathematical formulas (logical-mathematical)
- examine charts and graphs (spatial)
- observe the Law of Supply and Demand in the natural world, through the changing price of gasoline, for example (naturalist)
- look at the way the Law of Supply and Demand is expressed in your own body, using food as a metaphor (bodily-kinesthetic)
- reflect on how and when you might be able to afford something you desperately want, like a certain model of car (intrapersonal)
- write (or find) a song that helps you understand the law (musical).

CAREER OUTLOOK: *Be Hard-Working*

 I'm a great believer in luck, and I find the harder I work the more I have of it.
THOMAS JEFFERSON

Exhibit a work ethic. In college, you're at your best when you demonstrate your work ethic. The same will be true in your career. If you've learned that focused, dedicated work produces your best results in school, carry that lesson over to the world of work. Organizations prefer to hire winners, not slackers. Winners are motivated and reliable. They know how to kick into high gear when necessary. Not only is day-to-day performance important, but so is how you handle yourself at crunch time. Someone once said, "Every job is a self-portrait of the person who did it. Autograph your work with excellence." Your work ethic says a great deal about who you are.

You don't have to try all eight ways, but it's intriguing to speculate about various ways to learn that may work for you, rather than assuming you're doomed because your intelligences don't match your instructor's.

Use Intelligence-Oriented Study Techniques

What if your strongest intelligence is different from the one through which course material is presented? What can you do about it? Take a look at the following techniques for studying using different intelligences. Tweaking the *way* you study may make a world of difference.

Intelligence	Techniques
Linguistic --→	1. Rewrite your class notes. 2. Record yourself reading through your class notes and play it as you study. 3. Read the textbook chapter aloud.
Logical Mathematical --→	1. Create hypothetical conceptual problems to solve. 2. Organize chapter or lecture notes into a logical flow. 3. Analyze how the textbook chapter is organized and why.
Spatial --→	1. Draw a map that demonstrates your thinking on course material. 2. Illustrate your notes by drawing diagrams and charts. 3. Mark up your textbook to show relationships between concepts.
Bodily–Kinesthetic --→	1. Study course material while engaged in physical activity. 2. Practice skills introduced in class or in the text. 3. Act out a scene based on chapter content.
Musical --→	1. Create musical memory devices by putting words into well-known melodies. 2. Listen to music while you're studying. 3. Sing or hum as you work.
Interpersonal --→	1. Discuss course material with your classmates. 2. Organize a study group that meets regularly. 3. Meet a classmate before or after class for coffee and class conversation.
Intrapersonal --→	1. Keep a journal to track your personal reactions to course material. 2. Study alone and engage in internal dialogue about course content. 3. Coach yourself on how to best study for a challenging class.
Naturalistic --→	1. Search for applications of course content in the natural world. 2. Study outside (if weather permits and you can resist distractions). 3. Go to a physical location that exemplifies course material (for example, a park for your geology course).

Develop Your Weaker Intelligences

It's important to cultivate your weaker intelligences. Why? Because life isn't geared to one kind of intelligence. It's complex. A photo journalist for *National Geographic*, for example, might need linguistic intelligence, spatial intelligence, interpersonal intelligence, and naturalist intelligence. Being well-rounded, as the expression goes, is truly a good thing. Artist Pablo Picasso once said, "I am always doing that which I cannot do, in order that I may learn how to do it."

Use your multiple intelligences to multiply your success. Remember that no one is naturally intelligent in all eight areas. Each individual is a unique blend of intelligences. But the Theory of Multiple Intelligences claims that we all have the capacity to develop all of our eight intelligences further. That's good news!

How Do You Perceive and Process Information?

Style—we all have it, right? What's yours? Baggy jeans and a T-shirt? Sandals, even in the middle of winter? A signature hairdo that defies gravity? When it comes to appearance, you have your own style. You know it, and so does everyone who knows you.

Think about how your mind works. For example, how do you decide what to wear in the morning? Do you turn on the radio or TV for the weather forecast? Stick your head out the front door? Ask someone else's opinion? Throw on whatever happens to be clean? We all have different styles, don't we?

So what's a learning style? A learning style is defined as your "characteristic and preferred way of gathering, interpreting, organizing, and thinking about information."[11]

perceive become aware of

Here's one way of looking at things. The way you **perceive** information and the way you process it—your perceiving/processing preferences—are based in part on your senses. Which senses do you prefer to use to take in information—your eyes (visual-graphic or visual-words), your ears (aural), or all your senses using your whole body (kinesthetic)? Which type of information sinks in best? Which type of information do you most trust to be accurate?

To further understand your preferred sensory channel, let's take this hypothetical example. Assume a rich relative you didn't know leaves you some money, and you decide to use it to buy a new car. You must first answer many questions: What kind of car do you want to buy—an SUV, a sedan, a sports car, a van, or a truck? What are the differences between various makes and models? How do prices, comfort, and safety compare? Who provides the best warranty? Which car do consumers rate highest? How would you go about learning the answers to all these questions?

Marcela Barsse/MarsBars/
iStockphoto.com

Visual. Some of us would **look**. We'd study charts and graphs comparing cars, mileage, fuel tank capacity, maintenance costs, and customer satisfaction. We learn through graphic representations that explain what could have been said in normal text format.

Johanna Goodyear/
Dreamstime.com

Aural. Some of us would **listen**. We'd ask all our friends what kind of cars they drive and what they've heard about cars from other people. We'd pay attention as showroom salespeople describe the features of various cars. We learn through sounds by listening.

Nadezda Firsova/
iStockphoto.com

Read/Write. Some of us would **read** or **write**. We'd buy a copy of *Consumer Reports'* annual edition on automobiles, or copies of magazines such as *Car and Driver* or *Road and Track*, and write lists of each car's pros and cons. We learn through words by reading and writing.

Pascal Genest/iStockphoto.com

Kinesthetic. Some of us would want to **do it**. We'd go to the showroom and test drive a few cars to physically try them out. We learn through experience when all our senses are activated.

What would you do? Eventually, as you're deciding which vehicle to buy, you might do all these things, and do them more than once. But learning style theory says we all have preferences for how we perceive and process information.

© Holger Winkler/zefa/Corbis

Learning how to learn is life's most important skill.

Tony Buzan,
memory expert

VARK

EXERCISE 3.3

VARK Learning Styles Assessment

Choose the answer that best explains your preference and circle the letter. Please select more than one response if a single answer does not match your perception. ***Leave blank any question that does not apply.***

1. You are helping someone who wants to go downtown, find your airport, or locate the bus station. You would:
   a) draw or give her a map.
   b) tell her the directions.
   c) write down the directions (without a map).
   d) go with her.

2. You are not sure whether a word should be spelled "dependent" or "dependant." You would:
   a) see the word in your mind and choose by the way different versions look.
   b) think about how each word sounds and choose one.
   c) find it in a dictionary.
   d) write both words on paper and choose one.

3. You are planning a group vacation. You want some feedback from your friends about your plans. You would:
   a) use a map or website to show them the places.
   b) phone, text, or email them.
   c) give them a copy of the printed itinerary.
   d) describe some of the highlights.

(continued)

How Do You Perceive and Process Information? 63

4. You are going to cook something as a special treat for your family. You would:
   a) look through the cookbook for ideas from the pictures.
   b) ask friends for suggestions.
   c) use a cookbook where you know there is a good recipe.
   d) cook something you know without the need for instructions.

5. A group of tourists want to learn about the parks or wildlife reserves in your area. You would:
   a) show them Internet pictures, photographs, or picture books.
   b) talk about, or arrange a talk for them about, parks or wildlife reserves.
   c) give them a book or pamphlets about the parks or wildlife reserves.
   d) take them to a park or wildlife reserve and walk with them.

6. You are about to purchase a digital camera or cell phone. Other than price, what would most influence your decision?
   a) Its attractive design that looks good.
   b) The salesperson telling me about its features.
   c) Reading the details about its features.
   d) Trying or testing it.

7. Remember a time when you learned how to do something new. Try to avoid choosing a physical skill, like riding a bike. You learned best by:
   a) diagrams and charts—visual clues.
   b) listening to somebody explaining it and asking questions.
   c) written instructions—for example, a manual or textbook.
   d) watching a demonstration.

8. You have a problem with your knee. You would prefer that the doctor:
   a) show you a diagram of what was wrong.
   b) describe what was wrong.
   c) give you a pamphlet to read about it.
   d) use a plastic model of a knee to show what was wrong.

9. You want to learn a new software program, skill, or game on a computer. You would:
   a) follow the diagrams in the book that came with it.
   b) talk with people who know about the program.
   c) read the written instructions that came with the program.
   d) use the controls or keyboard and try things out.

10. I like websites that have:
    a) interesting design and visual features.
    b) audio channels where I can hear music, radio programs or interviews.
    c) interesting written descriptions, lists and explanations.
    d) things I can click on or try out.

11. Other than price, what would most influence your decision to buy a new nonfiction book?
    a) The cover looks appealing.
    b) A friend talks about it and recommends it.
    c) You quickly read parts of it.
    d) It contains real-life stories, experiences, and examples.

12. You are using a book, CD, or website to learn how to take photos with your new digital camera. You would like to have:
    a) diagrams showing the camera and what each part does.
    b) a chance to ask questions and talk about the camera and its features.
    c) clear written instructions with lists and bullet points about what to do.
    d) many examples of good and poor photos and how to improve them.

13. Do you prefer a teacher or a presenter who uses:
    a) diagrams, charts, or graphs?
    b) question and answer, talk, group discussion, or guest speakers?
    c) handouts, books, or readings?
    d) demonstrations, models, field trips, role plays, or practical exercises?

14. You have finished a competition or test and would like some feedback. You would like to have feedback:
    a) using graphs showing what you achieved.
    b) from somebody who talks it through with you.
    c) in a written format, describing your results.
    d) using examples from what you have done.

15. You are going to choose food at a restaurant or cafe. You would:
    a) look at what others are eating or look at pictures of each dish.
    b) ask the server or friends to recommend choices.
    c) choose from the written descriptions in the menu.
    d) choose something that you have had there before.

16. You have to give an important speech at a conference or special occasion. You would:
    a) make diagrams or create graphs to help explain things.
    b) write a few key words and practice your speech over and over.
    c) write out your speech and learn from reading it over several times.
    d) gather many examples and stories to make the talk real and practical.

Source: N. Fleming. (2001–2010). *VARK, a Guide to Learning Styles.* Version 7.0. Available at http://www.vark-learn.com/english/page.asp?p=questionnaire. Adapted and used with permission from Neil Fleming.

Scoring the VARK

Let's tabulate your results.

Count your choices in each of the four VARK categories.	(a)	(b)	(c)	(d)
	10	4	5	11
	Visual	Aural	Read/Write	Kinesthetic

Now that you've calculated your scores, do they match your perceptions of yourself as a learner? Could you have predicted them? The VARK's creators believe that *you* are best qualified to verify and interpret your own results.[12]

Using Your Sensory Preferences

Knowing your preferences can help you in your academic coursework. If your highest score (by 4 or 5 points) is in one of the four VARK modalities, that particular learning modality is your preferred one.[13] If your scores are more or less even between several or all four modalities, these scores mean that you don't have a strong preference for any single modality. A lower score in a preference simply means that you are more comfortable using other styles. If your VARK results contain a zero in a particular learning modality, you may realize that you do indeed dislike this mode or find it unhelpful. You might want to reflect on why you don't like to use this learning modality. To learn more about your results and suggestions for applying them, see Figure 3.1 for your preferred modality.

Most college classes emphasize reading and writing; however, if your lowest score is in the read/write modality, don't assume you're academically doomed.

VARK can help you discover alternative, more productive ways to learn the same course material. You may learn to adapt naturally to a particular instructor or discipline's preferences, using a visual modality in your economics class to interpret graphs and a kinesthetic modality in your chemistry lab to conduct experiments.

However, you may also find that you need to deliberately and strategically reroute your learning methods in some of your classes, and knowing your VARK preferences can help you do that. Learning to capitalize on your preferences and translate challenging course material into your preferred modality may serve you well. Remember these suggestions about the VARK, and try them out to see if they improve your academic results.

1. **VARK preferences are not necessarily strengths.** However, VARK is an excellent vehicle to help you reflect on how you learn and begin to reinforce the productive strategies you're already using or select ones that might work better.

	Everyday Study Strategies	Exam Preparation Strategies
VISUAL	• Convert your lecture notes to a visual format. • Study the placement of items, colors, and shapes in your textbook. • Put complex concepts into flowcharts or graphs. • Redraw ideas you create from memory.	• Practice turning your visuals back into words. • Practice writing out exam answers. • Recall the pictures you made of the pages you studied. • Use diagrams to answer exam questions, if your instructor will allow it.
AURAL	• Read your notes aloud. • Explain your notes to another auditory learner. • Ask others to "hear" your understanding of the material. • Record your notes or listen to your instructors' podcasts. • Realize that your lecture notes may be incomplete. You may have become so involved in listening that you stopped writing. Fill your notes in later by talking with other students or getting material from the textbook.	• Practice by speaking your answers aloud. • Listen to your own voice as you answer questions. • Opt for an oral exam if allowed. • Imagine you are talking with the teacher as you answer questions.
READ/WRITE	• Write out your lecture notes again and again. • Read your notes (silently) again and again. • Put ideas and principles into different words. • Translate diagrams, graphs, etc., into text. • Rearrange words and "play"with wording. • Turn diagrams and charts into words.	• Write out potential exam answers. • Practice creating and taking exams. • Type out your answers to potential test questions. • Organize your notes into lists or bullets. • Write practice paragraphs, particularly beginnings and endings.
KINESTHETIC	• Recall experiments, field trips, etc. Remember the real things that happened. • Talk over your notes with another "K" person. • Use photos and pictures that make ideas come to life. • Go back to the lab, your manual, or your notes that include real examples. • Remember that your lecture notes will have gaps if topics weren't concrete or relevant for you. • Use case studies to help you learn abstract principles.	• Role-play the exam situation in your room (or the actual classroom). • Put plenty of examples into your answers. • Write practice answers and sample paragraphs. • Give yourself practice tests.

2. **If you have a strong preference for a particular modality, practice multiple suggestions listed in Figure 3.1 for that particular modality.** Reinforce your learning by doing many things in that column.

3. **An estimated 60 percent of people are** multimodal. In a typical classroom of 30 students (based on VARK data):

multimodal prefer to use more than one sense

   > 17 students would be multimodal,

   > 1 student would be visual,

   > 1 student would be aural,

   > 5 students would be read/write,

   > 6 students would be kinesthetic,

   and the teacher would most likely have a strong read/write preference![14]

[handwritten note: MULTIMODAL: MORE THAN ONE PREFERANCE TO LEARN.]

4. **If you are multimodal, as most of us are, it may be necessary to use several of you modalities to boost your confidence in your learning.** Practice the suggestions for all of your preferred modalities.

5. **While in an ideal world, it would be good to try to strengthen lesser preferences, you may wish to save that goal for later in life.** Some experts suggest that college isn't the place to experiment. Grades count, and your continuing success will depend on how well you do. You may decide it's better to try to strengthen your current preferences now and work on expanding your lesser preferences later. This book will give you an opportunity to practice your VARK learning preferences—whatever they are—in each chapter. Ultimately, learning at your best is up to you.

Gaining the insights provided in this chapter and acting on them have the potential to greatly affect your college success. Understand yourself, capitalize on your preferences, build on them, focus, and learn!

VARK Activity — Complete the activity recommended for your preferred VARK learning style and bring it to class (or follow your instructor's instructions).

 Visual: Put together a collage of photos that represents how you learn. Post it on the course blog or website, assemble it on a posterboard, or make a PowerPoint slide show.

 Aural: Discuss your multiple intelligences and VARK preferences that affect learning with your friends or family. See if they can predict their own scores (generally). Access the CourseMate via www.cengagebrain.com/shop/ISBN/1439083908 to listen to the iAudio summary for this chapter.

 Read/Write: Write a one-paragraph summary of what you have learned about yourself as a result of reading this chapter.

 Kinesthetic: Use a variety of kinesthetic learning techniques to prepare for an upcoming quiz or exam in this class or another one. Did the techniques help you master the material? Report your results.

(from top to bottom) Marcela Barsse/MarsBars/iStockphoto.com; Johanna Goodyear/Dreamstime.com; Nadezda Firsova/iStockphoto.com; Pascal Genest/iStockphoto.com

What Role Does Your Personality Play?

One of the best things about college is having a chance to meet so many different types of people. At times you may find these differences intriguing. At other times, they may baffle you. Look around and listen to other students, and you'll start to notice. Have you heard students saying totally opposite things such as those listed here?

"There's no way I can study at home. It's way too noisy."

"There's no way I can study in the library. It's way too quiet."

"I'm so glad I've already decided on a major. Now I can go full steam ahead."

"I have no idea what to major in. I can think of six different majors I'd like to choose."

"My sociology instructor is great. She talks about all kinds of things in class, and her essay tests are actually fun!"

"My sociology instructor is so confusing. She talks about so many different things in class. How am I supposed to know what to study for her tests?"[15]

You're likely to run into all kinds of viewpoints and all types of people, but, differences make life much more interesting! We're each unique. Perhaps your friends comment on your personality by saying, "She's really quiet," or "He's a 'party animal'," or "He's incredibly logical," or "She trusts her gut feelings." What you may not know is how big a role your personality plays in how you prefer to learn.

The Myers-Briggs Type Indicator® (MBTI) is the most well-known personality assessment instrument in the world. Each year, approximately four million people worldwide get a look into their personalities, their career choices, their interaction with others, and their learning styles by completing it. If you are able to complete the full Myers-Briggs Type Indicator in the class for which you're using this textbook, or through your college counseling center or learning center, do so. You'll learn a great deal about yourself.

The Myers-Briggs Type Indicator shows you your preferences in four areas:

1. **What energizes you and where do you direct energy?** Do you get energy from other people (**E**xtravert) or do you go within yourself to find strength (**I**ntrovert)?

2. **How do you gather information and what kind of information do you trust?** Do you trust your senses and factually-based information (**S**ensor) or do you trust your gut feelings (i**N**tuition)?

3. **How do you make decisions, arrive at conclusions, and make judgments?** Do you think things through logically (**T**hinker) or do you care about how others react and feel (**F**eeler)?

4. **How do you relate to the outer world?** Do you prefer organization and structure (**J**udging) or do you like spontaneity and going with the flow (**P**erceiver)?

If you take the Myers-Briggs Type Indicator you should realize that it isn't about what you *can* do. It's about what you *prefer* to do. Here's an illustration. Write your name on the line first line.

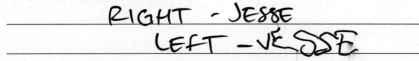

RIGHT - JESSE

LEFT - JESSE

Now put the pen in your other hand, and try writing your name on the second line. What was different the second time around? For most people, the second try takes longer, is messier, probably feels strange, and requires more concentration. But could you do it? Yes. It's just that you prefer doing it the first way. The first way is easier and more natural; the second way makes a simple task seem like hard work! It's possible that you might have to try "writing with your other hand" in college—doing things that don't come naturally.

In the "FOCUS Challenge Case," Tammy was described as outgoing (**E**xtraverted) and hands-on (**S**ensing) while Mr. Caldwell was described

" Each person is an exception to the rule. "

Carl Jung, psychiatrist
(1875–1961)

as reserved (**I**ntroverted) and theoretical (i**N**tuitive). It's unlikely that Mr. Caldwell will change his teaching style, and even if he did, students in his class have a variety of learning styles. Whose style would he try to match? Both Tammy's personality and Mr. Caldwell's are similar to the most common types found in college classrooms. Although you couldn't be sure without looking at actual MBTI scores, you'd expect Tammy to be an ESFP. ESFP's are outgoing, like facts as opposed to theories, pay attention to the feelings of others, and prefer exploring options to following a structure. Based on the clues in the Focus Challenge Case, you'd also expect Mr. Caldwell to be an INTJ—the opposite.

This chapter has covered learning from several different perspectives, and you now know more about yourself as a learner than you did before you read it. But you may be wondering: So how do Multiple Intelligences, VARK preferences, and personality traits (MBTI) work together to produce a unique learner? Although the three perspectives aren't intended to connect, let's look at this example to help you understand how each one would explain how people learn.

Let's say the person you sit by in your math class always asks you if you want to join his study group. Based on what you've learned in this chapter, you'd be more likely to say yes if you:

1. MI: have *interpersonal* (or social) intelligence

2. VARK: are an *aural* learner who likes to discuss things

3. MBTI: are *extroverted* (you get energy from other people)

The three perspectives don't overlap; they're different. That's why this chapter presents all three. Instead, each perspective explains how people learn in a different way.

While simply knowing about these three perspectives is good, it's important to go further and act on that knowledge. As a single learner in a larger class, you will need to adjust to the teaching style of your instructor in ways such as the following:

> **Translate for maximum comfort.** The way to maximize your comfort as a learner is to find ways to translate from your instructor's preferences to yours. If you know that you prefer feeling over thinking, and your instructor's style is based on thinking, make the course material come alive by personalizing it. How does the topic relate to you, your lifestyle, your family, and your future choices?

> **Make strategic choices.** While learning preferences can help explain your academic successes, it's also important not to use them to rationalize your nonsuccesses. An introvert could say, "I could have aced that assignment if the instructor had let me work alone! I hate group projects." Become the best learner you can be at what you're naturally good at. But also realize that you'll need to become more versatile over time. In the workforce, you will not always be able to choose what you do and how you do it. Actively choose your learning strategies, rather than simply hoping for the best. Remember: No one can learn for you, just as no one can eat for you.

> **Take full advantage.** College will present you with an extensive menu of learning opportunities. You will also build on your learning as you move beyond your general, introductory classes into courses in your chosen major—and across and between classes. Don't fall victim to the temptation to make excuses as some students do ("I could have been more successful in college if . . . I hadn't had to work so many hours . . . I hadn't had a family to support . . . my instructors had been more supportive. . . ." If, if, if. College may well be the most concentrated and potentially powerful learning opportunity you'll ever have. Ultimately, learning at your best is up to you.

ONLINE **TechKnow**

Improve Your Grade
Online Flashcards
Glossary

Have you ever thought about how you can use your VARK preferences for online coursework? Here are a few useful ideas.

- **If you're a visual learner,** capitalize on course material that comes to you as diagrams, charts, jpegs, and flowcharts—or better yet, take textual information and transform it into visual material to help you understand and remember it.

- **If you're an aural learner,** make the most of voiced-over lectures or narrated resources provided by the course—or find your own. Read the screen aloud as often as you can, and talk with others taking the same course.

- **If you're a read/write learner,** you'll be in your element for many online courses. But go beyond just reading the assigned online material by taking notes, making lists, and writing summaries of each lesson and activity.

- **If you're a kinesthetic learner,** the keyboard action will help, but also remember to get up and move around regularly—and connect your stretching or walking with what you've just learned online. Focus on the real-life examples provided in your online materials. You might also want to take advantage of gaming interfaces, drag and drop technology, interactive flash animations, simulations with 3D graphics, or virtual reality environments (e.g. http://secondlife.com/).

step 3 INSIGHT *Now* What Do You Think?

At the beginning of this chapter, Tammy Ko faced a series of challenges as a new college student. Now after learning from this chapter, would you respond differently to any of the questions you answered about the "FOCUS Challenge Case"? Using what you learned in the chapter, write a paragraph ending to Tammy's case study. What are some of the possible outcomes for her?

step 4 ACTION Your Plans for Change

1. Identify one new thing you learned in reading this chapter. Why did you select the topic you've selected? How will it affect what you do in your college classes?

2. How will you put the information from this chapter to good use, not only in this class, but in any others you're enrolled in this term?

3. List your learning and personality preferences as you discovered them in this chapter here:

   Multiple Intelligences _____

   VARK _____

   MBTI _____

   What do you think these preferences reveal about you and how you learn?

What did you **Learn?**

On a scale of 1 to 5, answer these questions now that you've completed this chapter.

1 = not very/not much/very little/low   5 = very/a lot/very much/high

How much do you know *now*?

Now rate your current level of knowledge about topics covered in this chapter.

Learning and the human brain

1   2   3   4   ⑤

Multiple intelligences

1   2   3   4   ⑤

Sensory preferences for learning

1   2   3   4   ⑤

Becoming a better learner

1   2   3   4   ⑤

How useful might the information in this chapter be to you?

How much do you think this information might affect your college success?

1   2   3   4   ⑤

How much do you think this information might affect your career success after college?

1   2   3   4   ⑤

How long did it actually take you to complete this chapter (both the reading and writing tasks)?

_4_ Hour(s) _10_ Minutes

 Challenge Yourself Online Quiz. To find out how much you've learned, access the CourseMate via www.cengagebrain.com/shop/ISBN/1439083908 to take the Challenge Yourself Online Quiz.

Compare these answers with your answers from the "Readiness Check" at the beginning of this chapter. How might the gaps between what you thought before starting the chapter and what you now think affect how you approach the next chapter?

chapter 4 Managing Your Time, Energy, and Money

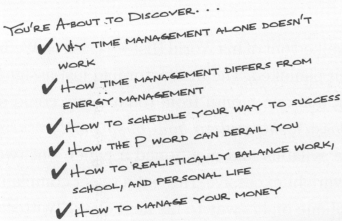

You're About to Discover. . .

✔ WHY TIME MANAGEMENT ALONE DOESN'T WORK

✔ HOW TIME MANAGEMENT DIFFERS FROM ENERGY MANAGEMENT

✔ HOW TO SCHEDULE YOUR WAY TO SUCCESS

✔ HOW THE P WORD CAN DERAIL YOU

✔ HOW TO REALISTICALLY BALANCE WORK, SCHOOL, AND PERSONAL LIFE

✔ HOW TO MANAGE YOUR MONEY

READINESS CHECK | What do you **Know?**

Before beginning this chapter, take a moment to answer these questions. Your answers will help you assess how ready you are to focus.

1 = not very/not much/very little/low   5 = very/a lot/very much/high

How much do you *already* know?

Rate your current level of knowledge about topics covered in this chapter.

Time management vs. energy management

1 2 ③ 4 5

Procrastination

1 2 ③ 4 5

Balancing work, school, and personal life

1 2 3 ④ 5

Money management

1 ② 3 4 5

How motivated are you to learn *more*?

In general, how motivated are you to learn the material in this chapter?

1 2 ③ 4 5

How much do you think this information might affect your college success?

1 2 3 ④ 5

How much do you think this information might affect your career success after college?

1 2 ③ 4 5

How ready are you to read *now*?

How ready are you to focus on this chapter—physically, intellectually, and emotionally? Which of these three areas is most challenging for you right now? Circle a number to represent it.

1 2 ③ 4 5

If any of your answers is below a 3, consider addressing the issue before reading.

Then, read the chapter carefully, while looking for ways to improve your focus.

Finally, how long do you think it will take you to complete this chapter? If you start and stop, keep track of the overall time.

__4__ Hour(s) __15__ Minutes

DEREK JOHNSON

A s Derek Johnson walked out of his World History class on Wednesday evening, he felt panicked. The instructor had just assigned a twelve-page paper, due one month from today. How could she? Derek thought. *Doesn't she realize how busy most returning students are?* The syllabus had mentioned a paper, but twelve pages seemed downright excessive. He sent a tweet complaining about it from his phone on his way to his next class. Twitter was quickly becoming Derek's favorite way to communicate.

MAKE
TO-DO
LIST!?

REMEMBER TO BUY
MOM A BIRTHDAY
GIFT!!!

REMEMBER:

COMPUTER TRAINING
CLASS FOR WORK ON
WEDNESDAY!

When Derek had decided to go back to college five years after he graduated from high school, he hadn't quite realized what a juggling act it would require. First, there was his family—his wife, Justine, his four-year-old daughter, Taura, and another baby due before winter break. Then there was his job, which was really quite demanding for what he earned. He hoped that an associate's degree in accounting would help him get a job as an accounting assistant and possibly even move into the management ranks, where the salaries were higher. Money was tight, and they always seemed to run out before payday. Add to that singing in his church choir, coaching the youth soccer league, competing in cycling races, and working out every morning at the gym. Derek had been a high school athlete, and physical fitness was a priority for him.

His head began to swim as he thought about all his upcoming obligations: his mother's birthday next week, his dog's vet appointment, his brother's visit, the training class he was required to attend for work. Something had to go, but he couldn't think of anything he was willing to sacrifice to make time for a twelve-page paper. Maybe he'd have to break down and buy one of those planners, but weren't most people who use those slightly, well . . . compulsive?

Still, the paper was to count as 25 percent of his final grade in the course. He decided he'd try and think of a topic for the paper on his way home. But then he remembered that his wife had asked him to stop at the store to pick up groceries. Somewhere on aisle 12, between the frozen pizza and the frozen yogurt, Derek's thoughts about his research paper vanished.

Community Center Gym Schedule

Monday	Tuesday	Wednesday	Thursday	Friday
Open Gym 6:30-8:30	Open Gym 6:30-8:30	Open Gym 6:30-8:30	Open Gym 6:30-8:30	Open Gym 6:30-8:30
Cycling Class 9:00-10:00	Taekwondo Class 9:00-10:00	Taekwondo Class 9:00-10:00	Kick Boxing 9:00-10:00	Cycling Class 9:00-10:00
Taekwondo Class 12:00-1:00	Yoga Class 12:00-1:00	Yoga Class 12:00-1:00	Yoga Class 12:00-1:00	Taekwondo Class 12:00-1:00
Yoga Class 3:00-4:00	Kick Boxing 3:00-4:00	Cycling Class 3:00-4:00	Taekwondo Class	Kick Boxing

HISTORY PAPER OUTLINE

INTRO...

The following week, the instructor asked the students in the class how their papers were coming along. Some students gave long descriptions of their research progress, the amazing number of sources they'd found, and the detailed outlines they'd put together. Derek didn't raise his hand.

A whole week has gone by, Derek thought on his way back to his car after class. *I have to get going!* Writing had never exactly been Derek's strong suit. In fact, it was something he generally disliked doing. Through a great deal of hard work, he had managed to earn a 3.8 GPA in high school—a record he planned to continue. A course in World History—a general education class that was not even a part of his major—was *not* going to ruin things! The week had absolutely flown by, and there were plenty of good reasons why his paper was getting off to such a slow start. Derek rarely wasted time, except for occasionally watching his favorite TV shows. But then again, with such a jam-packed schedule, he really felt the need to unwind once in a while. Regardless, he rarely missed his nightly study time from 11:00 p.m. to 1:00 a.m. Those two hours were reserved for homework, no matter what.

At the end of class two weeks later, Derek noticed that several students lined up to show the instructor the first drafts of their papers. *That's it!* Derek thought to himself. *The paper is due next Wednesday. I'll spend Monday night, my only free night of the week, in the library. I can get there right after work and stay until 11:00 or so. That'll be five hours of concentrated time. I should be able to write it then.* Despite his good intentions, Derek didn't arrive at the library until nearly 8:00 p.m., and his work session wasn't all that productive. As he sat in his library stall, he found himself obsessing about things that were bothering him at work. His boss was being difficult, and his coworkers were fighting among themselves. Finally, when he glanced at his watch, he was shocked to see that it was already midnight! The library was closing, and he'd only written three pages. Where had the time gone?

On his way out to the car, his cell phone rang. It was Justine, wondering where he was. Taura was running a fever, and his boss had called about an emergency meeting at 7:00 a.m. *If one more thing goes wrong . . .* , Derek thought to himself. His twelve-page paper was due in two days.

WORLD HISTORY
Fall Semester Syllabus

Instructor: Julia Alexander
Office: Main Hall 320
Email: Julia.Alexander@campusmail.edu
Phone: 555-3424
Office Hours: 12:30-3pm daily

red Textbook:
History, 6th Edition. By William J. Duiker and Jackson J. Spielvogel ISBN: 049

Exam:	10 @ 10 points each	100pts
nalysis:		100pts
ay:		50pts
		150pts
		100pts
		500pts

vilization and the Fertile Crescent
ne: *Agriculture and Mesopotamia*
vo: *The Nile Valley and the Near East*

Civilizations
ee: *The World of Homer*
: *Classical Greece and the Golden Age*
Rome: *The Rise of the Republic*
perial Rome
Rome: *The Fall of the Empire*
China and the Far East
he Indian Subcontinent

Accounting Associate

Job Description
We are currently looking for a qualified Accounting As
educational, and industry experience. This is an entry
graduates are encouraged to apply.

Job Responsibilities
- Ensure timely collection of vendor A/R
- Review, correct, and update sub ledger transactions a
- Transaction review
- Vendor follow-up and research
- Vendor disputes
- Inventory audits

CampusLibrary

FALL SEMESTER HOURS
Monday – Thursday: 8 am – Midnight
Friday – Saturday: 8 am – 8 pm
10 am – 4 pm

1. What do you have in common with Derek? What time, energy, or money management issues are you experiencing in your life right now?
2. Describe the time-wasters that are a part of Derek's schedule. Do you think procrastination is an issue for Derek? What's behind his failure to make progress on his paper?
3. Suggest three realistic ways for Derek to balance work, school, and personal life.

Time Management Isn't Enough

Before diving into the details of time management skills, let's clarify one important point. There's a sense in which the phrase *time management* is misleading. Let's say you decide to spend an hour reading an assigned short story for your literature class. You may sit in the library with your book propped open in front of you from 3:00 to 4:00 p.m. on the dot. But you may not digest a single word you're reading. You may be going through the motions, reading on autopilot. Have you managed your time? Technically, yes. Your planner says, "Library, short story for Lit 101, 3:00–4:00 p.m." But did you get results? Time management expert Jeffrey Mayer asks provocatively in the title of his book: *If You Haven't Got the Time to Do It Right, When Will You Find the Time to Do It Over?*. Now that's a good question!

"Time management" is not just about managing your time, it's about managing your attention. Attention management is the ability to focus your attention, not just your time, on a designated activity so that you produce a desired result. Time management may get you through reading a chapter of your textbook, but attention management will make sure that you understand what you're reading. It's about *focus*. If you manage your attention during that hour, then you've managed your time productively. Without attention management, time management is pointless.

Succeeding in school, at work, and in life is not just about what you do. It's about what gets done. You can argue about the effort you put into an academic assignment all you want, but it's doubtful your professor will say, "You know what? You're right. You deserve an A just for staying up late last night working on this paper." Activity and accomplishment aren't the same thing. Neither are quantity and quality. Just because the assignment asked for five pages and you turned in five, doesn't mean that you automatically deserve an A. Results count, so don't confuse being busy with being successful. Staying busy isn't much of a challenge; being successful is.

Here's a list of preliminary academic time-saving tips. However, remember that these suggestions won't give you a surefire recipe for academic success. To manage your time, you must also manage yourself: your energy, your behavior, your attention, your attitudes, *you*. Once you know how to manage all that, managing your time begins to work.

> In truth, people can generally make time for what they choose to do; it is not really the time but the will that is lacking.
>
> *Sir John Lubbock, British banker, politician, and archaeologist (1834–1913)*

➤ Have a plan for your study session; include suggested time limits for each topic or task.

> Pay attention to what gets you off track. If you come to understand your patterns, you may be better able to control them.

> Turn off your phone or tell other people you live with that you don't want to be disturbed if a call comes in for you. Let them know what time they can tell callers to call you back.

> If you're working on your computer, work offline whenever possible. If you must be online to check sources, don't give in to the temptation to check your social networking account or e-mail every ten minutes.

> Take two minutes to organize your workspace before beginning. Having the resources you need at your fingertips makes the session go much more smoothly, and you won't waste time searching for things you need.

> If you are in a study group, make sure everyone is clear about assigned tasks for the next session. Not knowing who's supposed to do what is a big time-waster for study groups.

> Learn to say no. Saying no to someone, especially someone you care about, can feel awkward at first, but people close to you will understand that you can't do everything.

> Focus. You can't do anything if you try to do everything. **Multitasking** may work for simple matters, such as scheduling a doctor's appointment while heating up a snack in the microwave. But when it comes to tasks that require brainpower, such as studying or writing, you need a single-minded focus.

> Slow down. Working at something a million miles a minute will most likely result in mistakes. If you rush, you may run out of time and end up settling for less than your best. Try to avoid the "headless chicken" phenomenon.

> Monitor how your life works. There are different ways to manage your time, and different ways work best for different people. Think of this analogy: Is time like ice or like water? A hard copy planner is a day-by-day record of solid blocks of time. But in today's world, solid blocks can melt away in seconds as events around us change. Managing time may be less like moving around ice cubes and more like "going with the flow." Many dynamic e-tools are available to help you on a minute-by-minute basis, if you stay on top of how time flows in your life.[1]

" Don't confuse activity with accomplishment. 'Time = Success' is a myth. "

Dr. Constance Staley, University of Colorado at Colorado Springs

multitasking doing two or more tasks at one time

Energy, Our Most Precious Resource

"We live in a digital time. Our rhythms are rushed, rapid-fire and relentless, our days carved up into bits and bytes. . . . We're wired up but we're melting down." So begins a bestselling book, *The Power of Full Engagement: Managing Energy,*

> Performance, health and happiness are grounded in the skillful management of energy.

Jim Loehr and Tony Schwartz,
from The Power of Full Engagement

Not Time, Is the Key to High Performance and Personal Renewal. The authors, Jim Loehr and Tony Schwartz, have replaced the term *time management* with the term *energy management.* Their shift makes sense. Since most of us are running in overdrive most of the time, energy is our most precious resource.

Energy management experts say you can't control time—everyone has a fixed amount—but you can manage your energy. And in fact, it's your responsibility to do so. Once a day is gone, it's gone. But your energy can be renewed.

It's clear that some things are energy *drains:* bad news, illness, interpersonal conflict, time-consuming hassles, a heavy meal, rainy days. Likewise, some things are energy *gains* giving you a surge of freshness: a new job, good friends, music, laughter, fruit, coffee. It's a good idea to recognize your own personal energy drains and gains so that you know how and when to renew your supply.[2] Energy management experts say it's not just about *spending time,* it's about *expending energy:*

> physical energy
> emotional energy
> mental energy
> spiritual energy

Of the four dimensions of energy, let's take a closer look at the first two. To do your very best academically, it helps to be *physically* energized and *emotionally* connected. Physical energy is measured in terms of *quantity.* How much energy do you have—a lot or a little? Emotional energy, on the other hand, is measured by *quality.* What kind of energy do you have—positive or negative? If you put them together into a two-dimensional chart with *quantity* as the vertical axis and *quality* as the horizontal axis, you get something like Figure 4.1.

FIGURE 4.1

The Dynamics of Energy[3]

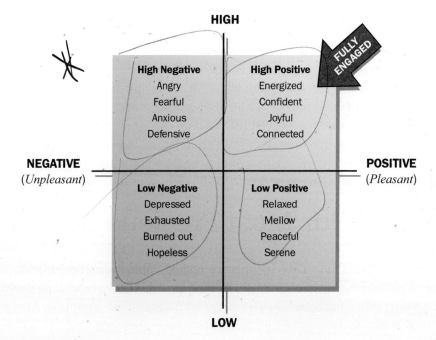

When you're operating in the upper right quarter of the chart with high, positive energy, you're most productive, which makes sense. The question is: How do you get there? How do you make certain you're physically energized and emotionally connected so that you can do your best, academically?

✳ Get Physically Energized

To make sure you're physically energized, try these suggestions.

1. **Snap to your body's rhythm.** Have you noticed times of the day when it's easier to concentrate than others? Perhaps you regularly crash in the middle of the afternoon, for example, so you go for a chocolate fix, or a coffee pick-me-up. Everyone has a biological clock. Paying attention to your body's natural rhythms is important. Plan to do activities that require you to be alert during your natural productivity peaks. That's better than plodding through a tough assignment when the energy just isn't there. Use low energy times to take care of mindless chores that require little to no brainpower.[4]

   — GET UP AND READY / SLEEP AND EAT

2. **Up and at 'em.** What about 8:00 a.m. classes? Don't use your body's natural rhythms as an excuse to sleep through class! ("I'm just not a morning person. . . .") If you're truly not a morning person, don't sign up for early morning classes. If you are coming off working a night shift, you may need some rest first. Sleeping through your obligations won't do much for your success—and you'll be playing a continual game of catch-up, which takes even more time. Some experts advise that you start your day as early as possible. Marking six items off your to-do list before lunch can give you a real high.[5]

3. **Sleep at night, study during the day.** Burning the midnight oil and pulling all-nighters aren't the best ideas, either. It only takes one all-nighter to help you realize that a lack of sleep translates into a drop in performance. Without proper sleep, your ability to understand and remember course material is impaired. Research shows that the average adult requires seven to eight hours of sleep each night. If you can't get that much for whatever reason, take a short afternoon nap. Did you know that the Three Mile Island nuclear meltdown in Pennsylvania in 1979 and the Chernobyl disaster in the Ukraine in 1986 took place at 4 a.m. and 1:23 a.m., respectively? Experts believe it's no coincidence that both these events took place when workers would normally be sleeping.[6]

4. **"Burn premium fuel."** You've heard it before: Food is the fuel that makes us run. The better the fuel, the smoother we run. It's that simple. A solid diet of carbs—pizza, chips, and cookies—jammed into the fuel tank of your car would certainly gum up the works! When the demands on your energy are high, such as exam week, use premium fuel. If you don't believe it, think about how many people you know get sick during time of high stress. Watch how many of your classmates are hacking and coughing their way through exams—or in bed missing them altogether.

Get Emotionally Connected

Physical needs count, to be sure, but emotional connections are part of the picture too. See if you agree with these suggestions.

1. **Communicate like it matters.** Sometimes we save our best communicating for people we think we have to impress: teachers, bosses, or clients, for example. But what about the people we care about most in our lives? Sometimes these people get the leftovers after all the "important" communicating has been done for the day. Sometimes we're so comfortable with these people that we think we can let it all hang out, even when doing so is *not a* pretty sight. Communicate as if everything you said would actually come true—"Just drop dead," for instance—and watch the difference! Communicating productively with people we care about is one of the best ways to replenish our energy.

2. **Choose how you renew.** Finish this comparison: Junk food is to physical energy as _____ is to emotional energy. If you answered "TV," you're absolutely right. Most people use television as their primary form of emotional renewal, but, like junk food, it's not that nutritious and it's easy to consume

Stressed Out?

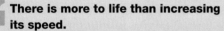

> **There is more to life than increasing its speed.**
>
> —MOHANDAS K. GANDHI, INDIAN SPIRITUAL LEADER
> (1869–1948)

What does the word *spirituality* mean to you? Do you picture a church, respond with the name of an organized religion, or think about looking inward or examining your life? According to a national study of 112,232 college students, four out of five first-year students are interested in spirituality, and nearly three-fourths report feeling a sense of connection with a higher power. Nearly half believe that college should help encourage their expression of spirituality.[7] Can college help you examine your values, find inner direction, ponder the meaning of life, and possibly lower your stress level?

Devon Stephens/iStockphoto.com

TRY IT!

Do you think paying attention to your spiritual health has the potential to lower your stress level? To help you think about your answer to this question, respond to the items below:

1. It's easy to get caught up in day-to-day details, like kids, jobs, and bills. But many experts believe that you can lower your stress level by taking time out to consider "life's bigger picture"—through yoga, meditation, prayer, or exercise, for example. Do you practice any of these? Do they help you manage stress?

2. Think about your college classes. Does "big picture" thinking come up (directly or indirectly) in any of them? If so, which class—and where has your thinking led you?

3. Sometimes spirituality is simply about freeing up your mind and slowing down long enough to think more deeply than usual. Make a promise to yourself to find time to do that this week, and then pay attention to the results. What were they?

too much. Try more engaging activities that affirm you: singing or reading or playing a sport.[8]

3. **Let others renew you.** Remember that people don't just make demands on your time, they can provide emotional renewal. There's pure joy in a child's laugh, a friend's smile, a father's pat on the back. These small pleasures in life are priceless—prize them!

We've focused on physical and emotional energy here, but remember that all four dimensions of energy—physical, emotional, mental, and spiritual—are interconnected. If you subtract one from the equation, you'll be firing on less than four cylinders. If you are fully engaged and living life to the fullest, all four dimensions of your energy equation will be in balance.

"I'll Study in My Free Time" … and When Is That?

EXERCISE 4.1

Where Did the Time Go?

How do you spend your time? Complete this self-assessment to find out how you spend your time. Fill in the number of hours you spend doing each of the following, then multiply your answer by the number given (7 or 5 to figure weekly amounts) where appropriate.

Number of hours per day

Sleeping: $\underline{7} \times 7 = \mathbf{49}$

Personal grooming (for example, showering, shaving, putting on makeup): $\underline{1} \times 7 = \mathbf{7}$

Eating (meals and snacks; include preparation or driving time): $\underline{3} \times 7 = \mathbf{21}$

Commuting Monday thru Friday (to school and work): $\underline{1} \times 5 = \mathbf{5}$

Doing errands and chores: $\underline{1} \times 7 = \mathbf{7}$

Spending time with family (parents, children, or spouse): $\underline{2} \times 7 = \mathbf{14}$

Spending time with boyfriend or girlfriend: $\underline{7} \times 7 = \mathbf{49}$

Number of hours per week

At work: **20**

In classes: **20**

At regularly scheduled functions (church, clubs, etc.): **2**

Socializing, hanging out, watching TV, talking on the phone, etc.: **20**

Now add up all the numbers in the far right column, and subtract your total from 168, the number of hours in a week.

168 – _____ = _____. *This is the total number of hours you have remaining in your week for that ever-important task of studying. You may wish to revise how much time you spend on other activities of your life, based on whether or not you're already short on hours without studying factored in.*

Ask ten students when they study, and chances are at least eight will reply, "in my free time." The strange thing about this statement is that if you actually waited until you had free time to study, you probably never would. Truthfully, some students are amazed at how easily a day can race by without ever thinking about cracking a book. This is why you should actually *schedule* your study time, but to do that, you should first be aware of how you're currently spending those twenty-four hours of each day.

Notice that Exercise 4.1 places studying at the bottom of the list, even though it's vital to your success in college. The exercise reflects a common attitude among college students, namely that studying is what takes place after everything else gets done. Where does schoolwork rank on *your* list of priorities?

If succeeding in college is a top priority for you, then make sure that you're devoting adequate time to schoolwork outside of the classroom. Most instructors expect you to study two to three hours outside of class for every hour spent in class. If it's a particularly challenging class, you may need even more study time. You can use the following chart to calculate the total number of hours you ought to expect to study—effectively—each week:

Credit hours for less demanding classes: _____ × 2 hours = _____ hours

Credit hours for typical/average classes: _____ × 3 hours = _____ hours

Credit hours for more challenging classes: _____ × 4 hours = _____ hours

Expected total study time per week = _____ hours

Remember, just putting in the time won't guarantee that you'll truly *understand* what you're studying. You need to ensure that your study time is productive by focusing your attention and strategically selecting study techniques that work best for you.

BOX 4.1 Lame Excuses for Blowing Off Class

Do you find yourself skipping class at times in order to do something else: getting an oil change for your car, soaking up the sun's rays, or socializing with a friend on the phone? If so, ask yourself this: Would you walk into a gas station, put a $50 bill down on the counter to prepay for a tank of gas, and then put in a dollar's worth and drive off? Absolutely not, you say?

Would you buy a $10 movie ticket and then just toss it in the trash because you decided there was something else you'd rather do on the spur of the moment? No way!

Why, then, would you purchase much more expensive "tickets" to class—the average cost of an hour in class may be as high as $100, $150, or $200 or more—and then toss them in the trash by not attending? Don't you value your money more than that? More importantly, don't you value yourself more than that?

The next time you're tempted to opt out of your scheduled classes, ask yourself if you really want to throw away money, in addition to the opportunity. Check your priorities, then put one foot in front of the other and walk into that classroom. In the long run, it's the best investment in your own future.

Schedule Your Way to Success

Time Monitor

Can you remember how you spent all your time yesterday? Using the following Time Monitor, fill in as much as you can remember about how you spent your time yesterday for the complete 24-hour period. Be as detailed as possible, right down to thirty-minute segments.

7:00 a.m. WAKE UP	3:00 PICK UP AIR	11:00 ROME TW
7:30 DRIVING	3:30 B & N	11:30 ROME TW
8:00 CLASS	4:00 STARBUCKS	12:00 a.m. SLEEP
8:30 CLASS	4:30 STUDY	12:30 SLEEP
9:00 BREAK	5:00 STUDY	1:00 SLEEP
9:30 CLASS	5:30 DRIVING	1:30 SLEEP
10:00 BREAK	6:00 HOME	2:00 SLEEP
10:30 CLASS	6:30 EATING	2:30 SLEEP
11:00 BREAK	7:00 STUDY	3:00 SLEEP
11:30 CLASS	7:30 GET TACOS	3:30 SLEEP
12:00 p.m. BREAK	8:00 EAT	4:00 SLEEP
12:30 CLASS	8:30 MOVIE	4:30 SLEEP
1:00 DRIVING	9:00 MOVIE	5:00 SLEEP
HOME 1:30 PICK UP AIR	9:30 ROME TW	5:30 SLEEP
2:00 ROME TW	10:00 ROME TW	6:00 SLEEP
2:30 DRIVING	10:30 ROME TW	6:30 SLEEP

THIS TIME COULD BE USED BETTER

Now monitor how you use your time today (or tomorrow if you're reading this at night), or your instructor may have you complete this Time Monitor for a several days. You can use the additional Time Monitor available in the appendix or create your own on a piece of paper. Again, be very specific. You will refer back to this exercise later in this chapter. At the conclusion of your record-keeping for this exercise, go back to Exercise 4.1 and check to see how accurate your estimates were.

There is no one right way to schedule your time, but if you experiment with the system presented in this book, you'll be on the right path. Eventually, you can tweak the system to make it uniquely your own. Try these eight steps, and schedule your way to success!

CURIOSITY: *CHOOSE TO CHOOSE!*

Have you ever thought about how many dozens, if not hundreds, of choices you make each day? From the second you wake up, you're making decisions, even about the simplest things, like whether to order a cappuccino or a latté; decaf, half-caf, or high-octane; nonfat, two-percent, or the real deal.

Psychologist and professor Barry Schwartz, in his book, *The Paradox of Choice: Why More Is Less*, believes that making non-stop choices can actually cause us to "invest time, energy, and no small amount of self-doubt, and dread." Choosing a new cell phone plan can take some people weeks while they research models of cell phones, minutes available, quotas of text messages, and Internet access, not to mention the fine print. Simply put: Being flooded with choices, while it feels luxurious, can be stressful and even unrewarding. Paralysis, anxiety, and stress rather than happiness, satisfaction, and perfection can be the result of too much "more."

Some of us, Schwartz says, are "maximizers"; we don't rest until we find the best. Others of us are "satisficers"; we're satisfied with what's good enough, based on our most important criteria. Of course, we all do some "maximizing" and some "satisficing," but generally, which are you?

Here are Schwartz's recommendations to lower our stress levels in a society where more can actually give us less, especially in terms of quality of life:

1. **Choose to choose.** Some decisions are worth lengthy deliberation; others aren't. Be conscious of the choices you make and whether they're worth the return on your investment. "Maximize" when it counts and "satisfice" when it doesn't.

2. **Remember that there's always greener grass somewhere.** Someone will always have a better job than you do, a nicer apartment, or a more attractive romantic partner. Regret or envy can eat away at you, and second-guessing can bring unsettling dissatisfaction.

3. **Regret less and appreciate more.** While green grass does abound, so do sandpits and bumpy roads. That's an important realization, too! Value the good things you already have going for you.

4. **Build bridges, not walls.** Think about the ways in which the dozens of choices you've already made as a new college student give you your own unique profile or "choice-print": where you live, which classes you take, clubs you join, campus events you attend, your small circle of friends, and on and on. Remember that, and make conscious choices that will best help you succeed.[9]

STEP 1: Fill Out a "Term on a Page" Calendar. Right up front, create a "Term on a Page" calendar that shows the entire school term on one page. (See Exercise 4.3.) This calendar allows you to see the big picture. You will need to have the syllabus from each of your classes and your school's course schedule to do this step properly. The following items should be transferred onto your "Term on a Page" calendar:

> Holidays when your school is closed

> Exam and quiz dates from your syllabi

> Project or paper deadlines from your syllabi

> Relevant administrative deadlines (e.g., registration for the next term, drop dates)

> Birthdays and anniversaries to remember

> Important out-of-town travel

> Dates that pertain to other family members, such as days that your children's school is closed or that your spouse is out of town for a conference—anything that will impact your ability to attend classes or study

" Take care of your minutes, and the hours will take care of themselves. "

Lord Chesterfield, British statesman and diplomat (1694–1773)

EXERCISE 4.3

Term on a Page

Take a few minutes right now to create your own Term on a Page using the charts in Figure 4.2.

Term FALL Year 20113

FIGURE 4.2

Term on a Page

Month: SEPT	Sunday	Monday	Tuesday	Wednesday	Thursday	Friday	Saturday

Month: OCTOBER	Sunday	Monday	Tuesday	Wednesday	Thursday	Friday	Saturday

Month: NOVEMBER	Sunday	Monday	Tuesday	Wednesday	Thursday	Friday	Saturday

Month: DECEMBER	Sunday	Monday	Tuesday	Wednesday	Thursday	Friday	Saturday

Month:	Sunday	Monday	Tuesday	Wednesday	Thursday	Friday	Saturday

STEP 2: Invest in a Planner. While it's good to have the big picture, you must also develop an ongoing scheduling system that works for you. Using the "It's all right up here in my head" method is a surefire way to miss an important appointment, fly past the deadline for your term paper without a clue, or lose track of the time you have left to complete multiple projects.

Although your instructor will typically provide you with a class syllabus that lists test dates and assignment deadlines, trying to juggle multiple syllabi—not to mention your personal and work commitments—is enough to drive you crazy. You need *one* central place for all of your important deadlines, appointments, and commitments. This central place is a planner—a calendar book with space to write in each day. Derek Johnson in the "FOCUS Challenge Case" expressed his view that planners are for nerds and worry warts. Not true! Most every successful person on the planet uses one.

When you go planner shopping, remember that you don't have to break the bank unless you want to. Many new college students find that an ordinary paper-and-pencil daily calendar from an office supply store works best. Having a full page for each day means you can write your daily to-do list right in your planner (more on to-do lists later), and that can be a huge help. Using an online calendar, like Google calendar, can work, too. But remember that unless you have a smart cell phone with Internet access, an online calendar won't be portable, and you'll have to remember to enter events later.

STEP 3: Transfer Important Dates. The next step is to transfer important dates for the whole term from your "Term on a Page" overview to the appropriate days in your planner. This may seem repetitious, but there's a method to the madness. While it's important to be able to see all of your due dates together to create a big picture, it's equally important to have these dates recorded in your actual planner because you will use it more regularly—as the final authority on your schedule.

CAREER OUTLOOK: *Be Disciplined*

> **Time is the coin of your life. It is the only coin you have, and only you can determine how it will be spent.**
>
> CARL SANDBURG

Manage your time, your money, and yourself. College is about self-responsibility. You're in charge of your education; you call the shots. If you manage your time and money, you can focus as you should on your courses. If you "spend" unwisely—in either area—you lose your focus and your performance slips. In your career, the same will be true, but the professional aspect of time and money management becomes even more important. For example, you may be required to plan and follow a project schedule and work within a department budget, or you may even be responsible for coming up with next year's budget. Learning to be a budget expert in your personal life may well ensure real success in your professional career. In many ways, your ability to manage time and money will affect your personal and professional future.

> Nothing is so fatiguing as the eternal hanging on of an uncompleted task.

William James, American psychologist and philosopher (1842–1910)

STEP 4: Set Intermediate Deadlines. After recording the important dates for the entire academic term, look at the individual due dates for major projects or papers that are assigned. Then set intermediate stepping-stone goals that will ultimately help you accomplish your final goals. Working backward from the due date, choose and record deadlines for completing certain chunks of the work. For example, if you have a research paper due, you could set an intermediate deadline for completing all of your initial research and other deadlines for the prewriting, writing, and rewriting steps for the paper.

STEP 5: Schedule Fixed Activities for the Entire Term. Next you'll want to schedule in all fixed activities throughout the entire term: class meeting times and reading assignments, religious services you regularly attend, club meetings, and family activities. It's also a great idea to schedule brief review sessions for your classes. Of course, sometimes you'll be going directly into another class, but ten-minute segments of time before and after each class to review your notes helps prepare you for any surprise quizzes and dramatically improves your ability to understand and remember the material.

STEP 6: Check for Schedule Conflicts. Now, take a final look at your planner. Do you notice any major scheduling conflicts, such as a planned business trip smack dab in the middle of midterm exam week? Look for these conflicts now, when there's plenty of time to adjust your plans and talk with your instructor to see what you can work out.

STEP 7: Schedule Flextime. In all the scheduling of important dates, checking and double-checking, don't forget one thing. You do need personal time for eating, sleeping, exercising, and other regular activities that don't have a set time frame. Despite your planner, life will happen. If you get a toothache, you'll need to see a dentist right away. Several times each week, you can count on something coming up that will offer you a chance (or force you) to revise your schedule. The decision of how high the item ranks on your priority list rests with you, but the point is to leave some wiggle room in your schedule.

STEP 8: Monitor Your Schedule Every Day. At this point, you've developed a working time management system. Now it's important to monitor your use of that system on a daily basis. Each night, take three minutes to review the day's activities. How well did you stick to your schedule? Did you accomplish the tasks you set out to do? Do you need to revise your schedule for the rest of the week based on something that happened—or didn't happen—today? This simple process will help you better schedule your time in the future and give you a sense of accomplishment—or of the need for more discipline—for tasks completed, hours worked, and classes attended.

To Do or Not to Do? There *Is* No Question

Part of your personal time management system should be keeping an ongoing to-do list. While the concept of a to-do list sounds relatively simple, here are a few tricks of the trade.

Before the beginning of each school week, brainstorm all the things that you want or need to get done in the upcoming week. Using this random list of to-do items, assign a priority level next to each one. The A-B-C method is simple and easy to use:

A = must get this done; highest priority

B = very important, but not absolutely necessary to get done immediately

C = not terribly important, but should be done right away (time-sensitive)

The two factors to consider when assigning a priority level to a to-do item are *importance* and **urgency**, creating four time zones. Use Figure 4.3 as a guide.[10]

urgency in need of immediate attention

FIGURE 4.3

Time Zones

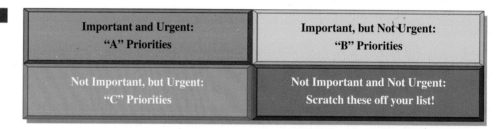

Important and Urgent: "A" Priorities	Important, but Not Urgent: "B" Priorities
Not Important, but Urgent: "C" Priorities	Not Important and Not Urgent: Scratch these off your list!

After you've assigned a time zone to each item, review your list of A and B priorities and ask yourself:

1. **Do any of the items fit best with a particular day of the week?** For example, donating blood may be a high priority task for you, yet you don't want to do it on a day when you have a sports event planned. That might leave you with two available days in the upcoming week that you can donate blood.

2. **Can any items be grouped together to make things easier?** For example, you may have three errands to run downtown on your to-do list, so grouping them together will save you from making three separate trips.

3. **Do any A and B priorities qualify as floating tasks that can be completed anytime, anywhere?** For example, perhaps you were assigned an extra long reading assignment for one of your classes. It's both important and urgent, an A priority item. Bring your book to read while waiting at the dentist's office for your appointment, a B priority. Planning ahead can really help save time.

4. **Do any priorities need to be shifted?** As the days pass, some of your B priorities will become A priorities due to the urgency factor increasing. Or maybe an A priority will become a C priority because something changed about the task. This is normal.

Items you've marked with a C must be decided on a case-by-case basis. But don't let their urgency convince you that you should do them before you accomplish items on your A and B lists. As for those not important and not urgent to-do items, scratch them off the list right now. Life is too short to waste time on unimportant tasks. Give yourself permission to focus on what's important. Since time is a limited resource, one of the best ways to guarantee a successful college experience is to use it wisely. If you don't already use these tools on a regular basis, give them a shot. What do you have to lose except time?

EXERCISE 4.4

So Much to Do—So Little Time

Assume this is your to-do list for today (Monday). Assign each item one of the four time zones described earlier: A, B, C (and strike through any items that are not urgent and not important). Finally, renumber the items to indicate which you would do first, which second, and so forth.

Start time: 9:00 a.m., Monday morning, during the second week of the fall term.

1. **B** Return Professor Jordan's call before class tomorrow. He left a message saying he wants to talk to you about some problems with the assignment you turned in.

2. _____ Pick up your paycheck and get to the bank before it closes at 5:00 p.m. this afternoon.

3. _____ Call your mother to find out how grandma is doing in the hospital.

4. _____ Start figuring out how to go about your new assignment at work. Your boss seems nervous about it.

5. _____ Call your favorite aunt. She lives overseas in a time zone seven hours ahead of yours. Today is her fiftieth birthday.

6. _____ Stop by the pharmacy to take advantage of discounted flu shots today only.

7. _____ Listen to the new music you downloaded yesterday.

8. _____ Leave a note asking your boy- or girlfriend/sibling/child to please stop leaving messes everywhere. It's really aggravating.

9. _____ Read the two chapters in your history textbook for the in-class quiz on Wednesday.

10. _____ Watch the first episode of the new reality TV show you've been waiting for at 9 p.m. tonight.

11. _____ Write a rough draft of the essay due in your composition class on Thursday.

12. _____ Invite an out-of-town friend to spend the weekend.

13. _____ Return the three library books that are a week overdue.

14. _____ Call your math Teaching Assistant and leave a message asking for an appointment during her office hours to get help with the homework due on Wednesday. Nearly everyone is confused about the assignment.

15. **A** Meet your best friend for dinner for his or her birthday at 6 p.m.

Outline the criteria you used for making your decisions. For example, did you base your answers on personal priorities, locations (combining tasks based on where you need to be to do them), urgency/importance, or some other principle? (Note that this exercise asks you to put these tasks in order, according to whatever principles from this chapter you choose—not to figure out how to multitask and accomplish several at once!)

How Time Flies!

According to efficiency expert Michael Fortino, in a lifetime, the average American will spend:

- Seven years in the bathroom
- Six years eating
- Five years waiting in line
- Three years in meetings

- Two years playing telephone tag
- Eight months opening junk mail
- And six months waiting at red lights[11]

What a waste of time! We can't do much about some of these items, but what *can* we do about other time-wasters? Plan—schedule—organize! Think about the issue of control in time management, and write in examples for the following:

1. Things you think you can't control, and you can't: **WEATHER**
2. Things you think you can't control, but you can: **GRADES**
3. Things you think you can control, but you can't: **TIME**
4. Things you think you can control, but you don't: **MYSELF**
5. Things you think you can control, and you can: **MY LIFE**

Perhaps you wrote in something like *medical emergencies* for (1). You could have written in *family or friends bothering you while you study* for (2). For (4), maybe you could control how much *time you waste online,* but you don't. And for (5), perhaps you wrote in *your attention.* You're absolutely right. But what about (3)? Did anything fit there? Are there things you think you can control, but you can't? Try and think of something that would fit into (3), and then think of creative ways you really could control this situation if you tried.[12] Have you ever thought about how much the issues of "control" and "time management" are related?

According to experts, there are four kinds of common problematic time management "Ps" in the world. When it comes to time management, control is generally a good thing. You take control and become more productive. But take a look at these four "P's." They exert control in ways that can bring counterproductive results!

- **The Preemptive.** Preemptives believe they are doing their best; in fact, they are continuously ahead of the game. They constantly, compulsively play "beat the clock." They're always way ahead of schedule. So what's wrong with that? Sometimes, nothing. But preemptives can gain a reputation of being non-team players, only out for themselves. They look like they're trying to impress everyone—or someone in particular, like the boss or teacher.

- **The People Pleaser.** People pleasers have the best of intentions, but they take on too much and sabotage their own effectiveness by trying to make others happy. Always saying yes to everyone may mean that there's no time left for their own work. Over time, they can even come to resent the very people they're trying to please and vice versa.

> **The Perfectionist.** Nothing is ever good enough for perfectionists. In effect, what they do is make other people play a waiting game, while they continue to tinker with their projects, trying to make them into some ideal they may never reach. They're control freaks, and they tend to lead anxiety-ridden lives.

> **The Procrastinator.** Procrastinators are adrenaline junkies. They put things off until the 11th hour and then make a mad dash for the finish line, trailing a long list of excuses. Often, the root cause of procrastination is fear. While the perfectionist will only accept an A+, the procrastinator is secretly afraid of not ever being able to achieve an A+. If he doesn't turn in an assignment, he can't find out just how good (or not) he is.[13]

© 2012 Cengage Learning. All Rights Reserved. May not be scanned, copied or duplicated, or posted to a publicly accessible website, in whole or in part.

EXERCISE 4.5

Are you a Preemptive, People-pleasing, Perfectionistic Procrastinator?

Do you know people who fit into each of these four problematic time management "P" categories? Do you? Work in groups or as a class to brainstorm ways of helping these people improve their time management skills. What advice would you give each type?

Preemptive

RELAX
SLOW DOWN
TAKE IT EASY.

People Pleaser

PLEASE SELF
RELAX
LIVE LIFE

Perfectionist

CHILL!
ACCEPT

Procrastinator

PICK IT UP!
COME ON!

(all images) Photos.com

The P Word. Read This Section *Now!* ... or Maybe Tomorrow ... or ...

Picture this: You sit down to work on a challenging homework assignment. After a few minutes, you think, *Man, I'm thirsty,* so you get up and get a soda. Then you sit back down to continue your work. A few minutes later, you decide that some chips would go nicely with your soda and you head to the kitchen. Again, you sit down to face the task before you, as you concentrate more on eating than on working. Ten minutes go by and a nagging thought starts taking over: *Must do laundry.* Up you go again and throw a load of clothes in the washer. Before long you're wondering where all the time went. Since you only have an hour left before class, you think, *Why bother getting started now? Doing this project will take much more time than that, so I'll just start it tomorrow.* Despite good intentions at the beginning of your work session, you've just succeeded in accomplishing zip, nada, nothing.

Congratulations! You—like thousands of other college students—have just successfully procrastinated! Researchers define procrastination as "needlessly delaying tasks to the point of experiencing subjective discomfort."[14] And according to researchers, 70 percent of college students admit to procrastinating on their assignments.[15]

You may be in the majority, but alas, in this case, there's no safety in numbers! Academic procrastination is a major threat to your ability to succeed in college. And procrastination in the working world can actually bring your job, and ultimately your career, to a screeching halt. Plenty of people try to rationalize their procrastination by claiming that they work better under pressure. However, the challenge in college is that during some weeks of the term, every class you're taking will have an assignment or test due, all at once, and if you procrastinate, you'll not only generate tremendous anxiety for yourself, but you'll lower your chances of succeeding on any of them.

EXERCISE 4.6

Who, Me, Procrastinate?

Procrastination is a habit. It may show up as not getting around to doing your homework (if you don't turn it in, you can't get a bad grade on it—which almost guarantees that you'll get a bad grade on it), not vacuuming the carpet because it takes too much energy to lug the machine around, or not getting to work on time because your job is boring. What about you? Think about the following ten situations, and put a check mark next to each one to indicate the degree to which you normally procrastinate:

	Always	Sometimes	Never
1. Doing homework		✓	
2. Writing a paper		✓	
3. Studying for tests	✓		
4. Reading class material		✓	
5. Meeting with your academic advisor	✓		
6. Texting/e-mailing a friend			✓
7. Playing a game/hanging out			✓
8. Going to see a movie you've heard about			✓
9. Meeting someone for dinner at a restaurant			✓
10. Watching TV		✓	

If you are like many students, you checked "always" or "sometimes" more often for the first five items than you did for the last five items. But procrastination isn't as simple as not procrastinating when you want to do something and procrastinating when you don't. You may actually hate vacuuming but decide to vacuum the entire house so that you don't have to face studying for a test. There are "layers" of procrastination and many reasons why people procrastinate. Which of these apply to you?

_____ Avoiding something you see as unpleasant   ☒ Not realizing how important the task is

☒ Feeling overwhelmed by all you have to do   ☒ Reacting to your own internal conflict

☒ Being intimidated by the task itself   _____ Protecting your self-esteem

☒ Fearing failure   _____ Waiting for a last-minute adrenaline rush

_____ Fearing success   _____ Just plain not wanting to

Procrastination has costs associated with it, like missed opportunities, lower grades, and disappointment. Quitting the procrastination habit is like quitting any other excessive, nonproductive thing in your life. If you want to minimize the "P Word" and its effects, consider putting yourself on this "10 Step Plan."

Step 1 – Admit that your procrastination is a problem.

Step 2 – Believe that it's up to you to fix it.

Step 3 – Make a decision to take control of your life.

Step 4 – Make an inventory of all the situations in which you procrastinate.

Step 5 – Examine all the reasons why.

Step 6 – Decide you're ready to change things.

Step 7 – Ask your friends and family to help you.

Step 8 – Concentrate on the rewards of not procrastinating.

Step 9 – Visualize success.

Step 10 – Notice the results!

Before you can control the procrastination monster in your life, it's important to understand *why* you procrastinate. Think about all the instances in which you don't procrastinate: meeting your friends for dinner, returning a phone call from a friend, going to the store. Why are those things easy to do, but getting started on an assignment is difficult until you feel the jaws of a deadline closing down on you?[16] The reasons for procrastinating vary from person to person, but once you know your own reasons for putting things off, you'll be in a better position to address the problem from its root cause.

The next time you find yourself procrastinating, ask yourself why. Procrastination hurts your chances for success and gives you ready-made excuses if you don't succeed: "It's like running a full race with a knapsack full of bricks on your back. When you don't win, you can say it's not that you're not a good runner, it's just that you had this sack of bricks on your back."[17] In addition to understanding why you procrastinate, try these ten procrastination busters to help you kick the habit.

1. **Keep track (of your excuses).** Write them down consistently, and soon you'll be able to recognize them for what they are. Own your responsibilities—in school and in the rest of your life.

2. **Break down.** Break your project into its smaller components. A term paper, for example, can be broken down into the following smaller parts: prospectus, thesis, research, outline, small chunks of writing, and bibliography.

> Things which matter most should never be at the mercy of things which matter least.
>
> *Johann Wolfgang von Goethe, German writer and scholar (1749–1832)*

Completing smaller tasks along the way is much easier than facing a threatening monster of a project.

3. **Trick yourself.** When you feel like procrastinating, pick some aspect of the project that's easy and that you would have to do anyway. If the thought of an entire paper is overwhelming you, for example, work on the bibliography to start. Starting with something—*anything*—will get you into the rhythm of the work.

4. **Resolve issues.** If something's eating away at you, making it difficult to concentrate, take care of it. Sometimes you must deal with a bossy friend, your kids vying for your attention, or something equally intrusive. Then get down to work.

5. **Get real.** Set realistic goals for yourself. If you declare that you're going to finish a twelve-page paper in five hours, you're already doomed. Procrastinators are sometimes overly optimistic. They underestimate how much time something will take. Make it a habit to keep track of how long assignments take you in all your courses so that you can be increasingly realistic over time.

6. **Be specific.** Instead of writing, "Finish chapter 10" in your planner, write exactly what you need to do, "Finish reading chapter 10, answer the discussion questions at the end, and e-mail my responses to my professor."

7. **Make a deal with yourself.** Even if it's only spending fifteen minutes on a task that day, do it so that you can see progress.

8. **Overcome fear.** Many of the reasons for procrastinating have to do with our personal fears. We may fear not doing something perfectly, or failing completely—or even the responsibility that comes with success to keep succeeding. But as Susan Jeffers, author and lecturer states, "Feel the fear, and do it anyway!"

9. **Get tough.** Sometimes projects simply require discipline. The best way to complete a tough task is to simply dig in. Become your own taskmaster, "crack the whip" and force yourself to focus on those things that are high priorities, but perhaps not your idea of fun.

10. **Acknowledge accomplishment.** We're not talking major shopping sprees at Neiman Marcus here. We're talking reasonable, meaningful rewards that match up with how much effort you invested. Go buy yourself a small treat, call your best friend in another state, take a relaxing soak in the bathtub, or do something to celebrate your accomplishments—big and small—along the way. Acknowledgment, from yourself or others, is a great motivator for tackling future projects.

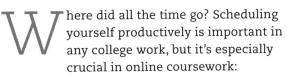

ONLINE **TechKnow**

Where did all the time go? Scheduling yourself productively is important in any college work, but it's especially crucial in online coursework:

- **Note your potential for peak performance.** Ever had a friend who was a "morning person" or a "night-owl"? Each of us has high energy times, and times during the day when we're zoned out on "auto-pilot." Learn to recognize when you're at your best, and find ways to schedule your online working sessions during those peak periods.

- **Read the "fine print."** You wouldn't buy a car without knowing the details of the contract, would you? When you sign up for an online course, your syllabus is your contract. It'll pay to read it carefully and note how much time this course will require, including reading, research, projects, tests, chats, and forums.

- **Make a calendar for yourself.** Write down exactly when online assignments must be done. Then mark on your calendar when you'll need to start each project ahead of time, and how long you estimate it will take you to get it done. Refer to this calendar every day—develop a partnership between yourself and your calendar as your main ally.

- **Work ahead.** What about cramming for tests? What about writing up assignments mere minutes before a deadline? In both cases, you'll do your best online work if you work ahead and submit assignments early. Use your contract (your syllabus) and your calendar wisely here—mark these tests and tasks at the beginning of the course and get them done ahead of time.

Beyond Juggling: *Realistically* Manage Work, School, and Personal Life

Your personal time management needs depend on who you are and how many obligations you have. Today's college students are more diverse than ever. Increasing numbers of college students are also parents, part-time employees, or full-time professionals, husbands or wives, community volunteers, soccer coaches, or Sunday school teachers. How on earth can you possibly juggle it all?

The answer? You can't. According to work-life balance expert Dawn Carlson, juggling is a knee-jerk coping mechanism—the default setting when time gets tight and it seems that nothing can be put on the back burner. If you, like millions of others, feel overworked, overcommitted, and exhausted at every turn, you may have already learned that you can't juggle your way to a balanced life. It's impossible.[18]

Now for the good news. Balance among work, school, and personal life is possible. All of us have three primary areas of our lives that should be in balance, ideally—meaningful work (including school), satisfying relationships, and a healthy lifestyle. In addition to work and relationships, we all need to take care of ourselves. See what you think of these five rebalancing strategies. The idea is you can't have it all, but you can have it better than you do now.

*Adapted from Sandholtz, K., Derr, B., Buckner, K., & Carlson, D. (2002). Beyond juggling: Rebalancing your busy life. San Francisco: Berrett-Koehler Publishing.

1. **Alternating.** If you use this strategy, your work-life balance comes in separate, concentrated doses. You may throw yourself into your career with abandon, and then cut back or quit work altogether and focus intensely on your family. You may give your job 110 percent during the week, but devote Saturdays to physical fitness or to your kids or running all the errands you've saved up during the week. Or you save Tuesdays and Thursdays for homework, and go to classes Mondays, Wednesdays, and Fridays. People who use this strategy alternate between important things, and it works for them. An alternator's motto is "I want to have it all, but just not all at once."

2. **Outsourcing.** Outsourcing, or paying someone else to do something for you, is another solution. An outsourcer's motto might be "I want to have it all, not do it all." This strategy helps you achieve work-life balance by giving someone else some of your responsibilities—usually in your personal life—to free up time for the tasks you care about most. If you have enough money, hire someone to clean the house or mow the lawn. If you don't, trade these jobs among family, friends, or neighbors who band together to help each other. Of course, there are ways this strategy could be misused by college students. Don't even think about outsourcing your research papers by having someone else write them or downloading them from the Internet with a charge card! Warning: This practice will definitely be hazardous to your academic health! In fact, your college career may be over!

3. **Bundling.** Bundling is efficient because it allows you to do two things at once. Examine your busy life and look for areas in which you can double dip, such as combining exercising with socializing. If your social life is suffering because you have too much to do, take walks with a friend so that you can talk along the way. A bundler's motto is "I want to get more mileage out of the things I do by combining activities."

4. **Techflexing.** Technology allows us to work from almost anywhere, anytime, using technology. If you telecommute from home several days a week for your job, you might get up early, spend some time on e-mail, go out for a run, have breakfast with your family, and then get back on your computer. In the office, you use instant messaging to stay connected to family members or a cell phone to call home while commuting to a business meeting. Chances are you can telecommute to your campus library and do research online, register for classes online, and pay all your bills online, including tuition. Use

> The trouble with the rat race is that even if you win, you're still a rat.

Lily Tomlin, comedian

technology, and the flexibility it gives you, to your advantage to merge important aspects of your life.

5. **Simplifying.** People who use this strategy have decided they don't want it all. They've reached a point where they make a permanent commitment to stop the craziness in their lives. The benefit of simplifying is greater freedom from details, stress, and the rat race. But there are trade-offs, of course. They may have to take a significant cut in pay in order to work fewer hours or at a less demanding job. But for them, it's worth it.[19]

These five strategies, used separately or in combination, have helped many people who are dealing with work, school, and family commitments at the same time. They all require certain trade-offs. None of these strategies is a magic solution.

But the alternative to rebalancing is more stress, more physical and emotional exhaustion, more frustration, and much less personal satisfaction. If you focus on rebalancing your life—making conscious choices and course corrections as you go—small changes can have a big impact. Work–life balance isn't an all-or-nothing proposition. It's an ever-changing journey. So take it one step at a time.

Time Is Money!

EXERCISE 4.7

How Fiscally Fit Are You?

Have you ever heard the phrase "time is money"? Before leaving subjects of time and energy management, let's look at how you manage your money as well. How good are you at managing your finances? Check one of the three boxes for each statement to get a sense of how financially savvy you are.

	Always true of me	Sometimes true of me	Never true of me
1. At any given moment in time, I know the balance of my checking account.	✓		
2. I use my credit card for particular types of purchases only, such as gas or food.		✓	
3. I pay off my bills in full every month.	✓		
4. I know the interest rate on my credit cards.	✓		
5. I resist impulse buying and only spend when I need things.		✓	
6. I have a budget and I follow it.		✓	
7. I put money aside to save each month.		✓	
8. When I get a pay raise, I increase the proportion of money I save.	✓		
9. I keep track of my spending on a daily or weekly basis.		✓	
10. I don't allow myself to get pressured by others into buying things I don't really need.		✓	

Look over your responses. If you have more checks in the "Never true of me" column than you do in either of the two others, you may be able to put the information you're about to read to good use!

People say that "time is money." It's true. If you're so efficient with your time that you can call more customers or sell more products, then time does equal money. If your company is the first to introduce a hot new kind of cell phone or a zippy fuel-efficient car, you win. Even if better models come out next year, they may fall flat because people have already invested.

Both time management and money management are key to your college success. Studies show that working too many hours for pay increases your chances of dropping out of college.[20] Many students find themselves working more so that they can spend more, which in turn takes time away from their studies. They may take a semester off from college to make a pile of money and then never come back. While there's evidence that working a moderate amount can help you polish your time and energy management skills, the real secret to financial responsibility in college is to track your habits and gain the knowledge you need to make sound financial decisions.

© Larry Harwood Photography. Property of Cengage Learning.

"I'd say it's been my biggest problem all my life . . . it's money. It takes a lot of money to make these dreams come true."

Walt Disney, American animator, entrepreneur, and philanthropist (1901–1966)

Create a Spending Log

Take a look at this student's spending log, then complete one for yourself. Money has a way of slipping through our fingers. Choose one entire day that is representative of your spending, and use the chart on the next page to keep track of how you spend money. Write down everything from seemingly small, insignificant items to major purchases, and explain why you made that purchase. Your log may look something like this student's:

TIME	ITEM	LOCATION	AMOUNT	REASON
8–9 a.m.	coffee and bagel	convenience store	$3.50	overslept!
9–10 a.m.	computer paper	office supply store	$2.50	English paper due
10–11 a.m.	gas fill-up	gas station	$65.00	running on fumes!
11 a.m.– 12 p.m.	burger and fries	fast-food restaurant	$6.00	lunch on the run
12–1 p.m.	toiletries, etc.	drugstore	$18.00	out of stock
1–2 p.m.	bottled water	convenience store	$2.50	forgot to bring
2–3 p.m.	supplies	bookstore	$12.00	forgot to get earlier
3–7 p.m.	WORK			
7-8 p.m.	pizza	pizza place	$12.00	meet friends
8–9 p.m.	week's groceries	grocery store	$61.50	cupboard is bare!
9–10 p.m.	laundry	laundromat	$5.00	washer broken
10–11 p.m.	STUDY TIME			
11 p.m.– 12 a.m.	weekend movie, online tickets, DVDs, cell phone upgrade	Internet retail websites, phone service	$129.00 $20.00	friend's recommendations, need more minutes

This student has spent $337 today without doing anything special! When you analyze his expenditures, you can find patterns. He seems to (1) forget to plan, so he spends money continuously throughout the day, (2) spend relatively large amounts of money online, (3) be particularly vulnerable late at night, and (4) spend money grabbing food on the run. These are patterns he should be aware of if he wants to control his spending. He could pack food from home to save a significant amount of money, for example. Now create your own chart.

TIME	ITEM	LOCATION	AMOUNT	REASON
8–9 a.m.				
9–10 a.m.				
10–11 a.m.				
11 a.m.–12 p.m.				
12–1 p.m.				
1–2 p.m.				
2–3 p.m.				
3–4 p.m.				
4–5 p.m.				
5–6 p.m.				
6–7 p.m.				
7–8 p.m.				
8–9 p.m.				
9–10 p.m.				
10–11 p.m.				
11 p.m.–12 a.m.				

What patterns do you notice about your spending? What kinds of changes will you try to make to curb any unnecessary spending?

The Perils of Plastic

The "newly minted" Credit Card Act of 2009 has changed some things about how credit cards work. In 2008 before the law went into effect, college students carried a balance of $3,173 (a ten-year high), and a full 82 percent kept paying on a balance every month.[21] Under the new law, credit cards cannot be issued to people under the age of 21 unless they have an adult co-signer or can show proof that they have enough income. College students will need permission from parents/guardians to increase their credit limits. And those under 21 will be protected from "sneaky" credit card offers unless they opt to get them. Read up on credible internet sites about the new law and the protections and restrictions it provides. If you already have a credit card or plan to get one, however, keep the following general advice in mind.

1. **Think about the difference between needs and wants.** You may think you need particular things so that your friends will like you ("Hey, let's stop for a burger"), so that you have a new item (like a new car you can't afford), or so that you look fabulous (like pricey manicures). Here's a rule of thumb: If buying something simply helps you move from acceptable to amazing, it's not an emergency. Do you really need a mocha latté every day? A regular old cup of coffee a day sets you back $500 per year!

2. **Leave home without it.** Don't routinely take your credit card with you. Use cash and save your credit card for true emergencies or essentials, like gas and groceries. Do you really want to risk paying interest on today's ice cream cone years from now?

3. **Don't spend money you don't have.** Only charge what you can pay for each month. Just because your credit card limit is $2,000 doesn't mean you need to spend that much each month. A vacation that costs $1,000 will take 12 years of minimal payments to pay off at an 18 percent interest rate. And that $1,000 trip will eventually cost you $2,115!

4. **Understand how credit works.** It's important to know the basics. In one study, 71 percent of new college students had no idea how much interest they were paying on their credit card bills.[22]

   Here are some terms you need to know:

   > **Credit reports.** Your credit history is based on (1) how many credit cards you owe money on, (2) how much money you owe, and (3) how many late payments you make. Bad grades on your credit report can make your life difficult later.

   > **Fees.** Credit card companies charge you in three ways: (1) annual fees (a fee you must pay every year to use the card); (2) finance charges (a charge for loaning you the money you can't pay back when your bill is due); and (3) late fees (for missing a monthly payment deadline). Think about what's most important to you—no annual fee, frequent flyer miles, lower interest rate—and shop around!

   > **The fine print.** How can you learn more? Read your credit card contract carefully. Credit card companies must give you certain important information, which is often on their website. Go to the Federal Reserve website for vital, bottomline information, and search online to find out more about ways the new law could affect you.[23]

5. **Track your expenses.** All kinds of tools—technology-based and otherwise—can help you discover where your money actually goes. To control your spending, use a credit card with caution or use a debit card.

6. **If you're already in financial trouble, ask for help.** Talk to an expert who can help you figure out what to do.[24]

BOX 4.2 **Top Ten Financial Aid FAQs**

Financial aid. Like all good things, you have to know how it works. You can think of financial aid as complicated and time-consuming, or it can be the one thing that keeps you in school. Take a look at these questions students often ask about the mysteries of financial aid. Most students need financial help of some kind to earn a college degree. Here is some information to help you navigate your way financially.[25]

1. **Who qualifies for financial aid?** You may not think you qualify for financial aid, but it's a good idea to apply anyway. You won't know until you try, and some types of aid are based on criteria other than whether or not you actually need the money.

2. **What does FAFSA stand for?** And where do I get a copy? FAFSA stands for Free Application for Federal Student Aid, and you can get a copy from your campus Financial Aid office, a public library, by calling 1-800-4-FED-AID, or by going to www.fafsa.ed.gov and filling out the FAFSA online.

3. **What types of financial aid exist?** You can receive financial aid in the form of scholarships, fellowships, loans, grants, or work-study awards. Generally, scholarships and fellowships are for students with special academic, artistic, or athletic abilities; students with interests in specialized fields; students from particular parts of the country; or students from minority groups. Typically, you don't repay them. Loans and grants come in a variety of forms and from several possible sources, either government or private. Typically, loans must be repaid. In addition, if you qualify for a need-based work-study job on or off campus, you can earn an hourly wage to help pay for school.

4. **When should I apply?** You can apply for financial aid any time after January 1 of the year you intend to go to college (because tax information from the previous year is required), but you must be enrolled to receive funds.

5. **Do I have to reapply every year?** Yes. Your financial situation can change over time. Your brothers or sisters may start college while you're in school, for example, which can change your family's status.

6. **How can I keep my financial aid over my college years?** Assuming your financial situation remains fairly similar from year to year, you must demonstrate that you're making progress toward a degree in terms of credits and a minimum GPA. Remember that if you drop courses, your financial aid may be affected based on whether you're considered to be a full-time or part-time student.

7. **Who's responsible for paying back my loans?** You are. Others can help you, but ultimately the responsibility is yours and yours alone. If your parents forget to make a payment or don't pay a bill on time, you will be held responsible.

8. **If I leave school for a time, do I have to start repaying my loans right away?** Most loans have a grace period of six or nine months before you must begin repayment. You can request an extension if you "stop out," but you must do so before the grace period ends.

9. **If I get an outside scholarship, should I report it to the Financial Aid office on campus?** Yes. They'll adjust your financial aid package accordingly, but those are the rules.

10. **Where can I find out more?** Your best source of information is in the Office of Financial Aid right on your own campus. Or call the Federal Student Aid Information Center at 1-800-433-3243 and ask for a free copy of *The Student Guide: Financial Aid* from the U.S. Department of Education.

YOU NEED TO STUDY

VARK Activity

Complete the activity recommended for your preferred VARK learning style and bring it to class (or follow your instructor's instructions).

 Visual: Buy a set of adhesive colored dots from a local office supply store. Go through your planner, putting red dots by A priority items, yellow dots by B priority items, and green dots by C priority items.

 Aural: Go to the National Public Radio website at www.npr.org and listen to a program about time management. Access the CourseMate via www.cengagebrain.com/shop/ISBN/1439083908 to listen to the iAudio summary for this chapter.

 Read/Write: Find a helpful library book on time management skills and summarize three pointers that don't appear in this chapter in a paragraph of your own.

 Kinesthetic: Find a YouTube or other online resource on time management that add to this chapter. Show your YouTube or "compete" with other "K" students to show the best one in class.

(from top to bottom) Marcela Barsse/MarsBars/iStockphoto.com; Johanna Goodyear/Dreamstime.com; Nadezda Firsova/iStockphoto.com; Pascal Genest/iStockphoto.com

At the beginning of this chapter, Derek Johnson, a frustrated and disgruntled student, faced a challenge. Now after reading this chapter, would you respond differently to any of the questions you answered about the "FOCUS Challenge Case"? Using what you learned in the chapter, write a paragraph ending to Derek's case study. What are some of the possible outcomes for Derek?

step
4 ACTION Your Plans for Change

1. What's the most important thing you learned in reading this chapter?
2. How will you apply the information you've learned to yourself to improve your time, energy, and money management?

REALITY CHECK | # What did you **Learn?**

On a scale of 1 to 5, answer these questions now that you've completed this chapter.

1 = not very/not much/very little/low   5 = very/a lot/very much/high

How much do you know *now*?

Now rate your current level of knowledge about topics covered in this chapter.

Time management vs. energy management

1   2   3   4   (5)

Procrastination

1   2   3   4   (5)

Balancing work, school, and personal life

1   2   3   4   (5)

Money management

1   2   3   4   (5)

How useful might the information in this chapter be to you?

How much do you think this information might affect your college success?

1   2   3   4   (5)

How much do you think this information might affect your career success after college?

1   2   3   4   (5)

How long did it actually take you to complete this chapter (both the reading and writing tasks)?

_____ Hour(s) _____ Minutes

 Challenge Yourself Online Quiz. To find out how much you've learned, access the CourseMate via www.cengagebrain.com/shop/ISBN/1439083908 to take the Challenge Yourself Online Quiz.

Compare these answers with your answers from the "Readiness Check" at the beginning of this chapter. How might the gaps between what you thought before starting the chapter and what you now think affect how you approach the next chapter?

chapter 5

Thinking Critically and Creatively

You're About to Discover...

✔ How focused thinking, critical thinking, and creative thinking are defined
✔ How a four-part model of critical thinking works
✔ How to analyze arguments, assess assumptions, and consider claims
✔ How to avoid mistakes in reasoning
✔ What metacognition is and why it's important
✔ How to become a more creative thinker

READINESS CHECK

What do you **Know?**

Before beginning this chapter, take a moment to answer these questions. Your answers will help you assess how ready you are to focus.

1 = not very/not much/very little/low   5 = very/a lot/very much/high

How much do you *already* know?

Rate your current level of knowledge about topics covered in this chapter.

Focused thinking

      1 2 3 4 5

Four-part model of critical thinking

      1 2 3 4 5

Arguments, assumptions, claims

      1 2 3 4 5

Critical versus *creative* thinking

      1 2 3 4 5

How motivated are you to learn *more*?

In general, how motivated are you to learn the material in this chapter?

      1 2 3 4 5

How much do you think this information might affect your college success?

      1 2 3 4 5

How much do you think this information might affect your career success after college?

      1 2 3 4 5

How ready are you to read *now*?

How ready are you to focus on this chapter—physically, intellectually, and emotionally? Which of these three areas is most challenging for you right now? Circle a number to represent it.

      1 2 3 4 5

If any of your answers is below a 3, consider addressing the issue before reading. Then, read the chapter carefully, while looking for ways to improve your focus.

Finally, how long do you think it will take you to complete this chapter? If you start and stop, keep track of the overall time.

_____ Hour(s) _____ Minutes

Desiree Moore

© Larry Harwood Photography. Property of Cengage Learning.

Simply put: Desiree Moore was a perfectionist. Her friends said she was "detail-oriented." Her family said she was compulsive. Truthfully, though, she hadn't been all that successful in high school because her assignments were always turned in late, if at all, because they were never "finished." She'd always ask her teachers how long a paper should be and what topic she should write about. She wanted to get things right. Her teachers always advised her to stop "tweaking": "You spend so much time revising your assignments that nothing ever gets done." But she found it hard to take their advice.

© Cengage Learning

Paralegal Associate's Degree Program

Courses offered:

- Introduction to the Law
- Torts & Personal Injury
- Contracts
- Legal Research, Writing & Civil Litigation
- Paralegal Ethics
- Criminal Law
- Business Law & Bankruptcy
- Constitutional Law

une the TOP PARALEGAL EXPERTS
RUNO

LESSONS

Paralegal Ethics Syllabus

Instructor: Samuel Courtney
Email Address: S.Courtney@campusmail.edu
Office Hours: MWF 8am–10am
Office Location: Main Hall 1020
Text: *Legal Ethics for Paralegals and the Law Office* (1st Edition) by Laura Morrison

Class Content:
- Understand ethical issues that paralegals may face
- Review the universal concepts of professional responsibility and ethical practices
- Define the roles of paralegals versus attorneys
- Recognize what activities constitute the
- Discuss possible solutions to ethical dilemmas

Class Method: Since philosophy is an important part of law, for our class method we will turn to one of the founding fathers of critical and philosophical thinking: Socrates. Consequently, we will be using the "Socratic method" when approaching course material. This means that instead of giving a lecture, I will ask you, the students, questions in order to create a lively discussion.

Grading: This course will include 3 exams, each worth 20% of your overall grade. There will also be 5 quizzes during the semester, all of which contribute to another 20% of your grade. Finally, class participation will count for the final 20% of your grade. It is imperative that you attend every class session, and that you are actively participating in class discussions.

Course Outline:
This course covers the basic principles governing the ethical practice of law for paralegals. Subjects explored include the unauthorized practice of law, confidentiality, paralegal-client relations, conflicts of interest, disciplinary procedures, advertising, fee splitting, billing, and misconduct in the law office.

High school had been so stressful that when she graduated, she took the first job that came along as a receptionist for a small law firm. When the two lawyers announced they were going to retire, she started to job hunt immediately. She found another job as a telemarketer. But being hung up on all day wasn't all that much fun, so eventually she quit. She tried waiting tables and cleaning houses, but those jobs didn't hold much appeal either. Before she knew it, more than a few years had gone by, and Desiree realized she didn't have much to show for it. She needed more specialized skills in order to get a better job. When she thought back over all the jobs she'd had since high school, she realized that working with the two law-

yers had been her favorite. So, Desiree decided to become a paralegal by earning a two-year degree at the big career college in town. She would be the first person in her family to go to college! It was a good career field, and she could investigate legal cases, draft documents, and do research working alongside an attorney.

Her first semester consisted of two night classes: "Introduction to Paralegal Careers" and "Paralegal Ethics." But "Paralegal Ethics" was a very challenging course. The instructor, Mr. Courtney, a retired lawyer himself, had announced on the first day of class that he believed in the Socratic method of teaching, by asking questions of students instead of lecturing. "Socrates, perhaps the

© Cengage Learning

greatest philosopher of all time," he announced the first day, "is the 'father' of critical thinking. In this class, you'll learn to think critically. *Learning to think* is what college is all about." Mr. Courtney began every class session with a hypothetical story, and he always randomly chose a student to respond. His openings went something like this:

> An attorney has just finished law school and opens a law office. He hires a legal assistant, just out of college. He is eager to begin his new career, but he is also nervous because he's starting from scratch.
>
> The lawyer's specialty is civil law, and several weeks go by before the phone even rings. His first potential client has a big problem. He wants to sue his next door neighbor for keeping old cars, junk, and trash in his front yard. When he's asked the neighbor nicely to clean up his property, the neighbor has refused in threatening tones. The teenage sons who live in the home have ties to local gangs and other neighbors are afraid. They all suspect the teenage boys of a series of unsolved robberies in the neighborhood. The neighborhood is getting a bad reputation, and home values in the area have fallen dramatically.
>
> The lawyer, who desperately needs the work, decides to take the case. However, when the client fills out the contract, his legal assistant notices that the client's zip code is the same as her boss's. In fact, she recognizes the street name as one that's in the subdivision

where the lawyer himself lives. Is this a problem? Would you say the lawyer has a "conflict of interest"? What should our legal assistant do?

One student responded with, "Yes, the lawyer lives in the same neighborhood as his client. He doesn't want his own property value to fall. According to our textbook, that's a conflict of interest." Another student said, "But the legal assistant should keep quiet and just do her job. She needs a paycheck. She shouldn't tell her boss what to do. It's none of her business." Mr. Courtney continued, "But what if the new client discovers that he and his lawyer live in the same neighborhood? Would the client see that as a possible conflict of interest? Could this damage the lawyer's legal career? What would *you* do if the legal assistant were you?" Mr. Courtney's questions seemed endless. Desiree's best friend suggested that she look him up on ratemyprofessors.com, but when she did, she found that students commented on how much they had learned from him.

"What's important in college is thinking through problems," he said. "There aren't always clear right and wrong answers. The process of learning to think can be just as important as the answer itself."

Frankly, that explanation didn't sit well with Desiree. *If there aren't right answers, why go to college? The instructor knows the right answers. Why doesn't he just tell us?* Perfectionists like Desiree were always most comfortable when things were straightforward. Without fail, she always left Mr. Courtney's class with a headache from thinking so hard.

New attorney opens office
-civil law

Potential client:
-wants to sue neighbor
-won't clean trash in yard
-possible gang connections

Attorney takes case
-but, attorney lives in same neighborhood!

PROBLEM!?

1. Do you have anything in common with Desiree, like an instructor who teaches in a way you find difficult to understand? What specific steps are you taking to help yourself succeed?
2. Do you agree with Mr. Courtney's statement that "there aren't always right answers"? If that's true, why is getting a college education so important?
3. Identify three things Desiree should do to get the most from Mr. Courtney's class.

Rethinking Thinking

Thinking is a natural, ongoing, everyday process we all engage in. In fact, we can't really turn it off, even if we try. We're always on. Everyone thinks all the time. We talk to ourselves in our heads. However, some experts say school teaches us how to just regurgitate what we've memorized, not how to think. Learning to think is what counts, and *focused thinking*—thinking critically and creatively—is what this chapter is about.

Picture this: You're in the library. It's late, and you're tired. You're supposed to be studying for your political science test, but instead of thinking about foreign policy, your mind begins drifting toward the vacation you took last summer, the great food you ate, and how much fun it was to be with your friends or family.

Would the mental process you're engaging in while sitting in the library be called *thinking*? For our purposes in this chapter, the answer is no. Here thinking is defined as a focused mental activity you engage in on purpose. You direct your thoughts toward a particular topic. You're the *active* thinker, not the *passive* daydreamer who is the victim of a wandering mind. Focused thinking involves zeroing in and managing your attention. It's deliberate, not accidental. You choose to do it for a reason.

Focused thinking is like a two-sided coin. Sometimes when you think, you *produce* ideas. That's what this chapter calls *creative thinking*, and that's something we'll deal with later. The other side of thinking requires you to *evaluate* ideas—your own or someone else's. That's *critical thinking*. The word *critical* comes from the Greek word for *critic* (*kritikos*), meaning "to question or analyze." You focus on something, sort through the information, and decide which ideas are most sensible, logical, or useful. When you're thinking critically, you're asking questions, analyzing arguments, assessing assumptions, considering

© Larry Harwood Photography. Property of Cengage Learning.

> **'Knowledge is power.' Rather, knowledge is happiness. To have knowledge, deep broad knowledge, is to know truth from false and lofty things from low.**
>
> *Helen Keller, American author, activist, and lecturer (1880–1968)*

claims, avoiding mistakes in reasoning, problem solving, decision making, and all the while, thinking about your thinking.

What Is Critical Thinking?

Critical thinking is a particular kind of focused thinking. It is purposeful, reasoned, and goal-directed. It's thinking that aims to solve problems, calculate likelihood, weigh evidence, and make decisions.[1] In that sense, movie critics are critical thinkers because they look at a variety of standards (screenplay, acting, production quality, costumes, and so forth) and then decide how a movie measures up. When you're thinking critically, you're not just being critical. You're on the lookout for both faults and strengths. You're looking at how things measure up.[2]

"
What we need is not the will to believe, but the will to find out.

Bertrand Russell, British philosopher, logician, and mathematician (1872–1970)

Critical thinkers develop standards they can use to judge advertisements, political speeches, sales pitches, movies—you name it.[3] Critical thinking is not jumping to conclusions; buying arguments lock, stock, and barrel; accepting controversial ideas no matter what; or ignoring the facts.

Unfortunately, some people are noncritical thinkers. They may be biased or closed-minded. Other people are *selective* critical thinkers. When it comes to one particular subject, they shut down their minds. They can't explain their views, they're emotional about them, and they refuse to acknowledge any other position. Why do they believe these things? Only if they understand the *why*, can they explain their views to someone else or defend them under fire. The importance of *why* can't be overstated. Some people, of course, have already thought through their beliefs, and they understand their positions and the reasons for them very well. Arriving at that point is the goal of anyone who wants to become a better critical thinker.

How **FULL** is your plate?

" Blessed are the flexible, for they shall not be bent out of shape. "

—MICHAEL MCGRIFFY, M.D.

When your plate is as full as yours probably is, sometimes you must *decide* to be flexible. You may not be able to do everything perfectly, as Desiree in the FOCUS Challenge Case wanted to. For her, procrastination was a way of giving herself permission to do a less than perfect job on a task that didn't require a perfect job in the first place.[4] For people like Desiree, developing flexibility can be a key to college success.

PhotostoGO.com

TRY IT!
Choose one item on your "to-do" list this week that can be shifted down the list, and one item that should be shifted up. What's *really* important? In class, discuss whether perfectionism is a problem for you, and if so, what you can do about it.

And Just Why Is Critical Thinking Important?

Here is a list of reasons why it's important to improve your critical thinking skills. Beside each entry, mark the degree to which you'd like to refine your critical thinking skills in each area. How important are each of these items to you? On a scale from 1 to 5 with 5 representing the highest degree, would you like to:

1. _____ **Become a more successful college student**? Most college courses require you to think critically (in answering essay questions, for example). In one study of over 1,100 college students, higher scores on critical thinking skills tests correlated highly with better grades.[5] Critical thinkers, for example, can ask better questions in class. There's even evidence that interaction with other students in activities outside of class can help you develop as a critical thinker.[6]

2. _____ **Become a better citizen**? Critical thinking is the foundation of a strong democracy. Voters must think critically about candidates' messages and whether they're likely to keep their campaign promises. It's easy to talk about balancing the budget, or lowering taxes, but the truth is these highly complex tasks are very challenging to carry out. The American public must sift through information and examine politicians' arguments in order to keep our democracy strong.

3. _____ **Become a better employee**? A workforce of critical—and creative—thinkers helps the American economy thrive and individuals become more successful. The U.S. Department of Labor reports that today's jobs require employees who can deal with complex issues, learn and perform multiple tasks, analyze and deal with a wide variety of options, identify problems, perceive alternative approaches, and select the best approach.[7] Employers are "practically begging" for employees who can "think, collaborate, communicate, coordinate, and create."[8]

4. _____ **Become a smarter consumer**? In today's world, everyone wants your money. If you bought everything advertised in magazines or on television, you'd run out of money very quickly. Critical thinking will help you evaluate offers, avoid slick come-ons, and buy responsibly.

5. _____ **Build stronger relationships**? Critical thinking helps us understand our own and others' actions and become more responsible communicators. Whether with friends or romantic partners, relationships take work. Sometimes you have to listen between the lines for important clues to figure out what your partner really means. Actually, critical thinking is at the heart of every relationship you care about.

6. _____ **Become a lifelong learner**? Your education doesn't end when you get your diploma. In many ways the real exams begin afterward when you put your classroom learning to the test on the job. And in today's world you must continue to learn as you transition through jobs—personally and professionally. You'll need to keep expanding your skills, no matter what your career is.

Look over your responses to these six items. Now rank them with one as your highest priority at this particular point in your life. Be prepared to explain how you rank ordered these six items in class.

A Four-Part Model of Critical Thinking

Now that we've defined critical thinking, let's ask an important related question: How do you do it? We'll look at the four primary components of critical thinking, and at the end of this chapter, we'll use a realistic news story, one that could take place near any college campus, to allow you to apply what you've learned through a memorable example.

Take a look at Figure 5.1 to preview the four-part model of critical thinking. You'll see right away that your reasoning skills underlie everything. They are

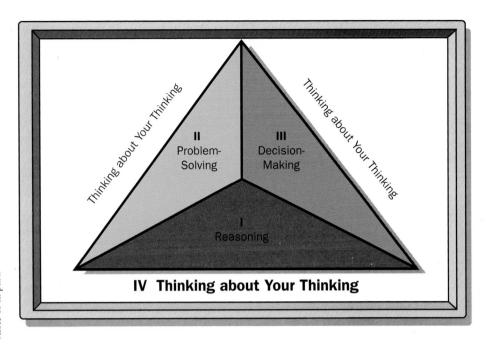

FIGURE 5.1

Critical Thinking Is Focused

Here's a four-part model of critical thinking. Your reasoning skills under-lie everything. They are the foundation upon which your problem-solving and decision-making skills rest, and your metacognitive skills, or thinking about your thinking, surround all the focused thinking you do.

the foundation upon which your problem-solving and decision-making skills rest, and your metacognitive skills, or thinking about your thinking, surround all the focused thinking you do.

I. Reasoning: The Foundation of Critical Thinking

Reasoning, the foundation of critical thinking, is the ability to reach a conclusion from one or more arguments. A strong argument is convincing because it offers **evidence** to back up its claim. If no one would disagree with what you're saying, it's not an argument. It's obvious. "Grass is green" is not an argument. But "Cows that are grass-fed make the best meat" is (if supporting evidence is provided). Do you see the difference?

evidence reasons why something is true, based on statistics, expert testimony, or examples

Think about your reasoning skills. How good are you at creating a sound argument? Let's say that you're trying to convince your friend that her cell phone conversation is making it difficult for you to study for a major exam. What evidence would you use to convince her? What's the likelihood of your success? Or how about this? How good are you at evaluating someone else's argument? For example, you're trying to decide whether an online discount is really a good deal. Would you take the advertiser's word for it or would you compare prices on your own?

Throughout the rest of this chapter, ask yourself: Are there ways I can improve my reasoning skills? As you think about your own skills, consider these reasoning nuts and bolts that are essential parts of creating and evaluating arguments.

Analyzing Arguments

Have you ever seen the *Monty Python Flying Circus* "Argument Sketch"? In this bizarre skit a man comes to an "argument clinic" to buy an argument. The two arguers—"professional" and customer—engage in a long, "yes, it is" "no, it isn't" squabble.

Critical thinking is about arguments. But most of us think of an argument as a back-and-forth disagreement. In the middle of the "Argument Clinic" sketch, however, the customer actually makes an important point. He says that they're not really arguing; they're just **contradicting** each other. He continues, "An argument is a connected series of statements intended to establish a **proposition**." That's the kind of argument that's related to critical thinking.

Critical thinking is about an argument that *one* person puts forth, not a squabble between two people. An op-ed piece in the newspaper contains an argument. (Op-ed stands for the page "opposite the editorial page" that features signed articles expressing personal viewpoints.) An attorney—whether prosecution or defense—will put forth a closing argument at the end of a trial.

Arguments are said to be inductive or deductive. *Inductive* arguments go from specific observations to general conclusions. In criminal trials, the prosecution puts together individual pieces of evidence to prove that the defendant is guilty: eyewitnesses put him at the scene, the gun store salesman remembers selling him a pistol, and his fingerprints are on the weapon. Therefore, the prosecutor argues that the defendant is guilty. Other arguments are said to be *deductive*, meaning they go from broad generalizations to specific conclusions. All serial killers have a particular psychological profile. The defendant has this psychological profile. Therefore the defendant is the killer.

What do arguments do? They propose a line of reasoning. They try to persuade. Arguments contain clear reasons to believe someone or something. Arguments say A plus B equals C. Once you understand what an argument is, you must also understand that arguments can be sound or unsound. If I tell you that two plus two equals four, chances are good that you'll believe me. If, on the other hand, I tell you two plus two equals five, you'll flatly deny it. If I say "Cats have fur." "Dogs have fur." "Therefore dogs are cats," you'll tell me I'm crazy—because it's an unsound argument.

The standard we use to test the soundness of arguments is logic, which is a fairly extensive topic. Let's just say for our purposes here that arguments are sound when the evidence for them is reasonable, more reasonable than the evidence against them. The important point is that a sound argument provides at least one good reason to believe. Let's look at an example:

I don't see why all students have to take an introductory writing course. It's a free country. Students shouldn't have to take courses they don't want to take.

John Lund/CORBIS

"

Few people think more than two or three times a year. I have made an international reputation for myself by thinking once or twice a week.

George Bernard Shaw, Irish literary critic, playwright, and essayist, 1925 Nobel Prize for Literature (1856–1950)

Based on our definition, is this example an argument? Why or why not? Is the statement "It's a free country" relevant? What does living in a free country have to do with courses that college students are required to take? Nothing. *Relevancy* is a condition needed for a sound argument.

Now look at this example:

I don't see why all first-year students have to take an introductory writing course. Many students have developed good writing skills in high school, and their entrance test scores are high.

Is this second example an argument? Why or why not? The first example doesn't give you a good reason to believe the argument; the second example does. A true argument must contain at least one reason for you to believe it.

Here's another warning. Not everything that sounds like an argument is one. Look at this example:

Everyone taking Math 100 failed the test last Friday. I took the test last Friday. Therefore, I will probably get an F in the course.

Is that a sound argument—or is something missing? Even though all three statements may be true, when you put them together they don't make a sound argument. What grade has this student earned on earlier math tests? How many tests are left in the course? What other assignments figure into students' grades? The information present may not be adequate to predict an F in the course. *Adequacy* is another condition needed for a sound argument. This alternative, on the other hand, is a sound argument:

Everyone taking Math 100 failed the test last Friday. I took the test last Friday. Therefore, I earned an F on the test.

When you're assessing the soundness of an argument, you must look for two things: *relevance* and *adequacy*.[9]

Not all arguments are sound. Have you ever heard this story? A scientist came up with a new study to find out what makes people drunk, using himself in the experiment. The study went like this. On Monday night, he drank three tall glasses of scotch and water, mixed in equal amounts. The next morning, he recorded his results: intoxication. On Tuesday night, he drank three tall glasses of whiskey and water. On Wednesday night, he drank three tall glasses of rum and water. On Thursday night, he drank three tall glasses of vodka and water. Each morning, his recorded results were the same. He had become drunk. His totally wrong conclusion? Water makes people drunk.

Not only is it important to be able to construct sound arguments, but it's also important to be able to recognize them. As a consumer in today's information society, you must know when to buy into an argument, and when not to.

Assessing Assumptions

When you're thinking critically, one of the most important kinds of questions you can ask is about the *assumptions* you or someone else is making, perhaps without even realizing it. Assumptions are things you take for granted, and they can limit your thinking. Consider this well-known puzzle, and afterward, examine how the assumptions you brought with you interfered with solving it.

One day Kerry celebrated her birthday. Two days later her older twin brother, Harry, celebrated his birthday. How could that be?

You may have solved this puzzle if you were willing to question the underlying assumptions that were holding you back. (The answer is upside down at the bottom of this page.)

People reveal their basic assumptions in what they say. If you listen carefully, you can uncover them. "Go on for a bachelor's degree after I finish here? No way! As soon as I get my associate's degree, I'm done!" This student's underlying assumption is that college itself isn't as important as what comes afterward (like making money). This student may sit through her classes without getting engaged in the subject matter, and she checks off requirements as quickly as she can. Too bad.

Considering Claims

Evaluating claims is one of the most basic aspects of reasoning. A claim is a statement that can be true or false, but not both. This is different from a fact, which cannot be disputed. What's the difference between a *fact* and a *claim*? Facts can't be disputed; claims can be true or false, but they must be one or the other, not both.

FACT: Ronald Reagan, Bill Clinton, and Barack Obama have been presidents of the United States during the last thirty years.

CLAIM: Bill Clinton was the most popular American president in the last thirty years.

The fact is obvious. The claim needs evidence to support it. As a critical thinker, it's important to use your reasoning skills to evaluate the evidence. Generally speaking, be wary of claims that

> are supported by unidentified sources ("Experts claim . . . ").

> are made by a person or company who stands to gain ("Brought to you by the makers of . . .").

> come from a a single person claiming his experience as the norm ("I tried it and it worked for me!").

> use a bandwagon appeal ("Everybody's doing it.").

> mislead with statistics ("over half" when it's really only 50.5 percent).

On the other hand, we must also keep an open mind and be flexible in our thinking. If you get good evidence to support a view that contradicts yours, be willing to change your ideas. One way to evaluate the validity of claims is to use the Critical Thinking Pyramid (Figure 5.2). Consider claims by asking these four key questions: "who?" "what?" "why?" and "how?" Figure 5.2 shows how the questions progress from level 1 to 3.

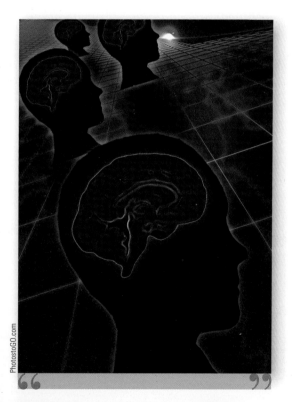

Photosto60.com

Great minds discuss ideas. Average minds discuss events. Small minds discuss people.

Eleanor Roosevelt, First Lady of the United States (1884–1962)

Kerry and Harry are not twins. Harry and his brother are twins, and they are older than Kerry.

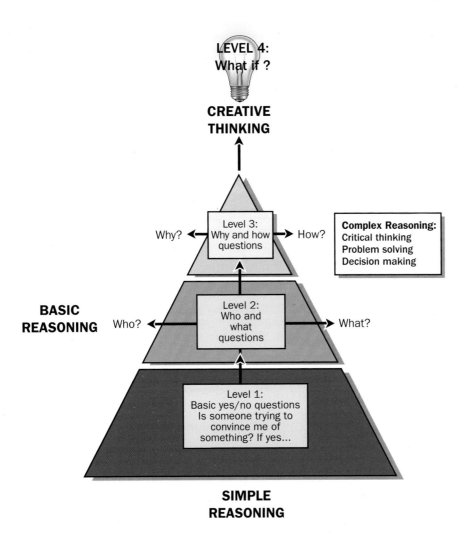

FIGURE 5.2

The Critical Thinking Pyramid

Source: Adapted from Hellyer, R., Robinson, C., & Sherwood, P. (1998). *Study skills for learning power*. New York: Houghton Mifflin, 18.

LEVEL 4:
What if ?

CREATIVE
THINKING

Level 3:
Why and how
questions

Why? ← → How?

Complex Reasoning:
Critical thinking
Problem solving
Decision making

**BASIC
REASONING**

Level 2:
Who and
what
questions

Who? ← → What?

Level 1:
Basic yes/no questions
Is someone trying to
convince me of
something? If yes…

**SIMPLE
REASONING**

Avoiding Faulty Reasoning

Although we can certainly improve our critical-thinking skills, it's impossible to be perfect critical thinkers 100 percent of the time. As thinkers, we make mistakes, and sometimes others try to trick us with bad arguments. It's important to cultivate both types of critical thinking skills: your *productive* skills, which you use as a speaker and writer when you "produce" ideas, and your *receptive* skills, which you use as a reader and listener when you "receive" others' ideas. As responsible communicators, we must understand what a sound argument is and know how to construct one ourselves. We must also understand what a defective argument is so that we avoid getting sucked in when we shouldn't.

Here is a top-ten list of logical fallacies, or false logic strategies, we can slip into—or others can use against us—if we're not careful. For each of the ten types, read through the example and then see if you can come up with one of your own.

1. **False cause and effect** (assuming one cause for something when other causes are possible, too)
   I moved back home from my own apartment last month. I've failed every exam I've taken since. Living at home is blowing my GPA!

> To treat your facts with imagination is one thing, but to imagine your facts is another.
>
> *John Burroughs, writer on ecology (1837–1921)*

A Four-Part Model of Critical Thinking   **113**

2. **Personal attack** (reacting to a challenge by attacking the challenger)

   How could anyone believe Mr. Courtney's views on ethics? We all know he's a very poor teacher.

3. **Unwarranted assumption** (taking too much for granted without evidence)

   You say college educations give women equal opportunities. I say they don't. Reply: It's true. I read it on a website.

4. **Emotional appeal** (appealing to someone's feelings in order to gain acceptance of an argument)

   If you care about all the people hurt in this tragic accident, you'll dig deep into your pockets and send in a donation now.

5. **False authority** (attributing your argument to someone else in a supposed position of power to get you off the hook)

   I'd really like to be able to change your grade, but my Department Chair doesn't like me to do that.

6. **Hasty conclusion** (jumping to a conclusion when other conclusions are possible)

   I'm sure that guy next to me in class stole my textbook when I wasn't looking. He's too cheap to buy his own.

7. **Straw man** (attempting to "prove" an argument by overstating, exaggerating, or oversimplifying the arguments of the opposing side)

   We should let students have more say in which courses they take. Reply: You actually want students to take any courses they want to? Oh, right, why don't we all just have a free-for-all instead?

8. **Shifting the burden of proof** (shifting the responsibility of proving an assertion to someone else because you have no evidence for what you assert)

   The policy forbidding any alcohol at campus events is working. Reply: No, it's not. Reply back: Oh yeah? Prove it.

9. **Oversimplification/overgeneralization** (reducing a complex issue to something very simple or stereotyping)

   College teachers have it made. They teach a couple classes a week for a few hours, and then they have free time the rest of the week. That's the kind of job I want!

10. **Either/or thinking** (taking only an extreme position on an issue when other positions are possible)

    Either we ban dating between students or we will be facing sexual harassment lawsuits.

    "

    Everyone is entitled to their own opinion, but not their own facts.

    Senator Daniel Patrick Moynihan (1927–2003)

Aspen Commons Apartment Complex Case Study

Great Bluffs Herald

Saturday, September 24, 2011

Start of School + Parties = Recipe for Death

Great Bluffs, Colorado It's that time of year again. The fall semester began last month at Great Bluffs Technical College, and again this year, a student died of alcohol poisoning within the first three weeks of classes. Dante Lewis, a resident of an apartment complex near the school, Aspen Commons, was found dead yesterday morning. The body of the collapsed GBTC student was found in a third-floor apartment. An anonymous call to 9-1-1 came in at 6:15 a.m.: "We've got a guy here. We can't wake him, and we know he drank way too much last night." Lewis was pronounced dead on arrival at Great Bluffs General Hospital. The incident represented the second death from alcohol poisoning at Aspen Commons in as many years. Roland Bishop, GBTC's new president, is said to deeply mourn the loss of another new student. "No student should die during his first few weeks of college—what should be one of the most exciting times of his life. It's insane and very, very sad."

The Aspen Commons Apartment Complex has been warned that student parties among underage residents, where alcohol is served, should be discouraged.

President Bishop will convene a cross-college panel of faculty, staff, and students to investigate the incident and decide if any action should be taken by GBTC. Professor Juan Cordova, Sociology Department Chairperson, will head the new committee. A report with specific recommendations to President Bishop is expected by the end of the term. Alcohol is to blame for the deaths of 1,875 college students per year, according to figures from the National Institute on Alcohol Abuse and Alcoholism. About 599,000 students between the ages of 18 and 24 are injured annually while under the influence of alcohol, more than 696,000 are assaulted by another student who has been drinking, and more than 97,000 students are victims of alcohol-related sexual assault or date rape.

The average age of students at Great Bluffs Technical College has dropped from 32 to 26 in recent years. Although some technical college students live at home, many others live on their own in the community. Because it is within walking distance to GBTC, Aspen Commons is a popular choice. President Bishop's office indicates that it may enter into negotiations with the Colorado Housing Authority and with Clifford Industries, owners of Aspen Commons, about banning alcohol in the complex and requiring tenants to sign a no-alcohol agreement.

After this article appeared in the Great Bluffs Herald, *many readers sent letters to the editor on September 25 and 26. Examine the following excerpts.*

Trevor Ryan, GBTC Student: "My first few weeks at GBTC have been awesome, and living at Aspen Commons has been totally cool—one of the highlights of my life so far. I'd do it all over again tomorrow. But I didn't want to live at Aspen Commons just for the parties everyone talks about. It's a great place to live. All the students who live there say so."

Carlos Cordova, GBTC Student: "This whole incident has been very hard on me. Dante was my roommate. We've known each other since we were kids, and we moved into an apartment right after we graduated from high school last spring. I still can't believe this happened to him. Yeah, I was drinking at the party where he got totally wasted, too. But I lost track of him when I went to bed around midnight. If I had just stayed around, I'll bet I could have prevented what happened."

Ross Riley, Building Manager, Aspen Commons: "As building manager, I've seen my fair share of parties over the years. Sometimes things get out of control. I get a call in the middle of the night and end up calling the cops. Other residents complain about the noise. But it's not the apartment complex's problem. We just put a roof over people's heads. They make their own decisions about how to live."

(continued)

Dr. Ruby Pinnell, ER Physician, Great Bluffs General Hospital: "As a doctor, I see all the damage today's young people are doing to themselves. The national study I spearheaded last year found that 31 percent of college students meet the clinical criteria for alcohol abuse, and 6 percent could be diagnosed as being alcohol-dependent. They don't realize that binge drinking could be risking serious damage to their brains now and actually cause increased memory loss later in adulthood. Many college males consume as many as 24 drinks in a row. These are very sad statistics."

Rufus Unser, Aspen Commons resident: "I've lived at Aspen Commons for 12 years now, and I'm just about to move into an assisted living facility because I'm 78 and my health is failing. I'm sick of rowdy parties, loud music late at night, and residents who run up and down the halls. I don't mind all the younger people who live in this complex, but I'd really like to get some sleep once in a while."

Sergeant Rick Fuller, Great Bluffs Police Department: "I've worked in the Great Bluffs Police Department for 15 years now, and I've seen a dramatic rise in the number of alcohol-related violence, crimes, and accidents. GBTC needs to do something. Their students are part of the problem, and they need to assume some responsibility."

Now that you've read the story from the Great Bluffs Herald *and the excerpts from letters to the editor, answer the following questions:*

1. What are the facts relating to the death of GBTC student Dante Lewis? How do you know they are facts and not claims?

2. Do you see logical fallacies in any of the letters to the editor of the *Great Bluffs Herald*? If so, which can you identify? What assumptions do the letter writers hold—right or wrong?

VARK Activity

Complete the activity recommended for your preferred VARK learning style and bring it to class (or follow your instructor's instructions).

 Visual: Create a collage that depicts each letter writer's point of view. Be certain to find a way to highlight the faulty reasoning.

 Aural: As a group, talk through the case. Focus on questions like these: Does the incident sound realistic? If you ran GBTC, how would you handle the situation?

 Read/Write: Write a press release sent from GBTC to local media outlets. How would you present this difficult situation to readers in the general public?

 Kinesthetic: Assume you are a member of President Bishop's new task force on alcohol policy. Role play members of the task force at their first meeting.

II. Problem Solving: The Basic How-To's

When you have to solve a problem, your critical thinking skills should move front and center. Perhaps you need to find a way to earn more money. You run short each month, and the last few days before payday are nerve-racking. What should you do? Use a shotgun approach and try many different strategies at once or come up with more precise way to get the best results? See if the following steps make sense to you and seem like something you might actually do.

" Education is nothing more, nor less, than learning to think! "

Peter Facione, professor, administrator, author, consultant, and critical thinking expert

iStockphoto.com/Geoffrey Hammond

STEP 1: Define the problem. What is the exact nature of the problem you face? Defining the exact nature of the problem is something you must do if you hope to solve it. For example:

> Is it that you don't meter your spending and run out of money long before the next paycheck?

> Is it that you don't have a budget and you spend money randomly?

STEP 2: Brainstorm possible options. List all of the possible solutions you can come up with. For example:

> Pack food from home instead of hitting the fast-food joints so often.

> Stop ordering in pizza four nights a week when you get the munchies at midnight.

> Ask your boss for a raise. You've been doing a good job.

> Look for a job that pays more. Tips at the Pancake House where you work don't really amount to much.

> Capitalize on your particular skills to earn extra money. If you're a whiz at math, you could sign on as a math tutor on campus.

STEP 3: Set criteria to evaluate each option. For example:

> *Distance* is important. Your car isn't very reliable, so it would be good to find a job you can walk or ride your bike to.

> *Good pay* is important. In the past, you've always had low-paying jobs. You need whatever solution you arrive at to be worth your while.

> *Time* is important. You're taking a challenging load of classes, and you need to keep up your grades to keep your scholarship.

STEP 4: Evaluate each option you've proposed. For example:

> Pack food from home. (This is a good idea because you've already paid for that food, regardless of which solution you choose.)

> Stop ordering pizza when the munchies hit at midnight. (This is also a good option because unplanned expenses like this can mount up fast.)

> Ask your family to borrow money. (You'd really like to avoid this option. You don't want to seem like you're trying to take advantage of them.)

> Get a job that pays more. (Unfortunately, your campus is half an hour from the center of town where all the posh restaurants are.)

> Capitalize on your particular skills to earn extra money. (Tutors are paid more than minimum wage, and getting a job on campus would be convenient.)

STEP 5: Choose the best solution. In this case, it looks like getting a job on campus could fit the bill!

STEP 6: Plan how to achieve the best solution. When you talk with your advisor about applying for a job as a math tutor, you discover that you need a letter of recommendation from a math instructor. You e-mail your math instructor and set up a meeting for later in the week. When the letter is ready, you make an appointment to schedule an interview, and so forth.

STEP 7: Implement the solution and evaluate the results. A month or two after you take on the tutoring job, you evaluate if this solution is really the best one. You may need to request more hours or different days. Or you may find that this job leads to a better one on campus. At any rate, you've used your critical thinking skills to solve a problem, systematically, logically, and effectively.

EXERCISE 5.3

Problem Solving for Yourself

Try out the seven-step problem-solving model for yourself. Think of a problem you're facing right now, and fill in your ideas for steps 1 through 7. When you're done, ask yourself whether filling in these steps helped you understand the problem and this problem-solving process better.

STEP 1: Define the problem.

_____

STEP 2: Brainstorm possible options.

_____

STEP 3: Set criteria to evaluate each option.

_____

STEP 4: Evaluate each option you've proposed.

_____

STEP 5: Choose the best solution.

_____

STEP 6: Plan how to achieve the best solution.

_____

STEP 7: Implement the solution and evaluate the results.

_____

> **Most people spend more time and energy going around problems than in trying to solve them.**
>
> HENRY FORD

Prove you're a problem solver. While taking your college classes, you learn problem-solving skills. Some of those problems are personal (who can I get to watch my kids at the last minute?), and some are academic (why was Edgar Allan Poe so "dark"?). On the job, everyone values the person who comes up with a workable solution when others are stumped. And your boss will value you more if you come up with solutions yourself or collaborate with your colleagues. Instead of, "What should we do about X?" say, "We're facing Problem X. Should we do A, B, or C?" You've proven that you've already thought about the problem and generated three possible solutions. That shows that you can think on your own and work with others to solve problems for the good of your organization.

III. Decision Making: What's Your Style?

The kinds of arguments we're discussing in this chapter lead to decisions, and it's important to make good ones! After you've evaluated an argument, you must often do something about it. Before you know it, you'll be deciding on a major if you haven't already, a career field, a place to live, a romantic partner—you name it.

When you have an important decision to make, your critical thinking skills should kick into action. The more important the decision, the more thoughtful the process of deciding should be. But people make decisions in different ways.

Alan J. Rowe and Richard O. Mason wrote a book called *Managing with Style* about four basic decision-making styles used by managers. Although you may not be a manager now, think about what your style may be when you do have a position of responsibility. Here are the four styles they describe. See which one sounds as if it might describe you.

Hemera Technologies/
PhotoObjects.net/Jupiter Images

> **Directive.** This decision-making style emphasizes the here and now. Directives prefer structure and using practical data to make decisions. They look for speed, efficiency, and results, and focus on short-term fixes. Directive decision makers base their decisions on experience, facts, procedures, and rules, and they have energy and drive to get things done. On the down side, because they work quickly, they are sometimes satisfied with simple solutions when something else might work better.

Ian Scott, 2009/Shutterstock.com

> **Analytical.** This decision-making style emphasizes a logical approach. Analyticals search carefully for the best decision, and they sometimes get hung up with overanalyzing things and take too long to finally make a decision. They are sometimes considered to be impersonal because they may be more interested in the

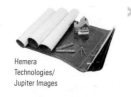

Hemera
Technologies/
Jupiter Images

problem than in the people who have it. But they are good at working with data and doing careful analysis.

> **Conceptual.** This decision-making style emphasizes the big picture. Conceptuals are adaptable, insightful, and flexible, and they look for interesting, new solutions. They are sometimes too idealistic, but they take risks and are very creative.

Ron Chapple/Index Open/
PhotostoGO

> **Behavioral.** This decision-making style emphasizes people. Behaviorals enjoy people and the social aspects of work. They use their feelings to assess situations, communicate well, and are supportive of others. On the other hand, they are sometimes seen as wishy-washy or are criticized because they can't make hard decisions or can't say no.

Whether you're in college to prepare for a career field or retool for a new one, eventually, you will have to make important decisions on a daily basis. It's useful to begin thinking about your decision-making style now.

ONLINE **TechKnow**

Improve Your Grade
Online Flashcards
Glossary

Remember, whether during an online group project or a week-by-week forum that everyone contributes to, your work represents you and your critical thought process. In both college and professional work, clear and courteous communication benefits both you and your colleagues and classmates. As you put together your online course contributions, always put your best "e-foot" forward.

• **Use complete words and spell them correctly.** Avoid the cute shortcuts devised for text messaging.

• **Be courteous, polite, and respectful of your classmates and your instructor.**

• **Concentrate on ideas, not on personalities.**

• **Phrase things such that others in your online class know you're praising their efforts while adding to and extending them.** Avoid sounding snide ("Oh sure, Randy and his kind may think so…"), abrupt ("That's just plain wrong!"), or demeaning ("That was a stupid thing to say, Sarah…").

• **Work to establish a feeling of teamwork while still being truthful and direct.** "I've been pleased to see how many of us are pitching in on this assignment…" establishes teamwork. "In our online discussions, I've noticed how often this one central fact comes up…" is direct.

IV. Thinking about Your Thinking

One of the most important aspects of critical thinking is that it evaluates itself. As you're solving problems, for example, you're thinking about how you're thinking. You're assessing your progress as you go, analyzing the strengths and weaknesses in your thinking, and perhaps even coming up with better ways to do it. We call that metacognition.

metacognition thinking about your thinking and learning about your learning

Novice or new learners don't stop to evaluate their thinking and make revisions. Expert or experienced learners do. Actually, whenever you're faced with learning something new, metacognition involves three elements. Ultimately, these elements should become the foundation of all your learning experiences so that you improve your metacognitive skills as you go.

> **Before: Develop a plan of action.** Ask yourself what you already know that can help you learn something new. What direction do you want to go in your thinking? What should be your first task? How much time should you give yourself? Talk through your plan with someone else.

> **During: Monitor your plan.** While you're working, ask yourself how you're doing. Are you staying on track? Are you moving in the right direction? Should you slow down or speed up? What should you do if you don't understand what you're doing? Keep track of what works for you and what doesn't. Assume responsibility for your own thinking and learning.

> **After: Evaluate the plan.** How well did you do? Did you do better than expected or not as well as you expected? What could you have done differently? Can you apply what you just did here to future tasks? Give yourself some feedback.[10]

And how is education supposed to make me feel smarter?

Homer Simpson, television cartoon character, The Simpsons

Becoming a Better Critical Thinker

Sharpening your critical thinking skills is vital because these skills underlie all the others in your academic toolkit. If you think well, you will be a better writer, a better presenter, a better listener, and a better reader. You will be more likely to engage more fully in your academic tasks because you will question, dig, analyze, and monitor yourself as you learn. Here are some suggestions for improving your skills. As you read them, think about yourself and how you learn.

1. **Admit when you don't know.** If you don't know enough to think critically about something, admit it, and then find out more. With the volume of information available in today's world, we can't possibly know everything about anything. But the good news is that information is everywhere. All you need to do is read, listen, point, and click to be well informed on many issues.

2. **Realize you have buttons that can be pushed.** We all have issues we're emotional about. That's normal. It's natural to feel strongly about some things, but it's also important to understand the reasons why so that you can tell your views to someone else. And of course, realize that you're not the only one with buttons. Your teacher, best friend, significant other, boss, and everyone else has them, too.

3. **Learn more about the opposition.** Many times, it's more comfortable to avoid what we don't agree with

If you have an apple and I have an apple and we exchange these apples, then you and I will still each have one apple. But if you have an idea and I have an idea and we exchange these ideas, then each of us will have two ideas.

George Bernard Shaw, Irish literary critic, playwright, and essayist, 1925 Nobel Prize for Literature (1856–1950)

and reinforce what we already believe. But part of being a well-educated person means learning about the history, backgrounds, values, and techniques of people you disagree with so that you can anticipate and deal with their arguments more effectively.

4. **Trust and verify.** During the Cold War, President Ronald Reagan liked to quote an old Russian saying to his Soviet counterpart, Mikhail Gorbachev: "Doveryay, no proveryay," or "Trust, but verify." Being a good critical thinker means achieving a balance between blind faith and healthy questioning.

5. **Remember that critical thinking is the foundation of all academic achievement.** There's nothing more important than learning to think critically. In college and in life, the skills discussed in this chapter will make you a better college student, a better citizen, a better employee, a smarter consumer, a better relational partner, and a better lifelong learner.

Creativity: "Thinking Outside the ... Book"

Do you believe this statement? *Everyone has creative potential.* It's true. Most of us deny it, however. "Me, creative? Nah!" We're often unaware of the untapped ability we have to think creatively. Try this experiment. Look at the following list of words, and divide the list into two (and only two) different categories, using any rules you create. Take a few moments and see what you come up with.

dog, salad, book, grasshopper, kettle, paper, garbage, candle

Whenever this experiment is tried, people always come up with very creative categories. They may divide the words into things that you buy at a store (dog, salad, kettle, paper, candle), things that move on their own (dog, grasshopper), things that have a distinct smell (dog, candle, garbage), words that have two consonants, and so forth. People never say it can't be done; they always *invent* categories. Revealing, isn't it? Our minds are hungry for the stimulation of a creative challenge.

The fact is that intelligence has more to do with coming up with the right answer, and creative thinking has more to do with coming up with more than one right answer. Often we get so focused on the *right* answer that we rush to find it instead of exploring all the possibilities. Creative thinking is thinking outside the box, or in terms of getting an education, perhaps we should call it thinking outside the book. Going beyond the obvious and exploring possibilities are important parts of becoming an educated person. Employers report that many college graduates today have spe-

> A mind that is stretched to a new idea never returns to its original dimensions.

Oliver Wendell Holmes, American poet (1809–1894)

cific skills, but that what they rarely see "is the ability to use the right-hand side of the brain—creativity, working in a team."[11]

In Figure 5.2, we looked at the Critical Thinking Pyramid. Creative thinking is at the top of the pyramid. It goes beyond critical thinking. It is predictive and multidimensional. It asks "What if …?" questions. Here are some interesting ones: "What if everyone was allowed to tell one lie per day?" "What if no one could perceive colors?" "What if colleges didn't exist?" "If you looked up a word like *squallizmotex* in the dictionary, what might it mean?"[12]

According to creativity expert Alan Rowe, our creative intelligence demonstrates itself in four major styles. Each of us has aspects of all four styles of creativity.

> **Intuitive.** This creative style is best described as *resourceful*. If you are an Intuitive, you achieve goals, use common sense, and work to solve problems. You focus on results and rely on past experience to guide your actions. Managers, actors, and politicians are commonly Intuitives.

> **Innovative.** This creative style is best described as *curious*. Innovatives concentrate on problem solving, are organized, and rely on data. They use original approaches, are willing to experiment, and focus on step-by-step inquiry. Scientists, engineers, and inventors typically demonstrate the Innovative creative style.

> **Imaginative.** This creative style is best described as *insightful*. Imaginatives are willing to take risks, have leaps of imagination, and are independent thinkers. They are able to visualize opportunities, are artistic, enjoy writing, and think outside the box. Artists, musicians, writers, and charismatic leaders are often Imaginatives.

> **Inspirational.** This creative style is best described as *visionary*. Inspirationals respond to societal needs, willingly give of themselves, and have the courage of their convictions. They focus on social change and the giving of themselves toward achieving it. They are often educators, motivational leaders, and writers.[13]

Which do you think is your predominant style? Think about how you can make the best use of your natural style. How will your creativity affect the major or career you choose? Most people have more than one creative style. Remember that motivation, not just intelligence, is the key to creativity. You must be willing to tap your creative potential and challenge yourself to show it.[14] According to *New York Times* best-seller, *A Whole New Mind*, "The future belongs to a very different kind of person with a very different kind of mind—creators and empathizers, pattern recognizers, and meaning makers. These people—artists, inventors, designers, storytellers, caregivers, consolers, big picture thinkers—will now reap society's richest rewards and share its greatest joys."[15]

Ten Ways to Become a More Creative Thinker

Becoming a more creative thinker may mean you need to accept your creativity and cultivate it. Consider these suggestions on how to think more creatively.

FIGURE 5.3

The Pillow Method

Position 1—I'm right and you're wrong.

Position 2—You're right and I'm wrong.

Position 3—We're both right.

Position 4—We're both wrong.

> A hunch is creativity trying to tell you something.

Frank Capra, Italian American film director (1897–1991)

1. **Find new eyes.** Find a new perspective on old issues. Here's an interesting example. Years ago, a group of Japanese schoolchildren came up with a new way to solve conflicts and build empathy for others' positions, called the Pillow Method. Figure 5.3 is an adaptation of it, based on the fact that a pillow has four sides and a middle, just like most problems. The middle or *mu* is the Zen expression for "it doesn't really matter." There is truth in all four positions. Try it: take a conflict you're having difficulty with at the moment, and write down all four sides and a middle.[16]

2. **Accept your creativity.** Many mindsets block creative thinking: "It can't be done!" "I'm just not the creative type." "I might look stupid!" Many people don't see themselves as creative. This perception can become a major stumbling block. If creativity isn't part of your self-image, you may need to change your image. Everyone has creative potential. You may have to learn how to tap into yours.

3. **Make your thoughts visible.** For many of us, things become clear when we can see them, either in our mind's eye or displayed for us. Even Einstein, a scientist and mathematician, had a very visual mind. Sometimes if we write something down or sketch something out, we generate a new approach without really trying.

4. **Generate lots of ideas.** Thomas Edison held 1,093 patents, still the record. He gave himself idea goals. The rule he set for himself was that he had to come up with a major invention every six months and a minor invention every ten days.

5. **Don't overcomplexify.** In hindsight, many of the most creative discoveries are embarrassingly simple. Biologist Thomas Huxley said, after reading Darwin's explanation of evolution: "How extremely stupid not to have thought of that!" But sometimes the most simple solution is the best one.[17]

6. **Capitalize on your mistakes.** Remember that Thomas Edison tried anything he could think of for a filament for the incandescent lamp, including a whisker from his best friend's beard. All in all, he tried about 1,800 things before finding the right one. Afterward he said, "I've gained a lot of knowledge—I now know a thousand things that won't work."[18]

7. **Let it flow.** Mihaly Csikszentmihalyi, the author of *Flow: The Psychology of Optimal Experience* and many other books on creativity, discovered something interesting. For his doctoral thesis, he studied artists by taking pictures of them painting every three minutes. He was struck by how engaged they were in their work, so engaged that they seemed to forget everything around them. He began studying other "experts": rock

William Whitehurst/CORBIS

climbers, chess players, dancers, musicians, surgeons. Regardless of the activity, these people forgot the time, themselves, and their problems. What did the activities have in common? Clear, high goals and immediate feedback. Athletes call it being in the zone. The zone is described as the ultimate human experience, where mind and body are united in purpose. Csikszentmihalyi's suggestions for achieving flow are these: Pick an enjoyable activity that is at or slightly above your ability level, screen out distractions, focus all your senses and emotions, and look for regular feedback on how you're doing.[19]

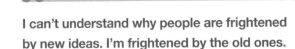

> I can't understand why people are frightened by new ideas. I'm frightened by the old ones.
>
> *John Cage, American Composer*
> *(1912–1992)*

8. **Bounce ideas off others.** One good way to become more creative is to use your family or friends as sounding boards. Sometimes just saying something out loud helps you understand more about it. Each person who provides a critique will give you a new perspective, possibly worth considering.

9. **Stop searching for the "right" answer.** This advice doesn't pertain to your upcoming math exam. But it does to apply to situations in which there are many ways to solve a problem. There may be more than one acceptable solution. A fear of making mistakes can hold you back.

10. **Detach your self-concept.** For most of us, creativity is often linked to self-concept. An idea is your brainchild, and you want it to win people over. You've invested part of yourself in giving birth to it. But there's nothing like self-criticism to shut down your creative juices. Your idea may not succeed on its own, but it may feed into someone else's idea and improve it. Or an idea you have about this problem may inform the next problem that challenges you. In the end, in addition to finding a workable solution, what's important is engaging in the creative process with others.

CONTROL: *YOUR TOUGHEST CLASS*

Look over the "10 Ways to Become a More Creative Thinker" in this chapter and choose one of these items to write about. Which piece of advice will be most useful to you? Is there a way you can use your natural creativity to improve your chances in your toughest class? For example, item 6 might be a good idea to use in your math class. When you get an exam back, look it over, analyze your mistakes, and then come up with creative new ideas to improve your score next time—now that you know what didn't work last time. Item 10 might be something to work on if you always fear the essays you write for your composition class won't measure up.

1. Find new eyes.
2. Accept your creativity.
3. Make your thoughts visible.
4. Generate lots of ideas.
5. Don't overcomplexify.
6. Capitalize on your mistakes.
7. Let it flow.
8. Bounce ideas off others.
9. Stop searching for the right answer.
10. Detach your self-concept.

DARIO JONES

© Larry Harwood Photography. Property of Cengage Learning.

© Mateusz Papiernik, 2010. Used under copyright from Shutterstock.com.

Evgeny Karandaev, 2010. Used under copyright from Shutterstock.com; -WOODOO-, 2010. Used under copyright from Shutterstock.com.

Ever since grade school, Dario Jones had been called a geek. It was a label he hated, but, honestly, most people probably thought of him that way. As a kid, Dario lived for computer games. He played them nearly every waking hour. In the morning, he'd shower in record time, throw on whatever clean clothes he could find, and use any spare minutes for computer games. When he got home, he'd log right back on again. His Dad tried threatening him: "You'll lose your eyesight and flunk out of school." Once he faked a sore throat and played World of Warcraft at home for a week, while his parents were at work. As he got older, his Dad warned: "You'll never get a date." But Dario wasn't worried. Second Life relationships were enough. Real-life relationships were too much trouble. Even now that he had been on his own for several years, his cyber life was much more exciting than his real life. Dario spent more time—even sacrificing precious hours of sleep—surfing the Internet, envisioning how he could improve websites, and grooming his MySpace page than he spent talking to any living being.

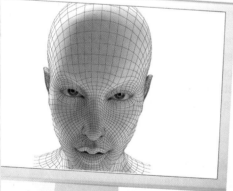

Mike Margol/PhotoEdit

Then one day the obvious truth dawned on him. Why was he wasting his time working in his Dad's auto body shop? The world of cars didn't really interest him. The world of cyberspace did. But somehow after high school, he hadn't thought about it much and went to work for his Dad because it was easy.

Eventually, Dario made a decision. Even though it had been a while since he had been in school, he needed to change his life. Being a web designer

Luciana Bueno, 2009. Used under license from Shutterstock.com.

was the right career for him. He drove to the college campus across town and parked in the parking lot. He sat in his car for a while, and then bit the bullet, walked through a big door, and talked with someone. As it turned out, that was the last official day to enroll for the semester. So with the help of a friendly advisor, who took him to the Financial Aid office and helped him fill out the application, Dario was in school again. He'd have to increase his hours at his Dad's auto body shop to afford tuition, but he thought it would be worth it.

But Dario quickly discovered that messing around with computers and studying computers were two very different things. His toughest class, required for his certificate program in web design, was a class called Fundamentals of Internet Business. Right off the bat, he discovered the course required a research paper. The assigned topic was Globalization and Internet Commerce. Even though he had always considered himself to be a technology expert, frankly, he didn't know where to start. *Step one*, Dario thought to himself, *is to Google*. He always Googled everything: the directions to a new Mexican restaurant—his favorite food—or some little-known fact that he wondered about, like how many Chihuahuas were sold in the United States last year. (He had just bought one.) But when he Googled "Internet Commerce," he got 22 million hits. *Better regroup*, he advised himself.

But how? Should he go to the library on campus, or try to do his research online in the comfort of his own apartment? Physically going to the library seemed unnecessary when so much information was available online. Then he had a flash of inspiration: Wikipedia. He found a page on "Electronic Commerce." At least that was a start—that is, until he looked at his instructor's handout on the assignment. Students were discouraged from using Wikipedia as a primary research source. The handout said "Information literacy is required." He got another idea: He'd close Wikipedia and go back to Googling. This time he'd try "Electronic Commerce." *Ah, only 7 million hits this time*. He was on a roll. He plugged in "E-Commerce," "E-Business," and "Globalization." He tried "Global Issues," but before he knew it, he found himself knee-deep in articles about "Global Warming." He was so far afield now that he couldn't find his way back to his topic. Should he shut everything down and start over or just give up?

Dario's paper was due the following day. At the last minute, he panicked. He found a few useful things online, and in the interest of time, he cut and pasted from the Internet until he'd filled five pages. At least he had something to turn in. He wondered if this was the way to do research and whether he'd broken any rules. *Well, at least there will always be fender-benders*, he thought pessimistically. But to be honest, a career smoothing out dents in other people's cars wasn't at all what he wanted to do with his life.

Christopher John Coudriet, 2009. Used under license from Shutterstock.com

© Cengage Learning

Fundamentals of Internet Business
CS 112

Research Paper Guidelines

TOPIC: Globalization and Internet Commerce

For this assignment you will write a 10 page research paper investig relationship between globalization and Internet commerce. You sho focus on how globalization has affected Internet commerce, but how relationship may be a two-way street. In other words, look at how commerce has changed the pace of globalization in the 21st century.

POTENTIAL AREAS OF RESEARCH FOCUS:

- What is Globalization?
- Free Trade
- ...national Corporations

© Cengage Learning

Fundamentals of Internet Business
CS 112

Instructor: Dr. Greg Otis
Office: Hansford Hall 230
Office Hours: T, W 2:00–4:00 PM

Description:
The Internet has fundamentally changed the ...

Wikipedia
http://en.wikipedia.org/wiki/Electronic_commerce
File Edit View Favorites Tools Help
Electronic commerce - Wikipedia, the free encyclopedia
Help us provide free content to the world by donating today!
article | discussion | edit this page | history

Electronic commerce
From Wikipedia, the free encyclopedia

Electronic Commerce, commonly known as (electronic marketing) e-commerce or eC ...sts of the buying and selling of products or services over electronic systems such ...conducted electronically has grown extra...

1. Do you have anything in common with Dario? Do you find doing research for papers like his to be easy or challenging?

2. The instructor's assignment required "information literacy." What is information literacy? Dario was tech-savvy, but did he have the right skills? Why or why not?

3. Did Dario plagiarize his paper—or did he simply find the sources he needed and use them? Give the reasons behind your answer.

4. In your view, is Dario addicted to technology? Can being too dependent on technology be a problem? Why?

Technology Skills: Wireless, Windowed, Webbed, and Wikied

Ah, technology . . . Does it make our lives simpler or more complicated? Like Dario, are you pulled into games like World of Warcraft? Do you live to text? Do you run, not walk, to any nearby computer to check your Facebook account? Or, on the other hand, do you hate the thought of facing your e-mail after you haven't had access for awhile? Did you find yourself answering "yes" to any of these questions—or maybe answering "yes" to all of them?

Many of us have a love-hate relationship with technology: We love the convenience but hate the dependence. But in college, your techno-skills will be another key to your success. You'll need to know things like how to produce an essay in Microsoft Word, how to give a PowerPoint presentation, and how to use course management systems like Blackboard. "Whoa! Wait a minute," you say. "I'm no expert at all of that!" You don't have to be an expert, but you do need to know the basics and be willing to learn more. Dario considered himself to be a technology expert, but his expertise was more about *entertainment* than *education*. In college, you'll be using technology to enhance your education.

ONLINE **TechKnow**

Improve Your Grade
Online Flashcards
Glossary

"It's on the Web, so it must be true!" Part of information literacy skills is evaluating the accuracy and usefulness of information you come across. As you read materials you find during online research, be careful to check the accuracy and authority of your sources.

- **Examine each article and each claim carefully to see where it comes from originally.** What original research came up with that finding? How reputable is the original source—can you find information about that source from other places?

- **Effective news editors follow this rule:** before a claim can be believed, it must be verified by two independent sources. Sometimes what looks like two sources is really only one source repeated. You may need to search for authenticity online before you use information that's readily available.

- **What about Wikipedia?** Many professors consider it a useful starting point in your research, but won't accept it as a critical reference. Best not to cite it in backing up your research. The best way to use Wikipedia is to use the bibliography and links at the bottom of the page, and do further research from there.

- **When you've been at your online research for a long time**—say over a half-hour—then it pays to take a break and think about what you've been finding. You'll find that short breaks strengthen your ability to critically assess what you've found.

- **Rule of thumb?** Don't use anything as a reference unless it has an author listed.

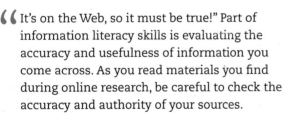

Your college may have invited you to enroll with a MySpace or Facebook invitation. Your school will provide you with an e-mail account and send you official college documents, like your tuition bill and weather alerts over e-mail. You will take entire courses or parts of courses online so that you can learn on your own time at your own pace. Many of your instructors will use course management systems, YouTube clips, streaming video, and websites in the classroom to increase your learning. (And the good news is that 70.4 percent of college students say it helps.[1]) So the time to start building your skills is now! Dario began researching his paper by Googling. Just how useful is the Internet to college students? The answer is: Just like anything else, the Internet has pros and cons.

The Internet: The Good, the Bad, and the Ugly

The Good Students who enter college right after high school are the leading consumers of digital technology in the United States.[2] In one study, 79 percent of college students reported that the Internet has had a positive impact on their college academic experience.[3] For many of us, the Internet is how we get our news, our research, our entertainment, and our communication. When it comes to all the potential benefits of the Internet, think about advantages like these:

> **Currency.** While some of the information posted on the Internet isn't up to date, much of it is current. This is especially important during a crisis or a national emergency, for example, when it's important to get news fast. Reports, articles, and studies that might take months to publish in books or articles are available on the web as soon as they're written.

currency timely

> **Availability.** The Internet never sleeps. If you can't sleep at 2:00 a.m., the Internet can keep you company. It can be a good friend to have. Unlike your real instructor who teaches other classes besides yours and attends marathon meetings, Professor Google is always in. For the most part, you can check your e-mail or log onto the Internet from anywhere, any time.

> **Scope.** You can find out virtually anything you want to know on the Internet from the recipe for the world's best chocolate chip cookie to medical advice on everything from Athlete's Foot to Zits. (Of course, real human beings are usually a better option for serious questions.)

scope range, capacity

> **Interactivity.** Unlike other media, the Internet lets you talk back. You can write a letter to the editor of a newspaper and wait for a reply, or you can push buttons on your phone in response to an endless list of menu questions ("If you want directions in English, press 1 . . .") and finally get to a real-live human being. But the Internet lets you communicate instantly and constantly. You can instant message to your heart's content, if you want to, add to your Facebook page daily, or edit a Wikipedia entry whenever you like.

> **Affordability.** As of December 2009, there were 1,802,330,457 Internet users worldwide; 234 million Americans are on the Net today.[4] For most of us, when it comes to the Internet, the price is right. After you buy a computer, and pay a monthly access fee, you get a great deal for your money.

For a list of all the ways technology has failed to improve the quality of life, please press three.

Alice Kahn, technology author

The Bad Too much of a good thing—anything—can be bad. When anything becomes that central to our lives, it carries risks. Here are some Internet dangers worth thinking about:

> **Inaccuracy.** Often we take information presented to us at face value, without questioning it. But on many Internet sites, the responsibility for checking the accuracy of the information presented there is yours. Bob's Statistics Home Page and the U.S. Census Bureau's website are not equally valid. Not everything published online is true or right.

> **Laziness.** It's easy to allow the convenience of the Internet to make us lazy. Why go through the hassle of cooking dinner when you can just stop for a burger on the way home? The same thing applies to the Internet. Why not just do what Dario did and find information somebody else has already posted on the Internet and use it? What's wrong with that? For one thing, if you don't give the rightful author credit, that's plagiarism, which can give you a zero on an assignment, or even cause you to fail a course. But another thing worth considering is that the *how* of learning is as important as the *what*. If all you ever did was cut, paste, and download, you wouldn't learn how to do research yourself. College helps you learn skills you will need later—critical thinking, research, and writing skills, for example—in your career. You may never have to give your boss a five-page paper on the humor of Mark Twain—as you might your literature instructor—but you may need to write a five-page report on your customers' buying trends over the last six months.

> **Overdependence.** A related problem with anything that's easy and convenient is that we can start depending on it too much. National studies report that many of us lack basic knowledge. We can't name the Chief Justice of the Supreme Court or the President of Pakistan. Without even realizing it, we may think: why bother learning a bunch of facts when you can just check quickly online? Are we so dependent on the Internet that we're relying on it for information we should learn or know?[5]

The Ugly The Internet can be used in foul ways. Spam, viruses, spyware, and phishing cost American consumers billions of dollars in damage last year, affecting 40 percent of U.S. households.[6] Take a look at one student's social networking page in Figure 6.1 and see if you can guess where things are headed.

Like the hypothetical Victoria Tymmyns (or her online name, VicTym) featured in Figure 6.1, some students publish inappropriate, confidential, and potentially dangerous information on their Facebook and MySpace pages. Victoria has posted her address, phone numbers, and moment-by-moment location. Look at the final entries on her page to find out what potential threat she may be facing. Aside from the risk of serious harm, other types of "danger" can result from bad judgment, too. What some students post just for fun can later cost them a job opportunity. If your webpage has provocative photos of you or descriptions of rowdy weekend activities that you wouldn't want your grandmother to see, remove them! (Employers regularly check these sources for insider information on applicants.) "Living out loud," as social networking is sometimes called, requires constant vigilance so that the details of your life aren't on display. Some recent research indicates that younger users are more

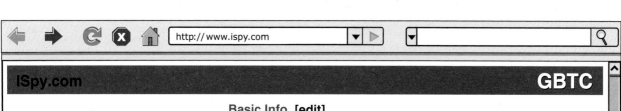

ISpy.com

[View More Photos of Me](#)

Status   edit

Doin' shots at Annie Oakley's!

RMSU Friends

425 friends at GBTC   See All

Seymore Bonz   **N.O. Body**

Friends in Other Networks

Cal (12)
UF (40)
CMU (6)
KSCC (7)
GBTC (425)

Basic Info [edit]

Name:	Victoria Tymmyns
Looking For:	A Good Time
Residence:	456 Pine Valley
Birthday:	June 12, 1990

Contact Info [edit]

Email:	VicTym@gbtc.edu
AIM Screenname	VicTym
Mobile:	719.111.1112
Current Address:	123 Fake St. Great Bluffs, CO 80900

Personal Info [edit]

Activities:	Drinkin' at "Annie Oakley's" every Fri. night. Karaoke at "All That Jazz" every Sat. night.
Favorite Music:	Black Flag, NIN, DK, the Clash
Favorite Movies	Shrek, Dracula

Work Info [edit]

Company:	Common Grounds Coffee Shop
Schedule:	Work M – F 7AM –2PM

The Wall [edit]

 N.O. Body wrote: at 11:00am August 1, 2010
Saw u dancing at Annie Oakley's!! Whatta hottie! We should meet.

 N.O. Body wrote: at 1:00pm August 1, 2010
Aw come on! U know u want to meet me!

 N.O. Body wrote: at 3:02pm August 1, 2010
Still no response? What 's up? Do u wanna play or not?

 Seymore Bonz wrote: at 4:27pm August 1, 2010
R we still hookin up w/the gang at Annie Oakley's tonight?
Meet you guys at the front door at 10.

 N.O. Body wrote: at 5:20pm August 1, 2010
Sounds fun. Maybe i'll see u there.

 Bay-Bee Face wrote: at 10:17pm August 2, 2010
Can you believe how we much we rocked last night? What was the deal with that guy who kept staring at us? He gave me the creeps!! You switched shifts w/Mary right? Working at 4?

 N.O. Body wrote: at 12:39pm August 2, 2010
Gee, BTW u were dressed, I just assumed u liked being stared at… U looked really cute at work.

 N.O. Body wrote: at 2:21pm August 3, 2010
What's the matter sweetheart? U looked unhappy to see me at work today. Why didn't u talk to me? BTW, nice house u got. Who knew you lived in such a nice neighborhood.

 N.O. Body wrote: at 12:57pm August 5, 2010
Nice dog u have. Ur parents must be outta town—no one's been home all night.

 N.O. Body wrote: at 7:26pm August 5, 2010
U never showed up for ur shift today. I waited all day for u. Saw your friends. They said somebody poisoned your dog. That's a shame—such a yappy little thing. I hate stuck-up women. Guess I'll just have to find u in person…

FIGURE 6.1

Fictional Ispy.com page

Companion, M. (2006). Victoria Tymmyns Ispy.com. Used with permission.

sensitive to keeping things offline than older users.[7] To avoid "social insecurity," keep these five useful suggestions in mind:

1. **Use a password with at least eight letters and numbers,** like FO34$&CuS.

It's noon. You decide to check your online life while you chow down a giant burrito. Three wall entries and five new requests from potential Facebook friends. *Who are these people?* you wonder. After a bit of browsing, you decide to update your photo albums by uploading several shots from your weekend adventures. Then you notice an amazing item on e-Bay that you've been looking for, and a bidding war is underway. You decide to join in, and you cast the winning bid. *Man, how am I going to pay for that?* you wonder. The clock ticks away. You order a new pair of shoes from your favorite website, and then check your watch. It's already 4:30. Four and a half hours have just gone by, and you have to catch the bus to get to campus in 10 minutes!

Does this scenario sound uncomfortably familiar? A few minutes start a chain reaction that stretches out for several hours. You hate to admit it, but you're caught in the Net, spending so much time on the Internet that you're neglecting other areas of your life. Just why is the Internet so addicting? Is it the novelty of things like Facebook or e-Bay? Is it because it allows us to do so much without moving from one spot? Is it because, like Dario, our real lives seem less interesting than the online potential? One user, who admits to spending 20 hours a week on Facebook, confessed "I'm an addict. I just get lost in Facebook. . . . My daughter gets so PO'd at me, and really it is kind of pathetic. It's not something I'm particularly proud of. I just get so sucked in." That's when you know you're really addicted."[8]

Are *you* addicted? Ask yourself these questions: Do you obsess about your online life and get nervous if you haven't checked your e-mail or Facebook account for a while? Do you spend more time with your online friends than your real friends? Do you interrupt yourself constantly to check your e-mail or chat electronically with someone while doing online research for your class projects? If the answers to the questions in this paragraph are yes, are you ready to consider that you may be overly dependent on the Internet?[9]

Don't get caught in the Net. Think about the impact it could have on your college success. Try these suggestions:

1. **Monitor your time online.** Estimate right now how much time you spend online per week. Then actually time yourself. Is your estimate accurate? Or are you way off base?

2. **Set limits.** Give yourself a hard-and-fast time limit, and stick to it.

3. **Shorten your online sessions.** Being online tends to distort time. You may think you've only been on for an hour, when three hours have actually gone by. Set an old-fashioned timer, and when it goes off, get up and do something else.

4. **Separate work and play online.** It's easy to find yourself on a fun-seeking detour when you're supposed to be working on a research paper. When work and play are combined, it's easy to lose track of what's what. You end up wasting time because it feels as if you're doing something productive when you really aren't.

5. **Take a tech vacation.** Without getting freaked out, think about this option: Turn off your computer for a day, and then extend the time to a week or more. Use a computer lab on campus to do your assignments, rather than tempting yourself to spend hours online at home. Train yourself to withdraw, little by little.

6. **Get a life.** Take up yoga, chess, or swimming. Make some new friends, start a relationship, or join a club on campus. Your real life might actually become more interesting.

7. **Talk to people who care about you—a family member or a counselor on campus.** Recognizing the problem and admitting it are the first steps. Being one-sided isn't healthy. There are experts and support groups available to help you deal with your problem and make your real life more fulfilling.[10]

2. **Don't include your full birth date.** Identity thieves can use this information.

3. **Take advantage of privacy controls.** Use the options provided to you, like choosing the "Friends Only" option. Be sure not to check the box for "Public Search Results". Search engines can find your Facebook profile on and off Facebook if you do.

4. **You wouldn't put a "No One's Home" sign on your door, so don't post it as your status.**

5. **Don't post your child's name in a caption.** If someone else does, remove it.[11]

What does all of this have to do with you? Everything! It's important to remember that the Internet itself is neutral. It can be used constructively or destructively, based on the choices you make. It can be an exciting, invigorating, essential part of your college experience. Use it wisely!

Use Technology to Your Academic Advantage

Despite the pros and cons, technology plays a big role in all of our lives, especially the lives of college students. A recent study of 30,616 students at both two-year and four-year colleges and universities reports that technology use is widespread in higher education. See how many of these items apply to you. For example:

Technology Ownership
98.4% of students own a computer
98.1% of students own a simple cell phone or smartphone
76.4% own an electronic music/video device
56.3% own an electronic game device

Technology Use
99.9% of students create, read, and use e-mail
98.6% write papers for classes
94.6% use the campus or library website
93.8% use presentation software
86.8% create spreadsheets
89.8 send texts
91.0% use course management systems, like Blackboard
90.3% use social networking sites, like Facebook
44.8% contribute to video websites
41.9% contribute to wikis
37.3% contribute to blogs[12]

What academic benefits does technology provide? In one major study, students noted that it helps them:

> Manage their courses

> Communicate with their instructors and classmates

> Improve their learning[13]

How Tech-Savvy Are You?

Let's look at some specific technology applications you'll need to know in college, including types of software, search engines, course management systems, and other class-related possibilities. Match the examples on the right to the descriptions on the left.

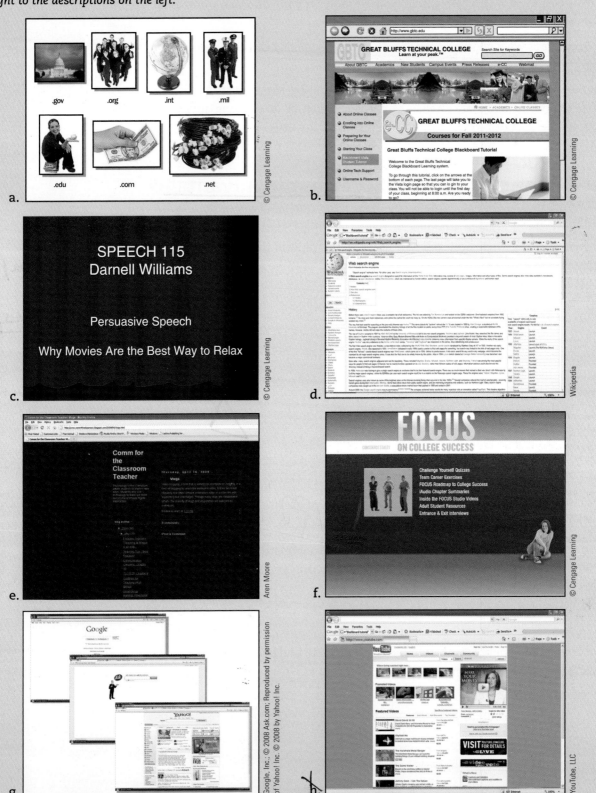

1. _A_ **Internet Domain Extensions**
Internet hostnames after the period in the URL (Uniform Resource Locator) describe where websites come from:
- **.gov** = U.S. government (such as www.irs.gov, the Internal Revenue Service or IRS)
- **.edu** = education (such as www.gbtc.edu, Great Bluffs Technical College)
- **.org** = organizations or businesses (such as www.democratic.org, the Democratic Party, or nonprofit organizations, like www.americanheart.org, American Heart Association)
- **.mil** = military (such as www.defenselink.mil, U.S. Department of Defense)
- **.com** = commercial, buying and selling (such as www.realtor.com, National Association of Realtors)
- **.net** = network or Internet provider (such as www.earthlink.net)
- **.int** = international organizations (such as Interpol, Council of Europe, or NATO)[14]

2. _C_ **Software**
College will require you to use several standard software applications to do your academic work:
- **Microsoft Word** allows you to type, edit, alphabetize, index, footnote, and do many other things to prepare papers for your classes.
- **Microsoft PowerPoint**, used as an electronic visual aid for oral presentations, allows you to create an on-screen guide for your listeners (and you, if you glance periodically and subtly for clues).
- **Microsoft Excel** spreadsheets are good for tabulating, record keeping, and organizing.

The industry standard for these applications is generally the Microsoft products listed here, although other possibilities exist. If you need help learning any of these applications, your campus techies, your instructors, or online tutorials (which can easily be found by Googling) can help. If you're a techie yourself, you can venture into other software applications like Flash, Camtasia, or iMovie to make your academic work look even more professional.

3. _G_ **Search Engines**
Different search engines work best for different purposes, but these three are the most popular recommendations:[15]
- **Google (www.google.com)** has a well-deserved reputation as the best search engine you can use. Its size is not disclosed anywhere, but it's generally thought to have the largest assets to search.
- **Yahoo (www.yahoo.com)** can also help you get excellent search results, or allow you to use any of the other specialized search features.

Ask (www.ask.com) became popular because it allowed you to ask virtually any question and get an answer.

4. _D_ **Wikis**
Wikis are today's online, editable encyclopedias. (The word wiki means "fast" in the Hawaiian language.) Wikipedia is the largest of these sites, and anyone can add information or change content (currently at 15 million articles in more than 270 languages on the Wikipedia site). On the other hand, be aware that inaccurate information can be added just as easily as accurate information. Never consider Wikipedia to be the final word on anything.

5. _B_ **Course Management Systems**
Many of your college classes will be conducted partially or wholly online, using a course management system, like Blackboard, eCollege, or Moodle. These shells help organize the online component of classes, and most students report having positive experiences with them. How do students use course management systems?
- To track grades, assignments, and tests
- To take sample tests and quizzes (or real ones)
- To get the course syllabus
- To turn in assignments online
- To access readings and other course materials
- To post to an online discussion[16]

6. _E_ **Blogs**
Web logs or blogs can be thought of as online journals that are typically one person's reactions to current events or cultural issues, for example. Or you can think of them as websites that someone changes every day.[17] Your instructors may post a question or comment and ask you to blog your responses online and to respond to your classmates' blogs. Everyone can get to know you by your online personality, and some students say they become better writers by reading other students' responses to their writing. And professional blogs can be a great way to stay current on the career you go into.

7. _F_ **YouTube**
YouTube is a video-sharing website where you can upload and watch video clips. You may want to insert one into a presentation you create as a class assignment or post one yourself related to your life as a student.

8. _F_ **Textbook Websites**
Textbook websites, like the one you're using for _FOCUS on College and Career Success,_ can contain information and activities to enrich your learning experience, like videos, quizzes, and iAudio chapter summaries. Use these resources to help you master course material.

Stressed Out? ....

W hat's keeping you up at night? Worry? Anxiety? Stress? According to sleep experts, you should be getting seven or more hours per night, or a minimum of forty-nine hours per week. Some students, like Dario from the FOCUS Challenge Case, choose to stay up until the wee, small hours of the morning. Or perhaps you have a baby at home who keeps you up at night or a job working the night shift. Stress and sleep are intricately related. Together, they combine to form a vicious circle: stress can keep you from getting sleep, and not getting enough sleep can interfere with your ability to cope with stress.

TRY IT!

Keep a sleep log for a week. When you wake up, write down the number of hours of sleep you've gotten.

| ____ | ____ | ____ | ____ | ____ | ____ | ____ |
| Sun. | Mon. | Tues. | Wed. | Thur. | Fri. | Sat. |

Are you surprised to see the actual numbers? Is there much variation from night to night? From weekdays to weekends? Formulate a new strategy to become better rested. Scientists now know that the amount of sleep you get can affect your health, your weight, and your grades![18]

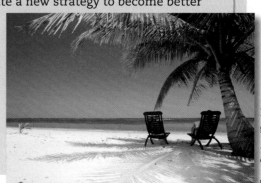

Devon Stephens/iStockphoto.com

BOX 6.1 Other Need-to-Know Technology Definitions

VPN (Virtual Private Network): You may need to go through particular steps to connect to your campus databases from home. Tech experts on your campus can show you how to do this, or there may be an online tutorial on your campus's website.

Podcasts: Many professors now record their lectures for you to review later. Or you can listen to *FOCUS on College and Career Success* and other textbooks' iAudio summaries for each chapter online.

PDF files: Using Adobe technology, you can create and edit documents that are formatted on your computer screen just as they would appear if they were published. PDFs look very

professional, and there may be a time when you are asked to create one for a particular class.

Web 2.0: Web 2.0 is not a new version of the Internet. It refers to creative uses of it, like Facebook, Wikis, and blogs, where instead of just reading passively, users help create the content.

Viruses, Worms, and Trojan Horses: Pranksters (or vicious cyber attackers, for that matter) can infiltrate campus technology systems and infect individual computers or shut down a campus system entirely. The solution? Don't open attachments with suspicious names or ones from people you don't know. And keep your antivirus software up to date!

Netiquette: Online Manners Matter

Being a professional student doesn't just apply to how you act in class, like asking questions if you're unclear or turning in your assignments on time. Online communication like e-mail has netiquette (or network etiquette) rules like these:

1. Don't send a message you don't want to risk being forwarded to someone else.

2. **Don't hit the "send" key until you've given yourself time to cool off, if you're upset.** You may want to edit what you've written.

3. **Don't forward chain e-mails.** At the very least, they're a nuisance, and sometimes, they're illegal.

4. **Don't do business over your school e-mail account.** Sending all 500 new students an invitation to your family's restaurant grand opening is off-limits. Besides, sending messages to lots of people at once is called "spam," and it can really gum up the works.

5. **Don't spread hoaxes about viruses or false threats.** You can get into big trouble for that.

6. **Don't type in all CAPS.** That's called SHOUTING, and it makes you look angry.

7. **Don't be too casual.** u no wat rly wrks? lol? ;>) Actually, what really works is good grammar and correct spelling. Your instructors consider e-mails to be academic writing, and they'll expect professionalism from you.

8. **Don't forget important details.** Include everything the reader needs to know. For example, if you're writing to an instructor, give your full name and the name of the course you're writing about. Professors teach more than one class and have many students.

9. **Don't hit the "Reply to All" key, when you mean to hit the "Reply" key.** Many e-mail message writers have been horrified upon learning that hundreds or thousands of people have read something personal or cranky that was meant for just one reader.

10. **Don't forget to fill in the subject line.** That gives readers a chance to preview your message and decide how soon they need to get to it.

EXERCISE 6.2

How *Not* to Win Friends and Influence People Online

All four of these e-mail messages from students violate the rules of netiquette. See if you can identify the rule number above that's been violated in each case.

From Matt   Rule:_____
> Professor X,
> I just looked at the online syllabus for Academic Success 101. Why didn't you tell us that our first paper is due on Monday? I will be very busy moving into a new apartment this weekend. Writing an essay for your class is the last thing I want to have to think about.

From Tiffany   Rule:_____
> Prof X,
> i didn't know u were makin us write a paper over the weekend. i won't be able to do it. i hop you don't mind.

From Xavier   Rule:_____
> PROFESSOR X,
> I CAN'T GET MY PAPER DONE BY MONDAY. LET ME KNOW WHAT I SHOULD DO.

(continued)

Taking Online Classes: E-Learning versus C-Learning

Here's one kind of technology you may well run into during your time in college. What do an American soldier in Afghanistan, a single mother of twin toddlers in California, and a victim of cerebral palsy in New York have in common? All three are taking the same online course in psychology. Instead of c-learning (traditionally, in the classroom), they're engaging in *distance education* or e-learning (electronically, online).

Of course, many of your college courses are hybrids or blended courses: they each have an online component and a classroom component. You e-mail your professor, use software to track your progress, upload assignments, and download handouts, along with the classroom part of the course. But if you haven't already, chances are you'll be engaged in distance learning in a totally online environment for more than one of your college classes. Distance education, as an entirely online class is sometimes called, is gaining momentum fast at colleges around the country, and the demand for these courses hasn't peaked yet.[19]

What are the differences between e-learning and c-learning? E-learning is sometimes defined as structured learning that takes place without a teacher at the front of the room. If you're an independent, self-motivated learner, e-learning can be a great way to learn, because *you* are in control.

> *You control when you learn.* Instead of that dreaded 8:00 a.m. class—the only section that's open when you register—you can schedule your e-learning when it's convenient for you. If you want to do your coursework at midnight in your pajamas, who's to know?

> *You control how you learn.* If you are an introvert, e-learning may work well for you. You can work thoughtfully online and take all the time you need to reflect. If you are an extravert, however, you may become frustrated by the lack of warm bodies around. Jumping into threaded discussions and chatting online may satisfy some of those needs. If you're a kinesthetic learner, the keyboard action may suit you well. Since you're working independently, you can do whatever you need to do to accommodate your own learning style.

Stockbyte/Getty Images

It was not so very long ago that people thought that semiconductors were part-time orchestra leaders and microchips were very small snack foods.

Geraldine Ferraro, Democratic politician

> *You control how fast you learn.* You know for a fact that students learn at different rates. With e-learning, you don't have to feel you're slowing down the class if you continue a line of questioning or worry about getting left in the dust if everyone else is way ahead of you.

E-learning can be a very effective way to learn, but it does require some adjustments. Here are some suggestions for making the best of your e-learning opportunities:

1. **Work to get course material.** Instead of listening to your professor lecture at the front of the room, you will have to get information yourself by downloading files or lecture notes. Some studies show that students work harder and longer online.

2. **Communicate your needs to your professor.** Your professor won't be able to see your 'huh?" looks when you don't understand something. Take direct action by e-mailing her, for example.

3. **Stay in touch with other students in the course.** Use e-mail to communicate with your cyber classmates to build an online **learning community**. They may be able to clarify an assignment or coach you through a tough spot.

learning community group of students who help one another learn

4. **Take notes.** When you're sitting through a lecture, you hand write notes to review later. Likewise, if you're reading lecture notes online, open a Word document and switch back and forth for your own note-taking purposes.

5. **Keep your antivirus program up to date.** When you upload assignment files, you run the risk of infecting your professor's computer with whatever viruses your computer may have. Make sure your antivirus software is up to date!

6. **Create a productive learning environment.** Since you'll most likely do your e-learning at home, make sure the environment is right for learning. If your computer is next to the TV or your kids are acting up to get attention, move to another location that's calm, well lit, and quiet.

7. **Use each login session as an opportunity to review.** Begin each online session by reviewing what you did or how much progress you made last time. Physically logging on can become a signal to take stock before moving forward with new course material.

8. **Call on your time management skills.** If your e-course is self-paced, you'll need to plan ahead, schedule due dates, and above all, discipline yourself to make continual progress. If you're sharing a computer with other family members, you'll need to create a master schedule. Remember that you may need to be online at particular times to engage in class chats or discussions.[20]

> 66 99
>
> **Any occurrence requiring undivided attention will be accompanied by a compelling distraction.**
>
> *Robert Bloch, American fiction writer, (1917–1994)*

Research Skills and Your College Success

Many of your class assignments in college will require you to conduct research. Why? Aren't you in college to learn from your instructors? Why do they ask *you* to do research on your own?

There are unanswered questions all around us in everyday life. Some questions are simple; others are complex. How much time will it take to get across town to a doctor's appointment during rush hour? What can you expect college tuition to cost by the time your kids are old enough to go? What are the chances that someone you know who has cancer will survive for five years? Research isn't necessarily a mysterious thing that scientists in white coats do in laboratories. Research is simply finding answers to questions, either real questions you encounter every day or questions that are assigned to you in your classes. Doing research on your own can be a powerful way to learn, sometimes even more so than hearing answers from someone else, even if those people are your instructors. Going off to a research expedition in the library may sound like exhausting busywork, but the skills you stand to gain are well worth the effort.

Conducting research teaches you some important things about how to formulate a question and then find answers. And it's not just finding answers so that you can scratch a particular assignment off your to-do list. It's about learning an important process. When you get into the world of work, your instructors won't be there to supply answers, so knowing how to figure things out on your own will be key to your success. So, exactly what is college-level research?

What Research Is *Not*	What Research Is
Research isn't just going on a "search and employ" mission. It's not just seeing what all you can find and then using it to check off an assignment on your to-do list.	**Research starts with a question.** If an assignment is broad, as Dario's was, you must come up with a specific question to research yourself. More about that later.
Research isn't just moving things from Point A (the library) to Point B (your paper).	**Research is a process with a plan.** A plan was something Dario lacked. He jumped in without a question—or a plan.
Research isn't random rummaging through real or virtual files to find out something.	**Research is goal-oriented.** You've formulated a question, developed a plan, and now you begin to find answers by using both online sources and ones that sit on your library's shelves.
Research isn't doing a quick Internet search. The cutting and pasting Dario did to fill up his five pages is actually plagiarism!	**Research often involves breaking a big question into several smaller ones.**[21]

Navigating the Library

You've probably heard this since you were a child: "The library is your friend." As a young child, it was exciting to go to the library, choose a book, check it out with your own library card, and bring it home to read. Now, being "exiled" to the library to do research for a paper may seem like torture that can ruin a perfectly good weekend. But if you look at things differently, it can be a mind-expanding trip into places unknown. The truth is: In college, the library should be more than just a friend. It should become your best friend! Beyond navigating the web to find research for your assignments, as many students do, it's important to learn your way around the actual, physical space of the library on your campus or in your community. The library has many useful resources, including real, very knowledgeable librarians who are there to help you. Asking a reference librarian for help can save you hours of unproductive digging on your own. Here are some of the resources your library offers and how you should use these resources when you're assigned a research project:

> **Card Catalog.** Explore your library's catalog that lists all of the books available to you. Card catalogs used to be actual cards in file cabinet drawers, but now most libraries put all the information about their holdings online. Go to your college's website, and from there, you can find your way to your college library's home page. Click on the library's catalog button. Let's say Dario follows these instructions and finds this book in his campus library's catalog: The Global Internet Economy, edited by Bruce Kogut. Cambridge, MA: MIT Press, 2003. The call number for the book is HC79.I55 G579, based on the Library of Congress classification system, which most college libraries use. (Some libraries, like your community's public library, may use the Dewey Decimal system. One advantage of the Library of Congress system is that books usually have the same number, no matter which library you find them in. That's not always true for the Dewey Decimal system.) The Library of Congress number identifies this item as a book about economics and information technology. Now, after identifying other possible useful books, Dario needs to make his way to campus and find the actual book on the shelf.

> **Databases.** If you go to your library's home page, you can link to the list of online databases it subscribes to. Databases identify articles from academic journals and sometimes contain entire articles online. Generally, different databases exist for different disciplines, for example:

Education	**ERIC** (Educational Resources Information Center)
Psychology	**PsycInfo**
Business	**Business Source Premier**

" I find that a great part of the information I have was acquired by looking up something and finding something else on the way.

Franklin P. Adams, American journalist and radio personality (1881–1960)

But more general databases also exist. Dario might want to search through:

Academic Search Premier

WilsonWeb OmniFile Full Text Mega

The key to making the most of databases is to find the right search words to plug into the database's search engine. That's where a short coaching session with a real reference librarian can be enormously helpful. You can have productive results or no results at all, just by slightly altering the search words you enter.

> **Stacks.** Physically walk through the stacks or collections of books and periodicals (journals, magazines, newspapers, and audiovisual resources, for example). Get to know the stacks in your library, and figure out how to find what you need. Look for the Library of Congress numbers posted on signs at the end of each row of books. When Dario finds the book he's looking for, he's likely to find other books in the library's "HC" section that would also be useful to him. That's why even though doing online research is convenient, there's no substitute for "being there."

CAREER OUTLOOK: *Be Resourceful*

 When action grows unprofitable, gather information.
URSULA K. LEGUIN

Know how to gather information and use it. In college, you're asked to develop your research skills. It's easy to think that each paper for a class is just another assignment to check off the list, when you're actually developing skills that will be critical to your success later. Whether in college or on the job, you don't just string together pieces of information when you do research for a paper or project. You analyze research through the "eyes" of the problem you're trying to address and your perspective on it. Then you weave ideas together to make an effective argument or proposal, and you anticipate counter-arguments and competing ideas as you develop yours. When the boss wants your thoughts on a new day-care program for your fellow employees, of course you'll want to research what works in similar organizations. What are the most common options out there? But you'll also want to consider the special needs of your colleagues, anticipate possible problems, and develop a proposal that takes both your research and your analysis into account.

Information Literacy and Your College Success

Much of the research you do for your college assignments will take place online. Information literacy is defined as knowing *when* you need information, *where* to find it, *what* it means, *whether* it's accurate, and *how* to use it. Simply put, it's "the ability to use technology to solve information problems." Information literacy includes five components, as seen in Figure 6.2. Think about them as a step-by-step process as we work through Dario's assignment.[22]

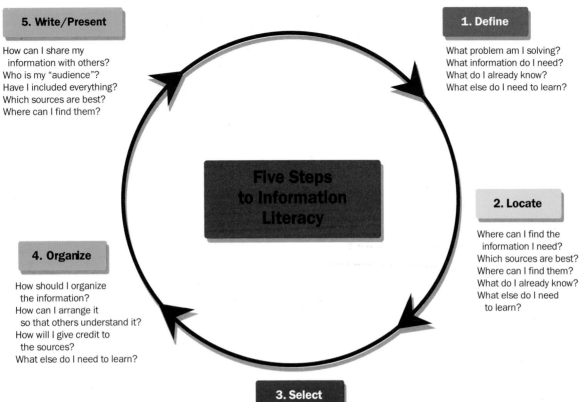

5. Write/Present

How can I share my
  information with others?
Who is my "audience"?
Have I included everything?
Which sources are best?
Where can I find them?

**Five Steps
to Information
Literacy**

1. Define

What problem am I solving?
What information do I need?
What do I already know?
What else do I need to learn?

2. Locate

Where can I find the
  information I need?
Which sources are best?
Where can I find them?
What do I already know?
What else do I need
  to learn?

4. Organize

How should I organize
  the information?
How can I arrange it
  so that others understand it?
How will I give credit to
  the sources?
What else do I need to learn?

3. Select

How can I best search
  these sources?
How will I record what
  I find?
How will I give credit to
  the sources?
What else do I need to learn?

FIGURE 6.2

Five Steps to Information Literacy

Source: Wood, G. (2004, April 9). Academic original sin: Plagiarism, the Internet, and librarians. *The Journal of Academic Librarianship*, 30(3), 237–242.

Step 1. Define

Define what the assignment requires of you. Dario was assigned a *research* paper. He wasn't being asked to **summarize** or *evaluate* a topic. He was asked to *find out about it*. But "Globalization and Internet Commerce" is a huge topic. He must narrow it down and decide which specific research question (or questions) he wants to focus on.

    If you were assigned the paper Dario was assigned, and you knew very little about "Globalization and Internet Commerce," you might start as he did, by Googling your topic to help you define it. But the Internet is huge and unstructured. There's really no way to organize that much information into simple, neat categories.[23] And how do you whittle down 22 million hits? According to a recent study, less than 1 percent of Google users look further than the first page of their Google results, regardless of how many hits they get![24]

    If you don't know anything about the topic you need to research—absolutely nothing at all—the Internet is a great place to start. You can type in "globalization" and "Internet commerce," and within the blink of an eye, information appears. The problem is that you now have too much information, and the challenge is knowing what to do next. Your college instructors will insist you go beyond the Internet and avoid relying too much on encyclopedias and Wikipedia. College requires you to do more research than you've probably done before, and to do it differently.

summarize condense a longer work into a few essential statements

Plans are only good intentions unless they immediately degenerate into hard work.

Peter Drucker, management expert (1909–2005)

bookmark a way to save and organize websites in your web browser

Dario could have used the websites that Google brought up to help him *define* a specific research focus, instead of being overwhelmed by the number of hits. Consider these more focused research topics or questions, which Google or Wikipedia could have led him to:

1. Five Reasons to Go Global with Your Website (Why is it a good idea?)

2. Online Retail Businesses Will Explode over the Next Ten Years (Where will it go in the future?)

3. Three Problems with Doing E-Business Internationally: Language, Shipping, and Money (What are the challenges of trying to make it happen?)

Let's take that last focused topic and run with it. Suppose you have an online business and you want to attract customers from around the world to expand it. That's a good idea, but how will you deal with translating what's on your website to other languages? How will you ship your product overseas for a reasonable cost? How will you deal with the exchange rate between the U.S. dollar and the currency used in other countries? Now we've taken a big, broad topic ("Globalization and Internet Commerce") and broken it down into three specific questions or subtopics to research. Your preliminary Google and Wikipedia searches can help you identify what the smaller chunks of your topic could be.

But they can't do *all* the work for you, and you can't stop there, as Dario did. You have to know what to do next. (If you think this process is challenging, you're not alone. In one study, only 35 percent of college students knew how to narrow a Google search!)[25]

Step 2. Locate

If you've identified electronic sources, bookmark them in a file labeled with the name of your project. If they're print resources, physically find them in the library. If they're not available in your own campus library, see if it participates in an interlibrary loan agreement among libraries. Your own library may be able to borrow the resource from another library. (But be aware that this process may take up to two weeks or so. That's why it's important to start your research projects early!)

Step 3. Select

The Information Age surrounds us with huge amounts of data of all kinds. With so much information available, how do we know what to believe? Whether or not it's true, we tend to think that if something is on television or in a book or online, it must be important. But in any of these cases, we need to exercise our critical thinking skills and turn them into critical searching skills. Just because information is published doesn't automatically make it right or true. In particular, some of the so-called research you encounter online may be bogus, containing inaccuracies or bias. You must read, interpret, and evaluate research to decide whether to use it. Use these five criteria to evaluate any website you come across:

1. **Currency.** How up to date is the information? Some websites don't list a date at the bottom of the screen (where copyright information is often found). If you don't see one, try using other hints on the site to get at how old the information is ("According to a study published in 1995 . . ."). You may find that you need to search for something more up to date.

2. **Accuracy.** How accurate is the information presented? If a website makes an unbelievable claim ("Grow a new head of hair in just six weeks!") or presents shaky statistics to make a case, it's important to be skeptical. Take responsibility to validate the information elsewhere.

3. **Authority.** Does the sponsor of the website have the credentials to post the information you see? Chances are "Steve's Picks" or "myfavoritemovies .com" is a collection of one person's opinions. Compare that to a film reviewer's site with information compiled by a professional film critic for a major newspaper. Which one would you trust more? You may not agree with Steve or the professional film critic, but one has credentials, and the other doesn't.

4. **Objectivity.** Does the website sponsor have a reason to convince you of something, or is it presenting unbiased information? If the site wants you to order something online because it claims to have better products than those you can buy at a store, for example, you should be suspicious.

   objectivity ability not to take sides, being neutral

5. **Coverage.** If a website just presents one side of an issue or a very small piece of a larger picture, check to make sure you're getting all the information you need. If you're left wondering, *but what about . . . ?* you're probably having the right reaction.

EXERCISE 6.3

Critical Searching on the Internet

With these five criteria in mind, choose one of the following two assignments to complete. Each one will ask you to use your critical searching skills.

Assignment 1: Create a list of three websites that pertain to your intended major. (If you're not sure of your major right now, choose one to explore anyway.) Evaluate the websites, using the five criteria, to see which ones seem most useful to you as a student.

Assignment 2: Compare websites with contradictory information. Choose a controversial subject such as abortion, the death penalty, religion, politics, or some other subject of interest. Find three websites on your topic and compare them on the five criteria. Which of the three websites gets the highest marks? Why?

Step 4. Organize

Now that you have located the information you need, using a variety of sources, and selected those that will be most useful to you in your research project, it's time to organize. Dario's paper will be easier to write now that he has created three subtopics: language, shipping, and money. He should begin taking notes on index cards or highlighting pieces of information he wants to quote word-for-word (giving credit to the author) or paraphrase (putting information into his own words). He can literally put the index cards, printed articles, and photo-copied pages from books he found while doing his research into three piles and work from those. Organization is the key to an excellent research paper. To help you keep track of the sources you find, you should follow these suggestions:

> **Pay attention to details.** Write the name of the book or article, author, place of publication, publisher, date, or URL at the top of an index card with your notes or on a photocopied page of information you plan to use. Here's an example of what two index cards (of the same paragraph) would look like:

[Ableson, H. Ledeen, K., & Lewis, H. (2008). *Blown to bits: Your life, liberty, and happiness after the digital explosion.* Boston, MA: Pearson Education, Inc.]

Direct Quote

"The Internet has caused drastic shifts in business practice. Customer service calls are outsourced to India today not just because labor costs are low there. Labor costs have always been low in India, but international telephone calls used to be expensive. Calls about airline reservations and lingerie returns are answered in India today because it now takes almost no time and costs almost no money to send to India the bits representing your voice." Blown to Bits, p. 12.

[Ableson, H. Ledeen, K., & Lewis, H. (2008). *Blown to bits: Your life, liberty, and happiness after the digital explosion.* Boston, MA: Pearson Education, Inc.]

Paraphrase

The Internet has changed the way we do business. We outsource everything from airline reservations to lingerie returns to people in places like India because the technology of cell phones has made long distance cheap.

If you have ideas of your own that don't come from any book, write them on cards or pages, too, and label them, "My Own Ideas."

> **Decide on an organizational format.** Once you have your note cards in stacks, decide on the organizational format that would be most effective. Dario's research focus on three different things—language, shipping, and money—lends itself to what's called a *topical* format. His research will fall into one of those three topics. If he were comparing Internet commerce in Europe, Asia, and North America, he might use a *compare and contrast* format. If he were going to present *solutions* to the three challenges he's addressing (language, shipping, and money), he'd use a *problem-solution* format. Decide how best to present your information, and then follow the format you choose.

Work is either fun or drudgery. It depends on your attitude. I like fun.

Colleen C. Barrett, President and Corporate Secretary, Southwest Airlines

Step 5. Write and Present

You've done your research, and now it's time to share it with the world (or at least your instructor) either through the written word, the spoken word, or both. Writing is much more complicated than just sitting down at your computer and letting your fingers do the talking. It's a three-stage process of prewriting, writing, and rewriting that works like this. As you read about the three stages of writing, think about how the process of writing a paper is like the process of preparing a speech.

Stage 1: Prewriting Much of what we've been discussing up to this point is called prewriting. It's all the work you do to get ready to write by defining, locating, selecting, and organizing, as we've just discussed. Aside from the various steps involved in prewriting, perhaps the biggest challenge most new college students face is constructing a strong thesis statement. *What's my paper's main idea in a nutshell?* Instead of just writing whatever happens to come out of your fingers, try to summarize your point in a single sentence—Dario's thesis might be: "Three problems with doing e-business internationally are language, shipping, and money."

Stage 2: Writing Have you ever sat down to write and suddenly gone blank? Sometimes that's called "writer's block." Some professional writers resort to unusual strategies to get themselves going. Victor Hugo supposedly wrote in his study at the same time every day—naked! His servant was ordered to lock away all of Hugo's clothes until he had finished each day's writing. Apparently, the method worked—among other things, he wrote *Les Misérables*.[26] But this technique may not be well received by your friends or family. A simpler way of starting is to just write freely about whatever comes into your head, whether it's on target or not. Say, for example, you've done all your prewriting work, but nothing's coming. Try just plunging in and recording your thoughts:.

I'm having trouble starting this paper because there's so much to talk about in terms of globalization and Internet commerce. Even though all businesses want to grow, there are lots of problems with doing worldwide business on the Internet. How can an American communicate with a French guy in Paris, when he doesn't speak French? How can that same American, who sells refrigerated meat, ship it to Paris? And how can he get paid in Euros, when what he needs are dollars?

Now stop and look at what you've written. If you take away the first sentence and play with what's left, you have the beginnings of a first draft.

Stage 3: Rewriting Take a close look at what you've said and how you've said it. Make wording changes that provide your reader with the clearest, most powerful writing possible. Correct grammar, punctuation, spelling, and appearance. But besides any technical fixes, you'll actually need to take a fresh look at what you've said. Rewriting is often called "*revision.*" It means not merely changing, but literally re-seeing, re-en*vision*ing your work. Sometimes students

66 **Don't agonize. Organize.** 99

Florynce Kennedy, American lawyer and African American activist

24' *READ THIS FOR QUE*

BOX 6.2 # PowerPoint or PowerPointless? Five Ways to Make Your Presentations Stand Out

ardniPhotographer, 2009/Used under license from Shutterstock.com

Instead of (or in addition to) writing a research paper, your instructor may require you to present your findings to the class in an oral presentation using PowerPoint as a tool. While PowerPoint has the potential to be a powerful visual aid, it can also be PowerPointless if some simple rules are ignored. Keep these five suggestions in mind to turn PowerPointless presentations you create for class assignments into powerful ones:

1. **DO use your whole brain.** When it comes to designing PowerPoint presentations, the challenge is to combine useful information with attractive design. You should never assume that PowerPoint razzle-dazzle is more important than content, but it's possible to aim for both. Think of it as using both sides of your brain—your logical left hemisphere and your creative right hemisphere. For example, if you're giving a presentation on becoming a teaching assistant, you might want to use a font that looks like this on your title slide. (Just make sure it's legible, even from a distance. A good rule of thumb is to use 24-point font size or larger and keep your fonts simple unless you have a particular reason to change them.) You also might want to include a high-quality graphic like this one here. Much of the clip art that's available won't give your presentation a professional look, but many different graphics packages offer high-quality, realistic images. Which of the following presentations would you rather listen to—Presentation 1 or Presentation 2?

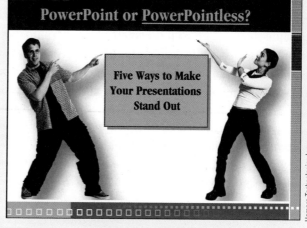

Presentation 1 — *PowerPoint or PowerPointless? Five Ways to Make Your Presentations Stand Out*
© Cengage Learning

Presentation 2 — *PowerPoint or PowerPointless? Five Ways to Make Your Presentations Stand Out*
Hemera Technologies Inc.

2. **DO use color to your advantage.** Use background colors to create a mood: soft colors for a subdued, quiet mood and bold colors for an energetic one. Choose an attractive color scheme and stick to it. That doesn't mean that every background on every slide must be the same. In fact, if you do that, your listeners may die of boredom. But if your title slide is blue, orange, and white, then use one, two, or all three of these colors in some hue or shade on every slide. Some speakers create PowerPoint presentations that seem fragmented and messy because the individual slides aren't connected visually. On a single slide, use contrasting colors to make particular points stand out.

3. **DON'T crowd your slides with text.** Your listeners won't pay attention to you if they're spending all of their time reading. Be kind, and spare them the trouble by limiting the text on your slides. Some of the most deadly PowerPoint presentations are those in which the speaker turns around, faces the screen, and just reads slide after slide. The only way your listeners can live through that is if oxygen masks drop from the overhead compartments!

4. **DON'T let your slides steal the show.** Always remember that YOU are the speaker. Your slides shouldn't be so fascinating that your audience ignores you. Gunshots and screaming sirens shouldn't be used as sound effects unless, of course, you're speaking on gun control or ambulance response times. Any special effects should be used sparingly to make a point, rather than to shock your listeners. Remember, too, to use graphics that relate to your topic.

5. **DO include a bibliography slide, both for words and images.** Some students assume that plagiarism only pertains to writing papers. Not so! Always give credit where credit is due. List your references, either on individual slides (if you use a direct quote, cite it) or on one slide at the end.

think they're revising when they're actually just editing: tinkering with words and phrases, checking spelling, changing punctuation. But the word *revision* actually means making major organizational overhauls, if necessary. According to many writing experts, that's what you must be willing to do.[27]

Perhaps the most powerful suggestion when it comes to rewriting is to separate yourself from what you're written. Step away and set it aside for a while. With new eyes, what you've written will look different. You can't use this recommendation as an excuse for a late paper ("I couldn't turn my paper in today because I need to wait before I rewrite."). But coming back later may cause this reaction: "What? I wrote that? What was I thinking?"

And finally, proofread, proofread, proofread! If your essay is littered with mistakes, your instructor may pay more attention to those than to your paper's brilliant ideas. Sometimes it also helps to proofread out loud, especially if you're an aural learner. Be positive there are no spelling errors, and be proud of the paper's final appearance—clean, type dark and crisp, margins consistent, headings useful, names and references correct. And remember that Spellcheck, for all its convenience, can let you down. If the word you use is an actual one, but not the right on, it will give its approval, regardless. (Did you catch the spelling error in that last sentence? Spellcheck didn't.)

EXERCISE 6.4

Technology Project: Group Ad

Working with two or three classmates and using PowerPoint, Flash, or iMovie, create a television ad (as professional-looking as possible) for the course for which you're using this book. Use text, images, and music. The advertisement shouldn't be long—two or three minutes, or the length of the song you use—but it should describe what the course is about and why other students should take it. Be as creative as you like! Once you've created your presentation, play your ad for the class.

Downloading Your Workload: The Easy Way Out?

EXERCISE 6.5

Plagiarism Survey[28]

When you're doing research for a class assignment, have you ever asked yourself questions like these? Jot down your own responses, and then see if you can find the answers as you continue reading this section. Then discuss them as a class.

1. How do I put things into my own words?
2. How do I give credit to sources I use?
3. How do I do research methodically in steps so that I don't run out of time, leaving plagiarism as an attractive alternative?
4. If an assignment feels as though it's busy work that has nothing to do with my life, is plagiarism really such a bad thing?
5. Isn't anything published on the Internet free, valid, and available to use?

One of the trickiest aspects of writing papers for your college courses can be expressed in these three words: *What is plagiarism?* First, you should understand the difference between *intentional* and *unintentional* plagiarism. Intentional plagiarism is deliberately downloading a paper from an online source or cutting and pasting text from a website or book, as Dario did, for example. However, you run the risk of committing unintentional plagiarism if you don't understand what plagiarism is or you forget which book you used so you don't cite the words you've borrowed from someone else. Intentional plagiarism is cheating, pure and simple. Technology today makes plagiarism all too convenient and easy, but by the same token, finding plagiarism in students' papers has become easy for instructors, too. The bottom line? Follow the guidelines you get from your instructors. And if you don't understand them or your instructor assumes you already know them, ask questions. Both intentional and unintentional plagiarism can hurt you academically. These FAQs will help.

Q1: If I just list all the sources I used in writing a paper in the bibliography, won't that cover everything? List all your sources in the bibliography at the end of your paper, but also mention that they are others' ideas as you present them. Generally, it's a good idea to cite the original author soon after you present that idea in your paper. In a research paper, it's also useful to name the authors ("According to Staley, college success skills are critical in the first year of college.") Each discipline uses a particular format to cite references. These are called *style sheets*, such as

> *MLA* (Modern Language Association) is often used in the humanities (English, art, and philosophy, for example).

> *APA* (American Psychological Association) is often used in the social sciences (psychology, communication, and sociology).

> *Chicago Manual of Style* is used in history.

Check with your instructor if you're not certain which one to use, and Google these terms to find the specifics of formatting.

Q2: Must I cite all my sources if I just put ideas into my own words? Yes, you must cite all your sources, even though you may think that your paper looks cluttered. In academic writing, you must cite all the information you use, whether you paraphrase it, quote it, or summarize it. Some students are even taught bad habits in high school, for example, "It's not plagiarism if you change every fifth word," so they write papers with a thesaurus close by. Unfortunately, that's not the way it works. Try reading what you'd like to paraphrase, and then cover the text with your hand and write what you remember. In this case, you'd still need to cite the reference, but since you're paraphrasing, you wouldn't use quotation marks.

Q3: But I didn't know anything at all about this subject before I started this assignment. Does that mean I should cite everything? Some ideas are common knowledge that need not be cited. For example, it's a well-known fact that the Civil War lasted from 1861 to 1865. If you cited this piece of common knowledge, who would you cite? Generally, however, your motto should be, "Better safe than sorry." As a rule, you must cite quotations, paraphrases, or summaries. If you use the exact words of someone else, put

REREAD THIS PAGE!

quotation marks around them, or if they're longer than four lines, indent them in a block. (And generally, only use long quotes if something has been said in a remarkable way.) Also cite specific facts you're using as support and distinctive ideas belonging to others, even if you don't agree with them.

 Q4: I've been doing a lot of reading for this paper. Now I'm not really sure which ideas came from others and which are my own. How do I avoid plagiarism? The best solution here is to take careful notes as you do your research and document where you found each piece of information. Avoid cutting and pasting text. That practice can backfire later when you can't remember what you've extracted and what represents your own thoughts and wording. And remember this: Plagiarism applies to speaking as well as writing!

> "Borrowed thoughts, like borrowed money, only show the poverty of the borrower."
>
> *Lady Marguerite Blessington, English socialite and writer (1789–1849)*

Now look back at your answers to the Plagiarism Survey in Exercise 6.5 at the beginning of this section and see if you would change any of them.

WHO.

EXERCISE 6.6

Plagiarism or Not?

In your opinion, is the following passage plagiarized? Compare these two examples:

Original passage: The emotional importance of a spoken message is conveyed by its semantic content ("what" is said) and by the affective prosody used by the speaker ("how" it is said). The listener has to pay attention to both types of information in order to comprehend the emotional message as a whole.

Source: Vingerhoets, G., Berckmoes, C., & Stroobant, N. (2003). Cerebral hemodynamics during discrimination of prosodic and semantic emotion in speech studied by transcranial doppler ultrasonography. *Neuropsychology, 17*(1), 93–99.

Student paper: The emotional importance of a spoken message is transmitted by its meaning ("what" is said) and by the emotional overtones used by the speaker ("how" it is said). The listener has to pay attention to both types of content in order to understand the entire emotional message.

Has this student committed plagiarism? Why or why not?

VARK Activity

Complete the activity recommended for your preferred VARK learning style and bring it to class (or follow your instructor's instructions).

 Visual: Draw an actual floor map of your library so that you know how to find sources easily.

 Aural: Interview a reference librarian on campus to find out specific ways she or he helps students do research. Access the CourseMate via www.cengagebrain.com/shop/ISBN/1439083908 to listen to the iAudio summary for this chapter.

 Read/Write: Find a quotation that sums up something important that you'll remember from this chapter, and bring it to class.

 Kinesthetic: Go to the library and find the "HC" section. Find three other books on Internet commerce and present the titles in class, along with photocopies of the book's covers, and their bibliographic information: title, author, place of publication, publisher, year of publication, and call number.

Rachel White

© Larry Harwood Photography. Property of Cengage Learning.

Bondarenko, 2010. Used under license from Shutterstock.com

All she ever wanted to be was a Mom. Rachel White loved kids. When she was one herself, she helped raise her six younger brothers and sisters. Her parents worked hard to support the family, so Rachel took over her mom's duties. With each new baby, Rachel got better at distinguishing between whiney cries, hurt cries, and hungry cries. It was Rachel who cooked their dinner most nights and took them to the park on Saturdays. It was almost as if they were Rachel's children. In fact, sometimes she pretended they were.

So as a senior, Rachel dropped out of high school and married her boyfriend, Mike. He loved kids, too, and when they found out they were expecting, he was as happy as she was that the "baby" was actually "babies." Twins ran in Mike's family, and it wasn't long until they had a real family with a little boy and a girl. But now with another baby on the way, Rachel realized that Mike's income wouldn't be enough. She wanted a big family like the one she'd grown up in, and she knew that getting an education was the best answer. The ideal career for a stay-at-home mom, she thought, would be to open a day care center in her own home. An associate's degree in Early Childhood Development would

provide credentials. So she studied at night, earned her GED, and enrolled in two evening classes at her local career college. Mike would be so proud of her.

Despite a 40-minute commute in heavy traffic, Rachel was excited about her first class, "Child Development I," as a new college student. But right away, several things caught her off guard. The young instructor was new to teaching, spoke with a foreign accent, and raced through the lecture. Since she'd been out of school for a while, Rachel felt as though she had forgotten how to be a student. As the instructor talked, she tried to take notes as quickly as she could, but how was she supposed to know what was important enough to write down? She looked around: What were other students writing? Was she the only one who couldn't keep up? The lecture began:

Sebastien Cote/iStockphoto.com

© Cengage Learning

Scott Bakal/Cengage Learning

Rachel White's Caring Hands Childcare

© Cengage Learning

TAKE ONE!!!

Caring Hands Childcare
719-555-5103

Caring Hands Childcare
719-555-5103

Caring Hands Childcare
719-555-5103

Caring Hands Childcare
719-555-5103

Caring Hands Childcare

Child Development I Syllabus
Instructor: Mary Kindler
Office: 343
Hours: Mon–Wed 10am–2pm

Course Description

This course is designed to give a general overview of childhood development and the processes that influence the physical, mental, emotional, and social growth of children through middle adolescence.

Course Objectives

© Cengage Learning

Child development is a process every child goes through. This process involves learning and mastering skills like sitting, walking, talking, skipping, and tying shoes. Children learn these skills, called developmental milestones, during predictable time periods. Children develop skills in five main areas of development: First, let's look at cognitive development. This is the child's ability to learn and solve problems. For example, this includes a two-month-old baby learning to explore the environment with hands or eyes or a five-year-old learning how to do simple math problems. Second, social/emotional development is the child's ability to interact with others, including helping themselves and self-control. Examples of this type of development would include a six-week-old baby smiling, a ten-month-old baby waving bye-bye, or a five-year-old boy knowing how to take turns in games at school. Third, speech and language development is the child's ability to both understand and use language. For example, this includes a 12-month-old baby saying his first words, a two-year-old naming parts of her body, or a five-year-old learning to say "feet" instead of "foots." Children also learn both fine and gross motor skills. Fine motor skills are the child's ability to use small muscles, specifically their hands and fingers, to pick up small objects, hold a spoon, turn pages in a book, or use a crayon to draw. Gross motor skills, on the other hand, are the child's ability to use large muscles. For example, a six-month-old baby learns how to sit up with some support, a 12-month-old baby learns to pull up to a stand holding onto furniture, and a five-year-old learns to skip.*

Rachel tried to pay attention to the instructor's words and copy down the writing scribbled all over the board, but her mind seemed to drift to the flyers she'd

*Based on http://www.howkidsdevelop.com/developSkills.html#dev

Shane White, 2010. Used under license from Shutterstock.com

create for her new day care business, or whether she should call Mike at the break to tell him the twins seemed to be coming down with a cold. Why was it so hard to focus? Rachel wondered whether she should bring her laptop to take notes that way, but somehow she knew she wouldn't be able to resist the temptation to check her Facebook page every 15 minutes or so. Information seemed to fly out of her instructor's mouth at mach speed, and frankly, she used the foreign accent as an excuse for her troubles. Taking notes that quickly was just plain impossible. She tried giving her quizzical looks to communicate "Slow down, please," but she probably couldn't see Rachel's face in the back of the room.

Since she didn't catch all of what the instructor was talking about, asking questions in class would only prove that she wasn't paying attention. Trying to read and take notes from the textbook chapters *before* class was hard with her active and noisy kids. Instead, she tried to look like she was paying attention in class so that no one knew that her brain wasn't really there.

Rachel had thought about trying to stop in during her instructor's office hours sometime, but she hated the thought of rush hour traffic. She could try making an appointment at another time, but did she really want to discuss how hard it was to concentrate in the class? It was too late in the term to drop the class, and she needed the credits for her degree. Still, she had to figure something out or this course was going to spoil her dream.

Constance Staley

1. Do have anything in common with Rachel? If so, how are you managing the situation so that you can be successful?
2. List five mistakes Rachel is making.
3. Now list five things that Rachel should do immediately to improve her childhood development classroom experience.

Get Engaged in Class

engagement emotional and psychological commitment to a task

No, this chapter isn't about buying a ring and getting down on one knee. It's about your willingness to focus, listen, discuss, ask questions, take notes, and generally dive into your classes. It's about being a full participant in your learning, not just a spectator sitting on the sidelines. It's about not just memorizing information for exams and then forgetting it. You see, the secret to college success hinges on this one word: **engagement**.

Think about this analogy. How did you learn to swim? Did you watch swimming on TV? Did you get advice from your friends about swimming? Did you just Google it? No, you probably jumped in and got wet, right? The same thing is true with your college classes. The more willing you are to jump in and get wet, the more engaged you'll be in the learning process.

[handwritten note: ENGAGE! MENTALLY PHYSICALLY.]

Dare to Prepare

If you want to get a head start on developing good academic habits in class, then start before you get there. Preparation separates students into two categories: those who excel at learning and those who don't. Although not all students see the value of preparation, do more than your classmates do—dare to prepare! Follow these suggestions and you'll find that it's easier to get engaged in class because you're ready.

[handwritten note: GET ENGAGED.]

1. **Look ahead.** By checking your course syllabus before class, you'll be prepared for the upcoming topic. You'll also avoid the "oops" factor of sitting down, looking around, and noticing that everyone else knows something you don't about what's supposed to happen today.

2. **Do the assigned reading.** If you have a reading assignment due for class, do it, and take notes as you read. Write in the margins of your textbook or on sticky notes. Or take notes using one of many convenient online note-taking tools while you read. Question what you're reading and enter into a mental conversation with the author. Having some background on the topic will allow you to listen more actively and participate more intelligently during any discussion: *Yes, I remember the chapter covering that topic*, you'll think when the instructor begins talking about something you recognize. Instead of hearing it for the first time, you'll *strengthen* what you've already read. According to one study, as few as one-third of your classmates will have done the assigned reading prior to class. That little known fact isn't a reason to excuse yourself from reading; instead it gives you insider information on how *you* can shine in class by comparison.[1]

> When you can do the common things of life in an uncommon way, you will command the attention of the world.
>
> —*George Washington Carver, 1864–1943, horticulturist, chemist, and educator*

PeR FAVOR STOP THE TYPOS.

> **You cannot truly listen to anyone and do anything else at the same time.**
>
> *M. Scott Peck, American author, (1936–2005)*

3. **Show up physically.** Not only is attending class important for your overall understanding of the material, but it may move your grade up a few notches. Even if attendance isn't required by your instructor, require it of yourself. Research says that missing classes is definitely related to your academic performance. And once you give yourself permission to skip one single class, it becomes easier to do it the next time, and the time after that. Studies indicate that on any given day, approximately one-third of your classmates will miss class, and that most students think that several absences during a term is "the standard."[2] Exercise good judgment, even if your classmates don't!

4. **Show up mentally.** Showing up means more than just occupying a seat in the classroom. It means thinking about what you bring to the class as a learner on any particular day. Do a mental "Readiness Check" when you arrive in class. If you're not ready, what can you do to rally for the cause?

5. **Choose your seat strategically.** Imagine paying $150 for a concert ticket, just like everyone else, and then electing to sit in the nosebleed section as high up and far away from the action as you could get. Sitting in the back means you're more likely to let your mind wander and less likely to hear clearly. Sitting in the front means you'll keep yourself accountable by being in full view of the instructor and the rest of the class. What's the best spot for great concentration? Front and center, literally—the "T zone"! In one study, students who sat at the back of a large auditorium were six times more likely to fail the course, even though the instructor had assigned seats randomly![3]

6. **Bring your tools.** Bring a writing utensil and notebook with you to every class. Your instructor may also ask you to bring your textbook, calculator, a blue book or scantron form for an exam, or other necessary items. If so, do it. Question: How seriously would you take a carpenter who showed up to work without a hammer, nails, and screwdriver? Get the point?

7. **Don't sit by your best friend.** Resist the temptation to sit next to your best buddy in order to catch up during class. Of course, it's important to have friends, but class is hardly the best time to devote yourself to helping your friendship blossom.

8. **Posture counts!** Your parents may have told you more than once as a kid: "Sit up straight!" Sitting up straight in class will help you develop a healthy mind. It's hard to focus when you're slouched into a position that screams, "I could really use a power nap right about now!" When your body says, "I'm ready to learn," your mind follows suit.

9. **Maintain your health.** Being sick can take its toll on your ability to concentrate, listen well, and participate. Prevent that from happening by getting enough sleep, eating well, and exercising. Remember, *energy management* is key to your ability to focus.

10. **Focus.** After sitting down in class each day, take a moment to clear your head of all daydreams, to-do's, and worries. Take a deep breath and remind yourself of the opportunity to learn that lies ahead. Think of yourself as a reporter at a press conference, listening carefully because you'll be writing a story about what's going on. You *will* be writing a "story"—often in response to an essay question on an exam!

Follow the Rules of Engagement.

Just as is the case with most places you can think of, college classrooms have rules about how to behave. You don't find people yelling in church or staring at other people in elevators or telling jokes at funerals. There are rules about how to behave in a variety of contexts, and college classrooms are no exception.

GAB – NO!

1. **Be aware that gab is not a gift.** In class, talking while others are speaking is inappropriate. And it's certainly not a gift—especially to your instructor. In fact, side conversations while your instructor is lecturing or your classmates are contributing to the discussion are downright rude. If you're seated next to a gabber, don't get sucked in. Use body language to communicate that you're there to learn, not to gab. If that's not enough, politely say something like, "I really need to pay attention right now. Let's talk more later, okay?" Don't let other students cheat you out of learning.

2. **Control your hunger.** If your class meets through a meal hour, get in the habit of eating before or after class. Crunching and munching in the classroom may get in the way of others' learning, not to mention the distraction caused by enticing smells. Instructors differ on their preferences here. It's a good idea to find out what your instructors' preferences are, and then abide by them.

3. **Turn off your cell phone, please!** There's a reason why people are asked to turn off their cell phones before concerts, athletic events, or movies. Imagine being in a jam-packed theater trying to follow the film's plot with cell phones going off every few seconds. You've paid good money to see a film. The same thing goes for your college classes.

4. **Better late than never?** Students arriving late and leaving early are annoying, not only to your instructor, but to your classmates. To them, it

looks like you don't value the other students or the class content. How would you like dinner guests to arrive an hour late, after you'd slaved over a hot stove all day? Your instructors have prepared for class, and they feel the same way. Build in time to find a parking place, hike to the building where class is held, or stop for a coffee. Do everything you can to avoid coming late and leaving early.

5. **Actively choose to engage, not disengage.** Engagement isn't something that just happens to you while you're not looking. It's a choice you make, and sometimes it's a difficult choice because the material isn't naturally appealing to you, or the course is a required one you didn't choose, or you're just in a bad mood. Choose to engage, anyway. Instead of actively choosing to disengage in class by sleeping through lectures, surfing the Internet, or texting friends, choose to engage by leaning forward, listening, finding your own ways to connect to the material, and thinking of questions to ask.

ACTIVELY CHOOSE TO ENGAGE.

CHOOSE IT!

LISTEN.

YOU CAN DO IT!

Listening with Focus

Listening with focus is more than just physically hearing words as they stream by. It's actually a complicated process that's hard work.

"Easy Listening" Is for Elevators— Focused Listening Is for Classrooms

Stores, restaurants, and elevators are known for their programmed, background easy listening music. Chances are you hardly notice it's there. Listening in class, however, requires actual skill, and you'll be doing a great deal of it as a college student. Experts estimate that the average student spends 80 percent of class time listening to lectures.[4]

Many of us think that listening is easy. If you happen to be around when there's something to listen to, you can't help but listen. Not so! Did you know that when you're listening at your best, your breathing rate, heartbeat, and body temperature all increase? Just as with physical exercise, your body works harder when you're engaged in focused listening. When all is said and done, listening is really about energy management. You can't listen well when your energy is zapped, when you've stayed up all night, or when your stomach is growling fiercely. Focused listening means that you are concentrating fully on what's going on in class.

Here are some techniques for improving your listening skills in the classroom. Read through the list, then go back and check off the ones you're willing to try harder to do in class this week. *TAKE IT EASY!*

> **Calm yourself.** Take a few deep breaths with your eyes closed to help you put all those nagging distractions out of your mind during class time.

> **Be open.** Keep an open mind and view your class as yet another opportunity to strengthen your intellect and learn something new. Wisdom comes from a broad understanding of many things, rather than from a consistently limited focus what's going on in your own world.

USE THOSE AROUND YOU TO LEARN.

© Larry Harwood Photography. Property of Cengage Learning.

" Politeness is the art of choosing among one's real thoughts. "

Adlai Stevenson II, U.S. Presidential candidate (1900–1965)

> **Don't make snap judgments.** Remember, you don't have to like your instructor's wardrobe to respect his knowledge. Focus on the content he's offering you, even if you don't agree with it. You may change your mind later when you learn more. Don't jump to conclusions about content *or* style.

> **Assume responsibility.** Speak up! Ask questions! Even if you have an instructor with an accent who's difficult to understand, the burden of understanding course content rests with you. You will interact with people with all sorts of accents, voices, and speech patterns throughout your life. It's up to you to improve the situation.

> **Watch for gestures that communicate "Here comes something important!"** Some typical examples include raising an index finger, turning to face the class, leaning forward from behind the lectern, walking up the aisle, or using specific facial expressions or gestures.

> **Listen for speech patterns that subtly communicate "Make sure you include this in your notes!"** For example, listen for changes in the rate, volume, or tone of speech, longer than usual pauses, or repeated information.

> **Uncover general themes or roadmaps for each lecture.** See if you can figure out where your instructor is taking you *while* he's taking you there. Always ask yourself, "Where's he going with this? What's he getting at? How does this relate to what was already said?"

> **Appreciate your instructor's prep time.** For every hour of lecture time, your teacher has worked for hours to prepare. Although she may make it look easy, her lecture has involved researching, organizing, creating a PowerPoint presentation, overheads, or a podcast, and preparing notes and handouts.

Listen Hard!

It's estimated that college students spend ten hours per week listening to lectures.[5] Instructors can speak 2,500–5,000 words during a fifty-minute lecture. That's a lot of words flying by at breakneck speed, so it's important to listen correctly. But what does *that* mean?

Think about the various situations in which you find yourself listening. You often listen to empty chit-chat on your way to class. "Hey, how's it going?" when you spot your best friend in the hallway is an example, right? Listening in this type of situation doesn't require a lot of brainpower. Although you wouldn't want to spend too much time on chit-chat, if you refused to engage in any at all, you'd probably be seen by others as odd, withdrawn, shy, or stuck up.

You also listen in challenging situations, some that are emotionally charged; for example, a friend needs to vent, relieve stress, or verbalize her anxieties. Most people who are blowing off steam aren't looking for you to fix their problems. They just want to be heard and hear you say something like "I understand" or "That's too bad."

KEEP KEEN.

How **FULL** is your plate?

Are you a fast food fanatic, mostly because it's fast? Do your days whiz by as you rush from thing to thing? Time management expert Edward Hallowell writes, "We go fast not just because we're busy, but because speed is fun. Speed grips attention. Speed excites. Speed speeds you out of boredom. Nothing is boring if it's fast enough." But what's the down side of speed? What do we lose? Are our lives long on stress and short on satisfaction?

Rafa Irusta, 2010/Used under license from Shutterstock.com

TRY IT!

As you go through this week, make a point of slowing down—and accomplishing more. Keep a record of something you do each day—slower, longer, and better—by consciously remembering that "slow and steady wins the race."

Listening to chit-chat and listening in emotionally charged situations require what are called **soft listening skills**. You must be accepting, sensitive, and nonjudgmental. You don't have to assess, analyze, or conclude. You just have to be there for someone else.

But these two types of listening situations don't describe all the kinds of listening you do. When you're listening to new information, as you do in your college classes, or when you're listening to someone trying to persuade you of something, you have to pay close attention, think critically, and ultimately make decisions about what you're hearing. Is something true or false? Right or wrong? How do you know? When you're listening to a person trying to inform you or to persuade you, you need **hard listening skills.** In situations like these you must evaluate, analyze, and decide.

One mistake many students make in class is listening the wrong way. They should be using their hard listening skills, rather than sitting back and letting information float over them. Soft listening skills don't help you in class. You must listen intently, think critically, and analyze carefully what you're hearing. It's important to note that neither listening mode is better than the other. They are each simply better suited to different situations. But soft listening won't get you the results you want in your classes. You don't need to be there for your instructor; you need to be there for yourself.[6]

You may find many of your classes to be naturally fascinating learning experiences. But for others, you will need to be convinced. Even if you don't find Intro to Whatever to be the most engaging subject in the world, you may find yourself fascinated by your instructor. Most people are interested in other people. What makes him tick? Why was she drawn to this field? If you find it hard to get interested in the material, trick yourself by paying attention to the person delivering the message. Sometimes focusing on something about the speaker can help you focus on the subject matter, too. And you may just find out that you actually do find this class to be valuable. While tricking yourself isn't always a good idea, it *can* work if you know what you're doing and why.

Get Wired for Sound

Increasingly instructors are providing podcasts and videocasts of their lectures so that you can *preview* the lecture in advance or *review* it after class. Some textbooks (like this one) offer chapter summaries you can listen to on the subway, in the gym, at home during a blizzard, or in bed while recovering from the flu via your computer or digital-audio player.

Regardless of your learning style, recorded lectures allow you to re-listen to difficult concepts as many times as needed. You can take part in the live action in class and take notes later while re-listening to the podcast. In one study, students who re-listened to a lecture one, two, or three times increased their lecture notes substantially each time.[7] Of course, recorded lectures aren't meant to excuse you from attending class, and in order to take advantage of them, you actually have to find time to listen to them. They're supplemental tools to *reinforce* learning for busy students on the go, which is virtually *everyone* these days.[8]

EVERYONES DOING IT! ....

Listening Tips if English Is Your Second Language

It's normal to feel overwhelmed in the classroom as a new student, but especially if your first language isn't English. The academic environment in higher education can be stressful and competitive. It's even more stressful if you're also dealing with a new and different culture. You will need to give yourself time to adapt to all of these changes. In the meantime, here are some suggestions for improving your ability to listen well in class:

- Talk to your instructor before the course begins. Let her know that English is not your native language, but that you're very interested in learning. Ask for any suggestions on how you can increase your chances of success in the class. Your instructor will most likely be willing to provide you with extra help, knowing you're willing to do your part to overcome the language barrier.

- Try to get the main points of your instructor's lecture. You don't have to understand every word.

- Write down words to look up in the dictionary later. Keep a running list and check them all after class. Missing out on one important term can hurt your chances of understanding something else down the line.

- Don't be afraid to ask questions. If you're too uncomfortable to ask during class, make use of your instructor's office hours or e-mail address to get your questions answered. Also, teaching assistants and peer tutors may be available to help you.

- Use all support materials available for the class. Find out if your instructor posts his notes on the course website or if they are available as handouts. Some instructors offer guided notes or skeleton outlines for students to fill in throughout the lecture. Some large lectures are videotaped for viewing by students at a later time. Make full use of podcasts of lectures, if they're available, so that you can listen more than once to portions you found confusing in class. Use any tools available to help reinforce lecture content.

- Team up with a classmate whose native language is English. Clarify your notes and fill in gaps.

- Form a study group with other classmates. Meet on a regular basis so that you can help one another. Remember: just because your native language isn't English doesn't mean you don't have something to offer the other members of your study group.

- Be patient. It will take some time to adjust to the accents of your various instructors. After a few weeks of class, you'll find it easier to understand what is being said.

- Practice your English comprehension by listening to talk radio or watching television or movies. You'll hear a variety of regional accents, for example, and broaden your understanding of American culture.

- Take an "English as a Second Language" course if you think it would help. It's important to keep up with the academic demands of college, and further development of your English skills may improve your comprehension and boost your confidence.

- If you continue to feel overwhelmed and unable to cope after several weeks in school, find out if your campus has an International Students Office, and enlist support from people who are trained to help.[9]

> The most basic and powerful way to connect to another person is to listen. Just listen. Perhaps the most important thing we ever give each other is our attention.
>
> *Rachel Naomi Remen,*
> *physician and author*

Identify Lecture Styles So You Can Modify Listening Styles

Regardless of how challenging it is to listen with focus, being successful in college will require you to do just that—focus—no matter what class or which instructor. Sometimes your instructors are **facilitators**, who help you discover information on your own in new ways. Other times they are **orators**, who lecture as their primary means of delivering information. If you're not an aural learner, listening with focus to lectures will be a challenge for you.

facilitators guides
orators public speakers

Chances are you won't be able to change your instructors' lecturing styles. And even if you could, different students react differently to different lecture styles. But what you can do is expand your own skills as a listener—no matter what class or which instructor. Take a look at the lecture styles coming up and see if you recognize them.

Sophie Louise Phelps, 2010. Used under license from Shutterstock.com

> **The Rapid-Fire Lecturer:** You may have found yourself in a situation like Rachel's with an instructor who lectures so fast it makes your head spin. Listening and taking notes in a class like this are not easy. By the end of class your hand aches from gripping your pen and writing furiously. Since there'll be no time to relax, you'll need to make certain you're ready for this class by taking all the suggestions in this chapter to heart. Read ahead so that you recognize points the instructor makes. Also take advantage of whatever **supplementary** materials this teacher provides in the way of audio support, online lecture notes, or PowerPoint handouts.

supplementary extra

NEVER MET A PROFESSOR LIKE THIS.

contemplate consider fully

ruminate to think over or meditate on

chew on to think about

pontificating speaking in an extremely dignified manner

NIK, 2010. Used under license from Shutterstock.com

HUMAN NATURE ←
PHILOSOPHY

narvikk/iStockphoto.com

· PUBLIC
SPEAKING
COURSE

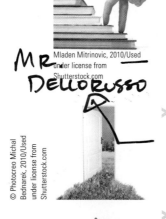

Kuzma, 2010/Used under license from Shutterstock.com

MR
DELLORUSSO

Mladen Mitrinovic, 2010/Used under license from Shutterstock.com

© Photocreo Michal Bednarek, 2010/Used under license from Shutterstock.com

Arkady, 2010/Used under license from Shutterstock.com

> **The Slow-Go Lecturer:** Instead of rushing, some lecturers move very slowly. They **contemplate**, **ruminate**, and **chew on** every word before they say each one. This lecturer proceeds so slowly that there are pauses—seconds long—between phrases, while he paces back and forth, **pontificating**. Your attention tends to drift because you become impatient and stop listening. Instead, discipline yourself to use the extra time to your advantage by predicting what's coming next or by clarifying what's just been said in your own mind.

> **The All-Over-the-Map Lecturer:** Organization is not this lecturer's strong suit. While the lecture may be organized in the lecturer's mind, what comes out is difficult to follow. In this case, it will be up to you to organize the lecture content yourself.

> **The Content-Intensive Lecturer:** This lecturer is hardly aware that anyone else is in the room, determined to cover a certain amount of material in a particular amount of time. This teacher may use specific language related to the subject that you will need to learn rapidly to keep up. Prepare yourself for a potentially rich learning environment, but be sure to ask questions right away if you find yourself confused.

> **The Review-the-Text Lecturer:** This lecturer will follow the textbook closely, summarizing and highlighting important points. You may assume it's not important to attend class, but watch out for this trap! Receiving the same information in more than one format (reading *and* listening) can be a great way to learn.

> **The Go-Beyond-the-Text Lecturer:** This lecturer will use class time to provide examples, tell stories, and bring in outside materials. Keeping up with reading in the text will be important so that you understand the additional information that you receive in class.

> **The Active-Learning Lecturer:** This lecturer may choose not to lecture at all or to alternate between short lectures and activities, exercises, and role plays. While you may find it easier to get engaged in this type of class, and you'll most likely appreciate the teacher's creativity, remember that you are still responsible for connecting what happens in class to the course material itself. You will need to read, digest, and process the information on your own outside of class.

YOUR TOUGHEST TASK

In Class: Think about the courses you're taking this term. Use the following form to analyze your various instructors' lecture styles. Be careful not to be too obvious as you listen and analyze their styles, of course, but after your chart is completed, decide what *you* can do as a listener to make adjustments in your toughest class. To get an idea of how to fill out the chart, look at what Rachel's entries for her child development class might have been. Doing this for all your classes may give you some insights about why one particular class is your toughest and help you modify your note-taking skills to what works best for that particular lecture style.

On the Job: Think about how this activity applies to listening at work, too—perhaps to listening to your boss. Have you ever noticed that some co-workers are harder to follow as you listen to them speak than others? This analysis sheet may help you find ways to adapt to those challenges at work.[10]

LECTURER STYLE ANALYSIS WORKSHEET			*No Forever* *No Never*
COURSES	**Example:** *Child Development 1*		
EMPHASIS Content, students, or both?	*Teacher emphasizes content, primarily. She lectures for the full class period with little student interaction.*	*KEEPS STUDENTS INTERESTED BUT KEEPING THE MATERIAL.*	
ORGANIZATION Structured or unstructured	*Lectures seem disorganized with notes written all over the board.*	*THE BOOK*	
PACE Fast, slow, or medium?	*Very fast*	*MODERATE*	
VISUAL AIDS Used? Useful?	*Board hard to see from the back of the room.*	*NOOOOOOO*	
EXAMPLES Used? Useful?	*She needs to provide more real examples that students can relate to.*	*GREAT!*	
LANGUAGE Terms defined? Vocabulary understandable?	*The language isn't too hard, but I can't focus on what she's saying.*	*MESSES UP ON WORDS*	
DELIVERY Animated via body language?	*Delivery style isn't lively and interesting. Instructor doesn't notice when students aren't paying attention.*	*NOT VERY. CRACKS JOKES THO*	
QUESTIONS Encouraged?	*She rarely pauses to take questions.*	*ALWAYS*	
Proposed adjustments in my toughest class:	*Make special arrangements to meet with the instructor outside her office hours.*		

Turn Listening Skills into Note-Taking Skills

EXERCISE 7.1

How Well Do You Listen?

Now that you've read about focused listening, see how the following statements apply to you. Check the box that most applies to what you usually do in the classroom. Use this self-assessment to develop a plan for improvement, particularly so that you're listening at your best to take careful, useful notes.

Listening Statements	Always True of Me	Sometimes True of Me	Never True of Me
I stay awake during class so that I can take good notes to use later while studying.	✓		
I maintain eye contact with the speaker.	✓		
I don't *pretend* to be interested in the subject.		✓	
I understand my instructor's questions.		✓	
I try to summarize the information in my notes.	✓		
I look for organizational patterns in the lecture and identify them in my notes (*e.g.*, causes and effects, lists of items).	✓		
I set a purpose for listening, like trying to capture all the key ideas and examples that explain them.		✓	
I don't daydream during class, leaving gaps in my notes.			✓
I try to predict the lecturer's next main point.		✓	
I take notes regularly.	✓		
I don't let external distractions such as loud noises, late-arriving students, etc. interfere with my note-taking.		✓	
I try to determine the speaker's purpose.		✓	
I recognize that the speaker may be biased about the subject, but I don't let that affect my note-taking.			✓
I write down questions the instructor poses during class.		✓	
I copy down main points and examples from the board or screen.	✓		
Total check marks for each column:	6	7	2

Add up the check marks in each column to learn the results of your analysis. Pay particular attention to the total in the "Always True of Me" column.

13–15 "Always True of Me": You're probably an excellent listener, both in the classroom and in other situations. Keep up the good work.

10–12 "Always True of Me": You are a good listener, but you need to fine-tune a few of your listening skills.

7–9 "Always True of Me": You need to change some behaviors so that you get more out of your classes.

6 or less "Always True of Me" or 7 or more "Never True of Me": You need to learn better listening skills if you want to achieve academic success in college.[11]

Listening in class is one thing. Taking notes is quite another. You must be a good listener to take good notes, but being a good listener alone doesn't automatically make you a good note-taker. Note-taking is a crucial and complex skill, and doing well on tests isn't based on luck. It's based on combining preparation and opportunity—in other words, knowing how to take useful notes in class that work for you.

Actually, one reason that note-taking is so important in the learning process is that it uses all four VARK categories: *visual* (you see your instructor and the screen, if overheads or PowerPoint slides are being used), *aural* (you listen to the lecture), *read/write* (you write what you see and hear so that you can read it later to review), and *kinesthetic* (the physical act of writing opens up a pathway to the brain). Have you ever thought about it that way before?

According to one study, 99 percent of college students take notes during lectures, and 94 percent of students believe that note-taking is important.[12] These are good signs, but are these students taking notes correctly, as a result of focused listening? If 99 percent of college students are taking notes, why isn't nearly everyone getting straight A's? Here are some reasons:

- Students typically record less than 40 percent of the lecture's main content ideas in their notes.[13]

- Only 47 percent of students actually review their notes later to see what they've written.

- Only 29 percent edit their notes later by adding, deleting, or reorganizing material.

- A full 12 percent do nothing other than recopy them verbatim. — *ME*

- Some students never do anything with their notes once they leave class![14]

Does note-taking make a difference? Absolutely. During lectures, it serves two fundamental purposes: It helps you understand what you're learning at the time and it helps you preserve information to study later. In other words, both the *process* of note-taking (as you record information) and the *product* (your notes themselves) are important to learning. There is strong evidence that taking notes during a lecture leads to higher achievement than not taking notes, and working with your notes later increases your chances for academic achievement even more. Studies show that if you take notes, you have a 50 percent chance of recalling that information at test time versus a 15 percent chance of remembering the same information if you didn't take notes.[15]

Different Strokes for Different Folks: Note-Taking by the System and Subject

Now that we know just how important listening and note-taking are, let's ask a crucial question. Exactly how do you take good notes? Interestingly, when it comes to note-taking, "different strokes for different folks" is literally true. Different note-taking systems work best for different lecture styles, different learning styles, and different subjects—math versus history, for example. If your instructor uses a "Rapid Fire" lecture style, you'll need to write quickly,

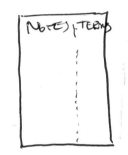

SYMBOLISIM.

perhaps using abbreviations, no matter which note-taking system you use. If your instructor is an "All-Over-the-Map" lecturer, you may have to create the connections on paper as she talks about all kinds of ideas.

No matter which note-taking strategy you choose to use in a particular situation, an important question to ask is: What constitutes good notes? The answer is: Writing an accurate, complete, organized account of what you hear in class (or read in your textbook, which is discussed later in this chapter). How do you know if your notes are good? Show them to your instructor and get input, or assess your strategy after you see your results on the first exam. Your note-taking skills should steadily improve as you evolve as a student.[16]

However you decide to take notes in a particular class, it's good to have some general goals:

1. **Capture main ideas.** Listen for an organizing pattern. Has the instructor been covering the subject by major time periods? Has she been listing contributors to the field by specific discoveries? What's her system? Listen for verbal clues your instructor emphasizes or repeats several times, notice what he writes on the board, or watch for major bullets or itemized steps on the screen. In the lecture Rachel was trying to focus on in class, her instructor made it easy to recognize main points by numbering them, "first," "second," and so forth. If portions of the lecture are highlighted verbally, these portions are probably important. Listen for signal words and phrases such as "There are three reasons . . ." "On the other hand . . ." "For example . . ." "In summary . . ."

2. **Note whether a handout accompanies lecture materials.** If so, chances are that the information is considered to be important. If the instructor interrupts the lecture to give more detailed examples from a handout, he must consider doing so important enough to take up class time. Keep all handouts, and assume they'll be worth reviewing at exam time.

3. **Write down examples or key words from stories that will help anchor the main points.** If you were a classmate of Rachel's, you may not remember exactly when the social/emotional milestone begins to develop in children, but writing down the instructor's story about something funny her own little girl did may help trigger your memory.

4. **When in doubt, write it down.** If you're not sure whether to write something down, use the motto, "Better safe than sorry." If you don't know a word the instructor uses, leave a blank to show you omitted something, or sound it out as you're writing and come back to it later. Put the lecture in your own words for the most part, but write down formulas, definitions, charts, diagrams, and specific facts verbatim. Also, write down good points made by classmates. Not all the words of wisdom in class will come from your instructor. If you've prepared for class by reading the assignment and listened to the lecture, and a classmate makes a point during a discussion that adds new information, write it down!

5. **Consider your learning style preferences.** If you're a visual learner, a note-taking system that works well for you may not work particularly well for a classmate who has a different learning style. Drawing all over your paper may help you see connections, while a classmate next to you is writing

the same information down in a structured outline format. If a note-taking system seems awkward to you even after you've tried it for awhile, you may be better off trying a different one.

6. **Create a shorthand system that works.** When you're taking notes quickly, as you often do in class, you won't have time to write out every word your instructor utters. Use abbreviations or a shorthand system that you create for yourself. The last thing you want is to look at your notes as you begin to study for an exam and wonder what you meant by a string of letters that makes no sense now. So make an abbreviation "dictionary" for yourself that you use regularly, like this:

Symbol	Meaning	Example
→	leads to, produces, causes, makes	Practice → perfect.
←	comes from, is the result of	Tsunamis ← earthquakes
↑	increased, increasing, goes up, rises	Taxes ↑ 100% last year.
↓	decreased, decreasing, lowering	Salaries ↓ 10% this year.
#	number	Retry problem #3.
@	at	Due @ 4:00p.m.
/	per	25 miles/gallon
p	page	Read p 99.
pp	pages	Study pp 99–105.
¶	paragraph	Revise ¶ #4.
w/o	without	They revised w/o reading carefully.
?	question	Answer ? 1.
w/i	within	There are problems w/i the tax laws.
i.e.	that is	The SAT, i.e. a college entrance exam, is challenging.
e.g.	for example	Professionals, e.g. doctors and lawyers, have advanced degrees.
etc.	et cetera, so forth	Clinton, Reagan, etc. were popular presidents.
b/c	because	We pay taxes b/c it's the law.
b/4	before	Incidents b/4 the attack.
esp.	especially	Tobacco, esp. cigarettes, causes cancer.
min.	minimum	The min. wage may go up.
max.	maximum	The max. number of people in an elevator is 8.
gov't.	government	The gov't. helped the people.
ASAP	as soon as possible	Complete your certificate program ASAP.
wrt	write	wrt #3 (write number 3)
yr / yrs	year, years	She's 18 yrs old.

Based on http://www.english-zone.com/study/symbols.html

So what are the various note-taking methods? What are the steps involved in using each one? Knowing your options, developing your skills, and learning flexibility as a note-taker are keys to your success.

Outlining

Outlining is probably the oldest, and perhaps the most trusted form of taking notes. The problem, of course, is that not all instructors speak from an outline. Rachel's instructor probably did, and if Rachel had been able to focus, outlining may have worked well. Here's what Rachel's notes would have looked like. She'd listen for key points, like the five developmental milestones, and list examples beneath each one, like this:

> **Child Development 1, Week 4**
>
> 1. Child development involves learning and mastering skills like sitting, walking, talking, skipping, and tying shoes.
>   A. Developmental milestones are learned during predictable time periods.
>   B. Children develop skills in five main areas of development:
>   1. Cognitive development: ability to learn and solve problems.
>   a. two-month-old baby learning to explore the environment with hands or eyes
>   b. five-year-old learning how to do simple math problems
>   2. Social/emotional development: ability to interact with others, including helping themselves and self-control.
>   a. six-week-old baby smiling
>   b. ten-month-old baby waving bye-bye
>   c. five-year-old boy knowing how to take turns in games at school
>   3. Speech/language development: ability to both understand and use language.
>   a. 12-month-old baby saying his first words
>   b. a two-year-old naming parts of her body
>   c. a five-year-old learning to say "feet" instead of "foots"

She's listed the instructor's main points and several examples below each point to help her remember what it's about. At the end of the lecture, she could have included a **summary** of her notes. Summarizing is an excellent way to make sure you've understood the gist of all the information you've written down.

summary a condensed version of the main points

> Summary:
>
> Children reach developmental milestones in five areas at fairly predictable ages. These five areas are cognitive, social/emotional, speech/language, fine motor skills, and gross motor skills.

Of course, if your instructor's lecture is less organized, you can elect to use an informal variation of outlining, like listing bullets, and perhaps even color-coding them so they're easier to remember, as shown here:

Child Development 1, Week 4

Child development = learning & mastering skills
- sitting
- walking
- talking
- skipping
- tying shoes

Children develop skills in five main areas of development:
1. Cognitive development: ability to learn and solve problems.
2. Social/emotional development: ability to interact with others, including helping themselves and self-control.
3. Speech/language development: ability to both understand and use language.

Even if your instructor is flashing PowerPoint slides on the screen, don't count on your memory to do all the work. You have to take notes yourself to help the information stick.

USE THE CORNELL

USE IT

The Cornell System

The Cornell system of note-taking, devised by educator Walter Pauk, suggests this. On each page of your notebook, draw a line from top to bottom about one and a half inches from the left edge of your paper. (Some notebook paper already has a red line there.) Take notes on the right side of the line. Your notes should include main ideas, examples, short phrases, and definitions, for example—almost like an outline.

Leave the left side blank to fill in later with key words or questions you'd like answered, as Rachel has done in Figure 7.1. After class as you review your notes, put your hand or a sheet of paper over the right side and use the words or questions you've written on the left side as prompts to see if you can remember what's on the right side.[17] By doing this to recall the lecture, you can get a good idea of how much of the information you've really understood.

Luck is what happens when preparation meets opportunity.

Darrell Royal, football coach

KEY WORDS AND QUESTIONS	SHORT PHRASES, EXAMPLES, DEFINITIONS
Child development	—Every child goes through.
Developmental milestones	—learning and mastering skills (sitting, walking, talking, skipping, tying shoes, etc.) — predictable time periods
Five main areas of development	1. Cognitive development Ability to learn and solve problems —two-month-old baby learning to explore the environment with hands or eyes —five-year-old learning to do simple math
Was it five main areas or six?	2. Social/emotional development Ability to interact with others, including helping themselves and self-control —six-week-old baby smiling —ten-month-old baby waving goodbye —five-year-old knowing how to take turns in games at school

FIGURE 7.1

Child Development Milestones: Cornell System Example

Mind Maps

An alternative to the Cornell system, or a way to expand on it, is to create mind maps. Mind maps use both sides of your brain: the logical, orderly left side and the visual, creative right side. What they're particularly good for is showing the relationship between ideas. Mind maps are also generally a good note-taking method for visual learners, and even the physical act of drawing one may help you remember the information, particularly if you're a kinesthetic learner. To give mind mapping a try, here are some useful suggestions:

1. **Use extra wide paper (11 × 17 or legal size).** You won't want to write vertically (which is hard to read) if you can help it.

2. **Write the main concept of the lecture in the center of the page.** Draw related concepts coming from the center.

3. **Limit your labels to key words so that your mind map is visually clear.**

4. **Use colors, symbols, and images to make your mind map livelier and more memorable.**

5. **Consider using software such as MindManager, MindManuals, Mind-Plugs, MindMapper, or MindGenius, which are all powerful brainstorming and organizing tools.** As you type, these programs will anticipate relationships and help you draw a mind map on screen.

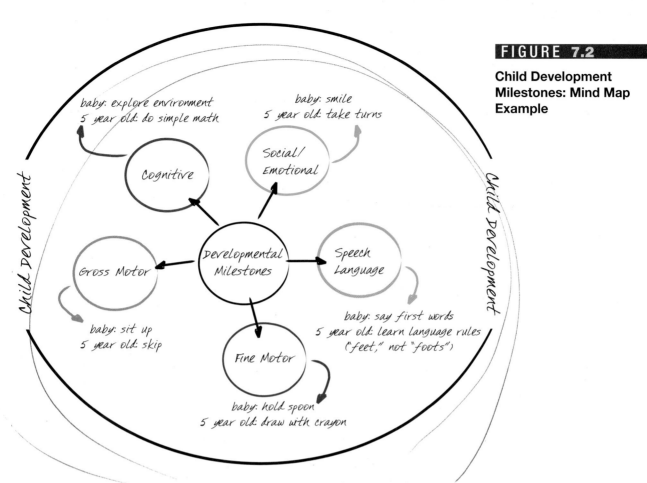

FIGURE 7.2

Child Development
Milestones: Mind Map
Example

Note-Taking on Instructor-Provided Handouts

PowerPoint Miniatures. Some instructors provide full-text lecture notes on-line or copies of their PowerPoint slides (three or six miniatures on a page). Instructors may hand out PowerPoint miniatures in class before the lecture, so you can follow along, hand them out after the lecture so that you still have to take your own notes but have the print outs of the miniatures as back-up, or e-mail them as attachments (see Figure 7.3). If you have copies of the Power-Point slides to use during class, write in specifics on the lines provided next to each slide miniature, more or less as you would if you were using the Cornell System. Put down examples that are discussed in class but don't appear on the slide, or a story that will help you remember a main point on a slide. If they're

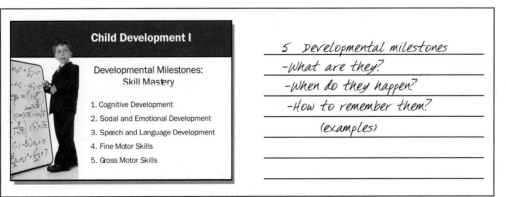

FIGURE 7.3

**Child Development
Milestones:
PowerPoint
Miniatures Example**

> **I make progress by having people around me who are smarter than I am and listening to them. And I assume that everyone is smarter about something than I am.**
>
> *Henry J. Kaiser, American industrialist (1882–1967)*

handed out after class, transfer your own notes to the PowerPoint fill-in lines. If they're e-mailed to you before or after class, make sure you use them. They're "insurance" that you have access to what appeared in class on the screen. Tools such as these can be a valuable resource, if you remember to use them. Don't rely on PowerPoints your instructors provide to the extent that you skip taking notes yourself in class altogether. Although it's helpful to have them available as a tool, you still need to take notes on your own to help you process the information you're listening to in class.

Guided Notes. Your instructor may actually help you to pay attention in class by providing what are called "Guided Notes," or copies of lecture outlines or PowerPoint miniatures with key words missing, so that you must listen closely to "fill in the blanks." In one study, students in a college algebra class who used guided notes with problem sets they worked out together in groups liked their math class and did much better than comparable students who weren't using guided notes.[18]

Parallel Note-Taking. Because many instructors today provide e-support for lectures, either through web notes, hard copies of onscreen slides, lecture outlines, or a full transcript, parallel note-taking may be particularly useful, if you go about it in the right way.[19] Here's how it works, ideally.

If they're available, print out lecture notes before class and bring them with you, preferably in a ring binder. As your instructor lectures, use the back (blank) side of each page to record your own notes as the notes from the ongoing, real-time lecture face you. You can parallel what you're hearing from your instructor with your own on-the-spot, self-recorded notes, using a Cornell format on each blank page. It's the best of both worlds! You're reading, writing, and listening at the same time, fully immersing yourself in immediate and longer-lasting learning. Figure 7.4 illustrates how parallel note-taking might look for Rachel in her childhood development class.

FIGURE 7.4

Child Development Milestones: Parallel Note-Taking Example

[Fill in the blank page during actual lecture.]

My In-Class Lecture Notes

Every child develops skills like learning to sit up, walk, talk, skip, and tie shoes.

These are called developmental milestones, and they happen to most children around the same age.

Children learn skills in five main areas of development: cognitive, social/emotional, speech/language, fine, and gross motor skills:

[Print out instructor's notes and place in binder.]

Instructor's Lecture Notes

Child development is a process every child goes through. This process involves learning and mastering skills like sitting, walking, talking, skipping, and tying shoes. Children learn these skills, called developmental milestones, during predictable time periods. Children develop skills in five main areas of development: First, let's look at cognitive development. This is the child's ability to learn and solve problems. For example, this includes a two-month-old baby learning to explore the environment with hands or eyes or a five-year-old learning how to do simple math problems. Second, social/emotional development is the child's ability to interact with others, including helping themselves and self-control. Examples of this type of development would include a six-week-old baby smiling, a ten-month-old baby waving bye-bye, or a five-year-old boy knowing how to take turns in games at school.

Note-Taking by the Book

So far this chapter has discussed taking notes in class. What about taking notes as you read from a textbook? Is that important, too? The answer: absolutely! It's easy to go on auto-pilot as you read and have no idea what you read afterwards! Instead, take notes in the margins, on sticky notes, or better yet, keep a spiral-bound notebook next to you, and fill it with your own words as you read. Jot down questions, summarize main points, or use the Cornell System. Actually, the best thing to do is to read a section, close the book, and write down what you remember. You'll prove to yourself what you absorbed and what you didn't. Then you can dive back into the textbook again and clarify concepts that are still fuzzy.[20]

CORNELL SYSTEM

Note-Taking by the Subject

Beyond figuring out which note-taking style seems to "fit" you best, think about times when the subject dictates that you vary your note-taking style. In your American History class, it may make sense to take your notes along a timeline of the beginning of World War II, for example (see Figure 7.5). Since your instructor and your textbook report key events that took place during World War II chronologically, along a time line, you might want your notes to reflect that.

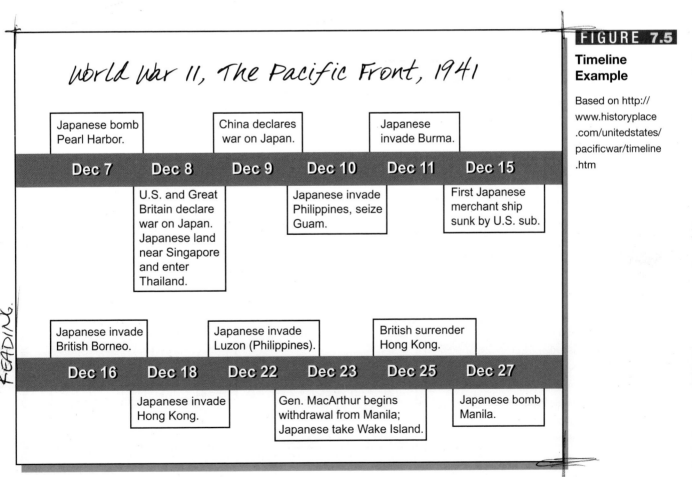

READING.

World War II, The Pacific Front, 1941

Japanese bomb Pearl Harbor.		China declares war on Japan.		Japanese invade Burma.	
Dec 7	**Dec 8**	**Dec 9**	**Dec 10**	**Dec 11**	**Dec 15**
	U.S. and Great Britain declare war on Japan. Japanese land near Singapore and enter Thailand.		Japanese invade Philippines, seize Guam.		First Japanese merchant ship sunk by U.S. sub.

Japanese invade British Borneo.		Japanese invade Luzon (Philippines).		British surrender Hong Kong.	
Dec 16	**Dec 18**	**Dec 22**	**Dec 23**	**Dec 25**	**Dec 27**
	Japanese invade Hong Kong.		Gen. MacArthur begins withdrawal from Manila; Japanese take Wake Island.		Japanese bomb Manila.

FIGURE 7.5

Timeline Example

Based on http://www.historyplace.com/unitedstates/pacificwar/timeline.htm

YOU NEED TO RE-READ THIS CHAPTER?!.

YES! △

However, in your college algebra class, you may want to take notes very differently. Let's say, for example, that your instructor lectures by working problems on a white board or by projecting them on the screen. Then you are asked to work a problem and then talk it over with a classmate next to you. You may want to divide up your notes into columns by proposing a solution and then showing how you arrived at your answer. Having a record of how you worked a problem can be a valuable aid later when you're studying for a test that will probably contain algebra problems very much like the ones you solve regularly in class. Write everything down, and skip a few lines if there's something you want to fill in later (see Figure 7.6).

Mind mapping, on the other hand, is particularly useful in criminal justice, physiology, biology, psychology, and education courses, where relationships between concepts are important.[21] Some students may make the mistake of thinking that mind maps are "scribbling," but the process of making connections on paper helps you make those same connections in your brain. Successful note-taking does mean "different strokes for different folks"—and different subjects. Be sure to make the right choices about which note-taking system makes the most sense for the course material being presented.

FIGURE 7.6

Math Note-Taking Example

From http://www.math.armstrong
.edu/MathTutorial/exerciseSoln/
LinearEqSoln/LinearEq1Soln/
13LinearEq1.html

Notes, College Algebra 100, Wednesday, Oct. 5

Determine which of the x values are solutions to the equation

$$x^4 + x^3 - 5x^2 + x - 6 = 0$$

a) $x = -3$ b) $x = -2$ c) $x = 1$ d) $x = 2$

STEPS TO SOLUTION	CALCULATIONS	RESULTS
1) Try answer a Substitute -3 into the equation for x and see if the equation is satisfied.	$(-3)^4 + (-3)^3 - 5(-3)^2 + (-3) - 6 \overset{?}{=} 0$ $81 \quad -27 \quad -45 \quad -3 -6 = 0$ $0 = 0$	YES since both sides are 0.
2) Try answer b Substitute -2 into the equation for x and see if the equation is satisfied.	$(-2)^4 + (-2)^3 - 5(-2)^2 + (-2) - 6 \overset{?}{=} 0$ $16 \quad -8 \quad -20 \quad -2 -6 = 0$ $-20 \neq 0$	NO since the two sides are unequal.
3) Try answer c Substitute 1 into the equation for x and see if the equation is satisfied.	$(1)^4 + (1)^3 - 5(1)^2 + 1 - 6 \overset{?}{=} 0$ $1 \quad +1 \quad -5 \quad +1-6 = 0$ $-8 \neq 0$	NO since the two sides are unequal.
4) Try answer d Substitute 2 into the equation for x and see if the equation is satisfied.	$(2)^4 + (2)^3 - 5(2)^2 + 2 - 6 \overset{?}{=} 0$ $16 \quad +8 \quad -20 \quad +2-6 = 0$ $0 = 0$	YES since both sides are 0.

"Focused" Multitasking   *1 THING AT A TIME*

One reason it's hard to focus in class is because of distractions. Like Rachel, you may be tempted to check your Facebook account or text someone about something that pops into your mind. Being pulled in different directions at once is what happens when you multitask. It breaks your concentration and disrupts your learning. Try this experiment instead. Let's call it "Focused Multitasking," meaning that all your attention is directed at one thing. Before you listen to an in-class lecture, divide into groups with each group trying out a different note-taking strategy presented in this chapter. For example, group 1 members should use outlines. Group 2 should use the Cornell System, Group 3 should create mind maps, etc. Then begin the lecture. The lecture could be your instructor lecturing about this chapter of FOCUS. Or it could be something different, like listening to an NPR podcast that the instructor or the whole class chooses. You are intentionally using all of your VARK preferences at once to focus on a single topic. After the lecture, take a quiz provided by your instructor and see which note-taking group's method earns the highest score!

Ask and You Shall Receive - *BIBLE REFERENCE*

Even if you listen carefully to every word your instructor utters, it's likely you won't understand them all. After all, your instructor is an expert in the subject you're studying, and you're new to it. At some point or other, you'll need to ask questions. Even though that makes sense, not all students feel comfortable asking questions in class. Why? See if you've excused yourself from asking questions for any of these reasons:

EXCUSES ARE EXPENISIVE.

Focus --

> I don't want to look stupid.
>
> I must be slow. Everyone else seems to be understanding.
>
> I'm too shy.
>
> I'll get the answer later from the textbook.
>
> I don't think my question is important enough.
>
> I don't want to interrupt the lecture. The instructor's on a roll.
>
> I'm sure the instructor knows what he's talking about. He must be right.

He who is ashamed of asking is ashamed of learning.

Danish Proverb

If any of these reasons for not asking questions in class applies to you, the good news is . . . you're in good company. Many students think this way. The bad news, of course, is that your question remains unasked, and therefore, unanswered.

The next time you find yourself in a situation where you don't understand something, consider these points.

1. **Remember that you're not in this alone.** Chances are you're probably not the only person in class who doesn't understand. Not only will you be doing yourself a favor by asking, but you'll also be helping someone else who's too shy to speak up.

2. **Ask academically relevant questions when the time is right.** As opposed to "Why do we need to know this?" or "Why did you make the test

so hard?" ask questions to clarify information. Don't ask questions designed to take your instructor off on a **tangent** (to delay the **impending** quiz, for example). If you're really interested in something that's not directly related to the material being covered, the best time to raise the question would be during your instructor's office hours.

HE MUST BE RIGHT!?

3. **Save *personally* relevant questions for later.** If your questions relate only to you (for example, you were ill and missed the last two classes), then don't ask in class. Set up an appointment with your instructor. You can also get answers by researching on your own, visiting or e-mailing your instructor, seeking out a teaching assistant or tutor, or working with a study group.

4. **Build on others' questions.** Your instructor isn't the only person who speaks in class. You must apply what you're reading in this chapter to listening to your classmates, too. Listen to the questions other students ask. Use their questions to spark your own. Perhaps another student has a unique way of looking at the issue being discussed that will spark an idea for a follow-up question from you. Remember, to your instructor, good questions indicate *interest*, not *ignorance*.

Remember, your college education is an investment in your own future. You're here to learn, and asking questions is a natural part of that learning experience. Don't be shy—put that hand in the air!

How Much Does Asking Questions Help?

To demonstrate the value of asking questions, try this in-class exercise. A student volunteer, or class "lecturer," will briefly replace the instructor to describe to the rest of the class two different, simple figures she draws herself. Each figure should take up a full piece of paper. The rest of the class must then reproduce the drawings as accurately as possible on their own paper as the class "lecturer" describes each figure during two rounds. The point of the exercise is to replicate the two figures the class "lecturer" has drawn as accurately as possible from her description alone. The lecturer can't show the class her drawings; she must simply describe them.

Round 1: The volunteer should turn her back to the group (so she can't see them and they can't see her), hiding her paper from view, and give the class instructions for drawing Figure 1. No questions from the group are allowed. Keep track of the exact amount of time it takes for the rest of the class to listen to the instructions and complete the drawing. If this were an exam, the class would have to redraw the figure as closely as possible to the original to get an "A."

Round 2: Next, the volunteer should now turn around and face the class, giving instructions for drawing Figure 2. Students may ask questions of the "lecturer" to make sure they're getting the drawing right. Again, note the exact amount of time taken.

After both rounds of the exercise are done, the "lecturer" should ask class members whether they think their drawings look like the two originals and count the number of students who think they drew Figure 1 correctly and the number of students who think they drew Figure 2 correctly. Then the "lecturer" should show the two original figures as drawn, and count the number of students who actually drew Figure 1 and Figure 2 correctly. Finally, as a group, discuss the two rounds and the value of asking questions in lecture classes. Even though questions take more time, the results are usually much better.

Elapsed Time	# Think Correct	# Actually Correct
Round 1		
Round 2		

Using Lecture Notes

Taking good notes is only part of the equation. To get the most value from your notes, you must actually *use* them. As soon as possible after class, take a few minutes to review your notes. If you find sections that are unclear, take time to fill in the gaps while things are still fresh in your mind. One instructor found that students who filled in any missing points right after class were able to increase the amount of lecture points they recorded by as much as 50 percent. And students who worked with another student to reconstruct the lecture immediately after class were able to increase their number of noted lecture points even more![22]

This part of the note-taking process is often overlooked, yet it is one of the most helpful steps for learning and recall. If you don't review your notes within twenty-four hours, there's good evidence that you'll end up re*learning* rather than re*viewing*. Reviewing helps you go beyond just writing to actually making sure you understand what you wrote. These three techniques help you get the best use of your notes: manipulating, paraphrasing, and summarizing.

> **Manipulating** involves working with your notes by typing them out later, for example. Some research indicates that it's not writing down information that's most important. Manipulating information is what counts. Work with your notes. Fill in charts, draw diagrams, create a mind map, underline, highlight, organize. Cut a copy of the instructor's lecture notes up into paragraphs, mix them up, and then put the lecture back together. Copy your notes onto flash cards. Manipulating information helps develop your reasoning skills, reduces your stress level, and can produce a more complete set of notes to study later.[23]

> **Paraphrasing** is a process of putting your notes into your own words. Recopy your notes or your instructor's prepared lecture notes, translating them into words you understand and examples that are meaningful to you. Paraphrasing is also a good way to self-test or to study with a classmate. If you can't find words of your own, perhaps you don't really understand the original notes. Sometimes students think they understand course material until the test proves otherwise, and then it's too late! Practice paraphrasing key concepts with a friend to see how well you both understand the material. Or ask yourself, if I had to explain this to someone who missed class, what words would I use?

> **Summarizing** is a process of writing a brief overview of all of your notes from one lecture. Imagine trying to take all your lecture notes from one class session and putting them on an index card. If you can do that, you've just written a summary. Research shows that students who use the summarizing technique have far greater recall of the material than those who don't.

Some students think that simply going over their notes is the best way to practice. Research shows that simply reading over your notes is a weak form of practice that does not transfer information into long-term memory.[24] You must actually *work with* the material, rearrange or reword it, or condense it to get the most academic bang for your buck. Active strategies always work better than more passive ones.

Note-Taking 4-M

Practice your note-taking skills by doing this. Immediately after class, or during the lecture if your instructor allows, compare notes with a classmate by following these four steps:[25]

1. Matching—look for content areas where your notes match those of your classmate's.

2. Missing—look for content areas where one of you has missed something important and fill in the gaps.

3. Meaning—talk about what this lecture means. Why was it included in the course? Do you both understand the lecture's main points?

4. Measuring—quiz each other. Measure how much you learned from the lecture. Give each other some sample test questions to see if you understand important concepts.

CAREER OUTLOOK: *Be Clear*

 A mighty thing is eloquence ... nothing so much rules the world.

POPE PIUS II

Speak and write well. Your college career may put more emphasis on these skills than any others. In today's world of abbreviated text messages (ays = Are you serious?; lol = laugh out loud; u = you; brb = be right back) and empty conversation ("And she's going. . . and I'm like . . . you know . . . whatever . . ."), you can become a super star on the job by just speaking and writing well. For example, if the boss wants someone to brief the staff on a new procedure, who will she choose? Someone who speaks like a high school student, or the person who sounds like an experienced professional? The ability to use both spoken and written language well—the language of educated and successful professionals—communicates to your colleagues and your supervisors that you think clearly and work effectively. And when the boss wants someone to deal with customers, partners, and suppliers, who will the boss choose? Those who are hard to understand and sound inexperienced, or those who have a solid command of the language and use it to clearly get their points across?

And in addition to speaking and writing well, learn to listen to what's really being said and why. With practice, you can listen past the bravado or baloney and get to the real message. We learn in the competitive world of business that poor speaking, writing, and listening skills will lead people to take their business elsewhere. When you communicate effectively and professionally, you help your organization succeed—and that helps you succeed!

VARK Activity

Complete the activity recommended for your preferred VARK learning style and bring it to class (or follow your instructor's instructions).

Visual: Color-code a set of notes you've taken in one of your current classes to mark important themes (blue highlighter for main points, yellow highlighter for examples, etc.).

Aural: Invite a classmate for coffee or a soft drink immediately after class to talk over the lecture you've just finished listening to. Did you hear the same thing? What do each of you consider the lecture's main points? Make sure you actually talk about the lecture! Access the CourseMate via www.cengagebrain.com/shop/ISBN/1439083908 to listen to the iAudio summary for this chapter.

Read/Write: Create a survey to hand out in one of your classes, asking students to identify their greatest note-taking challenges in one of their courses this term. Compile all the results and present them in the class for which you're using this textbook.

Kinesthetic: Conduct on-the-spot fake television news interviews on campus with a friend. Act like a reporter copying down information. Ask students for the number one reason they have trouble taking notes. Bring your results to class and role play giving the news report on TV.

(from top to bottom) Marcela Barsse/MarsBars/iStockphoto.com; Johanna Goodyear/Dreamstime.com; Nadezda Firsova/iStockphoto.com; Pascal Genest/iStockphoto.com

ONLINE TechKnow

Improve Your Grade
Online Flashcards
Glossary

When you're lost, you ask for directions, right? When you're not sure what to do or how to do it in your online coursework, ask for help.

- If you're not sure how to access information or use an online tool, ask your instructor. Remember, in an on-ground class, you can often benefit from the questions of others in the class. In an online environment, you don't have the benefit of other warm bodies around, so ask your instructor directly.

- If something isn't working the way you're told it should, ask your instructor or your IT helpdesk.

- If you're not sure what's required to fully complete an assignment, read your syllabus carefully. Usually, instructors are very helpful in describing exactly what they want—and don't want—in an assignment. But if reading the syllabus still leaves you with questions, go online to ask your instructor.

Taking notes for online courses can benefit from online technology. Such note-taking software as Evernote, Google Notebook, and Knowledge Notebook allow tremendous flexibility in taking, organizing, linking, and accessing notes, Web pages, images, sounds, and other data on your computer and phone. While working an online assignment in one window, you can take notes in another. Or if you prefer, you can toggle back and forth from readings to notes.

- You can import items from Webpages, add notes, images, to-do lists, PDFs, and more.

- You can search for printed or even handwritten text in images.

- You also have the ability to share these notes with classmates.

In an online environment, such note-taking software is a natural strength that you should take advantage of.[26]

step 3 — INSIGHT *Now* What Do You Think?

At the beginning of this chapter, Rachel White, a frustrated student, faced a challenge. Now after reading this chapter, would you respond differently to any of the questions you answered about the "FOCUS Challenge Case"? Using what you learned in the chapter, write a paragraph ending to Rachel's case study. What are some of the possible outcomes for Rachel?

step 4 — ACTION Your Plans for Change

1. What is the single most important point you will take from this chapter?
2. Do you have a class like Rachel's? What are you doing to cope?

REALITY CHECK

What did you Learn?

On a scale of 1 to 5, answer these questions now that you've completed this chapter.

1 = not very/not much/very little/low   5 = very/a lot/very much/high

How much do you know *now*?

Now rate your current level of knowledge about topics covered in this chapter.

Hard versus *soft* listening

       1 2 3 4 5

Lecture style analysis

       1 2 3 4 5

Cornell note-taking system

       1 2 3 4 5

Mind mapping

       1 2 3 4 5

How useful might the information in this chapter be to you?

How much do you think this information might affect your college success?

       1 2 3 4 5

How much do you think this information might affect your career success after college?

       1 2 3 4 5

How long did it actually take you to complete this chapter (both the reading and writing tasks)?

_____ Hour(s) _____ Minutes

 Challenge Yourself Online Quiz. To find out how much you've learned, access the CourseMate via www.cengagebrain.com/shop/ISBN/1439083908 to take the Challenge Yourself Online Quiz.

Compare these answers to your answers from the "Readiness Check" at the beginning of this chapter. How might the gaps between what you thought before starting the chapter and what you now think affect how you approach the next chapter?

8 Developing Your Memory

YOU'RE ABOUT TO DISCOVER. . .

✔ WHY MEMORY IS A PROCESS, NOT A THING

✔ HOW YOUR MEMORY WORKS LIKE A DIGITAL CAMERA

✔ HOW TO IMPROVE YOUR MEMORY USING TWENTY DIFFERENT TECHNIQUES

✔ HOW YOUR MEMORY CAN FAIL YOU

READINESS CHECK · What do you **Know?**

Before beginning this chapter, take a moment to answer these questions. Your answers will help you assess how ready you are to focus.

1 = not very/not much/very little/low   5 = very/a lot/very much/high

How much do you *already* know?

Rate your current level of knowledge about topics covered in this chapter.

Short-term versus long-term memory

1 2 3 4 5

Memory as a process

1 2 3 4 5

Memory improvement techniques

1 2 3 4 5

Causes for memory failures

1 2 3 4 5

How motivated are you to learn *more*?

In general, how motivated are you to learn the material in this chapter?

1 2 3 4 5

How much do you think this information might affect your college success?

1 2 3 4 5

How much do you think this information might affect your career success after college?

1 2 3 4 5

How ready are you to read *now*?

How ready are you to focus on this chapter—physically, intellectually, and emotionally? Which of these three areas is most challenging for you right now? Circle a number to represent it.

1 2 3 4 5

If any of your answers is below a 3, consider addressing the issue before reading. Then, read the chapter carefully, while looking for ways to improve your focus.

Finally, how long do you think it will take you to complete this chapter? If you start and stop, keep track of the overall time.

_____ Hour(s) _____ Minutes

KEVIN BAXTER

© Larry Harwood Photography. Property of Cengage Learning.

As he got ready for work one morning, it finally hit him. He took a long, close look at himself in the mirror, and frankly, he didn't like what he saw. Kevin Baxter was a forty-year-old father of three who was dissatisfied with his life. Yes, he earned a decent income as a construction foreman, and yes, his job allowed him to work outdoors. To Kevin, being cooped up in an office from eight to five every day was something he'd always wanted to avoid. Being outdoors, where you could see the sky, feel the sunshine, and breathe fresh air was what made him feel alive. The world outside was where he wanted to be, yet at the same time, he knew the world inside his head was withering away. Kevin realized he hadn't really learned much since high school. *I feel brain-dead; that's the best way to describe it,* he frequently thought. *I've run out of options, and I'm stuck.*

Clearly, dropping out of college his first semester twenty-two years ago had been the wrong decision for him. But at the time, he'd convinced himself that he wasn't college material. Besides, college had seemed so expensive, and he desperately wanted to be on his own and begin a life with Carol, his high school sweetheart. Unfortunately, that hadn't worked out well, either. Now he was a single dad whose children lived out of state. He very rarely saw them. Nothing had quite turned out as he had planned.

But in a way, his divorce had jolted him into the midlife crisis he needed to change things, and going back to college to earn a degree in architecture was the right decision for him now. He was sure of it. Working in construction, he frequently

Nadezda, 2010/Used under copyright from Shutterstock.com

Buturlimov Paul, 2010/Used under copyright from Shutterstock.com

Ingvar Bjork, 2010/Used under copyright from Shutterstock.com

Dmitriy Shironosov/Shutterstock.com

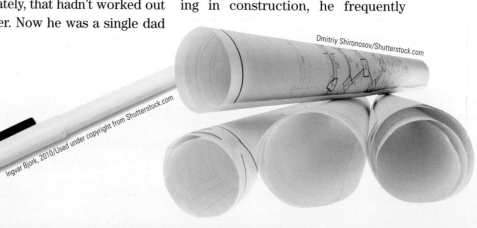

saw flaws in the architects' plans, and he'd often come up with better ideas. *This is a chance to start over again*, he thought to himself, *and I'm going to do it right this time.* So at forty, he quit his construction job and enrolled in his local career college. His first-term courses consisted of Introduction to Architectural Design, Introduction to Philosophy, Introduction to Rhetoric and Writing, and Introduction to Art. For Kevin, college would be an introduction to many new things. Underneath it all, he had to admit that he was proud of himself. *Going back to college at forty takes guts*, he congratulated himself. Who knows? He might even change majors and get an engineering degree before it was all over.

But halfway into the term, Kevin's confidence was shaken. Although he'd been a construction foreman on huge projects, after he got his first mid-term exam back, he wondered, *Am I too old to learn new things? I keep up with the reading, come to every class, do my assignments conscientiously, and study until I'm blue in the face! But things just don't seem to stick.* His exam didn't reflect the time he was investing, and frankly, he was embarrassed. Younger students without his years of experience were outperforming him. *That* bothered him. Kevin was getting discouraged about school and his academic capabilities.

Without a doubt, his most challenging class was philosophy. What did Socrates, Plato, Aristotle, Galileo, and Descartes have in common, and what separated them? Philosophy was unlike anything he had ever tried to learn. He'd read a chapter four, five, or six times, and feel sure he knew it, but when he faced the exam, it seemed as if he'd never studied at all. Of course, it didn't help that while he was trying to focus, his kids would call to talk about their problems or a telephone solicitor would interrupt his reading. He'd even bought a set of colored highlighters after watching a young student next to him, madly yellowing everything in his textbook right before class started, but that didn't seem to help either. He never had problems at work remembering details, like ordering materials and managing multiple construction teams, but trying to distinguish Plato, Aristotle, and Socrates was hard for him, and many of the new terms he was learning didn't really seem to have any relevance to his life. More than once on the exam, he just couldn't come up with a term that was on the tip of his tongue.

Kevin hated to admit it, but doubts were beginning to creep in. Maybe being a construction foreman was as far as he could ever go in life, and he should have left well enough alone. Maybe college was the last place he should be. Maybe he should have been satisfied with what he'd already achieved, instead of putting everything on the line for more.

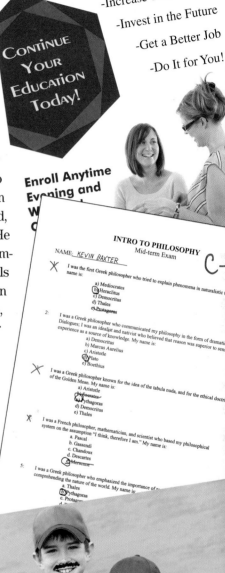

INTRO TO PHILOSOPHY
Mid-term Exam

NAME: KEVIN BAXTER   C–

1. I was the first Greek philosopher who tried to explain phenomena in naturalistic te... name is:
   a) Mediocrates
   b) Heraclitus
   c) Democritus
   d) Thales
   e) Protagoras

2. I was a Greek philosopher who communicated my philosophy in the form of dramatic Dialogues; I was an idealist and nativist who believed that reason was superior to sens... experience as a source of knowledge. My name is:
   a) Democritus
   b) Marcus Aurelius
   c) Aristotle
   d) Plato
   e) Boethius

3. I was a Greek philosopher known for the idea of the tabula nuda, and for the ethical doctri... of the Golden Mean. My name is:
   a) Aristotle
   b) Socrates
   c) Pythagoras
   d) Democritus
   e) Thales

4. I was a French philosopher, mathematician, and scientist who based my philosophical system on the assumption "I think, therefore I am." My name is:
   a. Pascal
   b. Gassendi
   c. Chandoux
   d. Descartes
   e. Mersenne

5. I was a Greek philosopher who emphasized the importance of ... comprehending the nature of the world. My name is:
   a. Thales
   b. Pythagoras
   c. Protagoras
   d. ...

the Big Question
A Short Introduction to Philoso...

Course Schedule
Career College
FALL SEMESTER
Baxter, Kevin

Course ID	Course Title	Hrs	Days	Meeting Times	Bldg	Room	Meeting Dates	Status	Instructor
ARCH 100	INTRO TO ARCHITECTURAL DESIGN	3.0	T	0500PM-0830PM	SCI BLDG	210	AUG 16 - DEC 16	ENROLLED	FRANKLIN, L
PHIL 101	INTRO TO PHILOSOPHY	3.0	M	0705-1020PM	MAIN HALL	105	AUG 16 - DEC 17	ENROLLED	FREDRICKSON
COMM 180	INTRO TO RHETORIC AND WRITING	3.0	S SU	0800AM-0400PM	MAIN HALL	412	OCT 2 - OCT 23	ENROLLED	WEDDLE
ART 110	INTRO TO ART	3.0	R	0705-1020PM	MAIN HALL	300	AUG 16 - DEC 17	ENROLLED	DALTON
	Credit Load:	**12.0**							

2 REACTION What Do *You* Think?

1. Do you have anything in common with Kevin? If so, how are you managing the situation so that you can be successful?

2. Why is Kevin experiencing problems remembering course content in his philosophy class? List five reasons you identify from the case study.

3. Is Kevin too old to learn? Why or why not?

4. Identify three memory techniques that Kevin should use to help him memorize all the names and terms he needs to know.

Memory: The *Long* and *Short* of It

EXERCISE 8.1

Subjective Memory Test

How would you rate your memory overall?

	Excellent		Good		Poor
	1	2	3	4	5

A. How often do the following general memory tasks present a problem for you?

	Never		Sometimes		Always
1. Names	①	2	3	4	5
2. Where I've put things	1	2	③	4	5
3. Phone numbers I've just checked	1	②	3	4	5
4. Words	①	2	3	4	5
5. Knowing if I've already told someone something	1	②	3	4	5
6. Forgetting things people tell me	1	2	③	4	5
7. Faces	①	2	3	4	5
8. Directions ← FLAWLESS— CLOSE TO	①	2	3	4	5
9. Forgetting what I started to do	1	②	3	4	5
10. Forgetting what I was saying	1	2	③	4	5
11. Remembering what I've done (lock the door, etc.)	1	2	③	⊗	5

B. How often do the following academic memory tasks present a problem for you?

	Never		Sometimes		Always
12. What I've just been reading	1	2	③	4	5
13. What I read an hour ago	1	②	3	4	5
14. What I read last week	1	②	③	4	5
15. Assignment/Exam due dates	1	2	③	4	5
16. Appointments with instructors	1	2	③	4	5
17. Assignment details	1	2	③	4	5
18. Factual information for exams	1	②	3	4	5
19. Theoretical information for exams	1	②	3	4	5
20. Information from readings for exams	1	2	③	4	5
21. Information from in-class lectures for exams	1	2	③	4	5
22. Including everything I should study for exams	1	2	③	4	5

These informal assessments may help you understand your own perceptions of how well your memory works. The lower your score on each portion, the better you perceive your memory to be. Do your scores for Part A and Part B differ? The general tasks in Part A are presented in the order of concern reported by older adults cited in one study (with the top items perceived as most problematic).[1] Are your priorities similar? Did your numbers drop as you went down the list?

In one recent study in which college students were asked which aspects of memory they most wanted to improve among general and academic tasks, the top three items were improving schoolwork or study skills, remembering what was read, and remembering specific facts and details.[2] Understandably, the academic aspects of memory were those most personally valued. Is that true for you, too? Are the items in Part B generally higher priorities for you now as a college student?

Most of us may not even realize just how important memory is. We talk about our memories as if they were something we own. We say we have good memories or bad memories, just like we have a crooked smile or a nice one. But no one would ever say, "Hey, that's one nice-looking memory you've got there!" in the same way they'd say, "Wow, you have a really nice smile!" Memory isn't a thing; it's a process. You can't see it or touch it or hold it. Even one specific memory has many different features: You can remember something by what you saw, smelled, heard, or felt. And even within one of these categories, individuals may differ in what they recall. You may be able to hum the movie's theme song, but your friend may remember conversations between the main characters almost word for word.

Don't believe it when someone claims to have a one-size-fits-all, magic formula to help you unlock the secrets of your memory. It isn't that easy. Still, there are techniques that can help you do your best academically. We can only begin to grasp the rich complexities of memory by understanding it as a process. However, it's important to recognize first that mastering memory depends on the answers to several questions like these:[3]

1. **Who is learning?** An algebra instructor and a beginning algebra student would approach memorizing the main points of an article on math differently.

2. **What needs to be learned?** How you learn your lines for a play would differ from how you learn to recognize paintings for your art appreciation test.

3. **How will learning be tested?** Learning information to *recall* uses different memory techniques than learning information to *recognize*. Recognition requires that you select from several possibilities; recall requires that you come up with memorized information on your own.

4. **How long must the information be remembered?** Learning your multiplication tables as a child is something that must remain with you throughout your life. You use it on a daily basis to do routine things like figure how much it will cost you to fill up your gas tank.

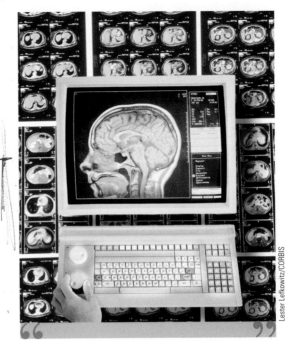

"The existence of forgetting has never been proved: We only know that some things don't come to mind when we want them.

Friedrich Nietzsche, German philosopher
(1844–1900)

YOU CAN IMPROVE YOUR MEMORY!

Test Your Memory

For a more objective assessment of your memory, try this test. Study the following list of words for up to one minute. Then cover them with your hand and see how many you can remember and list them in the right-hand column.

theory   *THEORY*

rehearsal   *RHEARSAL*

student   *BONE*

bone   *FROSBITE*

frostbite   _____   *ROSE*

camera   _____   *CAMERA*

rose   _____

calculus   *CALCULUS.*

lecture   *LECTURE*

How many words were you able to remember? Which words did you forget? Unfamiliar words? Words that had no meaning in your life? What memory techniques did you use to help you remember?

C Squared Studios/Photodisc/Getty Images

> 66 99
>
> **I have a photographic memory but once in a while I forget to take off the lens cap.**
>
> *Milton Berle, comedian*
> *(1908–2002)*

The Three R's of Remembering: Record, Retain, Retrieve

Improving your memory is easier if you understand how it works. Memory consists of three parts:

> your sensory memory

> your working memory (called short-term memory by some psychologists)

> your long-term memory

These three parts of the memorization process are connected to these three memory tasks, the "Three R's of Remembering"[4]:

> recording

> retaining

> retrieving

We'll compare the three R's of remembering to the process involved when taking pictures with a digital camera: record, retain, retrieve.

Your Sensory Memory: Focus

Before we discuss the first R of remembering—namely, *Record*—we have to talk first about focus. Before you even push the button to snap a picture, you have to focus on your subject. Most digital cameras today focus on things automatically, and unlike older cameras, you don't have to turn the focus ring until the image is clear. But you do need to decide what to focus *on*. What do you want to take a picture of? Where will you point the camera? When it comes to your college classes and the role your memory plays in your success, remember that focus doesn't come automatically. It requires consciously deciding where to direct your attention.

Imagine this: You're on your way to class. You walk through a crowded street corner and get brushed by people on all sides. Then you cross a busy intersection a little too slowly and get honked at by a speeding car. Finally, you see a billboard you've never noticed before: "I love you, Whitney. Will you marry me? Carl." *How romantic*, you think to yourself.

Three major sensations just passed through your *sensory memory* in this scenario, in this case, your *haptic* memory (touch, the crowd), your *echoic* memory (sounds, the car horn), and your *iconic* memory (sight, the billboard), all parts of your sensory memory. You have a different channel for each of these three senses. Most experts believe that your sensory memory retains an exact copy of what you've seen or heard—pure and unanalyzed—for less than a second.[5] Some of these images, or icons, will be transferred to your working memory.

To help you to focus, consider the following suggestions:

1. **Slow down; you move too fast.** Imagine trying to take a photo of something on the way to class if you were running. Everything would be a blur; trying to take a picture would be useless. Focus requires your full attention aimed at one thing at a time. Turn down the music, turn off the television, shut down the six windows open on your browser, and focus.

2. **Deal with it.** If something is driving you to distraction, maybe you need to take care of it first so that you *can* focus.

3. **Notice where you go.** Wandering thoughts are normal. When *your* attention wanders off, where does it go? Knowing your mental habits helps you to recognize the pattern and work on changing it.

4. **Watch for signals.** You'll probably take many different courses from different departments in your college and be exposed to literally thousands of facts. Not even a memory expert could master them all at once. You must be selective about focus. You're most likely to learn the subject material presented by your instructor and through your course readings. Your textbooks will guide you as you read by using bold fonts, different colors, charts, tables, and headings. Think of them as animated JPEGs on the page, calling out, "Hey, look at me!" In class, watch the instructor's body language; listen to her inflection; notice what gets written on the board or which PowerPoint slides stay on the screen longer than others. Plenty of subtle signals exist, but you have to pay attention to them.

RECORD.

HAPTIC - Touch
ECHOIC - Sound
ICONIC - Sight

analogy comparison

5. **Get help if you need to.** If you have been diagnosed with ADHD, your brain is wired somewhat differently, affecting your memory and your ability to concentrate.[6] If you've not been diagnosed with a learning disability, but your attention appears to be difficult to control and you're not sure why, get help from a counselor or learning specialist on campus or in your community.

RECORD   GET HELP YA FREAK!

Your Working Memory: Record

After you've focused your camera on your subject, you're ready to take a picture, right? But with a digital camera, you don't just click and walk away. You actually click and then review the picture on the small viewing screen to decide whether you want to save it or delete it.

Similarly, *recording* sensory impressions involves an evaluation process that takes place in your short-term or *working memory*. Your working memory is like a review screen, where you review recently acquired sensory impressions. In fact, your working memory is often involved in the focus process. In our example of you walking to class, which of these three specific sensations you just experienced are you likely to remember: the crowd, the car, or the billboard? To stay true to the camera **analogy**, which one would you take a picture of? It depends, right? You may remember the billboard because you plan to show it to someone else later, or the crowd because you hate crowded places, or the car horn because it scared you. Your working memory records something because it holds personal meaning for you.

The problem with working memory is that the length of time it can hold information is limited. You probably don't remember what you ate for dinner last Monday, do you? You'd have to reconstruct the memory based on other clues. Where was I? What was I doing? Who was I with?

The other problem with working memory is that it has limited capacity. It fills up quickly and then dumps what it doesn't need. If you look up a number in the campus directory, you can usually remember it long enough to walk over to the phone, right? A few minutes after you've dialed, however, the number is gone. Current estimates are that you can keep something in working memory for one to two minutes, giving your brain a chance to do a quick review, selecting what to save and what to delete.[7] Look at these letters and then close your eyes and try to repeat them back in order.

SAJANISMOELIHHEGNR

Can't do it? This task is virtually impossible because the string contains eighteen letters. Researchers believe that working memory can recall only seven pieces of information, plus or minus two.[8] (There's a reason why telephone numbers are prechunked for us.) Chunking these eighteen letters into five units helps considerably. Now look at the letters again and try to recall all eighteen.

SAJA NISM OELI HHEG NR

If we rearrange the letters into recognizable units, it becomes even easier, right?

AN IS MAJOR ENGLISH HE

And if the words are rearranged to make perfect sense, the task becomes simple.

HE IS AN ENGLISH MAJOR

The principle of chunking is also used to move information from your working memory to your long-term memory bank, and it's used in memorization techniques described later in this chapter.

Your Long-Term Memory: Retain and Retrieve

Once your camera's memory card gets full, you probably transfer the photos to your computer, or you print them out and put them in photo albums or picture frames. However, before you do that, you generally review the photos, decide how to arrange them, where to put them, whether to print them, and so forth. In other words, you make the photos memorable by putting them into some kind of order or context.

Just as you must transfer photos from your camera's memory stick to a more permanent location with more storage room, you must transfer information from short-term, or working, memory to long-term memory. You *retain* the information by transferring it, and this transfer takes place if you review and use information in a way that makes it memorable. It is this review process that we use when we study for a test. You transfer information to long-term memory by putting the information into a context that has meaning for you, linking new information to old information, creating stories or using particular memory techniques, or organizing material so that it makes sense. You can frame material you're learning by putting a mental border around it, just as you put pictures into frames.

Your long-term memory is the computer in which you store new knowledge until you need to use it. However, while the memories in long-term memory aren't easily disturbed, they can be challenging to *retrieve*.[9] Ideally, you'd like your memories to be readily available when you want to retrieve them, just like the pictures or digital images that you have transferred to your computer or put in a photo album (Figure 8.1). You can click on them to view them again, arrange them into a slideshow, or send them to your friends as attachments. If you just dump your photos onto your hard drive, or print them out and then put them into a box, with no organization or labeling system, how easy will it be to find a specific photo? Difficult, right? Retrieving information from your long-term memory can be equally challenging if you haven't organized your

> "A memory is anything that happens and does not completely unhappen."
>
> *Edward de Bono, creative thinking expert and author of Lateral Thinking: Creativity Step by Step*

[handwritten: WHAT CAN YOU DO?]

ONLINE **TechKnow**

Improve Your Grade
Online Flashcards
Glossary

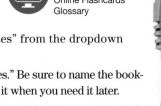

Having trouble remembering all the websites you need to access for your online course? One of the most useful tools available while reading or researching online is the "Bookmark" or "Favorite" function.

- When you need to keep track of numerous websites made available through your readings, select "Bookmarks" or "Favorites" from the dropdown menu.

- Then select "Add to favorites." Be sure to name the bookmark so you can easily find it when you need it later.

- Finally, use the "New Folder" or "Organize Favorites" functions to organize the many links you're collecting by topic, and place older links in more useful folders.

[handwritten: Today mm so Before]

information, or created mental labels that will help you retrieve them later. Good recall often depends on having a good storage system. The remainder of this chapter will be about how to *retain* information by transferring it from working memory into long-term memory and how to *retrieve* information when you need to.

FIGURE 8.1

Your Memory as a Digital Camera

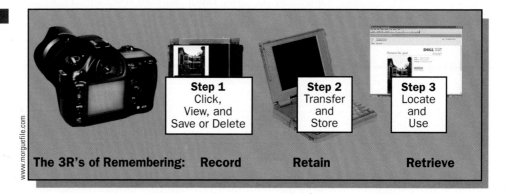

Twenty Ways to Master Your Memory

STUDY FOR QUIZ ON THURSDAY!

What can you do to sharpen your memory for the reading and test-taking you'll do in college? Try the following twenty techniques, grouped into five major categories (to help you remember them). These techniques are specifically designed to help you with the *retain* and *retrieve* parts of the memory process. As you consider each one, think about what you know about your own learning style.

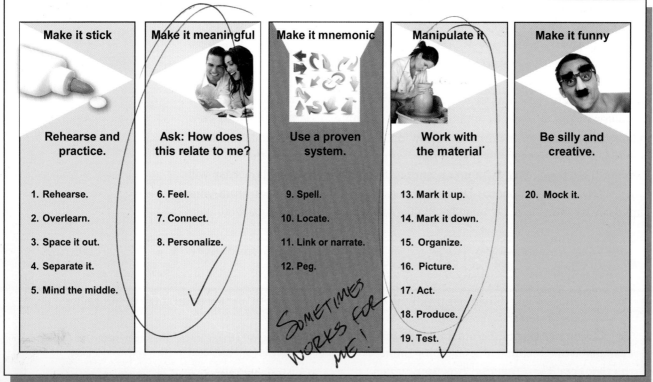

Feng Yu, 2009. Used under license from Shutterstock.com; Yuri Arcurs, 2009. Used under license from Shutterstock.com; Nishan Sothilingam/iStockphoto.com; IKO, 2009. Used under license from Shutterstock.com; Alex James Bramwell, 2009. Used under license from Shutterstock.com.

FIGURE 8.2

Twenty Ways to Master Your Memory

Make It Stick ~ MAKE IT STICK.

How do you actually move material from your working memory to your long-term memory? What will work best for you? Some techniques are more effective than others, but the following suggestions are a good start.[10]

PhotostoGO.com

FIGURE 8.3

Which of these two pictures are you more likely to remember—the simple or the elaborate?

1. **Rehearse.** Although it's not the most powerful memorization strategy available to you, especially by itself, repeating information helps. Nothing gets stored in your memory for long without practice. How did you learn those multiplication tables in fourth grade? Probably not by just reading them over once or twice.

   Memory experts distinguish between *maintenance* (or shallow) rehearsal and *elaborative* rehearsal. Maintenance rehearsal helps you keep something in working memory for a short time. Repeating a phone number twenty times while you look for your cell phone might help you keep it there for several minutes, but will you remember it tomorrow when you need to call again? Shallow rehearsal didn't work for Kevin in the "FOCUS Challenge Case," who just kept rereading course material. Elaborative rehearsal—actually working with the information—helps transfer information to long-term memory more effectively. Most of the techniques described in this chapter will focus on elaborative rehearsal techniques. Typically, we remember the elaborate over the simple (Figure 8.3).

2. **Overlearn.** Overlearning helps you truly hardwire information, so that you can practically work in autopilot. When you think you've learned something, don't automatically assume it's time to move on. Keep working at it. The more you continue to work at it, the greater your degree of mastery.[11]

3. **Space it out.** Many studies show that studying for several hours at a time, as opposed to one long stretch, is much more effective. Clearing your entire day so that you can study algebra for six hours isn't the best idea. Your anxiety level would mount over that time, and you'd get tired, keeping you from maximizing your memory. Instead, study in shorter spurts for several days leading up to the exam. Cramming may work in the short run, but your working memory will most likely dump what you think you've mastered right after the exam.

 REVERE

Twenty Ways to Master Your Memory **195**

4. **Separate it.** When you're tasked with learning similar, yet distinct, information, "bleeding" can occur. One body of knowledge can spill over into another. Imagine the confusion you'd experience if you tried to learn Spanish, French, Russian, and Chinese at the same time.

   Kevin from the "FOCUS Challenge Case" had trouble differentiating between Plato, Aristotle, and Socrates. He would have benefited from deliberately working to separate the three philosophers as he studied by making his own compare-and-contrast chart.

   Interference presents a particular problem for college students because the subject matter in different courses often overlaps; one course may contain information that's similar to another's. Knowledge is interconnected; that's not the issue. It's the challenge of keeping knowledge bases separate for exams. If your sociology test is on Wednesday and your psychology test is on Friday, study sociology on Tuesday and psychology on Thursday. But if both tests are on Friday, separating the two bodies of information will be a challenge. Differentiate your study sessions as much as possible by studying for each test in a specific location or at a particular time of day, for example.[12]

5. **Mind the middle.** Perhaps you've heard of the serial-position effect. Research shows that we tend to remember what comes first because of the impression it makes on us, and what comes last because it's most recent. But what's in the middle sometimes tends to get lost.[13] That's an important principle for you to know. If you need to memorize a list of items, or a timeline, for example, pay particular attention to the middle.

Make It Meaningful

Sometimes we make the mistake of creating artificial distinctions between thoughts and feelings, when in fact, emotions and personal connections play an important role in learning.

6. <u>**Feel.**</u> Emotions and memories can team up in powerful ways. A piece of new information that makes you feel happy, angry, or sad lights up your amygdala, a small area of your brain that serves as your emotional center of operations. If a novel makes you cry or laugh or actually feel fear, you're likely to remember the story. If course content hooks into career goals you care about, you're likely to commit more of it to memory. Human beings care about other human beings and themselves, so the emotional side of new information (which you may have to create yourself) is a strong magnet for your memory.[14] All American adults remember where they were on September 11, 2001. Emotions enhance memory and recall.[15]

7. **Connect.** Create associations between what you're trying to commit to memory now and what you already know. That's why doing the reading assignment before class is so useful. During the lecture, you can think to yourself, *Oh, I remember that . . . and that . . . and that.* When you learn new information, it's almost as if you "file" it between other files already in place. If you know where to put it, instead of just stuffing it somewhere, that helps. Connecting it to previous knowledge also helps you retrieve the memory later.

THE MATERIAL SHOULD BE ORGANIZED.

Socrates

8. **Personalize.** Find ways you can relate what you're memorizing to your own life. Okay, so you're thinking what do the plot and characters of *Pride and Prejudice*, a novel published by England's Jane Austen in 1813, possibly have to do with me now? Actually, there may be more similarities than you first think. Imagine the story taking place in your household. Do you have sisters? Does your mother worry about you marrying someone good enough for you? Do you have a close relationship with your father? Once you start actively searching for overlap, you may be surprised. This task is easier with some course content than others, but the very act of trying to do this may be useful.

CAREER OUTLOOK: *Be Skilled*

Numbers constitute the only universal language.
NATHANAEL WEST

Understand that numbers count. Unfortunately, math gets a bad rap. Many people approach math classes in college with "fear and loathing," when actually the ability to work with numbers is one key to success in the world of work. If you can understand spreadsheets or figure out a budget, you'll be ahead of the game. Some people de-emphasize the importance of financial and data management skills by referring to them as "bean-counting" or "number crunching," but people who know how to use numbers on the job are highly sought after.

Make It Mnemonic

Some of the oldest ways to master your memory are through the use of mnemonic (pronounced *ne MON ik*) devices, verbal or visual memory aids, first used by Greek orators around 500 B.C. Imagine trying to remember a speech that goes on for hours; you'd need to devise specific ways to train your memory to keep working (without a teleprompter!). Although mnemonic devices can become complicated and aren't a solution to all memory challenges, for some students, these specialized elaborative rehearsal strategies can work well.

9. **Spell.** Acronyms are the simplest type of mnemonic device, words you create by putting together the first letters of what you want to memorize. Let's say, for example, that you want to learn the first five items in the list of random words in Exercise 8.2: theory, rehearsal, student, bone, and frostbite. You could create a bizarre acronym such as <u>T</u>en <u>r</u>abbits' <u>s</u>oup <u>b</u>owls <u>f</u>ell. If you had vowels to work with, you may also be able to create an acronym you can pronounce, such as RAM for Random Access Memory.

acronym a short word made up of the first letters of a longer phrase, such as radar (radio detecting and ranging) or an abbreviation, like FBI for Federal Bureau of Investigation

10. **Locate.** The Loci (pronounced *LO si*) mnemonic system cues memory by using locations. Using the Loci system requires two steps. First, think of a familiar path, setting, or route. Perhaps you decide on the path from your apartment to the classroom where your exam will be given. On your way,

Have you ever watched a movie, wondering how *do* actors learn all those lines? Do they have super-human memory powers? The average movie-goer assumes that actors simply repeat their lines over and over until they learn them. However, actors themselves say that's not all there is to it.[16]

Actually, what actors are most concerned with is convincing you that they're not playing a role. But actors' contracts often require them to stick to the exact script, so how do they do it? Four of the techniques used by actors may also be useful to you as you try to commit course material to memory. Maybe you've even tried some of these techniques.

Chunking: Actors chunk their material into beats. For example, an actor might divide a half page of dialogue into three beats: to flirt, to sweet-talk, and to convince. In other words, the character would first flirt with the other actor, then sweet-talk him to lower his guard, and then convince him to do something he might not want to do. The results? Three chunks to remember instead of twelve lines of double-spaced text.

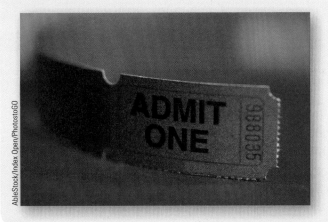

AbleStock/Index Open/PhotostoGO

Goal Setting: Notice that the chunks are based on goals, a strategy that also works well while you're studying. Actors ask themselves goal-oriented questions such as: "Should I be flirting with him here?" In the same way, you can ask yourself, "Am I trying to learn the underlying formula so that I can work other problem sets?" or "Should I be coming up with my own reasons for why the play is considered to be Shakespeare's best comedy?" When you ask yourself goal-oriented questions while you study, you steer your actions toward learning.

Moving: Going through the motions while rehearsing their lines helps actors memorize them. Imagine the hypothetical actor whose goals were to flirt, to sweet-talk, and to convince, glancing toward the other actor from across the room, moving closer and smiling, and then touching his arm while making the persuasive case. The actor must know the meanings behind the movements to give meaning to the lines. The meanings are tied to the movements, which are tied to the lines, and the lines become committed to memory. Likewise, when you study, moving around may help you learn. Even if you're not primarily a kinesthetic learner, pieces of information become tied to motions in ways that help you recall information.

Meaning: "Say what you mean" and "mean what you say" was Lewis Carroll's advice in *Alice's Adventures in Wonderland*. Researchers use the term active experiencing to refer to what actors do when they use all their physical, mental, and emotional channels to communicate the meaning of their lines to someone else, real or imagined. As you study course material, do the same thing. Imagine you need to communicate the information to someone you know who needs it.

you always pass distinct markers: the fountain in front of the big hotel, a tunnel that helps you bypass the freeway, the gym where you swim laps every morning, the hospital where someone you know had surgery, and the parking lot where you leave your car. Perhaps you want to use these five locations (fountain, tunnel, gym, hospital, and parking lot) to cue your memory to produce the first five items on our random list: theory, rehearsal, student, bone, and frostbite. You might picture saying hello to your science instructor, a "fountain" of knowledge who always says the word *theory* in class at least once. Then you might imagine conducting a *rehearsal* of a philharmonic orchestra in the tunnel, which would be a ridiculous sight and create a huge traffic jam. Then you envision *students* on a swim team thrashing about in the pool during a team practice. You know about a recent financial scandal involving the hospital so you imagine "skeletons" (*bones*) in the closet. And finally, you think of how terrible it would be to lose your apartment key and get a case of *frostbite* from spending the night in your car in the parking lot. Now without looking back, try it and see if it works for you. Of course, the optimal way the Loci system works is if the locations are familiar to *you*. Its main benefits are that it uses cues, connects things you already know about, and puts information in order, all of which aid in memory transfer and storage.[17] Or here's a simple example: perhaps you can remember the names of your classmates by simply paying attention to where they sit (the locations of their seats) each week.

11. **Link or narrate.** Instead of a Loci system, you can create a linking mnemonic to help you memorize a list. To do this, you must connect item A to item B, item B to item C, and so forth. Consider again the list of words you were challenged to remember and write down: theory, rehearsal, student, bone, frostbite, camera, rose, calculus, and lecture. Your visual links might go like this: (1) (theory + rehearsal) You imagine a *theoretician* at a *rehearsal* dinner. (2) (rehearsal + student) The *rehearsal* dinner is attended by *student* friends of the bride and groom. (3) (student + bone) One *student* is in a leg cast because of a broken *bone*, and so forth.

12. **Peg.** The Peg system uses rhyming syllables modified by England's John Sambrook in 1879.[18] Remember the old nursery rhyme, "One, two, buckle my shoe"? The Peg system uses these rhyming pairs:

one—bun	six—sticks
two—shoe	seven—heaven
three—tree	eight—gate
four—door	nine—wine
five—hive	ten—hen

To use the Peg system, create *specific* images for yourself. To continue with our example, you'd picture a *theoretical* treatise stuffed between the hamburger *bun*, an image of a teenage girl's *rehearsal* of how to walk in her first pair of stiletto high-heeled *shoes*, a *student* sprawled out studying under a weeping willow *tree*, and so forth. Other types of Peg systems have been devised, but the rhyming system is the most common.

Manipulate It

Although some of us aren't kinesthetic learns, all of us can benefit from memory techniques with a kinesthetic basis. Actively doing something with information is a better way to commit it to memory than being passive. If you had three hours to study a textbook chapter that takes one hour to read, what should you do: Read the chapter three times, or work with the material after reading it once? The second option is generally more effective. So what kinds of things should you *do*?

13. **Mark it up.** Be an active reader; interact with the text. People who are used to reading complex material—your instructors, for example—read slowly, chew on each word, and make notes in the margins, arguing, questioning, summarizing, or explaining. Take notes as you read, "talk" with the author, and write out your reactions. Highlighting can be somewhat helpful, but it's often not enough. It certainly wasn't for Kevin from the "FOCUS Challenge Case." Every time you reach for your highlighter, ask yourself why you want to highlight that passage. Why is it important? To commit information to memory, you must go beyond simply coloring.[19]

14. **Mark it down.** If you want to give yourself a break, don't bother committing something unimportant to memory. Just write it down. (Of course, you still have to remember where you put that piece of paper.) Writing something down is an obvious memory alternative; save your memory for more important tasks. If it's something you do want to remember, however, the physical act of writing itself can help. Unless the exam is open-book, however, actually bringing your notes with you at exam time could be "hazardous to your [academic] health!"

15. **Organize.** Arrange and rearrange the material you're trying to memorize. Outline it—putting concepts into an order or pattern can help you figure out important relationships. If you're trying to learn the responsibilities of the various branches of the government for your political science class, actually drawing a kind of written organizational chart is likely to help your essay answer flow better.

16. **Picture.** Drawings and mind maps can also be effective memory tools, particularly for visual learners. Think of drawing pictures to help you remember ridiculous visualizations or word associations. If you're trying to remember bones for your anatomy and physiology class, try Farsighted *Fibula*, Tempting *Tibia*, Party Girl *Patella*, Feathered *Femur*, and Pretty *Pelvis.*

17. **Act.** Consider putting motions to your memorizing. If you're trying to memorize a famous speech like Martin Luther King, Jr.'s "I Have a Dream," deliver it in front of a mirror. Write a short script and ask someone to play opposite you, if it helps you remember who said what to whom for an exam in history, or obviously, theater.

18. **Produce.** There's good evidence that putting things in your own words is highly beneficial to remembering.[20] Redeliver the instructor's lecture. Can you explain the concepts he explained, or do you stop after a few minutes because you are confused? Producing information requires you to dig deeper into your memory and benefits you and your memory beyond simple recognition tasks. One of the very best ways to produce is to teach something to someone else.

19. **Test.** Rather than assuming you remember something, test yourself. Create a multiple-choice, matching, or true-and-false test. Doing so requires you to ask what's important? Better yet, create essay questions that require you to organize and write what you know about a subject.

Make It Funny

Humor is an excellent memory-enhancing tool. Think about how easy it is to remember the plots of comedies you've seen at the movies or on television. For example, you may be able to remember conversations between *Friends* or *The Simpsons* cast members in shows you've watched once or twice, almost word for word, just because they tickled your funny bone.

20. Mock it. Experts on learning and the brain believe that the optimal condition for learning is *relaxed alertness*. Sounds like an oxymoron, doesn't it? How can you be relaxed and alert at the same time? Actually, it is possible when the challenge is high, but the threat is low—you're working hard, but you know you're learning.[21] What better way to create those conditions than to be a stand-up (or sit-down) comedian?

oxymoron combination of two words that mean opposite things

Think back to some of the funniest TV or movie scenes you've ever seen. They're probably still vivid in your memory. Ask yourself how you could apply your own humor to the material you're attempting to trigger your memory to learn. If you're having trouble separating Socrates and Plato, draw a picture of a crate full of socks next to Socrates' name and a can of PlayDoh® next to Plato's.

Create a David Letterman-like top-ten list of the reasons why Shakespeare's ten tragedies are tragic. Or put Shakespeare's *Romeo and Juliet* into contemporary slang so that you can remember what it is about. Or if you can never remember which character is from the Montague family and which is a Capulet, write a silly limerick to help you remember:

There once was a girl named Cap

Who fell for a guy and was hap

But her family and his

Wouldn't stand for the biz

So they both ended up playing taps.

Set it to music. Be imaginative. We tend to remember what's bizarre, funny, or even obscene![22]

How Our Memories (uh…hmmm…) Fail Us

Imagine this: You meet someone at a school reception who says, "Hey, I know you! Remember? We met a year ago—it was October—at that Halloween party, and we even went out a few times. I've never forgotten you." You rack your brain. This person doesn't even look familiar. You wonder, *Am I being confused with someone else? Am I crazy? I have no recollection at all!* Later, you comb through your calendar to reconstruct that month. You weren't even attending your current school then. It couldn't have been you.

Digital cameras can malfunction, files we've saved can become corrupted, and sometimes our memories fail us, too. We forget things or change them in our thinking. Think of how many times you have had to e-mail someone for a password because you've forgotten your original one.

Here are seven ways our memories fail us from *The Seven Sins of Memory: How the Mind Forgets and Remembers*. See how many cause you to say "yes" because you've experienced them, and think about which ones particularly apply most to Kevin from the "FOCUS Challenge Case."

1. **Fading.** Memories fade over time. You probably remember what you wore yesterday, but how about on October 5 a year ago? As time goes by, memories generally weaken.

2. **Absentmindedness.** Sometimes there's a disconnect between your focus and your memory. You were doing several things at one time—talking to the girl next to you after class and checking your cell phone while stuffing your backpack—and now you have no idea what you did with your history textbook. It's not that the information is lost over time; it probably never registered in the first place because your attention was elsewhere.

3. **Blocking.** It's right on the tip of your tongue, but you just can't quite retrieve it. You can see the face, but you can't dig up the name. But later that day, without even trying, suddenly it comes to you. Psychologists call it TOT, the Tip of the Tongue phenomenon. You feel as if you're about to sneeze, but can't, and the word—whatever it is—just won't come to you.

4. **Mistaking.** You say to your friend, "Hey, that was an interesting story you told me about the new girl in our writing class." "What story?" your friend replies. Someone told you something, but you're wrong about who it was. Or you read a passage in one book, but think you've read it in another. Or you've dreamed about something for so long that the fantasy actually becomes real in your mind. Your memory deceives you by mistaking one source for another or tricks you by inventing a memory where none actually exists.

5. **Inventing.** Sometimes you retain bits of information that you think are memories, but they really aren't. Here's an example: Perhaps your mother has told you the cute story about yourself as a two-year-old toddler so many times that you can now envision it, and you think you remember it. You were actually too young to remember anything, but the event has become real at someone else's suggestion.

bias based on your own personal feeling or belief

6. **Bias.** Sometimes we knowingly, or more often unknowingly, rewrite history. We insist on some detail that, if we had the ability to go back in time to verify it, is actually wrong. Perhaps someone has caught you in a trap in one of those instances by finding a piece of real evidence, and you've had to back down and admit that your memory is off a bit.

persistence keeping at it; not letting go; continuing

7. **Persistence.** Another way that memory bothers us is by nagging. You'd really like to forget something, but you just can't. You wake up in a cold sweat at 3 a.m., remembering the embarrassing thing you did at work or said in class. You'd like to be able to push the memory away, but it won't budge.

While these seven memory faults are aggravating and inconvenient at times, they also have value. Persistence may serve as a reminder to be more

How **FULL** is your plate?

> **Make use of time, let not advantage slip.**
> —WILLIAM SHAKESPEARE

When it comes to managing your time, perhaps the biggest challenge is actually doing it. That may sound like talking in a circle, but think about it: You buy a planner, fill in due dates, color code the level of priority of various items, and devote a substantial amount of time to getting yourself organized. Then you lose the planner, leave it in your car, or don't remember to take it out of your backpack when you get home. You can't find the time to actually open the planner meant to help you use the planner you've planned to use. Follow through and remember Shakespeare's wisdom: "let not advantage slip"!

Paul Maguire, 2010/Used under license from Shutterstock.com

careful next time. Fading is the result of memory efficiency. Why waste time recalling outdated, insignificant details we no longer need? Chances are you can't recall something because you haven't needed to recently, and the memory connection has weakened. (This can happen if you don't keep up with your coursework. When it's exam time, and you haven't looked at your notes for weeks, the memory of what you'd studied long ago may have faded.) Generally, we remember what we need to remember in order to survive in the environment in which we live. We get the basics of things, and often the rest falls away. The point, however, is to take charge of the process of remembering![23]

Deepen Your Memory

The point of this chapter is this: In a classic study conducted in the mid-1970s, two Swedish scholars decided to find out the difference between effective and ineffective learners. They gave students this task: read an essay, summarize it, and solve a problem. Then they interviewed the students to find out how they had approached the task.

The interviews revealed two types of learners. One group of students said things like, "I just tried to remember as much as I could" or "I just memorized what I read." Other students said, "I tried to look for the main idea" or "I looked for the point of the article." The professors who conducted the study then characterized the difference between *surface-level processing*, looking at words and numbers alone, and *deep-level processing*, searching beneath the surface for underlying meaning.[24] To become a truly focused learner, you must process information as you go. Dig deep!

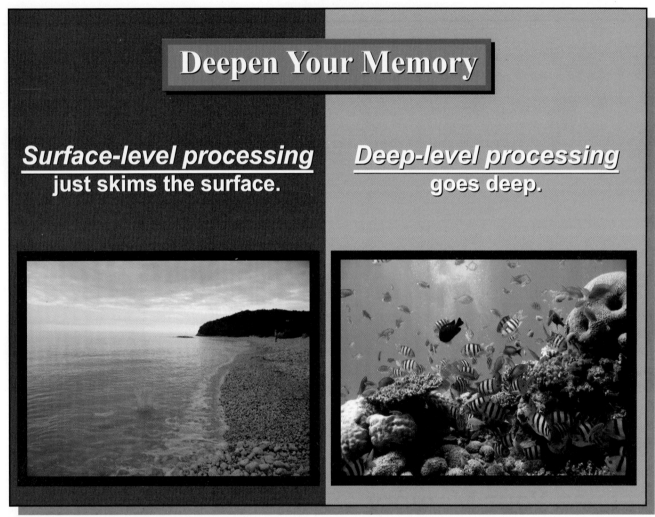

Nathan B. Dappen, 2009/Used under license from Shutterstock.com; Elisei Shafer, 2009/Used under license from Shutterstock.com.

FIGURE 8.4

**Memory Processing:
Skipping a Stone versus
Deep Sea Diving**

The true art of memory is the art of attention.

*Samuel Johnson, British poet, essayist, and biographer
(1709–1784)*

VARK Activity

Complete the activity recommended for your preferred VARK learning style and bring it to class (or follow your instructor's instructions).

 Visual: Create a diagram that shows all of the steps a student should go through when memorizing challenging material for an exam.

 Aural: Reconstruct one of your instructor's lectures and then present the lecture yourself to someone else. Access the CourseMate via www.cengagebrain.com/shop/ISBN/1439083908 to listen to the iAudio summary for this chapter. Write down three ideas that stuck in your head.

 Read/Write: Check out a library book on memory, and summarize a major section that's important to understanding memory as a process.

 Kinesthetic: Demonstrate three memory techniques that work for you in front of your classmates, and let them guess what you're trying to portray.

step 3 INSIGHT *Now* What Do You Think?

At the beginning of this chapter, Kevin Baxter, a frustrated and discouraged returning adult student, faced a challenge. Now after reading this chapter, would you respond differently to any of the questions you answered about the "FOCUS Challenge Case"? Using what you learned in the chapter, write a paragraph ending to Kevin's case study. What are some of the possible outcomes for Kevin?

step 4 ACTION Your Plans for Change

1. What's the most important thing you learned in reading this chapter? Why was it memorable?
2. Which memory techniques will you try as you study for your next exam?

On a scale of 1 to 5, answer these questions now that you've completed this chapter.

1 = not very/not much/very little/low   5 = very/a lot/very much/high

How much do you know *now*?

Now rate your current level of knowledge about topics covered in this chapter.

Short-term versus long-term memory

        1   2   3   4   ⑤

Memory as a process

        1   2   3   4   ⑤

Memory improvement techniques

        1   2   3   4   ⑤

Causes for memory failures

        1   2   3   4   ⑤

How useful might the information in this chapter be to you?

How much do you think this information might affect your college success?

        1   2   3   4   ⑤

How much do you think this information might affect your career success after college?

        1   2   3   4   ⑤

How long did it actually take you to complete this chapter (both the reading and writing tasks)?

   _____ Hour(s) _____ Minutes

 Challenge Yourself Online Quiz. To find out how much you've learned, access the CourseMate via www.cengagebrain.com/shop/ISBN/1439083908 to take the Challenge Yourself Online Quiz.

Compare these answers with your answers from the "Readiness Check" at the beginning of this chapter. How might the gaps between what you thought before starting the chapter and what you now think affect how you approach the next chapter?

FOR MIDTERM:
READ CHAPTERS
2-9!!

work, or everything else she had to do.

Back in grade school, Katie had been labeled as a slow reader. She was never in the top reading group, and although she resented the label, she didn't quite know what do to about it. The last time reading had actually been a subject in school was sixth grade. Now, eight years later, she was enrolled in a developmental reading class. Would it really help her?

One of Katie's best friends, Amanda, was an Elementary Education major who loved to read. In fact, that's all she ever seemed to do. Her other best friend, Brittney, however, had a different strategy. "There's so much required reading in all my classes that I don't even know where to start," Brittney admitted, "so I just don't do it. I go to class, listen to the lectures, and write down what the instructor has said on the essay tests. Katie, just learn to 'play the game'!"

Besides her developmental reading class, Katie was enrolled in an introduction to psychology class. She knew she'd have plenty of reading to do there, and her friend Brittney's strategy definitely wasn't going to work. Professor Harris-Black had assigned a shocking number of chapters to read in their thick textbook for the first exam. She didn't even go over the reading in class, and her lectures were about all sorts of things, much of which wasn't even related to the reading. Whenever Katie sat down to read a chapter, she found what to her were unfamiliar words and long, complicated phrases. The instructor had suggested that students read with a dictionary at their sides, but who'd ever want to keep stopping to look up words? You'd never finish!

With a midterm exam coming up in her psychology class next week, Katie was beginning to panic. She'd only read one of the nine chapters assigned. In fact, she hadn't made it through the first chapter when she got discouraged and gave up. She knew the essay questions would be challenging. Winging it wouldn't work, and choosing to "watch the movie" instead of reading the book wasn't an option. Exactly what did psychology have to do with hospitality, she puzzled, and why did she have to take this course in the first place?

The night before the test, Katie decided to get serious. She sat down at her desk, armed with her yellow highlighter. As she began reading, however, she realized she didn't know exactly what to highlight since she didn't really understand what she was reading. Looking back at the page she had just finished, she saw that she had basically highlighted everything.

Exasperated, Katie told herself that she couldn't go to bed until she'd finished reading everything, no matter when that was. She started with the second chapter, since she'd read the first one, and by morning, she'd be as ready as possible. Anyway, whether or not she did well wasn't up to her—it was up to Professor Harris-Black. She was the one making up the test.

Getting a good grade on her Introduction to Psychology midterm exam was probably out of the question, but if she could just manage to pass, Katie knew she would have to settle for that. On the other hand, she secretly hoped that maybe she'd just luck out.

MONDAY
Class 10-12   Class
Practice @ 4
Evening   Class
TUESDAY
Lab 11-1   Group project   Work
meeting @ 3
WEDNESDAY
Work 9-5   SATURDAY
Softball
Campus
3pm
Evening   Movie Night!   Evening

Psychology
Recommended Reading List

Treating the Troubled Family
    Ackerman, N.W.
The Care and Feeding of Ideas
    Adams, J. L.
Kinds of Minds
    Dennett, D.C.
The Dreaming Brain
    Clifford, James
Guilty by Reason of Insanity
    Lewis, D.O.
The Evolution of Consciousness
    Ornstein, R.
Beginner's Guide to Jungian Psychology
    Robertson, R.
Anger: The Misunderstood Emotion
    Tavris, C.

Study Strategies for Students with Dys[...]

- **Take advantage of multi-sensory learning me[...]**
  Study diagrams, look at charts
  Listen to the instructor's words
  Combine sensory input to create a more complete pict[...]

- **Read through superficially first**
  Look at the title page and intro
  Note the major headings and bullets
  Skim through the text to get the main ideas

- **Read out loud**
  Read out loud while highlighting, then read what y[...]
  Listen to your voice as you emphasize important [...]

- **Organize your workspace**
  Categorize papers and books for each subject
  Color-code assignments and papers to make o[...]

- **Improve your work methods**
  Brainstorm at the beginning of a project
  Set priorities and outline your work strateg[...]

- **Prepare for tests**
  Be sure to attend all classes leading up to [...]
  for clues and try to determine the [...]

1. Do you have anything in common with Katie? If so, in what ways, specifically?
2. Katie is probably an intelligent student, but she has decided that she dislikes reading and studying, so she avoids it. How important will these two skills be as she continues to pursue a college degree? Is she likely to succeed her second time around?
3. How would you characterize Katie as a student? Identify five specific problems described in this case study that could interfere with her college success.
4. Identify three specific things Katie should do to get her college career on track.

Who Needs to Read?

What's so important about reading? Teachers seem to think it's important, but times have changed, haven't they? Now you can just skim predigested information on websites, get a summary of the day's news from television, and watch movies for entertainment. Who needs to read? Look around the next time you're in a doctor or dentist's waiting room. You'll see some people staring at the TV screen mounted on the wall, others plugged into iPods, and still others working with their smart phones. A few may be skimming through magazines, but does anyone ever pick up a book to actually read it cover to cover anymore? Does it matter?

The answer, according to many experts, is a definite yes, it does matter![1] Reading helped create civilization as we know it and taught us particular ways of thinking.

One fairly predictable result of doing anything less often is that eventually you may not do it as well. Practice helps you improve. Even an Olympic athlete who doesn't stick with training gets rusty after a while. As students read less, their reading skills deteriorate and they don't enjoy doing it. On the other hand, the better you get at reading, the more you may enjoy it. Falling down every ten minutes the first time you get on skis isn't all that much fun, but once you can zip down the mountain like a pro, you begin to appreciate the sport.

Like Katie from the "FOCUS Challenge Case," reading may not be your favorite pastime. You may feel about reading like many people do about eating cauliflower. You know it's good for you, but you'd prefer to avoid it. However, this chapter wouldn't be worth its weight in trees if it didn't try to convince you otherwise. One aspect of reading Katie particularly dislikes is that reading is not a social or physical activity. You can read with someone else in the room, of course, or talk about what you read afterward with other people, but basically, reading is something you do alone.

> **You don't have to burn books to destroy a culture. Just get people to stop reading them.**
>
> *Ray Bradbury, science fiction writer*

Stressed Out?

> **In times of great stress or adversity, it's always best to keep busy, to plow your anger and your energy into something positive.**
> —LEE IACOCCA, AMERICAN BUSINESSMAN (1924–)

Stress . . . it's all in your head. That's what some people say. Stress is what you feel when your mind reacts to tough challenges. They even say some stress is good for you. But when stress goes unchecked, there's always the possibility you'll blow up like Mt. Vesuvius. How can you tell when you're about to reach that point? Is it when the stress that was in your head spreads to other parts of your body? Your immune system goes haywire and you come down with the cold of the century? Your headache is debilitating or your back feels like six kids are jumping on it? _Feel_ the stress!

Devon Stephens/iStockphoto.com

TRY IT!

Keep track of when your body tells you to deal with the stress in your life. Write down your top three symptoms here:

1. _____
2. _____
3. _____

Lee Iacocca says that the best way to deal with stress is to channel negative energy into something positive in your life, something you want to achieve, something you value—like getting a college education. This week, pay attention to symptoms of unchecked stress and take positive action!

It's a solitary activity that involves you, words on a page, an invisible author, and your brain. You need to do it with a minimum of physical movement. Reading while playing a game of volleyball would be tough to pull off.

If you enjoy reading, congratulations! When you settle in with an exciting novel, you can travel to the far corners of the Earth, turn back the clock to previous centuries, or fast-forward to a future that extends beyond your lifetime. Whether or not you enjoy reading, it will be one of the primary skills you need to cultivate in college. According to one study, 85 percent of the learning you'll do in college requires careful reading.[2] First-year students often need to read and comprehend 150–200 pages per week in order to complete their academic assignments.[3]

What's more, reading skills go hand in hand with writing skills, which makes them even more important. The better you get at reading, the more likely you are to achieve academic success. Many of your classes will require intensive reading of complex material, including **primary sources** by original authors and **scholarly research**. If you complete reading assignments, and your classmates don't, think about how much ahead of the nonreaders _you_ will be! But how do you become a better reader?

Read Right!

What do we know about reading? How _should_ you tackle your many reading assignments in college? Consider these twelve

2 TERMS

1

primary sources works written by authors themselves, like the autobiography of Benjamin Franklin (that he wrote himself)

scholarly research articles in academic journals, like the studies about reading and college students, footnoted at the end of the last paragraph

> It matters, if individuals are to retain any capacity to form their own judgments and opinions, that they continue to read for themselves.
>
> _Harold Bloom, literary critic_

essential points.[4] As you read, put checkmarks next to items you see as potential areas of improvement for yourself as a reader:

1. _____ **Understand what being a good reader is all about.** Reading isn't a race. Remember the old children's story about the tortoise and the hare? The turtle actually won the race because he plodded along, slowly and steadily, while the rabbit zipped all over the place and lost focus. The moral of that story applies to reading, too. Reading is a process; understanding is the goal. The point isn't simply to make it through the reading assignment by turning pages every few minutes so that you can finish the chapter in a certain amount of time. Reading requires you to back up occasionally, just like when you back up a DVD to catch something you missed: "What did he say to her? I didn't get that."

   Students sometimes mistakenly think that good readers are speed-readers, when it's really about focus.[5] Science fiction writer Isaac Asimov once wrote, "I am not a speed reader. I am a speed understander." On the other hand, reading too slowly can be a problem, too. If you chew (with your eyes) on every word and huff and puff along as you go, your mind can wander. Before you know it, you've let a thousand other thoughts intervene, as Katie Alexander did, and you have no idea where you are. The average reader reads at a rate of approximately 250 words per minute with a 70 percent comprehension rate. Time yourself on an upcoming paragraph in this chapter, and then see if you can talk through what you've just read and convince yourself that you understand it.[6] The point is to be efficient so that you can actually get all your reading done for all your classes.

EXERCISE 9.1

Keeping a Reading Log

Is there a book you'd really like to read? Perhaps it's a book about which people say, "Oh, the book is much better than the movie!" Perhaps it's an author you've heard about: a famous politician, actor, or singer. Select a book to read for pleasure this month, and keep a reading log of how many pages you read each day and how long you stick with it. After you finish the book, write a letter about the book and the process of reading it to your instructor and classmates. There's evidence that reading something you choose yourself can be an important force in becoming a better reader![7]

2. _____ **Take stock of your own reading challenges.** Which of the following are reading issues for you? Rank order your top five with 1 as your most difficult challenge.[8]

   ___ boredom   ___ surroundings   ✓ vision   ___ fear   ___ speed
   ___ fluency   ___ comprehension   ✓ fatigue   ___ time   ___ level
   ✓ amount   ___ retention   ___ interest   ✓ laziness   ___ motivation

   Many people find reading challenging. You may have worked with an impatient teacher as a youngster, or you may have been taught using a method that didn't work well for you—factors that still cause you problems today. Reading involves visually recognizing symbols, transferring those visual cues to your brain, translating them into meaningful signals—recording, retaining, and retrieving information (here's where your memory kicks in)—and finally using these meanings to think, write, or speak. Reading challenges can be caused by *physical factors* (your vision, for example) and *psychological factors* (your attitude). If you want to become a better reader in the future, it's a good idea to assess honestly what's most challenging about the process for you right now.[9]

3. _____ **Adjust your reading style.** Reading requires flexibility. Contrast these two situations: reading the menu on the wall at your local fast-food joint and poring over the menu at a fancy, high-end restaurant. You'd just scan the fast-food menu in a few seconds, wouldn't you? You wouldn't read word by word and ask: "Is the beef in that burger from grass-fed cattle?" "What, exactly, is in the 'special sauce'?" If you did, the counter clerk would probably blurt out, "Look, are you going to order something or not?" That kind of situation requires quick skimming. But you'd take some time to study the menu at a pricey restaurant you might go to with friends and family to celebrate a special occasion. It's an entirely different situation, and the information is more complicated. And if it's a fancy French restaurant, you might even need to ask the definitions of some terms like *canard* (duck) or *cassoulet* (a rich, hearty stew). That kind of situation requires slow, considered study, word by word. You're going to pay for what you choose, and you want the best results on your investment. That's true about college, too. You're investing in your college classes, so reading right is important!

You'll face an enormous amount of reading in your combined college classes. The question is, what's fast food (to carry through with the example) and what's fine dining? According to research on reading, good readers know the difference and adjust their reading styles.[10]

Reading a new popular new detective novel is something you should whip through, but reading the first chapter of your philosophy textbook would require more concentration. Likewise, some of the reading you'll do in college is fast food. You just need to skim to get the main points and then move on to the next homework item on your agenda. However, much of the reading you'll do in college is fine dining. That's why it's important to devote more time to reading and studying than you think you'll actually need. You'll be able to "digest" what you're reading much better.

4. _____ **Have a "conversation" with the author.** In every book you read, the author is trying to convince you of something. Take this book, for example. We have been engaged in a conversation all the way through. What do you know about me? What am I trying to persuade you to think about or do? Even though I'm not right in front of you in person on every page, you are forming impressions of me as you read, and I'm either convincing you to try the suggestions in this book or I'm not. As you read any book, argue with the author ("That's not how I see it!"), question her ("What makes you say that?"), agree with her ("Yes, right on!"), relate something

"Perhaps the most valuable result of all education is the ability to make yourself do the thing you have to do, when it ought to be done, whether you like it or not.

Thomas Henry Huxley,
British biologist (1825–1895)

commentary a record of your opinion

she said earlier to something she's saying now ("But what about …?"). Instead of just coloring with your yellow highlighter, scribble comments in the margins, or keep a running **commentary** in a notebook. Reading is an active process, not a passive one in which the words just float by you. In fact, mark up this page right now! How do you decide what's really important? One thing you can do is ask your instructor in this course to show you his or her mark-ups in this book, and see if the two of you agree on what's important.

5. _____ **Dissect the text.** Whether you did it virtually online or physically in a real lab, dissecting or cutting up those little critters in your biology class helped you figure out what was what. The ability to dissect text is important in reading. As you read and make notes in the margins, write *what* and *why* statements. Try it: beside each paragraph on this page, write a one-sentence summary statement: a *what* statement. Put the author's words into your own words. Then write another sentence that focuses on *why* the paragraph is included. Does the paragraph contain *evidence* to make a point? Is it an *example* of something? If you can tackle this recommendation, you'll do wonders for yourself when exam time rolls around.

EXERCISE 9.2

Marginal Notes

Go back through the section of this chapter on reading that you just completed. Make notes to yourself in the margins (or on another sheet of paper) about why you underlined a word, phrase, or section. Why did you consider that part to be important? Knowing the answers to these questions is more important than the act of "coloring."[11]

6. _____ **Make detailed notes.** You'll be much more likely to actually master a challenging reading assignment if you keep a notebook beside you and take full-blown notes as you read. Or go online and use a note-taking tool like evernote.com. The old rule of thumb still applies: read, close the book, and write down what you remember. Then go back into the book and check.[12] The physical act of writing or typing can help you remember it later.

7. _____ **Put things into context.** Reading requires a certain level of what's called **cultural literacy**. Authors assume their readers have a common background. They refer to other books or current events, or historical milestones, and unless you know what they're referring to, what you're reading may not make sense to you. An example you might be familiar with is how the television show *Seinfeld* made real words that everyone now knows and uses out of fake ones: *yada yada yada*, for example. Those words are now part of our cultural literacy that have meaning for you and everyone you know, probably, but may not for people from another culture. They know the literacy of their own culture instead.

cultural literacy core knowledge—things that everyone knows—that helps put things into context and give them meaning

8. _____ **Don't avoid the tough stuff.** Much of the reading you'll do in college includes complicated sentences that are difficult to work your way through. When you read complex passages aloud, you may stumble because you don't immediately recognize how the words are linked into

phrases. But practicing reading aloud is one way you can become more conversant with difficult language. Many instructors teach their students a common approach to reading and studying called SQ3R:

Survey—Skim to get the lay of the land quickly.

Question—Ask yourself what, why, and how questions. What is this article or chapter about? Why is it included? How might I use this information?

Read (1)—Go ahead now and read the entire assignment. Make notes in the margins or even create a study guide for yourself.

Recite (2)—Stop every now and then and talk to yourself. See if you can put what you're reading into your own words.

Review (3)—When you've finished, go back and summarize what you've learned.

Try it right now with this section of the chapter, "Read Right."

Survey—What is this section of the chapter about, generally? When you preview a chapter or section of a textbook, look for color, highlighting, italics, layout, bullets—anything that communicates, "This is important!"

Question—What's the point of including it? Why is it here? How can it help you?

Read (1)—Now read the bullets in this section carefully, making "what" and "why" comments in the margins.

Recite (2)—At the conclusion of each bullet, summarize the point out loud, and decide if this is an item you should put a checkmark next to, indicating that it's something you should work on.

Review (3)—When you're finished with the whole section, see if you can summarize what you've learned from reading it.

> Parents should play an inestimable role in children's learning to read and learning to love to read.
>
> —*Barbara Swaby*

9. _____ **Learn the language.** Every discipline has its own perspective and its own vocabulary. In many of the introductory classes you take, you'll spend a good deal of time and effort learning terms to be used in classes you'll take later. In order to study *advanced* biology, everyone has to learn the same language in *introductory* biology. You can't be calling things whatever you want to call them. You call it a respiratory system, but your classmate calls it a reproductive system. In college you will be introduced to various subjects or disciplines as you take what are often called general education or core courses. It's important to get to know a discipline.

10. _____ **Bring your reading to class.** Some of your instructors will infuse the outside course readings into their lectures. They may preview the readings in class, talk about their importance, or create reading worksheets for use in small groups. If they don't, however, it's up to you to integrate them. Bring up the reading in class, ask questions about it, and find

out how it relates to particular points in the lecture. Doing so is an important part of being responsible for your own learning.

11. _____ **Ask for a demonstration.** If a textbook reading assignment for a course baffles you, ask your instructor for a mini-lesson in how to proceed. Sometimes all it takes is for the teacher to give the entire class (or just you) some pointers. For example, the instructor may help you come up with "What" and "Why" statements or tell you where she would stop to write something in the notebook she keeps beside her.

12. _____ **Be inventive!** Students who are the best readers invent strategies that work for them. Perhaps you're an auditory learner. Reading assignments aloud might drive people you live with crazy (so find a place where you can be alone), but it might be the perfect way for you to learn. If you're a kinesthetic learner, you might make copies of particular passages from your textbook and lecture notes, and build your own scrapbook for a course. Or cut up the instructors's lecture notes into small puzzle pieces and reassemble them. Using what you know about yourself as a learner is a big part of college success, so don't just do what everyone else does or even follow your instructor's advice word for word, if it doesn't work for you. Figure out what does, and then do it!

Re Read Chapter.

 Learn everything you can, anytime you can, from anyone you can—there will always come a time when you will be grateful you did.

SARAH CALDWELL

Study Up. In college, you are encouraged to learn deeply, not just memorize facts. Transfer this principle to the workplace. On the job, learn the ins and outs of your industry. If, for example, you are a healthcare or law enforcement professional, strive to know more than just the details of your day-to-day work. Learn about your department's history, what your employing agency stands for, its vision and values, and the reputation it has earned from customers, clients, and citizens. It's easy to get tunnel vision and lose sight of the bigger picture. But when you keep up on your profession, and even on new events—the "news"—of what's happening in your industry, you show your colleagues and supervisors that you care about your job and your organization's future. All other things being equal, when there's a promotion coming up, the person who has shown a pattern of "studying up" on the organization will be the person most often promoted.

"Elementary, My Dear Watson": Build Your Reading Skills

Remember Sherlock Holmes, that great fictional detective? His sidekick, Dr. Watson, didn't always grasp clues in the instinctive, speedy way Sherlock Holmes did. Holmes would size up a situation immediately, while Watson scratched his head and asked, "How did you know that?" Holmes would reply, "Elementary, My

Dear Watson." In other words: "Once I reveal the clue to you, you'll see. It's easy." For Holmes, detective work was second-nature.

Some people think reading should be second-nature since we've all been doing it for many years now. Someone may understand an article they've just read immediately, while others ask "How did you know that?" about something in the same passage. Learning to recognize the clues helps. We'll look at some clues to help you become a better reader. It's not always as easy as it looks, especially in college. Books and articles you need to read for your classes are often challenging, and they can require a lot of self-discipline to read. Perhaps you're in a developmental reading class to boost your skills. Or perhaps a language other than English is your native tongue. If so, this section of the chapter can be especially useful to you.

Put English under the Magnifying Glass

One way to become a better reader is by gaining a deeper understanding of how English works. If you've been speaking it all your life, it seems natural. You open your mouth and speak, without pausing to think over every word choice. But even for many people who learned to speak English as children, *reading* English is a bigger challenge. Just what are some of the specific challenges?

Sounds. English is spoken as a first or second language by 1.8 billion people. It's the designated "official" language in 53 countries.[13] English varies somewhat from one region of the country to another. If you live in the South, "pa" (as in "I'll have a slice of apple 'pa'") may be something you eat for dessert; in another part of the country, it's what you call your dad. The sound "tsk" you make when you mean "What a shame . . ." (tsk, tsk . . .) is an actual sound that might be the first sound in a word in other languages. In fact, when you were a six-month-old baby, you could pronounce almost any sound that exists in any language. But as you learn to speak as a young child, you discard sounds that aren't a part of your native language.

You already know a good deal about English that you're not even aware you know. If you entered a contest to name a new laundry detergent, you'd automatically use the "rules" for how English operates. For example, you know that you can't clump too many consonants together at the beginning of an English word, and you know that some sounds just don't go together, like "f" and "z." You'd never come up with "Buy new Fzuthoox!" People in the supermarket couldn't even pronounce it to ask a stocker, let alone find it on Aisle 9. If you're a new speaker of English, go to a website on English sounds and play the MP3 files. You can hear "pure" English online.[14]

Syllables. Things get more complicated when sounds combine into syllables, like prefixes or suffixes. Some syllables are easy to understand, like the difference between the prefixes *pre-* and *post-* in preseason game versus postseason game. Or you know when you see the word *co-presenters*, that more than one person will be speaking. Other times, syllables are just plain puzzling. For example, typically, the prefix "in-" means "not." But why do *flammable* and *inflammable* mean exactly the same thing? Or when someone says your help is *valuable* or *invaluable*, that both remarks are equally complimentary? Go

figure. Learning basic prefixes, suffixes, and word roots can help you decipher unfamiliar words you encounter in your reading.

Spelling. Here's where many of us get tripped up—and Spellcheck isn't always the solution. (Did you notice the missing letter in the word spelled by the blocks?) To make things especially messy, English has many exceptions to its rules. Take a look at the Curiosity box in this chapter to see some humorous examples of just how varied spelling is in English. When you try reading the poem out loud, you'll get the point quickly.

Vocabulary. Reading is about words. That's why it's important to put some muscle into your vocabulary. When you study a foreign language, your first task is to learn new vocabulary words so that you have something to say: "What time is it?" or "Where is the train station?" or "How much does this cost?" It's just as important, especially in college, to fill your mind with new words, too.

One of the best things you can do to become a better reader is to make friends with your dictionary. Even though it's annoying to stop every few minutes to look up a word, it's absolutely necessary. Sometimes it's important to break your stride, stop, and look up a word or phrase because what follows in the reading is based on that particular definition. Other times, these strategies might be appropriate:

> Keep a stack of blank index cards next to you and write down the unknown word or phrase, the sentence it appears in, and the page number. Then when you have a sizable stack, or when you've scheduled a chunk of time, look up the whole stack.

context words, sentences, and/or paragraphs around an unknown word that help you unlock its meaning

> Try to guess the word's meaning from its **context** that helps to reveal its meaning. Remember Lewis Carroll's "Jabberwocky" poem from *Through the Looking-Glass*? Even though the poem contains fabricated words, when you read it, you infer that something was moving around sometime, somewhere, right?

> > ***'Twas brillig*** ['twas usually indicates a time, as in 'twas daybreak],

> > ***and the slithy toves*** [we don't know what *toves* are, but *slithy* sounds like a combination of slimy and slithering]

Often you can infer a word's meaning from how it's used or from other words around it, but not always. Many of your courses will require you to learn precise meanings for new terms. If you can't detect the meaning from the context, use your dictionary—and see it as a friend, rather than an enemy.

EXERCISE 9.3

Word Hunt

You'll notice that this book defines some words that relate to your college education in the margins. That's not only a convenience; they're included to help remind you to stop and look up words as you read assignments for your other courses. Which other words are you looking up on your own as you read FOCUS? Highlight all the additional words you needed to look up in this chapter and bring your list to class to compare with your classmates' lists.

Hints on Pronunciation for Foreigners

I take it you already know
Of laugh and bough and cough and dough?
Others may stumble but not you,
On hiccough, thorough, laugh and through.
Well done! And now you wish, perhaps,
To learn of less familiar traps?

Beware of heard, a dreadful word
That looks like beard and sounds like bird,
And dead: It's said like bed, not bead—
For goodness' sake don't call it "deed"!
Watch out for meat and great and threat
(They rhyme with suite and straight and debt.)

A moth is not a moth in mother
Nor both in bother, broth in brother
And here is not a match for there
Nor dear and fear for bear and pear,
And then there's dose and rose and lose—
Just look them up—and goose and choose,
And cork and work and card and ward,
And font and front and word and sword,

And do and go and thwart and cart—
Come, come, I've hardly made a start!
A dreadful language? Man alive.
I'd mastered it when I was five.

—T.S.W. (only initials of writer known) or possibly
written by George Bernard Shaw

Go ahead. Try reading this poem aloud. Even if English is your first language, you probably had to pause and think about how to say a word occasionally. Most anyone would. English isn't exactly the easiest language in the world to learn, non-native English speakers say. It's filled with perplexing irregularities. Think about the courage it would take to pursue a college degree by reading and writing in a language other than your native tongue. If English is your first language, could *you* do it in German or Arabic or Hindi? That being acknowledged, what strategies can ESL (English as a Second Language) students use to help with challenging reading assignments?

1. **Remember that spoken English differs from the written English you'll find in textbooks and academic articles.** In casual conversation, you'll hear, "And she's … like, 'wow!' and I'm … like, 'really?'" If you read that in a book, you'd have no idea what the speakers were communicating about. But if you're standing next to the people doing the talking in the hallway, you have a chance of figuring it out. Learning to speak informally in conversation is very different from learning to read textbooks for your courses. Address these questions to your instructor or study-group mates instead.

2. **Ask your English-speaking friends and instructors to coach you.** For example, ESL speakers sometimes struggle with the hundreds of idioms found in English. Idioms are groups of words with their own meaning. For example, "I have a frog in my throat" means your voice is hoarse, not that you literally have swallowed a green amphibian. Idioms must be learned as a set of words in order to communicate their intended meaning. If you change one word ("I have a toad in my throat"), the idiom doesn't work. Considering how many idioms English has and how freely English speakers use them without thinking about it, non-native speakers may find learning them all to be a challenge. You'll more likely hear idioms spoken, rather than read them. If you're an international student, ask about unique phrases that don't make sense to you.

3. **Use the Internet or an online course to improve your language skills.** According to one study, international students in an online course made significant gains in their language skills, compared with a control group of students who sat through the same course in a classroom. Online courses provide good exposure and practice in your reading and writing skills via e-mail, web searching, threaded discussions, and online postings.[15]

4. **Try explaining what you're reading to someone else.** Talking something through while you're reading, especially with a native English speaker, can help you clarify meanings on the spot—and may help the other student achieve better comprehension, too.

5. **Mark up the textbook so that you can pursue difficult passages in greater detail later.** Insert question marks in the margins. Read with your English–native tongue dictionary in front of you.

6. **If you get completely stuck, find another book that may explain the concepts differently, or take a break and let your brain continue to work on it while you're doing something else.**

Search for Clues: Develop Your Skills of Detection

We can move beyond the realm of sounds and words into the realm of sentences, inferences, main ideas, and patterns. Being a good reader is like being a good detective. You have to watch for subtle clues and draw conclusions.

Inferences. Combining words into "complete thoughts" gives us sentences, and they can be complicated, too. The mere arrangement of words in a sentence can make a difference. From sentences and paragraphs, we create meaning and make **inferences**. For example, language experts talk about the difference between active and passive voice, often detectable by how words are arranged. For example:

> Mom (noticing the dent in the front fender): "Did you drive the car?"
>
> You: "Yes, I drove the car." (Active voice, as in "I admit it.")

Compare that answer with "Um, the car was driven [by me]." (Passive voice, as in "the car was practically driving itself . . . ")

There's an inference (or conclusion) behind Mom's question, right? The dent is most likely your fault. Even a slight change in intonation or emphasis can make a difference in what two nearly identical sentences mean. Take this sign, for example, hanging in the ~~men's room of a restaurant~~: "We aim to please. You aim, ~~too, please~~."

inference a conclusion reached from hints or clues about something

---

EXERCISE 9.4

Two-Way Inferences

Part I. *Find a photo for this quote and bring it to class with you.*

> *"The secret of joy in work is contained in one word—excellence. To know how to do something well is to enjoy it."*
>
> *—Pearl Buck, Pulitzer Prize-winning American author, 1892–1973*

Part II. *Find a quote for the photo on the right and write it in the caption box accompanying the photo.*

Daniel Bobrowsky/iStockphoto.com

Stay on the Case: Put Clues Together

Reading longer sections of text requires that we look beyond sentences, down into the "guts" of a passage. This is where reading becomes interesting. How do you move beyond sounds, syllables, and words—the building blocks of language—toward understanding? The place to start is by finding the **main idea**. How do you do that?

main idea central message a writer is trying to get across

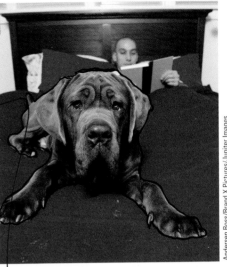

> "Outside of a dog, a book is man's best friend. Inside of a dog, it's too dark to read."
>
> *Groucho Marx, American comedian, actor, and singer (1890–1977)*

> Look for hints that identify the topic or subject being discussed.

> Look for words and phrases that are repeated.

> Look for a thesis statement or topic sentence that summarizes the passage.

> Look for evidence of the author's opinion on what's being written about.

How do you know if the main idea is worth buying into? Where can you find the evidence that supports the idea and makes it believable?

> Look for statistics, testimony from an expert, or examples.

And how do you detect inferences?

> See if you can uncover a generalization that could be made after reading the passage.

> Ask how the passage overall relates to you.

EXERCISE 9.5

Paragraph Analysis

Here are three passages from Katie Alexander's psychology textbook. You will need to know the answers to these six questions by the time you finish reading each paragraph.

Paragraph A

1. What's the difference between a Type A personality and a Type B personality?
2. Which personality type is most beneficial to a person's health and well-being?

Paragraph B

3. What is learned helplessness?
4. Where does learned helplessness come from?

Paragraph C

5. What are the three personality characteristics that make up hardiness?
6. How can being hardy help college students?

(When you read assignments for your classes, skipping ahead to the questions that will be asked of you afterward can be a good way to make sure you read more closely.) Below each paragraph, list the main idea, the supporting evidence for the main idea, and any inferences you detect.

(continued)

Paragraph A

Would you consider yourself more of a Type A personality, a person who is aggressive, competitive, and driven to achieve? Or do you characterize yourself as more of a Type B personality, a person who is more relaxed, easygoing, patient, and flexible? . . . Cardiologists Meyer Friedman and Ray Rosenman were the first to examine the connection between personality and heart disease. They suspected that personality or behavior patterns may play a role in the lives of men who were more likely to develop heart disease, and in men more likely to die from a heart attack. To test their idea, the researchers gathered a sample of 3,000 men between the ages of 35 and 59 with no known health problems. Each man was interviewed, and based on the man's behavior during the interview, each was designated as a Type A personality, a Type B personality, or somewhere in between. The majority of the sample fell somewhere in between, but in comparing the two types over the next decade, Friedman and Rosenman found that Type A personalities were two to three times more likely to have suffered a heart attack.

Topic: _CORRELATION OF HEART PROBLEMS TO PERSONALITY TYPE._

Main idea: _TYPE A PERSONALITIES ARE PRONE TO HEART PROBS._

Supporting evidence: _THE STUDY AND INTERVIEW TAKEN._

Inference: _"_ _"_

Paragraph B

Research supports the notion that college students who feel helpless are less likely to persist, more likely to give up easily, and as a result earn poor grades and report unhappiness. Adults and adolescents who react to stress by feeling at a loss to do anything about the situation are more prone to depression and other stress problems. Learned helplessness also has been documented in children with a history of reading failure. It can develop in elderly people in nursing homes who are not given choices about their daily activities and routines. In all of these situations, the expectation of failure and lack of control are what influence one's perceived level of stress, one's subsequent response to stress, and ultimately, one's mental and physical health.

Topic: _CORRELATION OF ONE'S ACADEMIC PREFORMM WITH DEPRETION_

Main idea: _THE EFFECT OF DEPRESSION ON STUDENS._

Supporting evidence: _THE FAILURE OF STUDENS._

Inference: _DEPRESSION SEVERLY EFFECT A STUDENT IN EVERY ASPECT_

Paragraph C

Do you view stressors as challenges rather than as threats? For example, if you try out for the soccer team one year and do not make it, do you try out again the next year or do you simply give up? Do you stay committed to the pursuit of your goals and values? If you fail an exam, do you go and get help, or do you just assume that you'll never understand the material and withdraw from the class—possibly spoiling your chance at a college degree? Do you believe that your actions influence the outcome of a situation? Your answers to these questions outline three factors that appear to be related to health: challenge, commitment, and control. . . . The "three Cs" taken together were labeled by psychologists Salvatore Maddi and Suzanne Kobasa as the hardy personality. This term resulted from Kobasa's research on upper-level executives and attorneys who had experienced considerable stress over a three-year period. Those who exemplified hardy traits were less likely to get ill during this time of stress. Even Type A people who scored high on measure of hardiness were less likely to get ill compared with Type A people who scored low on hardiness.

Topic: _THE EFFECT OF STRESS ON INDIVIDUALS_

Main idea: _HIGHER STRESS LEVELS LEAD TO A DECREASE IN HEALTH._

Supporting evidence: _ATTORNEYS GETTING SICK_

Inference: _STRESS SEVERLY EFFET TYPE A PEOPLE._

Paragraphs adapted from Pastorino, E., & Doyle-Portillo, S. (2006). *What is psychology?* Belmont, CA: Cengage Learning, p. 602–604.

BOX 9.1 Learning Disability? Five Ways to Help Yourself

Perhaps you were diagnosed with Attention-Deficit/Hyperactivity Disorder (ADHD) or dyslexia as a young child. If you're beginning your college career with a learning disability (LD), you're not alone. In a college or university with an enrollment of 25,000 students, for example, approximately 550 of those students have learning disabilities.[16] By some estimates, two-thirds of students with diagnosed LDs continue on to college after high school.[17] Does a learning disability mean all the odds are against you? No, but there are some important steps you must take to help yourself. Successful college students with LDs recognize, understand, and accept these steps, and develop compensating strategies to offset them.

1. If you've been previously diagnosed with a learning disability, bring a copy of your evaluation or Individualized Education Plan (IEP) with you to campus. Some schools require documentation in order to use the institution's support services.

2. Locate the support services office on your campus and use it. These services are free and can make all the difference in your success.

3. Learn more about your specific LD. Read about it. Visit credible websites. Understanding the ins and outs of what you're up against is important.

4. If you need special accommodations such as taking exams somewhere other than the classroom, schedule an appointment with your instructors early in the term to let them know. Having a learning disability doesn't mean you're required to do less work, but you'll get the support you need in order to do your best.

5. Remember that the advice in this book, which is helpful to all college students, can be even more useful to anyone with a learning disability. Time management strategies and study skills tailored to your specific LD are key.

Don't let fear of failure immobilize you. Instead, keep your eye on the goal and take charge of your own learning.[18]

Meta-what? Metacognition, Reading, and Studying

Talk about needing to use a dictionary! What does the word *metacognition* mean? *Meta* is an ancient Greek prefix that is often used to mean *about*. For example, metacommunication is communicating *about* the way you communicate. ("I feel humiliated when you tease me in front of other people. Can you *not* do that?")

Since cognition means thinking and learning, metacognition is thinking about your thinking and learning about your learning. It's about identifying your learning goals, monitoring your progress, backing up or getting help when you're stuck, forging ahead when you're in the groove, and evaluating your results. Metacognition is about knowing yourself as a learner and about your ability (and motivation) to control your own learning. Some things are easy for you to learn; others are hard. What do you know about yourself as a learner, and do you use that awareness *intentionally* to learn at your best?[19]

These questions may seem simple, but how do you know:

1. When you've finished a reading assignment?

2. When your paper is ready to turn in?

3. When you've finished studying for an exam?

Do You Know How to Study?

To what extent do these ten statements apply to you? Write the number for each statement on the line preceeding it.

Never		Sometimes		Always
1	2	3	4	5

3 1. I keep going with things I have to learn, rather than skipping over what I don't understand.

3 2. When I'm studying something difficult, I realize when I'm stuck and ask for help.

3 3. I make a study plan and stick to it in order to master class material.

5 4. I quiz myself as I'm studying to see what I understand and what I don't.

4 5. I talk through my problems, understanding things while I study.

5 6. After I study something, I think about how well it went.

4 7. I know when I learn best: morning, afternoon, or evening, for example.

4 8. I know how I study best: alone, with one other person, in a group, etc.

3 9. I know where I study best: at home, at the library, at my computer, etc.

4 10. I believe I'm in control of my own learning.

Now tally your scores on this informal instrument. If you scored between 40 and 50 total points, you have excellent metacognitive skills. If you scored between 30 and 40 points, your skills are probably average. However, note any items you rated down in the 1 to 2 range, and then continue reading this section of the chapter carefully.

When you're eating a meal, you know when you're full, right? But when it comes to academic work, how do you know when you're done? Some students resort to answers like this to the question, "How do you know when you're done?" Look at the range of students' answers:

> I just do.
> I trust in God.
> My eyelids get too heavy.
> I've been at it for a long time.
> My mom tells me to go to bed.
> I understand everything.
> I can write everything down without looking at the textbook or my notes.
> I've created a practice quiz for myself and get all the answers right.
> When my wife or girlfriend drills me and I know all the answers.
> When I can teach my husband everything I've learned.
> When I've highlighted, recopied my notes, made flash cards, written sample questions, tested myself, etc.

You can see that their answers become increasingly reliable as you progress down the list.[20]

Metacognition is about having an "awareness of [your] own cognitive machinery and how the machinery works."[21] It's about knowing the limits of your own learning and memory capabilities, knowing how much you can accomplish within a certain amount of time, and knowing what learning strategies work for you.[22] Know your limits, but at the same time, stretch.

Becoming an Intentional Learner: Make a Master Study Plan

What's your favorite class this term? Or let's turn the question around: What's your least favorite class? Becoming an educated person may well require you to study things you wouldn't *choose* to study. Considering all you have to do, including your most and least favorite classes, what would making a master study plan look like? You've "been there, done that" all through your schooling, but do you *really* know how to study?

To begin, think about what you have to think about. What's your goal? Is it to finish your English essay by 10:00 P.M. so that you can start your algebra homework? Or is it to write the best essay you can possibly write? If you've allowed yourself one hour to read this chapter, but after an hour, you're still not finished, you have three choices: keep reading, finish later, or give up entirely. What's in your best interest, honestly? See if you find the following planning strategies helpful.

1. **Make sure you understand your assignments.** Understanding is critical to making a master plan. You can waste a great deal of time trying to read your instructor's mind after the fact: "Did she want us to *analyze* the play or *summarize* it?" When you leave class, make sure you're clear on what's been assigned.

2. **Schedule yourself to be three places at once.** Making a master plan requires you to think simultaneously about three different time zones:

   <u>The past:</u> Ask yourself what you already know. Is this a subject you've studied before? Have your study habits worked well for you in the past? How have you done your best work—in papers, on exams, on projects?

   <u>The present:</u> Ask yourself what you need to learn now. How interested are you in this material? How motivated are you to learn it? How much time will you devote to it?

   <u>The future:</u> Ask yourself how you'll go about learning it. Will you learn it using the strategies that work best for you? Which learning factors will you control? Will you do what you can to change what's not working?[23]

© Larry Harwood Photography. Property of Cengage Learning.

3. **Talk through your learning challenges.** There's good evidence that talking to yourself while you're studying is a good thing. Researchers find it helps you figure things out: *Okay, I understand the difference between a neurosis and a psychosis, but I'm not sure I can provide examples on my psychology test.* Once you've heard yourself admit that, you know where to focus your efforts next.[24]

4. **Be a stickler.** Sticklers pay attention to details. They want to make sure everything is absolutely right. Have you ever thought about how important accuracy is? For example, if you were 99 instead of 100 percent accurate, that would mean that:

   > 500 airplanes in U.S. skies each day wouldn't be directed by air traffic controllers.[25] Disastrous!

   As you read and study, remember this example. Be thorough. Read the entire assignment. Pay attention to details. If you make a mistake, for example in solving a math problem, figure out exactly what went wrong, so that you don't hold on to a bad academic habit. Rework the problem at least twice, write a few sentences describing the right way to solve it, and try another problem similar to it to see if you really understand.[26] Accuracy counts!

5. **Take study breaks.** The human attention span is limited, and according to some researchers, it's shrinking, rather than expanding.[27] Plan to take brief scheduled breaks to stretch, walk around, or grab a light snack every half hour during study sessions. Of course, it's important to sit down and get back to work again. Don't let a quick study break to get a snack multiply into several hours of television viewing that wasn't in the plan.

6. **Mix it up.** Put a little variety into your study sessions by switching from one subject to another, or from one mode of studying—for example, reading, self-quizzing, writing—to another. Variety helps you fight boredom and stay fresh (unless, of course, you're on the verge of a breakthrough).

7. **Review, review, review!** Review your course material often enough that you can retain and retrieve information at the level expected by your instructor. If you have to start fresh each time you come to class, trying to work from what you remember from the last class, you'll always feel behind.

8. **Find a study buddy.** Find a classmate who also values studying, and commit to keeping one another focused during study sessions. Go beyond just studying together. Create quizzes and hypothetical test questions for each other, and use your study partner to keep you on track.

9. **Estimate how long it will take.** Before starting an assignment, estimate the amount of time you will need to complete that assignment (just

as you do at the start of each chapter of this book), and then compare that estimate with the actual amount of time the assignment took to complete. Getting into this habit helps you develop realistic schedules for future projects.

10. **Vary your study techniques by course content.** Studying productively is more than just learning a few general rules that apply to any type of subject matter. You need to zoom in on whatever subject or discipline it is that you're studying. Look over the pages of your textbook. Does the material synch with your learning style? Is it text-heavy (read/write)? Do graphs or charts explain the text and seem important? Are color-coding or bulleting used to call your attention to particular items (visual)? If the material isn't presented as you'd prefer, what can you do to "translate"? For example, if you're a kinesthetic learner, can you make flash cards? Can you create and complete practice tests? If you learn by listening, can you read the material aloud (aural)? And finally, what kind of exam (multiple-choice, essay, problem sets, etc.) does the material lend itself to? What are you likely to need to know and what will you be asked to do on an exam? When you study math, it's important to do more than read. Working problem sets helps you actually develop the skills you need. When you study history, you study differently. You might draw a timeline of the events leading up to World War I, for example.[28]

11. **Study earlier, rather than later.** Whenever possible, study during the daytime, rather than waiting until evening. Research shows that each hour used for study during the day is equal to one and a half hours at night. Another major study showed that students who study between 6:00 P.M. and midnight are twice as likely to earn A's as students who put off their studying until after midnight.[29]

12. **Create artificial deadlines for yourself.** Even though your instructors will have set deadlines for various assignments, create your own deadlines that precede the ones they set. Finish early, and you'll save yourself from any last minute emergencies that may come up, like crashed hard drives or empty printer cartridges.

13. **Treat school as a job.** If you consider the amount of study time you need to budget for each hour of class time, and you're taking 12–15 credits, then essentially you're working a 36–45 hour/week job on campus. Arrive at "work" early and get your tasks done during "business hours" so you have more leisure time in the evenings.

14. **Show up.** Once you've decided to sit down to read or study, really commit yourself to showing up—being present emotionally and intellectually, not just physically. If you're committed to getting a college education, then give it all you've got! Get help if you need it. If you have a diagnosed learning disability, or believe you might, find out where help is available on your campus. One of the best ways to compensate for a learning disability is by relying on metacognition. In other words, consciously controlling what isn't happening automatically is vital to your success.[30]

"Disciplined" Studying

For the three textbook pages here, describe how you would go about studying the material, based on the disciplines of math, psychology, and music.

---

2   **Chapter P**   Preparation for Calculus

P.1 Graphs and Models

- Sketch the graph of an equation.
- Find the intercepts of a graph.
- Test a graph for symmetry with respect to an axis and the origin.
- Find the points of intersection of two graphs.
- Interpret mathematical models for real-life data.

The Graph of an Equation

In 1637 the French mathematician René Descartes revolutionized the study of mathematics by joining its two major fields—algebra and geometry. With Descartes's coordinate plane, geometric concepts could be formulated analytically and algebraic concepts could be viewed graphically. The power of this approach was such that within a century of its introduction, much of calculus had been developed.

The same approach can be followed in your study of calculus. That is, by viewing calculus from multiple perspectives—*graphically*, *analytically*, and *numerically*—you will increase your understanding of core concepts.

Consider the equation $3x + y = 7$. The point $(2, 1)$ is a **solution point** of the equation because the equation is satisfied (is true) when 2 is substituted for x and 1 is substituted for y. This equation has many other solutions, such as $(1, 4)$ and $(0, 7)$. To find other solutions systematically, solve the original equation for y.

$$y = 7 - 3x \qquad \text{Analytic approach}$$

Then construct a **table of values** by substituting several values of x.

x	0	1	2	3	4
y	7	4	1	-2	-5

Numerical approach

From the table, you can see that $(0, 7)$, $(1, 4)$, $(2, 1)$, $(3, -2)$, and $(4, -5)$ are solutions of the original equation $3x + y = 7$. Like many equations, this equation has an infinite number of solutions. The set of all solution points is the **graph** of the equation, as shown in Figure P.1.

NOTE Even though we refer to the sketch shown in Figure P.1 as the graph of $3x + y = 7$, it really represents only a *portion* of the graph. The entire graph would extend beyond the page. ∎

In this course, you will study many sketching techniques. The simplest is point plotting—that is, you plot points until the basic shape of the graph seems apparent.

EXAMPLE 1 **Sketching a Graph by Point Plotting**

Sketch the graph of $y = x^2 - 2$.

Solution First construct a table of values. Then plot the points shown in the table.

x	-2	-1	0	1	2	3
y	2	-1	-2	-1	2	7

Finally, connect the points with a *smooth curve*, as shown in Figure P.2. This graph is a **parabola**. It is one of the conics you will study in Chapter 10. ∎

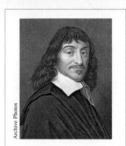

RENÉ DESCARTES (1596–1650)

Descartes made many contributions to philosophy, science, and mathematics. The idea of representing points in the plane by pairs of real numbers and representing curves in the plane by equations was described by Descartes in his book *La Géométrie*, published in 1637.

Graphical approach: $3x + y = 7$
Figure P.1

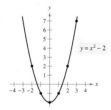

The parabola $y = x^2 - 2$
Figure P.2

Calculus, 9th Edition, by Ron Larson and Bruce H. Edwards

This textbook page shows how the visual parts of the page are key to understanding the read/write parts. How would you study this?

_____

_____

studies of the brain. Case studies lack formal control groups. This, of course, limits the conclusions that can be drawn from clinical observations.

Survey Method

Sometimes psychologists would like to ask everyone in the world a few well-chosen questions: "Do you drink coffee? How often per week?" "What form of discipline did your parents use when you were a child?" "What is the most dishonest thing you've done?" Honest answers to such questions can reveal much about people's behavior. But, because it is impossible to question everyone, doing a survey is often more practical.

In the **survey method,** public polling techniques are used to answer psychological questions (Tourangeau, 2004). Typically, people in a representative sample are asked a series of carefully worded questions. A **representative sample** is a small group that accurately reflects a larger population. A good sample must include the same proportion of men, women, young, old, professionals, blue-collar workers, Republicans, Democrats, whites, African Americans, Native Americans, Latinos, Asians, and so on as found in the population as a whole.

A *population* is an entire group of animals or people belonging to a particular category (for example, all college students or all single women). Ultimately, we are interested in entire populations. But by selecting a smaller sample, we can draw conclusions about the larger group without polling each and every person. Representative samples are often obtained by *randomly* selecting who will be included (▶▶ Figure 1.11). (Notice that this is similar to randomly assigning participants to groups in an experiment.)

How accurate is the survey method? Modern surveys like the Gallup and Harris polls are quite accurate. The Gallup poll has erred in its election predictions by only 1.5 percent since 1954. However, if a survey is based on a biased sample, it may paint a false picture. A *biased sample* does not accurately reflect the population from which it was drawn. Surveys done by magazines, websites, and online information services can be quite biased. Surveys on the use of guns done by *O: The Oprah Magazine* and *Guns and Ammo* magazine would probably produce very different results—neither of which would represent the general population. That's why psychologists using the survey method go to great lengths to ensure that their samples are representative. Fortunately, people can often be polled by telephone, which makes it easier to obtain large samples. Even if one person out of three refuses to answer survey questions, the results are still likely to be valid (Hutchinson, 2004).

Internet Surveys

Recently, psychologists have started doing surveys and experiments on the Internet. Web-based research can be a cost-effective way to reach very large groups of people. Internet studies have provided interesting information about topics such as anger, decision making,

Survey method The use of public polling techniques to answer psychological questions.

Representative sample A small, randomly selected part of a larger population that accurately reflects characteristics of the whole population.

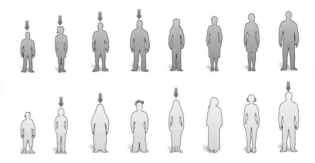

▶▶ **FIGURE 1.11** If you were conducting a survey in which a person's height might be an important variable, the upper, nonrandom sample would be very unrepresentative. The lower sample, selected using a table of random numbers, better represents the group as a whole.

44 CHAPTER ONE

Psychology: A Journey, 4th Edition by Dennis Coon and John O. Mitterer

How would you study this?

_____

_____

(continued)

Measures

As you performed the different meters, you may have lost your place momentarily. Even if you didn't, you can see that it would be difficult to play a long piece of music without losing one's place. For this reason, music is divided into **measures** with vertical lines called **bar lines**.

A bar line occurs immediately before an accented pulse. Thus, duple meter has two pulses per measure, triple meter has three pulses per measure, and quadruple meter has four pulses per measure. The following example shows the common meters again, this time with bar lines included. Notice how much easier it is to read and perform the meter when it is written this way.

Double bar lines have a special meaning: Their two most common uses are to signal the beginning of a new section in a large work and to mark the end of a work. Put double bar lines at the end of any exercises or pieces you write.

MUSIC IN *Action*

Hearing Pulse and Meter

As members of the class listen, clap a steady pulse without any noticeable accents. Slowly change the pulse to duple, triple, or quadruple meter. You may want to have a contest to see how quickly members of the class can detect the shift to a measured pulse.

Note Values

Learning to read music involves mastering two different musical subsystems: pitch notation and rhythmic notation. Pitch is indicated by the placement of a note on a five-line staff (the higher the note on the staff, the higher the pitch). You will learn about that later in this chapter. Rhythm, on the other hand, is written with

---

A Creative Approach to Music Fundamentals, 10th Edition, by William Duckworth

Learning this textbook page would require not just visual and read/write skills, but also kinesthetic and aural skills as the author suggests clapping out the rhythms.

How would you study this?

_____

_____

Finally, what have you learned about studying and about yourself as a learner by completing this exercise?

> **Education is learning what you didn't even know you didn't know.**
>
> —Daniel J. Boorstin, American historian, 1914–2004

Sprinting to the Finish Line: How to Study When the Heat Is On

© Larry Harwood Photography. Property of Cengage Learning.

Let's be realistic. Planning is important, but there will be the occasional time when you'll have to find some creative ways to survive the onslaught of all you have to study. You'll need to prioritize your time and make decisions about what to study. When you do need to find a way to accomplish more than is humanly possible, keep these "emergency preparedness" suggestions in mind:

1. **Triage.** With little time to spare, you must be efficient. Consider this analogy: If you're the physician on duty in the ER, and three patients come in at once, who will you take care of first: the fellow with strep throat, the woman with a sprained wrist, or the heart attack victim who needs CPR? Making decisions about priorities is called triage. Of all the material you need to study, ask what is most important, moderately important, and least important. For example, if you are earning an A– in art history, a B+ in geography, and a C– in math, you know which course most needs your attention. Evaluate the material and ask yourself which topics have received the most attention in class and in the textbook. Then focus your study time on those topics, rather than trying to study everything.[31]

2. **Use every spare moment to study.** If flashcards work for you, take your flashcards with you everywhere, like your daily bus ride or the laundromat, for example. Organize your essay answer in your head while you're filling up at the pump. It's surprising: Small amounts of focused time do add up.

3. **Give it the old one-two-three-four punch.** Immerse *all* your senses in the precious little amount of time you have to study: *read, write, listen,* and *speak* the material.

4. **Get a grip on your gaps.** Honesty is the best policy. Rather than glossing over what you don't know, assess your knowledge as accurately as possible, and fill in the gaps.

5. **Cram, but only as the very last resort.** If you're ultrashort on time due to a real emergency, and you have studying to do for several classes, focus on one class at a time. Be aware: If you learn new information that is similar to something you already know, the old information can interfere. So if you're studying for a psychology test that contains some overlap with your sociology test, separate the study sessions by a day. Studies also show that cramming up to one hour before sleeping can help to minimize interference.[32] Nevertheless, continually remind yourself: What's my goal here? Is it to just get through twenty-five pages or is it to truly understand?

A Final Word about Reading and Studying

Albert Einstein said this: "Never regard study as a duty, but as the enviable opportunity to learn . . ." Reading and studying are what college is all about. Take his advice: Consider the opportunities before you to become an educated person and take advantage of them all.

⌐ ONLINE **TechKnow**

Improve Your Grade
Online Flashcards
Glossary

In "Lazy eyes: How we read online," Michael Agger has come up with a clever list of suggestions for successful online writing:

- Bulleted lists
- Occasional use of **bold** to prevent skimming
- Short sentence fragments
- Explanatory subheads
- No puns
- Did I mention lists?

While funny, these suggestions are also useful. Writing that will be read online should be easy to read from a small screen—and these suggestions can help busy readers better manage online reading. For reading online coursework more effectively, try these suggestions:

- **Choose a default font** designed for screen reading, e.g., Verdana, Trebuchet, Georgia.
- **Minimize reflections.**

- **Use a good monitor**. Don't make it too bright or have it too close to your eyes.
- **Read when you can focus best.** Choose those times of the day when you know you're sharpest for reading, retaining, and learning.
- **Rest your eyes** for 10 minutes every 30 minutes.
- **Take action.** When you've read something you know will be useful, use it right away. Experience strengthens understanding and retention.
- **Be aware of visual cues.** Bold text, *italics*, lists, charts, and graphs can be especially helpful when scanning or reviewing online material.
- **Print out or bookmark pages of special interest**. And be sure to develop a well-organized filing system.
- **Take notes.** Find a useful online note-taking tool (such as Evernote™) or physically write down in your own words what you've found important.
- **Avoid Internet distractions.**[33]

VARK Activity

Complete the activity recommended for your preferred VARK learning style and bring it to class (or follow your instructor's instructions).

 Visual: Make a chart comparing how much time you spend on three things this week: talking on your cell phone, watching TV, and studying. Which activity has the longest line?

 Aural: Access the CourseMate via www.cengagebrain.com/shop/ISBN/1439083908 to listen to the iAudio summary for this chapter. Then repeat three main points you heard.

 Read/Write: Make a stack of index cards with words you couldn't define in this chapter. Look them up in the dictionary and write out the definitions. Then compare your stack with the ones of other classmates.

 Kinesthetic: Access the CourseMate via www.cengagebrain.com/shop/ISBN/1439083908 to watch the FOCUS TV episode for this chapter and answer the questions.

(from top to bottom) Marcela Barsse/MarsBars/iStockphoto.com; Johanna Goodyear/Dreamstime.com; Nadezda Firsova/iStockphoto.com; Pascal Genest/iStockphoto.com

step 3 INSIGHT *Now* What Do You Think?

At the beginning of this chapter, Katie Alexander, a frustrated and disgruntled student, faced a challenge. Now after reading this chapter, would you respond differently to any of the questions you answered about the "FOCUS Challenge Case"? Using what you learned in the chapter, write a paragraph ending to Katie's case study. What are some of the possible outcomes for Katie?

step 4 ACTION Your Plans for Change

1. What, in particular, from this chapter will you put to the test immediately in some other class?
2. In what ways might the information in this chapter help you become more successful in this class? What results are you expecting and how will you achieve them?

What did you **Learn?**

On a scale of 1 to 5, answer these questions now that you've completed this chapter.

1 = not very/not much/very little/low   5 = very/a lot/very much/high

How much do you know *now*?

Now rate your current level of knowledge about topics covered in this chapter.

Focused reading

        1 2 3 4 5

Study skills and techniques

        1 2 3 4 5

Metacognition

        1 2 3 4 5

Intentional learning

        1 2 3 4 5

How useful might the information in this chapter be to you?

How much do you think this information might affect your college success?

        1 2 3 4 5

How much do you think this information might affect your career success after college?

        1 2 3 4 5

How long did it actually take you to complete this chapter (both the reading and writing tasks)?

_____ Hour(s) _____ Minutes

  Challenge Yourself Online Quiz. To find out how much you've learned, access the CourseMate via www.cengagebrain.com/shop/ISBN/1439083908 to take the Challenge Yourself Online Quiz.

Compare these answers with your answers from the "Readiness Check" at the beginning of this chapter. How might the gaps between what you thought before starting the chapter and what you now think affect how you approach the next chapter?

© Larry Harwood Photography. Property of Cengage Learning.

You're About to Discover. . .

✔ Why you should change your thinking about tests
✔ What to do before, during, and after a test
✔ Why cramming doesn't always work
✔ What test anxiety is and what to do about it
✔ How to take different kinds of tests differently
✔ How cheating can hurt your chances for success

READINESS CHECK | What do you **Know?**

Before beginning this chapter, take a moment to answer these questions. Your answers will help you assess how ready you are to focus.

1 = not very/not much/very little/low   5 = very/a lot/very much/high

How much do you *already* know?

Rate your current level of knowledge about topics covered in this chapter.

Steps to complete before, during, and after a test

    1 2 3 4 5

Cramming

    1 2 3 4 5

Test anxiety

    1 2 3 4 5

The downside of cheating

    1 2 3 4 5

How motivated are you to learn *more*?

In general, how motivated are you to learn the material in this chapter?

    1 2 3 4 5

How much do you think this information might affect your college success?

    1 2 3 4 5

How much do you think this information might affect your career success after college?

    1 2 3 4 5

How ready are you to read *now*?

How ready are you to focus on this chapter—physically, intellectually, and emotionally? Which of these three areas is most challenging for you right now? Circle a number to represent it.

    1 2 3 4 5

If any of your answers is below a 3, consider addressing the issue before reading. Then, read the chapter carefully, while looking for ways to improve your focus.

Finally, how long do you think it will take you to complete this chapter? If you start and stop, keep track of the overall time.

_____ Hour(s) _____ Minutes

© Larry Harwood Photography. Property of Cengage Learning.

thepiwko/Shutterstock.com

Joe Cloud

"*Joe College," that's me*, Joe Cloud kept thinking to himself. His long-awaited opportunity to go to the technical college near the reservation had finally arrived. Even though he was living at home, somehow he knew life in college would be vastly different. He would be different, too, he had convinced himself—somehow more outgoing, more athletic, more popular, more successful—more of everything.

kavram/Shutterstock.com

Growing up in his town of 1,000, he had been the basketball king, the after-school grocery store shelf stocker, and the smartest guy in his high school of thirty-five. He was leaving a trail of victories behind him, and everyone in town appeared to have a stake in his future success in college. As the end of the summer approached, whenever people saw him in the grocery store, they'd yell out, "Hey, Joe, when are you starting college?"

Much to his parents' delight, Joe had even won a scholarship that would pay for all of his expenses. The condition, of course, was that he would be successful, graduate, and give back to the community in some capacity. Joe hoped to earn a pre-teaching associate's degree, and see how much he liked working as a teacher's assistant. If he liked it, he'd continue on for a four-year teaching degree, and then teach and coach athletics at his own high school.

Now that his college classes were in full swing and midterms were approaching, Joe was beginning to feel the stress. Generally, things were going well, except for his killer algebra course, a general education requirement. There weren't many students in the course, but compared with other teachers, Professor Crow was unusually businesslike and aloof. Joe was building up a great deal of anxiety over the course. Never before had he failed at anything, and if he didn't keep his grades up, he'd lose his scholarship.

The first week had been a review of what he had learned in his high school algebra class. But things became more challenging quickly. The pace quickened to the point that Joe found himself frantically trying to keep up. Math had never been his best subject, but by applying himself and hitting the books, he'd always been able to squeak by.

However, as the midterm exam approached, Joe began experiencing a funny sensation when he entered class each week. As he approached the door, his breathing became shallow and rapid, his heart was pounding, and he felt light-headed when he sat in his seat. He finally had to get up and leave before passing out. Unfortunately, it was exam review day, too.

That evening, he talked over his experience with his friend, Sam. "I've been telling you to eat breakfast!" Sam said. "You have to start rolling out of bed earlier, man!" But deep within

© Cengage Learning

himself, Joe knew his problem was more than just skipping breakfast. His reaction to each class session had become progressively worse. *There's no way I'll pass this course*, he thought. Although he hated to admit it, algebra had become so distasteful that Joe hadn't cracked the textbook since the day he had to get up and leave. He knew cramming was a bad idea, but he spent an hour or so online researching how to cram, anyway, since had given himself no choice.

The night before the midterm, Joe figured he'd study all night and forget about everything else that was due the next day. As the clock ticked into the wee hours of the morning, he was making himself a cup of instant coffee every forty-five minutes. It was hard to focus, but the test was tomorrow, and he figured he had to pull an all-nighter if he wanted to pass at all. Mr. Crow had said the test would consist of algebra problems with the answers in multiple-choice format, so Joe got out his highlighter and started reading the textbook chapters.

The morning of the exam, Joe woke up suddenly with a feeling of dread weighing him down. When he glanced at his alarm clock, he saw that he had overslept. The exam would start in fifteen minutes. His palms were sweaty, and his heart was racing again. He leapt out of bed, threw on some clothes, and ran out the door. When he got to class, he noticed that he'd forgotten his calculator. When he sat down, a student next to him leaned over and whispered, "I am totally freaked out about this test, aren't you?" That didn't help.

Joe finally worked up the nerve to look at the first question and realized he couldn't answer it. Frantically, he paged through the rest of the exam. It all looked unfamiliar. His seat gave him a perfect view of another student's answer sheet one row down and over. He struggled with the temptation. It was the longest fifty minutes of his life, and when Mr. Crow called "time," Joe slumped back into his chair.

The next week when the exams were handed back, Joe expected the worst—and he got it. What he stared at was the worst grade he'd ever gotten on any test in his entire life. Disgusted, he threw his exam in the trash can at the front of the classroom on his way out. *Why is there so much emphasis on exams in college, anyway? I'll never have to take a test again when I get out of here*, he muttered to himself. He was only halfway through his first term, and his scholarship was already on the line.

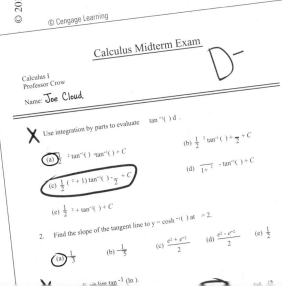

Calculus Midterm Exam

Calculus I
Professor Crow

Name: Joe Cloud

D-

X Use integration by parts to evaluate $\tan^{-1}(\ )\,d$.

(a) $\frac{1}{2}^2\tan^{-1}(\ )-\tan^{-1}(\ )+C$

(b) $\frac{1}{2}^2\tan^{-1}(\ )+\frac{}{2}+C$

(c) $\frac{1}{2}(^2+1)\tan^{-1}(\ )-\frac{}{2}+C$

(d) $\frac{}{1+^2}-\tan^{-1}(\ )+C$

(e) $\frac{1}{2}^2+\tan^{-1}(\ )+C$

2. Find the slope of the tangent line to $y=\cosh^{-1}(\ )$ at $=2$.

(a) $\frac{1}{3}$ (b) $\frac{1}{\sqrt{5}}$ (c) $\frac{e^2+e^{-2}}{2}$ (d) $\frac{e^2-e^{-2}}{2}$ (e) $\frac{1}{2}$

wikiHow.com

Back Forward Stop Refresh Home AutoFill Print Mail

Address: http://www.wikihow.com/Cram-for-a-Test

Microsoft Web Sites MSN Web Sites Apple

wikiHow
The How-to Manual That You Can Edit

Home > Categories > Education and Communications > Learning Techniques and Student Skills > Tests and Exams

Related wikiHows
- Get a Cloud Grade on a Math Test
- Study Better
- Cheer Yourself up After a Crummy Test
- Ace Your Next Test

Ads by Google

How to Cram for a Test

Whoops! It's the night before the big exam, and you haven't done a lick of studying all semester. Looking back on it, you know that you should have been hitting the books all those nights you were watching t.v., but there's nothing you can do about it now. Don't throw in the towel yet, though—it's time to get cramming.

While cramming probably won't get you an "A," it can definitely save you from an "F." So suck it up and get ready for a long, hard night. And vow to be a better student from now on.

Steps

1. Find out what you really need to study. If your teacher holds a review session before the exam, take advantage of the opportunity. You'll find out what topics the teacher thinks are important, and you'll have the opportunity to ask questions (although if you're having to cram, you probably have not done much studying at this point). Many teachers hand out study guides; be sure to use them. While that won't tell you everything that will be on the test, you'll at least be able to focus on the key topics.

MOUNTAIN FOODS

1. Do you have anything in common with Joe? If so, how are you managing the situation so that you can be successful?
2. What should Joe have done differently *before, during,* and *after* the exam?
3. Does Joe have test anxiety? Why or why not?
4. Does cramming work? Why or why not?
5. Do you think most students would have cheated to save their scholarships? Why or why not?

Testing 1, 2, 3...*Show What You Know*

Let's face it, life would be very different without grades in college, or time clocks on the job, or performance reviews throughout your career, wouldn't it? You wouldn't have to show up at work if you didn't feel like it, and you'd get a paycheck anyway. You wouldn't have to do a good job because no one would care. And you wouldn't have to write papers, or give presentations, or take tests in college. Not only would you benefit by having more free time, but your instructors wouldn't have to work their way through stacks of papers assigning grades, either. What a wonderful world that would be—or would it? Realistically, it would probably bring total chaos.

Life's not like that. Results count. **Accountability** is the bottom line. Achievement is taken seriously. Like Joe in the "FOCUS Challenge Case," you may be thinking, "I'll never have to take another test once I get out of here," but exams are actually realistic representations of life's requirements. The experience of taking a test is similar to running a critical meeting or giving a high-stakes presentation on the job. You'll need to walk into the room, ready to show what you know, and answer unanticipated questions. Exams help you compare your progress with that of other students and to your instructor's set of expectations about what all students should know.[1] On the job, every day will be a test of your skills and abilities, and you'll get your "grade" when your supervisor gives you a review of your performance over the last six months or year. Tests are inevitable; so rather than complain about them, perhaps we should change the way we think about them.

The first step of test-taking, of course, is to make sure you're prepared. All of the information in this chapter is worthless if you haven't gone to class or read the textbook or taken good notes during lectures. Miracles, by their very definition, are in very short supply. Nothing can substitute for being **conscientious** about your work. Think about preparing for an exam as you would for an athletic event. Imagine running the 26 mile, 385 yard Boston Marathon. You'd have to work for months to develop the stamina you would need to finish successfully. You wouldn't want to just show up for kicks and wing it. If you did, at the very least, you'd probably pull a muscle. At the very worst, they'd carry you away on a stretcher.

The same principle holds true for exams in college. In order to have the stamina required and avoid the "injury" of not doing well, tests require this same kind of step-by-step, long-term preparation.

accountability understanding the consequences of doing a good job or a poor one

conscientious dedicated to doing your best

Think about taking tests as a three-stage project with a beginning, middle, and end. What do you do *before* the test to get ready? What do you do *during* the test to do your best? What do you do *after* the test to ensure a productive learning experience you can use for future exams?

Before the Test: Prepare Carefully

As you read the upcoming sections about *before*, *during*, and *after* a test, evaluate how many of these suggestions apply to you. Put a plus sign (+) in front of each item you already do regularly and a check mark (✓) in front of items you could start doing more regularly to improve your test-taking skills.

1. _____✓_____ **Begin preparing for an exam on the first day of class.** Nothing can replace consistent, regular study before and after each class. If you work along the way, then when it comes time for the exam, you will be much more ready and much less in need of last-minute heroics. Keep up with the reading, even if there are things you'd rather be doing.

2. _____✓_____ **Identify the days and times of all your exams for the whole term up front.** At the beginning of the term, record the days and times of all the exams in all your courses—even finals, which will seem very far off—in your planner, cell phone, or online calendar. You'll thank yourself many times over for completing this essential task.

3. _____+_____ **Find out exactly what the test will cover.** There's nothing more terrifying than having a classmate next to you say something like this before the exam begins, "I can't believe this test covers the entire first six chapters," when you thought it only covered the first four chapters. Clarify whether handouts will be included, previous quiz questions—anything you're not sure of. Phone, text, or e-mail other students, or better yet, ask your instructor questions like these: How long will the test be? What material will it cover? Which topics are most important? It's also a good idea to ask about **criteria** that will be used in grading. Do punctuation and grammar count? Will you be asked to turn in your notes or draft so that the instructor can see your work? Will there be an in-class review? All these questions are usually fair game.

4. _____✓_____ **Understand that specific types of preparation are required for specific types of tests.** As described in later sections in this chapter, objective and subjective tests should be approached differently. Online tests require that you know the answers to important questions up front. For example, will the test time out? Must you complete the exam once you start, or can you save your answers and come back to finish later? Should you compose essay answers elsewhere and paste them into the online exam so that you don't lose all your work in case of a technology hiccup?

Christina Ripp wins the 2003 Boston Marathon Women's Wheelchair Division

criteria standards

5. _____ **Make a study schedule.** How many days are left to study? What will you accomplish each day? Don't decide you'll use whatever time is left over to study for your test. Usually there isn't any time left over.

6. _____ **Begin serious reviewing several days before the test.** The best strategy is paying regular attention to class material, just as you take care of other things you care about, like your car or your dog. After each lecture, work with your notes, revising, organizing, or summarizing them. Then several days before the exam, step up your effort. Divide up the work by days or study blocks. Begin putting your lecture notes and reading notes together. Make flashcards, outlines, charts, summaries, tables, diagrams, whatever works for your learning style and fits the material.

7. _____ **Maximize your memory.** Research indicates that specific techniques help transfer information from short-term to long-term memory. Remember to "Make It Stick" (rehearse, overlearn, space it out, separate it, and mind the middle), "Make It Meaningful" (feel, connect, and personalize), "Make It Mnemonic" (spell, locate, link or narrate, and peg), "Manipulate It" (mark it up, mark it down, organize, picture, act, produce, and test), and "Make It Funny" (mock it).

8. _____ **Get everything ready the night before.** To calm your nerves, lay out your clothes the night before the exam and pack your book bag with things you'll need: several pencils, erasers, scrap paper, your calculator, and a watch that works. Remove as much hassle as you can from test day.

9. _____ **Manage your energy so that you're ready to focus and work quickly.** You've heard it before, but if you're exhausted or feverish, you're not as likely to "show what you know" as you will if you're healthy and rested. Don't resort to things like drinking cup after cup of coffee to stay awake. "All-nighters" are something students brag about, but they catch up with you, and they're a bad habit to get into. According to one expert, "for every hour of sleep we lose, we drop one IQ point."[2] A series of all-nighters during midterms or final exams can seriously impair your intellectual performance.

If you would hit the mark, you must aim a little above it.

Henry Wadsworth Longfellow,
American poet (1807–1882)

10. _____ **Don't give in to a nonproductive, negative attitude.** Emotions are contagious. Stay away from other students who are freaked out or pessimistic about the exam. Think—and feel—for yourself. Make sure your self-coaching is productive ("I've studied this section for an hour; if it's on the exam, I'll nail it."), rather than punishing ("I'm so stupid. Why didn't I keep up with the reading?").

11. _____ **Study with other students.** When you teach something to someone else, you must first learn it thoroughly yourself. Why not study with other students? You can take turns teaching one another, comparing class notes, and making practice exams for each other. For most of us, talking things through helps us figure them out as we go. But don't wait to be invited; take responsibility and start a

Comstock/Jupiter Images

study group yourself. And if you're concerned that a study group of several students may degenerate into a social club, study with just one other person—find a study buddy and commit to doing the work.

12. _____ **Remind yourself of your long-term goals.** Why are you going to college? All this hard work is worth something or you wouldn't be doing it. Keep your sights on the finish line! Enjoy the feeling of accomplishing something now that contributes to your goal-oriented success later.

13. _____ **Arrive at the classroom early, but not too early.** Get there early enough to get a seat where the lighting is good and you won't be distracted by other students, but don't arrive so early that you build up excessive anxiety during a long wait.

14. _____ **Don't pop pills to stay awake.** You may know students who use Ritalin, Adderall, Vicodin, and OxyContin as study aids. This is a bad idea. When these drugs are used for the wrong reasons, they can help you stay awake for hours and enter a dreamy state. The potential side effects include insomnia, nausea or vomiting, dizziness, palpitations, headaches, tremors and muscle twitching, even seizures. With such horrible potential health risks staring you in the face, not to mention possible legal sanctions if you obtain these drugs without a prescription, why not make things simple? Just study.[3]

15. _____ **Don't let open-book or take-home tests lull you into a false sense of security.** What could be easier than an open-book test? What could be better than taking a test in the comfort of your own home? Actually, these two types of tests require more preparation than you'd expect. Time is the issue here. If you're unfamiliar with the material, flipping through pages of notes or skipping around in the textbook won't help. Create a reference guide or page tabs for yourself so that you can find various topics in your notes or textbook and use your time efficiently.

16. _____ **Don't mess with success.** If you're doing well and earning the grades you deserve, don't discard what is working for you. Honestly assess the efficiency and effectiveness of your current practices, and then decide what ideas from this chapter you should add to your test-taking preparation routine.

Cramming: Does "All or Nothing" Really Work?

Imagine yourself as the actor in the following scenarios. Compare these situations to cramming for tests.

> You haven't called your significant other since last year. Suddenly you appear at her door with candy, flowers, concert tickets, and dinner reservations at the most exclusive restaurant in town. You can't understand why she isn't happier to see you.

> You don't feed your dog for several months. When you finally bring him a plate loaded with ten T-bone steaks to make up for your neglect, you notice he's up and died on you. Oops!

Of course, these situations are ridiculous, aren't they? How could anyone ever neglect such basic necessities of life? There's an important point to be made here. Many things in life require continuous tending. If you ignore them for a time, catching up is next to impossible. Your college courses should be added to the list.

Believe it or not, some students give themselves permission to follow this all-or-nothing principle of cramming in their academic work. They sail along without investing much time or energy in their studies, and then they try and make up for lost time right before an exam by cramming. The word *cram* provokes a distinct visual image, and rightly so. Picture yourself packing for a vacation in a warm, sunny place and hardly being able to close your suitcase because it's crammed full. You can't decide what to bring so you bring everything you can think of.

The same holds for cramming for a test. You try to stuff your brain full of information, including things you won't need. Since you haven't taken the time to keep up with learning as you go, you try to learn everything at the last minute. Cramming is an attempt to overload information into your unreliable working memory. It's only available for a very short time. However, there are other reasons why cramming is a bad idea:

> Your anxiety level will rise quickly.

> Your sleep will suffer.

> Your immune system may go haywire.

> You may oversleep and miss the exam altogether.

Stressed Out?

> **For fast-acting relief, try slowing down.**
> —LILY TOMLIN, COMEDIAN

Stress—a six-letter dirty word. We complain about it and try to avoid it, but we don't seem to be able to eliminate it from our lives. Some stress is good for you. Olympic athletes, for example, subject themselves to unbelievable stress, and they achieve excellence. It's true that stress can produce results. Short-term stress—giving a speech or doing a tough math problem in your head—can actually bring out the best in you. But, long-term stress such as living through a devastating hurricane or taking care of a sick relative can take its toll. Short-term stress "revs up" your immune system and protects you, but long-term or chronic stress tears it down, making you more vulnerable to illness.[4] What's so stressful about college? Plenty! Grades, workload, exams, tough classes, finances, family problems that interfere with your academic work—you name it. You can't get rid of stress in your life, but what *can* you do about it? Sometimes you can 1) Change the stressful situation, 2) Change your reaction to stress, 3) Keep up with your schoolwork so that falling behind doesn't become a major stressor, or 4) Become a better problem-solver.

TRY IT!

Keep a stress diary for a week. Record what causes you stress each day and how strongly you react. How high was your stress level? What did you do about it? After a week, you'll have good information about what causes you stress and how you handle it. Summarize your results, what you learned in doing this experiment, and what actions you can take in the future to better manage the stress in your life.

Devon Stephens/iStockphoto.com

Despite the warnings here, most students cram at some time or other while taking college courses, and doing so may even give them a temporary high and make them feel like they're suffering for a cause.[5] But generally, slow and steady wins the race.[6]

Test-Taking: High Anxiety?

Test anxiety—what is it? And, more importantly, does it affect you? While most people think of text anxiety as a negative, the truth is, it's natural to be anxious before, during, and even after an exam. Most everyone is. In fact, some anxiety is useful. The adrenaline rush that accompanies anxiety can keep you alert and focused.

EXERCISE 10.1

Test Anxiety Survey

What is test anxiety? What are the symptoms? Do you have it? Fill out the following informal survey to determine whether or not you may have test anxiety. For each of the twelve statements, rate your degree of agreement or disagreement.

1	2	3	4	5
Disagree Completely	Disagree Somewhat	Unsure	Agree Somewhat	Agree Completely

1. I cringe when I suddenly realize on the day of an exam that a test is coming up. _____ 4

2. I obsess about the possibility of failing an upcoming exam. _____ 3

3. I often experience disappointment, anger, embarrassment, or some other emotional reaction during an exam. _____ 4

4. I think that instructors secretly get enjoyment from watching students squirm over exams. _____ 2

5. I experience physical symptoms such as an upset stomach, faintness, hyperventilation, or nausea before an exam. _____ 2

6. I tend to zone out during exams; my mind goes blank. _____ 2

7. I feel extreme pressure to please others by doing well on exams. _____ 1

8. If I'm honest, I'd have to admit that I really don't know how to study for tests. _____ 3

9. I'd much rather write a paper or give a presentation than take an exam. _____ 1

10. I usually fear that my exam grade will be lower than that of other students. _____ 2

11. After taking an exam, I obsess on my performance, going over and over questions that I think I may have missed. _____ 1

12. I convince myself that I'm not good at taking exams even though I often do fairly well on them. _____ 1

TOTAL (add up your score) _____ 26

If your score equals 49–60, you are a likely candidate for test anxiety. For suggestions on how to manage your anxiety, read on.

If you scored between 37 and 48, you have some signs of anxiety and may need help in managing your stress level.

If you scored 36 or below, you most likely experience a normal amount of anxiety and have already developed coping skills to help you.

© Chase Jarvis/Photodisc/Getty Images

"Positive thinking will let you do everything better than negative thinking will."

Zig Ziglar, motivational speaker and author

cognitive thinking

emotional feeling

behavioral doing

physiological your body reacting bodily

For some students, like Joe Cloud, test anxiety takes over and sabotages their efforts. They may say, "I knew it all before the test, but when I saw the questions, everything I knew vanished before my very eyes." These students experience fainting spells or even gastric distress that requires them to make a quick exit from the room. Some of them may be reacting to prior bad experiences with exams. Others may put intense pressure on themselves because they're perfectionists. Clearly, there's evidence from medical science that too much anxiety can work against you. Corticosterone, a hormone released during times of extreme stress, can actually hurt your ability to retrieve information from long-term memory.[7] Regardless of the reason, the first part of the solution is understanding exactly what test anxiety is. It has four different, yet related, components in terms of what you think, feel, and do, as well as how your body reacts:[8]

> **cognitive aspects**—nonproductive thoughts that run through your head before, during, and after an exam ("I have to get an A on this test. If I don't, I'll flunk out of school.")

> **emotional aspects**—negative feelings you experience related to the exam (disappointment, frustration, sadness, and so on)

> **behavioral aspects**—observable indications of stress (fidgeting, drumming your fingers on the desk, and so on)

> **physiological aspects**—unhelpful physiological reactions (dry mouth, butterflies in your stomach, your heart pounding in your chest, and so on)

Since you can't expect the tests you take in college to change for your sake—to reduce your anxiety—the possibility for change must come from within *you*. Consider these suggestions as they relate to the four indicators of test anxiety.

Cognitive

> **Understand your testing strengths and challenges, based on your learning style.** Although research indicates that most students prefer multiple-choice tests over essay tests, you have your own strengths and preferences.[9]

> **Don't catastrophize!** Stop yourself from engaging in negative, unproductive self-talk. It's easy to imagine worst-case scenarios: "If I fail this exam, I'll probably fail the exams in all my courses and flunk out of college, and if I don't go to college, I'll probably end up as a homeless person, begging for change on the street." Negative thinking can easily spiral downward, and before you know it, you're thinking about major life catastrophes and the end of the world. Although some exams do have crucial outcomes, it's important to put things in perspective.

Emotional

> **Monitor your moods.** Your emotions change based on many factors; they vary by type, intensity, and timing.[10] If you eat well and get enough sleep before an exam, your moods are more likely to be stable than if you skip meals, give in to sugar highs and lows, and pull all-nighters. An eight-hour sleep debt will cause your mood to take a nosedive.[11]

> **"Park" your problems if you can.** When you go into a store, you leave your car outside in the parking lot and come back to it when you're finished shopping. Think about how that example can relate to taking a test. Park your problems for a while. Focus on your work, and challenge yourself to do your best.

Behavioral

> **Relieve some stress with physical activity.** Expend some of that extra, pent-up energy before the exam. Sprint to class or take a walk to clear your head in the hour before the test begins.

> **"Step out of your life" by spending time outdoors.** Being in the outdoors is liberating. It's easy to forget that when you're spending large amounts of time in classrooms or at work.

Physiological

> **Teach yourself how to relax.** Relaxation training can be used to overcome test anxiety. As simple as it sounds, that may involve learning how to breathe. Watch a new baby sleep, and you'll see instinctive, deep, even breathing in which only the baby's stomach moves up and down. As adults, when we're anxious, we breathe rapidly and shallowly, which doesn't sufficiently oxygenate our brains.

> **Seek help from a professional.** An expert who works with anxiety-ridden college students can diagnose your problem and help you visualize success or take steps to overcome your fears.

Reduce Math Anxiety and *Increase* Your Test Scores

Let's zero in on a particular type of test anxiety that plagues many college students. Honestly, most people feel some twinge of anxiety about working a complex set of math problems on an exam. But if your level of anxiety interferes with your test success, you may suffer from math anxiety. One expert estimates that roughly 20 to 25 percent of college students are in that category.[12] Some estimates are that as many as 85 percent of college students in introductory math classes experience some degree of math anxiety.[13]

If you're one of them, admitting the problem is the first step. Next, it's important to understand how math anxiety can work against you during exams so that you can do something about it. The most effective strategies to cope are direct and uncomplicated.[14]

Think back; perhaps you can pinpoint where your fears began. It may have been a teacher or a class or a particular test. Experts believe math anxiety is *learned*, and that it's up to you to "unlearn" it.

Why and how does math anxiety affect people? Try this experiment: multiply 86×7. To arrive at the answer, you must first multiply 6×7, make note of the 2, and carry the 4. Then you must multiply 7×8 and add the 4 to arrive at 602. Notice the steps involved in this simple math problem. You have to keep certain numbers in your head while you continue to work through it, which is often the case with math. Your working memory allows you to pull it off.

Working memory is your short-term, temporary-storage, limited-space memory. It's the memory you use to hold certain pieces of information—your brain's scratchpad—keeping them available for you to work with and update.[15] A task like multiplying 639×924 would be too much for most people's working memories, but some people have more capacity than others. Here's the kicker: Math anxiety actually eats up your working memory.

Why? Managing anxiety takes up working memory space that could be used to solve math problems. When you reduce your anxiety, you have more room to use your working memory productively. Math anxiety also causes people to take longer to do math and to make more mistakes.[16] It's not the case that you use up your working memory because you think and think and think about how to work the problem and get the right answer. Instead, your working memory is hijacked by negative thoughts, causing you to choke.[17]

The solution? Practice for stressful exams under pressure. Set a timer, and tell yourself you must finish before it goes off. Make a game of it: for every question you miss on a practice exam, you must put a quarter in the kitty and pay off your friend, spouse, or mom. In other words, practicing in an equally stressful environment (or nearly so) can help during the actual test.[18] Since math anxiety is a learned fear, it can be unlearned.

As you study for math tests, keep these five suggestions in mind.

1. **Get to know your calculator (like it's your best friend).** If your instructor allows you to use a calculator in class, learn its functions inside and out. Even though today's calculator can do amazing things, it won't help you much during an exam if you don't know how to use it. Your graphic calculator can plot graphs, solve several equations at once, and you can even program it to run customized applications. But it can't do those things on its own; it requires you to run it. So part of your study strategy should be to learn what your calculator can do and become so familiar with it that using it is almost second-nature.

2. **Concentrate on *comprehension*, not *memorization*.** Memorizing formulas or rules won't help you if you don't know how to apply them. This formula, $a^2 + 2ab + b^2 = (a+b)^2$, is a good thing to know about factoring in algebra, but on a test it wouldn't help you factor $w^2 + 8w + 16$ unless you knew exactly how to apply the formula, step by step. Here's a sample practice problem, showing the steps you should learn to feel comfortable with:

Problem: / (EW).

Simplify: $5(a - 4) + 3 = 8$

Solution:

Step 1: Remove the brackets	**Step 2: Isolate variable a**
$5a - 20 + 3 = 8$	$5a = 8 - 3 + 20$
	$5a = 25$
	$a = 25/5$
	$a = 5$
	Answer: $a = 5$

3. Maximize opportunities to practice. Homework isn't just busywork; it's practice so that you can succeed. Besides homework, you can find countless web sites with practice tests online. Here's an example of a question you might encounter on a test:

Question: There are 2000 liters of water in a swimming pool. Water is filling the pool at the rate of 100 liters per minute. How much water, in liters, would be in the swimming pool after m minutes?

Answer: The amount of water added to the pool after m minutes will be 100 liters per minute times m, or $100 \times m$. Since we started with 2000 liters of water in the pool, we add this to the amount of water added to the pool to get the expression $2000 + (100 \times m)$.

Having experience reformulating problems like this means that you know how to extract the math from the words used to describe the math. If you can translate a word problem into a mathematical expression, then you can easily plug in any value to get an answer, given a specific value for m. But in order to do that, you need to understand what you're doing. "Practice makes perfect" may be hard to actually accomplish, but it's important to keep practicing in small chunks. Most experts recommend that you take math classes that meet more than once a week, just for the regular practice.[19]

4. Make flash cards. The simple act of creating the flashcards will help commit the information to your memory. And if no one is available to help you go through the flash cards, go through them yourself, and write down the answers as you go.

$$\frac{a/c}{b/c} = \frac{a}{b}$$

The act of writing this fact on a flashcard reminds you to look for commonalities in the denominator and numerator.

5. Hit the "redo" button. Mistakes are invitations to "do it right" the next time. For example, if you get a homework problem wrong, figure out why, rework the problem, write down a sentence about the right way to solve it, and then work a similar problem to prove to yourself that you understand now. Don't just skip it, or convince yourself that you'll probably get it right next time. It's called "self-regulated learning" and it works.[20]

We all have ability. The difference is how we use it.

Stevie Wonder, singer and composer

During the Test: Focus and Work Hard

During an exam, the heat is on! Do you use these strategies? If not, which ones can you incorporate to improve your performance? Put a plus sign (+) in front of each item you already do regularly and a check mark (✓) in front of items you could start doing more regularly to improve your test-taking skills.

1. _____ **Jot down what you don't want to forget right away.** When you first receive your exam, turn it over and jot down everything you want to make sure you remember—mnemonic devices, charts you've created—assuming, of course, that writing on the test is allowed. Some students treat the exam itself as if it were a sacred document, but marking up your exam is usually allowed. Circle key words and strike through answers you eliminate.

2. _____ **Preview the exam.** Just going through all the questions may help you review terms you know. And you'll notice which questions are easier and which are harder right away. It's also likely that reading sample questions will trigger your memory and help you come up with information you need. After the first few minutes, you may relax a bit, and answers will come to you more easily.

3. _____ **Start with what you know.** Make sure you get credit for answers you know; don't waste time early on struggling with the more difficult questions. This strategy will also boost your confidence and help you relax. Studies show that running up against extremely difficult test questions at the beginning of a test can actually hurt your ability to answer simpler questions later on.[21]

4. _____ **Weigh your answers.** Allocate your time based on the relative weight of the questions. Don't wrestle with one question for ten minutes when it's only worth one point. Go on to one that's worth more.

5. _____ **Read directions thoroughly.** Misreading or skipping the directions altogether can be a lethal mistake. Remember that your instructor can't read your mind. ("But that's not what I meant!") Slow down and make sure you understand what you're being asked to do.

6. _____ **Read questions carefully.** Sometimes skipping over a word in the sentence (or filling one in where there isn't one) will cause you to jump to a false conclusion. Don't let your eyes (or your brain) play tricks on you!

7. _____ **If the test has a mixed format, complete the multiple-choice questions first.** Often instructors create exams using both *objective* (multiple-choice, true-false) questions and *subjective* questions (fill in the blank, essay). Generally, objective questions ask you to *recognize* answers from several alternatives, and subjective questions ask you to *recall* answers from memory. A multiple-choice question may remind you of something you want to include in an essay. Keep a pad of paper nearby during the exam. Jot down ideas as you answer multiple-choice questions. You'll feel more confident and do a better job if you keep a running list of ideas that occur to you as you go.

8. _____ **Explain your answer to a confusing question in the margin of your test.** You may point out a problem your instructor wasn't aware of or get partial credit.

9. _____ **Change your answers if you're convinced you're wrong.** Despite advice you've probably always received from teachers and classmates alike, changing answers when you're sure you've made a mistake is usually a good idea, not a bad one. In one study, less than 10 percent of students made changes that decreased their scores, while 74 percent made changes that increased their scores.[22]

10. _____ **Ask your instructor for clarification.** If the exam appears to have a typo or something seems strange, ask your instructor to clarify for you. Of course, if you ask for the definition of a word that is a clue, you probably won't get an answer, but if you have a legitimate question, don't be afraid to ask.

11. _____ **Pay attention to "aha" moments.** Don't let your "aha" moments turn into "oh, no" moments. If you remember something you couldn't think of earlier, go back to that question and finish it right away.

12. _____ **Don't give in to peer pressure.** If, while you're working away, you look around and see that many students are leaving because they're already finished, don't panic. Take as much of the allowed time as you need. Everyone works at a different rate.

13. _____ **Save time for review.** When you're finished, go back over all your answers. Make sure you've circled the right letter or filled in the correct bubble. Be certain you've made all the points you intended to make in your essay. Look at your work critically, as if you were the instructor. Careless errors can be costly!

14. _____ **Be strategic about taking online tests.** Often tests posted online are timed. If you're taking a distance education course or a classroom course with an online test component, watch for e-mail announcements that tests have been posted, and note particular instructions. When will the test expire and disappear? Can you reenter the test site and redo answers before you hit the submit button? Can you take tests together with other students? With online tests, of course, the other recommendations in this chapter for true-false or multiple-choice tests apply as well.

Taking Objective Tests

Many of the exams you'll take in college will be objective, rather than subjective, tests. Let's examine the best strategies for taking objective tests.

True-False: Truly a 50–50 Chance of Getting It Right?

Exam questions that test your ability to remember are always more challenging than questions that test your ability to recognize the right answer. T or F?

True-false tests may seem straightforward, but they can be tricky. You assume you have a 50–50 chance of answering correctly. But don't forget, you also have a 50–50 chance of answering incorrectly. Sometimes the wording of the statements makes the *process* of taking true-false tests more challenging than their *content*. Consider these helpful guidelines:

> **Watch for parts of statements that make the entire statement false.** The statement must be all true to be "true," and a few words may make an otherwise true statement "false." Here's an example:

> Derek Bok, who was president of Harvard University for thirty years, once said, "If you think education is expensive, try ignorance." T or F

The main part of the statement is true; the quotation does belong to Derek Bok. But Bok wasn't president of Harvard for a full thirty years, making the entire statement false.

> **Assume statements are true until you can prove them false.** Statistically, exams usually contain more true answers than false ones. You have a better than 50 percent chance of being right if you guess "true." But teachers vary; yours may not follow the norm.

> **Watch for *absolutes*; they often make a statement false.** Words like *always*, *never*, and *entirely* often make otherwise true statements become false. "You can *always* get an A on an exam if you study for it." Unfortunately, no.

> **Look for *qualifiers*; they often make a statement true.** On the other hand, words like *sometimes*, *often*, and *ordinarily* often make statements true. "You can *sometimes* get an A on an exam if you study for it." Fortunately, yes.

> **Remember that negatives can be confusing.** Is this statement true or false? "Students who don't lack motivation are likely to excel." "Don't lack" really means "have," right?

Multiple *Choice* or Multiple *Guess*? Taking the Guesswork Out

> Which of the following statements is (are) true?
>
> a. Richard Greener, who became Harvard's first African-American graduate in 1870, later became a lawyer, educator, and distinguished U.S. consul and diplomat.
>
> b. Elizabeth Blackwell, who graduated from Geneva Medical College in New York, was the first woman in the United States to earn a medical degree.

I am easily satisfied with the very best.

Winston Churchill, Prime Minister of England (1874–1965)

Image Source(RF)/Corbis

> c. Oberlin College was the first U.S. college to admit women and the last to admit African-American students on an equal footing with Caucasians.
>
> d. a and b
>
> e. a, b, and c

Are multiple-choice tests difficult for you? Often what's difficult about multiple-choice tests has more to do with the structure of the test than the content. Studying for these tests requires a particular approach, and if you master the approach, you'll find taking multiple-choice tests to be much easier. You can actually think of them as similar to true-false tests. [The correct answer to the question, by the way, is (d).]

> ➤ **Think of answers on your own before reading your choices.** You may get hung up on the wording of an answer. Answer it on your own so that you can recognize it, no matter how it's worded. You may want to do this by covering up the alternatives first, and then going ahead after you know what you're looking for. Sometimes the alternatives will differ by only one or two words. It's easy to become confused.

> ➤ **Line up your test and answer sheet.** This sounds like a simple suggestion, but getting off a line can be very disruptive when you have to erase like crazy and start over!

> ➤ **Determine the TPI (time per item).** Divide the number of questions by the allotted time. If there are seventy-five questions to answer in an hour, you know that you'll need to work faster than one question per minute. Remember to save some time for review and revision at the end, too.

> ➤ **Don't decide answers based on the law of averages.** If you flip a coin three times, and it comes up "heads," most of us assume it's probably time for "tails" to come up next. Likewise, on exams, if you've answered (d) for three questions in a row, you may think it's time for an (a), (b), or (c). It may not be.

> ➤ **Use a process of elimination and guess if there's no penalty.** Some instructors subtract points for wrong answers, but if you do guess, guess wisely. And don't skip questions. Always mark something unless you're penalized for doing so. Take a look at this example:

> Before you write an answer on an essay test, you should do all but the following:
>
> a. Read all the questions.
>
> b. Begin with the hardest question.
>
> c. Look at what the questions are asking you to do, specifically.
>
> d. Underline key words in the question.

You know that you should do (a). Reading all the questions before you start is a must. You know that option (d) makes sense, and so does (c).

But you're not quite sure about option (b). You can eliminate (a), (c), and (d), so (b) must be the right answer based on a process of elimination. As you work, eliminate answers that you know are incorrect by marking through them ~~like this~~.

> **Look for highly similar pairs.** Sometimes two options will differ by a single word or the order of words. Often one of these is the right choice.

> **Look for contradictory answers.** If two statements are complete opposites, one of them is often the right choice.

> **Watch out for tricks intended to separate the prepared from the unprepared!** For example, avoid answers that are true in and of themselves, but not true when attached to the first part of the question being asked. For example, imagine this question option on a multiple-choice exam:

> Global warming is considered to be a serious issue among some scientists because:
>
> a. Former President Bill Clinton describes global warming as a greater threat to the world than terrorism.

While Clinton did say this in a 2006 speech, it is not the reason for scientists' concern, so (a) isn't the correct answer.[23] Two other tips: generally, when numbers are in each alternative, choose numbers in the middle range. Choosing answers that are longer and more descriptive usually pays off, too.

> **Consider each answer as an individual true-false question.** Examine each option carefully, as if you had to decide if it were true or false, and use that process to decide which answer is correct.

ONLINE **TechKnow**

Improve Your Grade
Online Flashcards
Glossary

It's test time. Nervous? Most of us are, right before the big exam. But there are things you can do to make online testing a more productive and a less anxious experience:

- **Prepare: Don't cram.** Use your syllabus and calendar to set aside time to study for your test during each lesson. If the exam is "open book," have your study materials in reach and tabbed with key words so you can find what you need quickly. Organize your notes by topic. And for timed tests, make sure no one will enter your study room and break your concentration.

- **Take advantage of online resources.** Be aware of which tools and resources your online instructor has allowed for use during the test. Realize that when designing the course, instructors know you'll have access to many online materials while you're taking it—so don't

expect that just because an online exam is open book, it will be easy. If possible, run a "practice test" using potential questions and all the resources you know you'll have. Test your technology, too—make sure everything works.

- **Pace yourself.** Know the beginning and ending times, and divide questions and tasks so you have enough time for each. Many online exams are only available for a specific amount of time, so have everything ready before you start. If you'll need water or coffee, get it ready ahead of time.

- **Stay calm.** Anxiety can result in mistakes and slower work. So get a good night's sleep, eat a good meal, stick to your computer routines, and tell yourself you'll do well. If your online course allows you to choose your time, pick one when you know you're usually at your best.[24]

> **Be careful about "all of the above" or "none of the above" options.**
> While instructors sometimes make these options the correct ones, it's
> also possible they resort to these options because making up enough
> possible answers is challenging.

> **Watch for terms that have been emphasized.** Look for key terms
> that appeared in your lecture notes and in chapters of the text. These
> words may provide links to the correct answer. Remember when taking
> multiple-choice tests that you are looking for the *best* answer, not simply
> the *right* one.[25]

EXERCISE 10.2

Multiple-Choice Test

Answer the following multiple-choice questions. Beneath each question, identify which of the principles of test-taking from this chapter you are using to identify the correct answer.

1. "I know of no more encouraging fact than the unquestionable ability of man to elevate his life by conscious endeavor." These words were said by:

   a. Bill Clinton

   b. Abraham Maslow

   c. Ronald Reagan

   d. Henry David Thoreau

   _____

2. Which of the following statements about the ACT test is not true?

   a. The ACT includes 215 multiple-choice questions.

   b. ACT results are accepted by virtually all U.S. colleges and universities.

   c. Students may take the ACT test as many times as they like.

   d. None of the above.

   _____

3. Which of the following suggestions about preparing for college is (are) true?

   a. Get involved in co-curricular activities in high school.

   b. Always take challenging courses that show your effort and ability.

   c. Involve your family in your decisions and preparation for college.

   d. Find a mentor, a teacher, or a counselor who can give you good advice.

   e. All of the above.

[Answer key: (d), (d), (e)]

Short-Answer, Fill in the Blank, and Matching Tests

Short-answer tests are like essay tests, which we'll discuss shortly, in many ways. You're required to come up with an organized, thoughtful answer on your own. But instead of a long essay, you only need to write a paragraph or two. Is that easier? It may be, but sometimes it's just as hard or harder to say what you need to say in fewer words. Generally, however, the suggestions for essay tests hold.

For fill in the blank tests, first think the statement through. What does it mean? Try inserting different words. Which one sounds best? Which one was used during lectures or appeared in the textbook? If one word looks awkward, try another one. Although it's not a completely reliable hint, look at the number of words, placement of spaces, and length of the space. If you don't know the exact terminology the question is looking for, insert your own words. You may at least earn partial credit.

Matching tests require particular strategies, too. First of all, you must determine whether items should be used only once or if they can be reused. If it's not clear from the test directions, ask for clarification. Match the items you're certain about first and cross them out if once only is the rule. If you mismatch an item early on, all your subsequent choices will be wrong, too.

Taking Subjective Essay Tests

> Essay Question: Please discuss the value of brain research in relation to our current knowledge of how learning takes place.

Essay questions are difficult for some students because details are required. Rather than being able to *recognize* the correct answer, you must be able to *recall* it totally from your own memory. Here are some recommendations you should consider:

> **Save enough time for essays.** If the test has a mixed format with different types of questions, it's important to save enough time to write well-thought-through essays. Often objective questions such as multiple-choice or true-false only count a point or two, but, essay questions often count into the double digits.

> **Read all the questions before you start.** To sharpen your focus and avoid overlap, give yourself an overview of all the questions before you start writing.

> **Make brief notes.** Somewhere on the exam or on scratch paper, write a brief plan for your responses to essay questions. A few minutes of planning may be time well spent. As you plan your answer, keep basic questions in mind—*who, what, when, where,* and *why*—as an organizing framework.

thesis your main point

> **State your thesis up front.** How will you handle this question? What's your plan of attack? Your first paragraph should include your basic argument in a thesis statement.

assertions statements you claim to be true

> **Provide support for your thesis.** Writing an answer to an essay question requires you to make assertions. However, it's not enough that you assert things; you must try to prove that they are true. If your thesis asserts that college students cheat more today than they did when your parents went to college, you must present evidence—statistics, examples, or expert testimony—to demonstrate that what you're asserting is true.

> **Zero in on the verb.** The heart of an essay question is its verb. Take a look at this list and think about how each verb dictates what is required:

> **Analyze**—break into separate parts and examine or discuss each part

> **Compare**—examine two or more things, find the similarities and differences (usually you emphasize the similarities)

> **Contrast**—find the differences between two or more things

> **Critique, criticize, or evaluate**—make a judgment, describe the worth of something

> **Define**—provide the meaning (usually requires a short answer)

> **Describe**—give a detailed account, list characteristics or qualities

> **Discuss**—describe a cause/effect relationship, the significance of something, the pros and cons, or the role played by someone or something

> **Enumerate**—list qualities, characteristics, events, and so on

> **Explain**—similar to discuss

> **Illustrate**—give concrete examples

> **Interpret**—comment on, give examples, provide an explanation for, discuss

> **Outline**—describe the plot, main ideas, or organization of something

> **Prove**—support an argument with evidence from the text or class notes

> **Relate**—show the relationship or connection between two things

> **State**—explain in precise terms

> **Summarize**—give a condensed account of key points, reduce to the essential components

> **Trace**—describe a process or the development of something

> **Use terms from the course.** Perhaps more than any other type of exam, an essay test allows you room to truly display your knowledge. Use the opportunity! Reflect new terms you have learned, and tie your answer directly to course content.

> **Rifle your answer, don't shotgun.** Here's an analogy: A shotgun fires many small metal pellets. A rifle fires a single bullet. When writing an essay answer, some students write down everything they know, hoping that something will be correct. You may actually lose points by doing this. It's better to target your answer and be precise.

> **Generalize if you're unsure of small, exact details.** You can't quite remember, was it 1884 or 1894? The best idea is to write, "Toward the end of the nineteenth century" instead of choosing one of the two and being wrong.

> **Follow all the rules.** When answering an essay question, it's important to be as concise yet thorough as possible. Number your ideas ("There are *three* major . . . "). Avoid slang ("Wordsworth elaborated . . . " not "Wordsworth *jazzed up* the poem."). Refer to researchers or authors or

you'll graduate with so-so grades, and you'll never be able to compete for the jobs you've always wanted. Besides getting away with it here just helps prepare you for the business world where things are *really* cutthroat!"

> You hear about an entrepreneurial student who operates an underground paper-writing service. For $20 a page, he will guarantee you the grade you want (based on the grade you already have going in the course so that your paper won't raise the instructor's suspicions), and he "doctors" each sentence so that the source can't be found on the Internet. You have four papers, a presentation, and an exam all due the same week, and one or two papers would only run you around $150 to $200. That's not all that much considering the tips you make as a server. Hmm....

How did you respond to these three scenarios? Are you aware of cheating schemes at your school? Could students you know be the ones these scenarios were written about? Notice that these students have practical-sounding reasons for what they are doing. If you want to cheat, it's not hard, and you can always blame someone else. What's the harm? You get better grades, your teachers think they're doing a good job, your school brags about the fine academic record of its students, and you pat yourself on your back for skillfully managing a very busy, demanding life. Everyone wins, right? Wrong.

According to some studies, fifty years ago, one in five college students admitted to cheating. Today's figures range from 75 to 90 percent. Here's some straight talk about cheating:[27]

1. **Remember that cheating snowballs.** What started as secretly pocketing some kid's CD or glancing at your neighbor's reading test in grade school turns into writing a math formula between your fingers or hiding the names of the constellations under your shirt cuff in middle school. Then these violations as a kid turn into full-fledged, sophisticated rule-breaking as students "download their workload" in high school and knowingly violate their school's Academic Integrity Policy in college. Where does it stop?

2. **Instead of saving time, cheating can take time.** Everyone is busy. Most students are working at jobs for pay in addition to taking classes. How can anyone get everything done that needs to get done? But instead of devising elaborate cheating schemes, which take time to design, why not just use that time to study?

3. **If you cheat now, you'll pay later.** Sooner or later, cheating will catch up with you. You may get past your math instructor this time, and you may even get good grades on others' work you turn in as your own. But someday your boss will ask you to write something, or do some research, or use a skill a student is expected to have mastered in college, and you won't know where to start.

4. **If you do get caught, cheating may do you in.** Some students cheat because they know other students have gotten away with it. Cheating for them is a thrill, and not getting caught is like winning or beating the system. Roll the dice and see what happens, they say. But you should know that instructors are in the know these days. Academic hallways are abuzz with

faculty talk about cheating. If you do get caught, your academic career may come to an abrupt halt.

5. **Cheating is just plain wrong.** You may or may not agree with this point, but it deserves some serious consideration. How would you like to be cheated out of money that's owed you or days off that are due you? The Golden Rule may sound old-fashioned, but the fact that it's been around for a long time with roots in a wide range of world cultures tells you something. "Intellectual Property" and "Academic Integrity" may not be as tangible as money you deserve or eight hours of free time, but they are things that are increasingly protected by every college.

" For nothing can seem foul to those that win.

William Shakespeare, British poet and playwright (1564–1616)

What are your personal **ethical standards**? Are you willing to cut corners? Would you cheat to achieve top grades in college? What kind of "devil's bargain" would you be willing to strike?

ethical standards agreements about what is right and wrong

Some students today believe that technology is a tool, and using technology to avoid work isn't cheating, it's just plain smart. Some experts call it the "technological detachment phenomenon." These students think: schoolwork is just busywork, so if you download homework answers, buy a paper online, or collaborate with other students over the Internet when the assignment calls for your own work, you're just saving valuable time. They think the pervasiveness of technology somehow justifies cheating. But cheating, no matter how you do it, is still cheating--and the person you're cheating most is yourself. One student went to a campus computer lab and happened to find another student's homework saved there. So he changed the name to his own name, and turned the assignment in as his own. But he mistakenly forgot to change the name on one page. Busted.[28]

If you're tempted, remember this. Learning is about *doing*, not figuring out ways *not to do*, and sooner or later, cheating costs you—big time! Don't cheat yourself out of learning what you need to learn in college. Learning is not all about *product*—the exams, papers, grades, and diplomas themselves—it's about *process*, too. The process involves gaining skills that will prepare you for life after college. That's a goal worth working toward.

You can't go through life devising elaborate schemes, or hiring someone else to do your work for you, or rationalizing about finding a way to beat the system because you're too busy to do your own work. Cheating in your college classes now just makes it that much easier to risk cheating your employer—and yourself—later on the job. Look through newspapers or watch the evening news to see who's been caught lately. It's a competitive world out there, but more and more companies find that having a good reputation, which comes from being honest, is good business. Integrity starts now: *earn what you learn.*[29]

" A man's errors are his portals of discovery.

James Joyce, Irish novelist (1882–1941)

You are the only one who can use your ability. It is an awesome responsibility.

ZIG ZIGLAR

Go for extra credit. In some of your courses, your instructors may give extra credit. You could be allowed to do something extra, beyond the requirements on the syllabus, to raise your grade. But what's extra credit in terms of your career? On the job, you have "extra credit" when you develop abilities that stand out. You speak German and no one else does, so when something needs translating, you're the go-to person. You know how to use Excel spreadsheets to organize complicated information and make it useful. Or you're so exceptional at PowerPoint that you're affectionately referred to as the "PowerPoint King." Think of what your special talent might be, and come up with a plan to develop and practice that ability. Find ways of showing others that your talent is helpful to the organization. Mention your special gift in interviews, and give examples of when it has been useful in the past. Volunteer to take on tasks where you can use your special skills to make a difference. In your professional career as well as in school, go for "extra credit."

After the Test: Continue to Learn

After you finish an exam and get your results, you may be thrilled or discouraged. Regardless, exams can be excellent learning experiences if you take these steps. Put a plus sign (+) in front of each item you already do regularly and a check mark (✓) in front of items you could start doing more regularly to improve your test-taking skills.

1. _____ **Analyze your results.** Conduct a thorough analysis of your test results. For example, an analysis like this one might tell you what kinds of questions are most problematic for you.

Type of Question	Points Earned/Right	Points Deducted/Wrong	Total
Multiple-Choice	32	3	35
Fill in the Blank	15	2	17
True-False	20	8	28
Essay	10	10	20
Total	77	23	100

Or analyze your results by comparing how many lecture questions there were versus textbook questions to find out where to concentrate your efforts on future tests. Or do an analysis by chapter to tell you where to focus your time when studying for the final exam.

2. _____ **Read your instructor's comments and take them to heart.** After an exam, ask yourself: What was the instructor looking for? Was my writing ability part of the issue? Does the test make more sense now than it did while I was taking it? Are there instructor's com-

ments written on the test that I can learn from? What do the results of this exam teach me about preparing differently, perhaps, for the next test?

3. _____ **Explain your grade to yourself.** Where did you go wrong? Did you misread questions? Run out of time? Organize essay answers poorly? Does the grade reflect how much time you studied? If not, why not? Did test anxiety get the better of you? On the other hand, if you studied hard and your grade reflects it, that's an explanation, too!

4. _____ **Be honest.** It's easy to get caught up in the blame game: "I would have gotten a better grade if the exam had been fairer, if the test had been shorter, if the material hadn't been so difficult, if I'd had more time to study...." Your instructors have heard every excuse in the book: "my dog ate my notes," "a relative died," "a family emergency made it impossible to study," "my hard drive crashed," you name it. Of course, sometimes crises do overtake events. But rather than pointing fingers elsewhere if you're disappointed with your results, take a close look at what you can do differently next time.

5. _____ **Make a specific plan for the next test.** Most courses have more than one exam. You'll probably have an opportunity to apply what you've learned and do better next time.

6. _____ **Approach your instructor politely if you believe your exam has been mismarked.** Sometimes teachers make mistakes. Sometimes they're interrupted while grading and forget to finish reading an essay answer, or the answer key is wrong, or they make a mistake adding up points. Even if the scoring is correct, it may be a good idea to approach your instructor for help about how to improve your next test score.

7. _____ **Reward yourself for good (study) behavior.** After you've worked hard to prepare and the exam is over, reward yourself—take in a movie, go out with friends, do something to celebrate your hard work.

Non scholae sed vitae discrimus. (We do not learn for school, but for life.)

Lucius Annaeus Seneca, Roman philosopher and statesman (4 B.C.–A.D. 65)

VARK Activity

Complete the activity recommended for your preferred VARK learning style and bring it to class (or follow your instructor's instructions).

Visual: Make a flow chart to show how you will proceed *before*, *during*, and *after* the next test in one of your more challenging classes. Personalize the chart to show exactly what you will actually do.

Aural: Talk to yourself as you study for an upcoming exam that will challenge your test-taking knowledge and skills. Ask yourself questions that you predict will appear on the exam and answer them aloud. Access the CourseMate via www.cengagebrain.com/shop/ISBN/1439083908 to listen to the iAudio summary for this chapter. 🔊

Read/Write: Write a press release describing your ideal performance on an upcoming exam. For example, "Southern first-year student aces exam by trying new study techniques" and then describe the new techniques used.

Kinesthetic: Make up a challenging practice test for an upcoming actual exam, and time yourself while taking it to create some of the stress you'll face during the exam.

At the beginning of this chapter, Joe Cloud, a frustrated and disgruntled student, faced a challenge. Now after reading this chapter, would you respond differently to any of the questions you answered about the "FOCUS Challenge Case"? Using what you learned in the chapter, write a paragraph ending to Joe's case study. What are some of the possible outcomes for Joe?

step
4 ACTION Your Plans for Change

1. Which type of tests do you find most difficult—multiple-choice, true-false, or essay, for example? Within that particular portion of the chapter, which strategies that you read about will you try on your next exam?
2. Many students have negative attitudes toward tests. What could they do to change their outlook and learn to see tests as opportunities, rather than threats?
3. What piece of helpful information, based on your own experience, would you add to this chapter? How has it changed the way you prepare for or actually take tests?

| REALITY CHECK | What did you **Learn?** |

On a scale of 1 to 5, answer these questions now that you've completed this chapter.

1 = not very/not much/very little/low   5 = very/a lot/very much/high

How much do you know *now*?

Now rate your current level of knowledge about topics covered in this chapter.

Steps to complete before, during, and after a test

      1 2 3 4 5

Cramming

      1 2 3 4 5

Test anxiety

      1 2 3 4 5

Negative effects of cheating

      1 2 3 4 5

How useful might the information in this chapter be to you?

How much do you think this information might affect your college success?

      1 2 3 4 5

How much do you think this information might affect your career success after college?

      1 2 3 4 5

How long did it actually take you to complete this chapter (both the reading and writing tasks)?

      _____ Hour(s) _____ Minutes

 Challenge Yourself Online Quiz. To find out how much you've learned, access the CourseMate via www.cengagebrain.com/shop/ISBN/1439083908 to take the Challenge Yourself Online Quiz.

Compare these answers with your answers from the "Readiness Check" at the beginning of this chapter. How might the gaps between what you thought before starting the chapter and what you now think affect how you approach the next chapter?

chapter 11 Building Relationships, Valuing Diversity

You're About to Discover...

✔ *What emotional intelligence is*
✔ *Whether your EI can be improved*
✔ *How to improve communication with people you care about*
✔ *Why diversity enriches our lives*
✔ *What cultural intelligence is and why it's important*
✔ *How globalization changes our world*

READINESS CHECK — What do you **Know?**

Before beginning this chapter, take a moment to answer these questions. Your answers will help you assess how ready you are to focus.

1 = not very/not much/very little/low   5 = very/a lot/very much/high

How much do you *already* know?
Rate your current level of knowledge about topics covered in this chapter.

Emotional intelligence
    1 2 3 4 5

Conflict management
    1 2 3 4 5

Types of diversity
    1 2 3 4 5

Cultural intelligence
    1 2 3 4 5

How motivated are you to learn *more*?

In general, how motivated are you to learn the material in this chapter?
    1 2 3 4 5

How much do you think this information might affect your college success?
    1 2 3 4 5

How much do you think this information might affect your career success after college?
    1 2 3 4 5

How ready are you to read *now*?

How ready are you to focus on this chapter—physically, intellectually, and emotionally? Which of these three areas is most challenging for you right now? Circle a number to represent it.
    1 2 3 4 5

If any of your answers is below a 3, consider addressing the issue before reading. Then, read the chapter carefully, while looking for ways to improve your focus.

Finally, how long do you think it will take you to complete this chapter? If you start and stop, keep track of the overall time.

_____ Hour(s) _____ Minutes

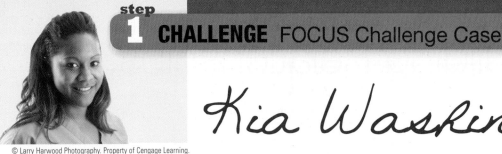

Kia Washington

A t first, Kia Washington was frustrated. Then she was scared. Then she was furious. How could her husband, James, manage to get laid off after only six months on the job? It had been a good job, too, in the construction industry, and it qualified them for their first house loan. A home of their own was a dream come true for Kia, especially after moving around as a military spouse for the first three years of their marriage. Now, how would they possibly afford it? To make matters worse, it wasn't long before Kia found out that she was staring possible unemployment in the face, too, at the manufacturing plant in town.

Photos.com

Tiplyashin Anatoly, 2009/ Used under license from Shutterstock.com

Recently, there had been talk of starting a family; maybe it would help bring some stability to their relationship, they'd even thought. But now that seemed out of the question. So Kia had enrolled at the career college close to home in their nursing program to become a pediatric nurse and work with children. Nursing was a stable profession, and jobs were plentiful. Security was what Kia wanted most in her life.

Financial turmoil had put considerable stress on their already rocky marriage, but there were other outside stressors, too. Both families had objected to an interracial marriage, but Kia and James didn't care. "It's not about race or the color of someone's skin," Kia remembered telling her mother. "It's about what's inside." Most of their friends were totally fine with the idea, but their families seemed to be stuck in another decade. And now, with talk about starting a family, they had turned up the heat again. *Why can't they be more open-minded*, Kia often thought. She was accepting of other family members' differences, like her older brother William's gay relationship. Her family had never accepted Will's boyfriend even though he and his partner had been in a stable relationship for five years. *Inclusiveness*, as she once heard it called, was not her family's strong suit.

Growing up, Kia's family life had been rocky. Her parents, who probably cared for each other deep down,

© Cengage Learning

Nursing Degree Requirements

		(18 credits)
al Education		4 credits
201	Human Anatomy and Physiology I	4 credits
202	Human Anatomy and Physiology II	4 credits
204	Microbiology (with lab)	3 credits
3 121	English Composition I	3 credits
235	Human Growth and Development	
		(14 credits)
rst Semester		3 credits
AT 103	Pharmacology Calculations	8 credits
UR 109	Fundamentals	2 credits
	Basic Concepts of Pharmacology	1 credit
		(20 credits)

just couldn't get along. As a child, Kia sometimes hid in her bedroom to wait out the arguments. Their decision to divorce had actually come as a relief. Despite trouble at home, Kia had been a very good student in high school. Perhaps because home was a difficult place, she threw herself into her studies. She liked to read anything she could get her hands on, and doing homework had been a good escape. But her family had no money, so college was never part of the plan. Instead, it was a plan she was now making for herself. So far, the only real problem looked like it would be finding a lab partner in her Anatomy and Physiology class. No one had approached her about teaming up yet. She hoped it wasn't because she was the only minority student in the class. On the other hand, she had to admit that she kept to herself and hadn't really spoken up in class at all. Was that it?

Regardless, the one constant in her life had been James. When she looked back she wasn't quite sure how she and James ended up together. They were very different people, beyond just being of different races. But throughout all of her high school years, Kia and James had been inseparable. James also happened to look like a movie star, and he was the funniest person Kia knew. So when they graduated, getting married seemed to be the natural next step. Some of the time, they got along fairly well, and fights were over quickly. Whenever a conflict came

up, Kia exploded and James just took it. He was the proverbial nice guy and she often felt as if she was on an emotional roller coaster. Often her temper got the best of her. Trying to communicate her way through a disagreement never seemed worth it to Kia. Fighting had been a fact of life with her parents, and Kia had never learned how to "fight fair." She'd spit out a few rude comments and then walk away. Fortunately, James never seemed to hold a grudge.

But two weeks ago, they'd had the worst fight ever on the phone about the layoff. Suddenly she heard herself yelling into the phone, saying things she knew she'd regret. James managed to get the words "control freak" out, and then this time he hung up. His texts and calls suddenly stopped, and he hadn't been home since. And she had missed her anatomy and physiology class both weeks since then because she was so upset about the fight. *Why does this have to be so hard?* Kia kept asking herself. All she wanted to do was make a better *future* for herself. But right now the most important thing she had to do was get through the *present. My life is a soap opera,* she thought. And to anyone watching right now, she was right.

Budget for this Month	
Car Insurance	$100
Car Payment	$200
Groceries	$150
Rent	$650
Utilities	$150
Cell phones, Internet	$350
Total	$1600

Real Estate Agent

Michelle Jenson
Residential Specialist
Accredited Buyer Representative (ABR)

515-555-1531 ext. 1200
Cell: 515-555-1822
Fax: 515-555-1582

Call me when you want to see some

Me, age 8 ☺

© Cengage Learning

BIOLOGY LAB ASSIGNMENT: ENZYME CA

Lab Objectives

1. Measure the rate of an enzyme.
2. Calculate rate.
3. Describe titration.
4. Collect and graph data.
5. Make hypotheses based on data.

DATA TABLE

	Initial H$_2$O$_2$ in Beaker before Catalase	Remaining H2O2 in Beaker after Catalase	T D
10 seconds	10 mL		
30 seconds	10 mL	9 mL	
60 seconds	10 mL	7 mL	
90 seconds	10 mL	4 mL	
120 seconds	10 mL	2 mL	
180 seconds	10 mL	1 mL	
		0 mL	

GRAPH

ImageryMajestic, 2010. Used under license from Shutterstock.com

James Steidl, 2010/Used under license from Shutterstock.com

1. Do you have anything in common with Kia? As you read her story, do you identify with portions of it—or do you know anyone else in college who would?
2. Kia's life is complicated, just like the lives of many college students. Identify five specific problems described in this case study that could interfere with her college success.
3. To have done so well in school, Kia must be an intelligent person. But is her emotional quotient (EQ) different from her intelligence quotient (IQ)? Why or why not?
4. Kia's relationship with James is an important one in her life. What is she doing to contribute to the problems in the relationship? Will the relationship survive? If so, what would it take?
5. Identify three things Kia should do to get her college success and her life on track.

The Heart of College Success

EXERCISE 11.1

How Would You Respond?

Read these five scenarios and identify your most likely reactions.[1]

1. You peer over a classmate's shoulder and notice she has copied your online response from a class chat and submitted it as her paper in the course, hoping the instructor won't notice. What do you do?
   a. Tell the student off to set the record straight, right then and there.
   b. Tell the instructor that someone has cheated.
   c. Ask the student where the research for the paper came from.
   d. Forget it. It's not worth the trouble. Cheaters lose in the end.

2. You're riding on a plane that hits a patch of extreme turbulence. What do you do?
   a. Grab hold of the person in the next seat and hold on for dear life.
   b. Close your eyes and wait it out.
   c. Read something or watch the movie to calm yourself until things improve.
   d. Panic and lose your composure.

3. You receive a paper back in your toughest course and decide that your grade is unacceptable. What do you do?
   a. Challenge the instructor immediately after class to argue for a better grade.
   b. Question whether or not you're really college material.
   c. Reread the paper to honestly assess its quality and make a plan for improvement.
   d. Deemphasize this course and focus on others in which you are more successful.

4. While kidding around with your friends, you hear one of them tell an offensive, racial joke. What do you do?
   a. Decide to ignore the problem and thereby avoid being perceived as overly touchy.
   b. Report the behavior to your advisor or an instructor.
   c. Stop the group's conversation. Make the point that racial jokes can hurt and that it's important to be sensitive to others' reactions.
   d. Tell your joke-telling friend later that racial jokes offend you.

5. You and your romantic partner are in the middle of a heated argument, and you're losing your temper. What do you do?
   a. Stop, think about what you're trying to communicate, and say it as clearly and neutrally as possible.
   b. Keep at it because if the issue generated that much emotion, it must be important to get to the bottom of it.
   c. Take a twenty-minute time out and then continue your discussion.
   d. Suggest that both of you apologize immediately and move on.

Collge is a time of transition; it can be an emotionally challenging time. Even if you're a returning student who's been on your own for years, college will require you to make some major adjustments in your life. Trying to do so without the internal resources you need may be overwhelming, as it was for Kia Washington in the "FOCUS Challenge Case." When it looked as if the relationship that was most important to her was falling apart, so did she.

Here's a fundamental truth: College isn't just about your head. Yes, academics are the reason you're in college, but your heart plays a critical role in your success, too. From friends to family members to professors to romantic partners, how you handle relationships can make or break you academically. Emotional reactions to troubling circumstances have the raw potential to stop you dead in your tracks. As may be the case for Kia Washington, who most likely has the *academic* skills required for success, *nonacademic* issues can interfere.

In college and in life, your EQ (emotional quotient), or *emotional intelligence*, can be just as important as your IQ (intelligence quotient). Studies show that first-year students often feel overwhelmed and lonely. Begin now to refine the emotional skills you'll need to face whatever challenges come your way.

Perhaps you've found yourself in settings such as those described in Exercise 11.1. You might need more actual details to make the best choice in these five scenarios, but according to some experts, choice (c) is the most emotionally intelligent one in each case. Do you agree? How do *you* make decisions such as these? What constitutes an emotionally intelligent response?

> **Our emotions are the driving powers of our lives.**
>
> *Earl Riney, American clergyman*
> *(1885–1955)*

© Larry Harwood Photography. Property of Cengage Learning.

What Is Emotional Intelligence?

Many experts believe that intelligence takes many forms. Rather than a narrow definition of intelligence, they believe in Multiple Intelligences: Linguistic, Logical-Mathematical, Spatial, Kinesthetic, Musical, Interpersonal, Intrapersonal, and Naturalistic.[2] Emotional intelligence may well be a combination, at least in part, of *intrapersonal* and *interpersonal* intelligences.

Emotional intelligence is a set of skills that determines how well you cope with the demands and pressures you face every day. How well do you understand yourself, empathize with others, draw on your inner resources, and encourage the same qualities in people you care about? Emotional intelligence involves having people skills, a positive outlook, and the capacity to adapt to change. Emotional intelligence can propel you through difficult situations.

The bottom line? New research links emotional intelligence to college success, and learning about the impact of EI in the first year of college helps students stay in school.[3]

As you read about the five scales of emotional intelligence, begin thinking about yourself in these areas. As each scale is introduced, ask yourself whether you agree or disagree with the sample statement from a well-known emotional intelligence instrument as it pertains to you.[4]

Intrapersonal Skills (Self-Awareness)

"It's hard for me to understand the way I feel." Agree or disagree?

Are you in tune with your emotions? Do you fully realize when you're anxious, depressed, or thrilled? Or do you just generally feel up or down? Are you aware of layers of emotions? Sometimes we show *anger*, for instance, when what we really feel is *fear*. (For example, Kia was in the habit of screaming angrily at her husband, James, when she probably desperately feared losing him.) Are you emotionally strong on your own, rather than depending on others for your happiness? Do you realize that no one else can truly make you happy, that you are responsible for creating your own emotions? How well do you understand yourself and what makes you tick?

Interpersonal Skills (Relating to Others)

"I'm sensitive to the feelings of others." Agree or disagree?

Are you aware of others' emotions and needs? Do you communicate with sensitivity and work to build positive relationships? Are you a good listener? Are you comfortable with others, and do you have confidence in your relationships with them?

Stress Management Skills

"I feel that it's hard for me to control my anxiety." Agree or disagree?

Can you productively manage your emotions so that they work *for* you and not *against* you? Can you control destructive emotions? Can you work well under pressure? Are you in control, even when things get tense and difficult?

Adaptability Skills

"When trying to solve a problem, I look at each possibility and then decide on the best way." Agree or disagree?

Are you flexible? Do you cope well when things *don't* go according to plan? Can you switch to a new plan when you need to? Do you manage change effectively? Can you anticipate problems and solve them as they come up? Do you rely on yourself and adapt well?

General Mood

"I generally expect things will turn out all right, despite setbacks from time to time." Agree or disagree?

Are you optimistic and positive most of the time? Do you feel happy and content with yourself, others, and your life in general? Are you energetic and self-motivated? Do people tell you you're pleasant to be around?

From EQ-i: Post Secondary version. Reprinted by permission.

resilience the ability to bounce back from difficulties

learned optimism a way of thinking that helps you stay optimistic and potentially improves your mental and physical health

Emotional intelligence affects every part of our lives. For example, researchers study related concepts: "hardiness," "resilience," and "learned optimism."[5] Some people are more resistant to stress and illness. Hardy, resilient, optimistic people are confident, committed to what they're doing, feel greater control over

> ❝
> **Managing your emotions is an inside job.**
>
> *Doc Childre and Howard Martin, performance experts*
> ❞

their lives, and see hurdles as challenges. Emotional intelligence is part of the reason why.

Looking back at the "FOCUS Challenge Case," we can see that Kia Washington probably lacks strong emotional intelligence. Her level of skill in these five areas may help explain her difficulty controlling her moods, communicating with James, managing stress, adjusting to college, and being positive and optimistic about working through her problems. Will she be academically successful? What do you think?

Emotional intelligence and its five scales are important in all aspects of life, including your future career.[6] When *Harvard Business Review* first published an article on the topic in 1998, it attracted more readers than any article in the journal's previous forty years. When the CEO of Johnson & Johnson read it, he ordered copies for the company's 400 top executives worldwide.[7]

Why? Emotional intelligence is a characteristic of true leaders. Immediately after the first shock of the September 11, 2001, tragedy, the world tuned in to a press conference with New York's Mayor Rudy Giuliani. He was asked to estimate the number of people who had lost their lives in the World Trade Center collapse that day, and his reply was this: "We don't know the exact number yet, but whatever the number, it will be more than we can bear." In that one sentence, Giuliani demonstrated one of the most important principles of true leadership. Leaders inspire by touching the feelings of others.[8]

Can Emotional Intelligence Be Improved?

Everyone wants well-developed emotional intelligence, but how do you get it? Can EI be learned? While researchers admit that genes definitely play a role, most experts believe that emotional intelligence can be increased. One of the most convincing pieces of evidence is from a study that followed a group of students over seven years. Students assessed their emotional intelligence, selected particular areas to strengthen, and then each created an individual plan to develop them. Seven years later, their competencies remained high.[9]

If you believe what this chapter says about the importance of emotional intelligence and college success, you're probably asking yourself what you can actually help you fight illness and depression, boost your brain power, and even prolong your life. In one study, students were taken to the bottom of a steep hill while wearing a heavy backpack. They were asked to guess how steep the hill was. Students standing next to friends, rather than by themselves, thought the hill looked much less steep, and friends who had known each other longer guessed it was even less steep. Researchers wrote that "People with stronger friendship networks feel like there is someone they can turn to. Friendship is an undervalued resource. The consistent message of these studies is that friends make your life better." If that's true, then how you communicate with them is more important than you may even realize.[17]

Or consider family members. These people make up the core of who you really are. Your kid brother may drive you crazy at times, and a parent may seem to smother you, but generally, these people care about you most. Often we "let it all hang out" with family members, perhaps because we know they'll overlook our flaws. When we're tired or stressed, this is often where we "veg" or vent. But because of the central, lasting role they play in our lives, they deserve more quality communication than we sometimes give them.

Classmates and instructors, too, deserve your best communication, even when you disagree with what they're saying in class. You may see your instructors as either friendly or unfriendly, but you'll need to make the first move to get to know them, rather than the other way around. Take the initiative to meet them during their office hours and bring up points from class that you'd like to know more about. It's unlikely a professor will single you out ("John, you looked puzzled when I got to the part of the chapter on pages 160–170. Did you understand what I was talking about?"). That could happen, but it's unlikely. You have many classmates, and your instructor may not be able to pay attention to each individual student. It'll be your job to go to your professor to ask questions or get help. You'll want to get to know your classmates, too, to make your classes more engaging. You're likely to work with them on class projects. Do some of your best communicating here. Chances are your group-mates—and the group's grade—will depend on it. Participate, do your part, and keep your word. No one will appreciate it if you promise to come to every planning meeting outside of class and turn out to be a no-show every week. And if you volunteer to do the group's PowerPoint and then don't come through in the end, you'll get a reputation that may follow you

But something students often wonder about is how to connect the dots. What's the big picture? Knowledge isn't quite as neat as departments and boxes; it's messy. It overlaps and merges. Despite the divisions and abbreviations colleges use to divide up knowledge, you might be able to take a somewhat similar course in visual art as an art course, a computer science course, or a communication course. You've probably noticed that you sometimes hear something discussed in one of your classes that's also being discussed in another one. Knowledge is interconnected. College in a Box isn't an accurate way of looking at things.

Even though each academic discipline has its own history and identity and way of asking questions and finding answers, the disciplines aren't as distinct as your class schedule might lead you to believe.

It takes courage to grow up and become who you really are.

e. e. cummings, American poet (1894–1962)

How Do the Disciplines Connect?

The Circle of Learning (see Figure 12.2) illustrates the interconnectedness of knowledge. Although this circle could be drawn in many different ways, using many different traditional academic disciplines, here is an example to get you thinking.[2]

It works like this. Let's start at the top of the circle with *math*, which is a basic "language" with rules and conventions, just like spoken language. You manipulate numbers and operations and functions, just as you manipulate sounds and words and sentences. Now, move clockwise around the circle.

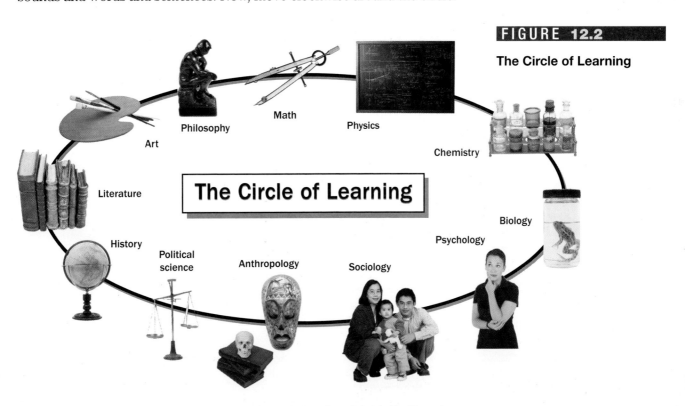

FIGURE 12.2

The Circle of Learning

"Never mistake knowledge for wisdom. One helps you make a living; the other helps you make a life.

Sandra Carey, consultant and lobbyist

Math is the fundamental language of *physics*, one branch of which studies atomic and subatomic particles. When atoms combine into molecules, such as carbon dioxide, the academic discipline involved is called *chemistry*. Chemicals combine to create living organisms studied in *biology* courses. Living organisms don't just exist, they think and behave, leading to the study of *psychology*. They also interact in groups, families, and societies, which you study in *sociology*. You can also study units of living beings throughout time and across cultures in the discipline of *anthropology*. These units—people—who live and work together are typically governed or govern themselves, leading to *political science*. Let's keep going.

When an account of peoples and countries and their rulers is recorded, you study *history*. These written accounts, sometimes factual or sometimes fictional (for pleasure or intrigue) comprise the study of *literature*. Literature is one way to record impressions and provoke reactions—poetry is a good example—through the use of words. But images and symbols can do the same things—enter *art*. A particular question artists ask is "What is beauty?" otherwise known as aesthetics, which is also a particular topic of study in *philosophy*. Philosophy also includes another subspecialty called number theory, one of the earliest branches of pure mathematics. And now we're all the way around the Circle of Learning, arriving right back at *math*.

That's a quick rundown. Of course, many academic disciplines don't appear on this chart, but they could and should. The point isn't which disciplines are represented. Instead, the Circle of Learning demonstrates that academic disciplines are interconnected because knowledge itself is interconnected. *Anthropology* (understanding people throughout time and across cultures) can provide an important foundation for *political science* (how people

CONTROL: *YOUR LEARNING*

YOUR TOUGHEST TASK

In Class: Think about your most challenging class this semester. Is it a general education course or one required for your major? If it's a general education course, make a list of all the ways this course can help you either to further your career or to become a well-educated person. If this course is one in your major, ask yourself why the challenge is so great. Do you understand the course content? Do you see how it connects with the content in other courses? Do you keep

up with readings and assignments? Can you follow your instructor's teaching style? Send your instructor in this class an e-mail indicating your specific efforts to do your best and detailing your progress.

On the Job: Assume your boss has just assigned you a challenging new task, one that will ask you to call on what you have learned in many different classes or disciplines. What might that task be? Describe it, along with knowledge you'd need from at least five academic disciplines.

are governed or govern themselves), and *history* (a record of peoples and countries and rulers) can be one basis for understanding *literature.* Using what you're learning in one discipline can lead to deeper understanding in another, and although some of your instructors will help you connect the dots, putting it all together is basically your responsibility.

In your career, you'll need to use knowledge without necessarily remembering in which course you learned it. You'll be thinking critically and creatively, solving problems, and calling upon all the skills you're developing in all the courses you're studying in college. The bottom line is that connections count. Recognize them, use them, and strengthen them to reinforce your learning.

How to Choose a Major and a Career

Like many students, you probably put value in how well college prepares you for a profession.[3] Choosing a college major and directing yourself toward a prospective career can be stressful. Many students feel pressure to make the right decision—and make it right now! You might hear conflicting advice from family members that put a high priority on financial success above other important factors, for example, and feel overwhelmed by the number of possibilities from which to choose.[4] You may know what you want to do with the rest of your life right now, but many of your classmates don't, and even if they *say* they do, they may well change their minds. Yes, these decisions are important. But where do you start? The decision-making process should involve these critical steps. If you're still deciding, or even if you think you already have, consider how they apply to you.

Photosto60.com

“ ”

The self is not something that one finds. It's something one creates.

Thomas Szasz, Professor Emeritus in Psychiatry, State University of New York Health Science Center, Syracuse

How **FULL** is your plate?

“ **The laws of science do not distinguish between the past and the future.** ”

—STEVEN W. HAWKING

People talk about something being a real "slice of life." They mean that whatever they're talking about is a realistic snapshot in time. What did you do with today's slice of life? Were you realistic in what you expected of yourself? Did you pay attention to the things and people that are most important to you? Did you make progress toward the future you're trying to create?

Irafael/Shutterstock.com

TRY IT!

Keep track of how productively you "carve up" your time this week and be prepared to be accountable to your instructor and classmates next week. Keep a journal of each day's biggest accomplishment and most distracting obstacle, and see if you recognize patterns. Create one time management pointer of your own to share with your classmates.

Step 1: Follow Your Bliss

In an ideal world, which major and career would you choose? Don't think about anything except the actual content you'd be studying. Don't consider career opportunities, requirements, difficulty, or anything else that might keep you from making these choices in an ideal world. What are you passionate about? If it's skateboarding, think about which majors might apply. Majoring in physics would help you understand skateboard "flight paths," spin, and angles. Majoring in landscape architecture would allow you to design skateparks. Majoring in journalism would put you in a good position to write for a skateboarding magazine.

Like Ethan Cole from the "FOCUS Challenge Case," you may be wondering what to do with your life. Perhaps the *idealist* in you has one potential career in mind and the *realist* in you has another. The $300,000 salary you'd earn as a surgeon may look very compelling until you consider the years of medical school required after college, the time invested in an internship and residency, and the still further years of specialization. It takes long-term commitment, dedication, and resources—yours or borrowed ones—to make that dream come true. Do these factors lessen the appeal?

Perhaps there's conflict between your ideal career and someone else's idea of an ideal career for you. Comedian Robin Williams once said, "When I told my father I was going to be an actor, he said, 'Fine, but study welding just in case.'"

And perhaps you just don't know yet. If that's the case, don't panic. Despite the increased pressure these days to choose the right major because of rising tuition and a changeable economy, Ethan Cole is right: It's hard to have it all figured out from the start.[5]

One thing is certain: You'll be a happier, more productive person if you do what *you* want to do *and* pursue it vigorously. When it comes to success, ability (*Can* you do it?) and effort (Are you *willing* to invest what it takes?) go hand in hand. Whatever your motivation, remember this. It's unusual for people to become truly successful halfheartedly. There are undeniable emotional and psychological components involved in success. Wayne Gretzky, called the greatest player in the history of hockey, once said, "God gave me a special talent to play the game . . . maybe he didn't give me a talent, he gave me a *passion*."

CAREER OUTLOOK: *Be Reliable*

 If you can absolutely be relied upon; if when you say a thing is so, it is so; if when you say you will do a thing, you do it; then you carry with you a passport to universal esteem.

GRENVILLE KLEISER

Do what you'll say you'll do. When you're given a task, complete it on time and with real quality. When you say you'll do something, do it. In college, your professors rely on you to get assignments done on time and according to their instructions. And when working on team projects, your classmates must be able to trust not only your intentions, but your results. This character trait, reliability, is a cornerstone of professional achievement and recognition. When your colleagues and supervisors learn that they can trust you to do what you say you'll do, you become recognized—and rewarded—as a valuable member of the team.

Having said that, what if your "bliss" just isn't feasible? You'd give anything to play for the NBA, but you're five foot two and female. You dream of being a rock star, but you can't carry a tune. Then it may be time to set aside the dream and get real. Maybe then it's time to translate—or shift—your dreams into goals.

When the statistics are against you, achieving success isn't impossible, but it might take more than expert skill. It might also take some luck, very specific planning, and perseverance.

Step 2: Conduct Preliminary Research

Has it ever occurred to you that you may not have all the facts—accurate ones—about your ideal major? Do you know what it *really* takes? Have you gotten your information from qualified sources—or are you basing your opinion on your friend's reaction to one course he took?

Try an experiment. Choose three majors you're considering, one of which is your ideal major, and send yourself on a fact-finding mission. To find out if you're on target, get the answers to the following ten questions for each of the three possibilities. Go to the physical location (department) where each major is housed, and interview an instructor. The experiment requires legwork; don't just let your fingers do the clicking.

1. What is the major or certificate?

2. Who is the interviewee?

3. What is the name of the academic department where this major is housed? Where are the department offices physically located on campus?

4. Which introductory courses in this major would give you information about your interests and abilities?

5. Which specialized courses in this major interest you? (List three.)

6. What courses do you have to complete before you can major in the subject?

7. How many students major in this discipline on your campus?

8. Which required course in the major do students usually find most challenging? Which is most engaging? Which is most valued? Why?

9. How would the interviewee describe the reputation of this department on campus? What is it known for?

10. From the interviewee's perspective, why should a student major in this discipline?

After you complete your interviews, review the facts. Did you change any of your opinions based on what you learned?[6]

> **Follow your bliss and be what you want to be. Don't climb the ladder of success only to find it's leaning against the wrong wall.**
>
> *Dr. Bernie Siegel, physician and writer*

> **The privilege of a lifetime is being who you are.**
>
> *Joseph Campbell, American professor and writer (1904–1987)*

How to Choose a Major and a Career **303**

Bryan Allen/CORBIS

Step 3: Take a Good Look at Yourself

What Are Your Job Preferences?

Take a good look at yourself and answer the following questions about how you prefer to work. Rank each item 1 or 2 based on your general preference. While many careers, if not most, require both, your task is to decide which of the two you prefer. (Mark 1 for your highest preference.)

I prefer to work at a job:

1. Alone	_____	With other people	_____
2. Indoors	_____	Outdoors	_____
3. With people	_____	With equipment or materials	_____
4. Directing/leading others	_____	Being directed/led by others	_____
5. Producing information	_____	Managing information	_____
6. In an organized, step-by-step way	_____	In a big-idea, big-picture way	_____
7. Starting things	_____	Completing things	_____
8. Involving a product	_____	Involving a service	_____
9. Solving challenging problems	_____	Generating creative ideas	_____
10. Finding information	_____	Applying information	_____
11. Teaching/training others in groups	_____	Advising/coaching others one-on-one	_____

Now look at your eleven first choices. Identify several career fields that come to mind that would allow you to achieve as many of them as possible.

Here's a bottom-line question: For you—as Dr. Bernie Siegel would say—what *is* the "right wall" to lean your ladder of success on? How do you know? Many first-year college students don't know. They don't have enough experience under their belts to plan for a lifetime. They're in college to *discover*. It all comes down to questions this book has been asking you all along: Who are you? And what do you want? If you're unsure of how to proceed in your decision making, follow these recommendations to see if they help you bring your future into focus.

Send in the SWOT Team! A SWOT analysis is an excellent way to begin taking a good look at yourself in relation to your future. SWOT stands for Strengths, Weaknesses, Opportunities, and Threats. SWOT analyses are typically used in business, but creating one for yourself may be useful when it comes to deciding on a college major and a career. Make a chart with four sections, label each one, and fill them in as objectively as you can.

> **Strengths** are traits that give you a leg up. These are talents you can capitalize on and qualities you can develop.

> **Weaknesses** are traits that currently work against you. You can, however, work to reduce or eliminate them.

> **Opportunities** are conditions or circumstances that work in your favor, like a strong forecast for the future of your prospective career.

> **Threats** are conditions that could have bad effects. Some of these factors are beyond your control; however, sometimes you can figure out ways to make them matter less.

As you create your own chart, begin with two basic questions:

What kinds of forces will impact your potential career?

Internal—forces inside you, such as motivation and skill

External—forces outside you that may affect your success: the job market or economy, for example

What kind of influence can these forces exert?

Positive—some forces will give you a boost toward your goals

Negative—other forces will work against you[7]

Let's complete a SWOT analysis for Ethan and his dream of becoming a professional skateboarder. Of course, you might say that, technically, he doesn't need an academic degree for that particular career. But if he wants to pursue related, more traditional careers—design a new skatepark or write for a skateboard magazine, for example—he would need knowledge from design and writing to finance and marketing. Besides, college isn't just about jobs, it's about living a fuller life as a well-educated person.

Look back at the "FOCUS Challenge Case," and see if you agree with the basic SWOT analysis shown in Figure 12.3.

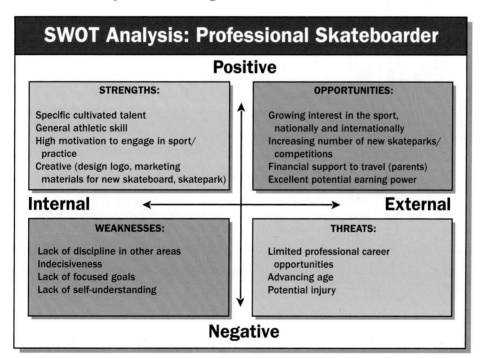

SWOT Analysis: Professional Skateboarder

Positive

STRENGTHS:
Specific cultivated talent
General athletic skill
High motivation to engage in sport/
  practice
Creative (design logo, marketing
  materials for new skateboard, skatepark)

OPPORTUNITIES:
Growing interest in the sport,
  nationally and internationally
Increasing number of new skateparks/
  competitions
Financial support to travel (parents)
Excellent potential earning power

Internal ← → **External**

WEAKNESSES:
Lack of discipline in other areas
Indecisiveness
Lack of focused goals
Lack of self-understanding

THREATS:
Limited professional career
  opportunities
Advancing age
Potential injury

Negative

FIGURE 12.3

SWOT Analysis

Looking at his SWOT analysis, what would you conclude? Is professional skateboarding a good career for him? In your view, do the opportunities outweigh the threats? For example, does the possibility of earning big bucks outweigh the risks of possible injuries? If not, could he move toward other potential careers, perhaps some that also involve skateboarding? "Ethan remembered liking geometry, he was good at creative writing, he played the drums like a real jazz musician, and he was an incredible artist." Do you see potential majors for him in college? Sports management? Kinesiology? Architecture? Journalism? Jazz studies? Creative writing? What should Ethan do?

Step 4: Consider Your Major versus Your Career

Which comes first, the chicken or the egg? The major or the career? Silly question? The obvious answer, of course, is that you must first major or earn a certificate in something in college before you can build a career on it. But the question isn't as straightforward as it seems.

Should you choose a major based on an intended career? Perhaps you know you want to be a science teacher, first and foremost. You don't know whether to get an associate's degree in physical science or an associate of arts degree in teaching. You like all sciences, but teaching is your real interest. If you major in science, which one should you emphasize (see Figure 12.4)?

FIGURE 12.4

Which Science Should a Science Teacher Major In?

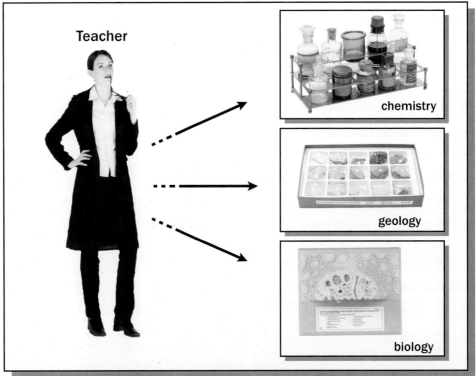

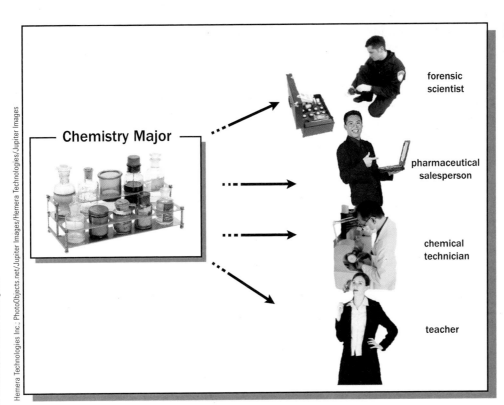

FIGURE 12.5

Which Career Should a Chemistry Major Choose?

Or instead, should you choose a major first, and then decide on a career? Say you made a firm decision to major in chemistry when your favorite science teacher did "mad scientist" experiments for the class in eighth grade. But at this point, you're not certain of the professional direction you'd like to pursue. Chemistry is your passion, but should you apply your chemistry degree as a forensics expert, a pharmaceutical salesperson, a chemical technician, or a teacher (see Figure 12.5)? You could enter some of these career fields with an associate's degree, but others might require a four-year degree.

So which comes first—major or career? It depends.[8] The answer sounds uncertain, and it's meant to. Although some professional degree programs put you into a particular track right away (nursing, for example), generally either direction can work well. Doors will open and close for you, and as you gain more knowledge and experience, you'll narrow your focus. As you learn more about your chosen major, you'll also learn about its specific career tracks. But it's important to remember that a major doesn't have to lock you into one specific career. And you can always narrow or refocus your area of emphasis by earning your bachelor's degree and continuing your education beyond that.[9]

What's Your Academic Anatomy? Thinking about your academic anatomy is a simple way to begin to get a handle on what you find fulfilling. If you had to rank order the four parts of you listed in Figure 12.6, what would you put in first place? Second, third, and last? To get yourself thinking, ask these questions:

1. Do you find fulfillment by using your *head*? Do you enjoy solving complex problems or thinking through difficult situations? Do you like to reason things out, weigh evidence, and think critically? Someone working toward a paralegal certificate might fit this category.

2. Do you find it satisfying to work with matters of the *heart*? Are you the kind of person others come to with problems because you listen and care? Does trying to make others happy make you happy? A nursing major might be what students with this preference choose, for example.

3. Do you like to create things with your *hands*? Do you enjoy making art? Doing hands-on projects? Building things out of other things? A drafting major who designs and builds models might be what students with this preference choose, for example.

4. Do you excel at physical activities that involve your *whole body*? Are you athletic? Do you like to stay active, no matter what you're doing? A physical therapy major who goes on to work in a rehabilitation facility helping stroke victims relearn to walk might be what students with this preference choose, for example.

ONLINE **TechKnow**

Improve Your Grade
Online Flashcards
Glossary

How do I find a job? Increasingly, job searches (and even applications) may take place on the Internet. Such powerful job-search sites as Monster.com, TheLadders.com, and Job.com can help in your job searches in many ways:

- Such sites help you search for jobs by category and location.
- They help you apply with features such as "Create Your Resume," "Job-Hunt Strategy," and "Plan Your Career."
- They also help you market yourself, plan for interviews, and test potential salaries using online salary calculators.

Many of the strengths you've developed while taking online courses—self-discipline, scheduling, focus, working ahead—will come in handy as you search for and start on that new job. Increasingly the skills that are useful in tomorrow's workplace are often the skills you've sharpened in your college work. And the online courses and concentrations you complete may well prepare you for work in a growing field. Perhaps you've already chosen your career field; but if not, it may help you to know this information about five of the fastest growing occupations in the next decade:

- **Networks systems and data communications analysts** perform tasks in data communication systems like the Internet. This is the fastest growing occupation with a 53% increase in the number of jobs.
- **Computer software engineers** develop, design, test, and evaluate the systems that operate our computers. This area will experience an increase of 45%.
- **Financial analysts and advisors** share expertise on investment strategies. This area will grow by 39%.
- **Substance abuse and behavioral counselors** offer counseling to people dealing with problems such as alcohol, tobacco, drugs, gambling, and eating disorders. This area should grow by 34%.
- **Physical therapist assistants** help treat victims of accidents or people with disabilities. This area will grow by 30%.[10]

FIGURE 12.6

What's Your Academic Anatomy?

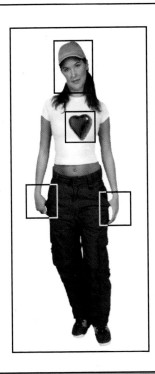

Another way of analyzing your preferences is by considering your "Academic Anatomy." What do you find most satisfying? Working with your

Head?
Heart?
Hands? or
Whole Body?

Now look at your academic anatomy rankings. Of course, the truth is that "all of you" is involved in everything you do. And achieving balance is important. But what are your priorities? This type of simple analysis can be one way of informing you about who you are and where you should be headed.

However, no system for choosing a major is perfect. In fact, most are imperfect at best. Here are four things to consider.

1. Sometimes students who don't select a likely major based on their "anatomical preferences" can still be successful. A whole-body person (like Ethan Cole probably is) may decide to major in art (using his hands). But he'll have to find other ways to meet his whole-body needs unless he becomes a sculptor involved in creating large constructed projects.

2. You may intentionally choose an unlikely major. Perhaps art (using your hands) comes so naturally to you that you decide to major in science (using your head). You need the challenge to stay fully involved in getting your education. While it may sound unlikely, it's been known to happen.

3. You may choose an unlikely major because one particular course turns you on. You had no idea majoring in this subject was even possible, and you didn't know what it entailed. But you find studying it fascinating—so you shift gears to focus all your attention on it.

4. You may be equally engaged, no matter what. You love subjects that require using your head, hands, heart, and whole body. The anatomy of learning is less important to you than other factors—a teacher whose enthusiasm is contagious, for example.[11]

© Larry Harwood Photography. Property of Cengage Learning.

Are you fit company for the person you wish to become?

Anonymous

Ethan's rankings would probably go something like this: (1) whole body, (2) hands, (3) heart, and (4) head. And just because "head" is in last place for him doesn't mean he's doomed in college. A career as a financial analyst sitting behind a desk probably wouldn't be his cup of tea, for example. But it may well be yours. As you decide, you may want to consider whether your choice is "anatomically correct."

Whatever major or career you're aiming for—or still looking for—make sure you follow the four steps outlined in this chapter and create the future you want.

EXERCISE 12.2

Get a Job!

Bring an employment ad from a newspaper or Internet website to class, perhaps for a job that's related to your prospective career. After carefully considering your individual ads in small groups of three or four, create an employment ad for the "job" of college student. For example, "_____ College seeks applicants with excellent skills in oral and written communication, problem solving, time management, and technology for positions as professional students preparing for a variety of future opportunities...." Your ad should list particular job requirements, benefits, information about your institution, and so on, and be as much like a real ad as possible. When your group is finished constructing its ad, present it to the entire class.[12]

VARK Activity	Complete the activity recommended for your preferred VARK learning style and bring it to class (or follow your instructor's instructions).

 Visual: Select a quotation from this chapter that was particularly memorable to you. Create a poster of the quote, using large font and graphics, to hang on a wall in your room.

 Aural: Talk through the Circle of Learning aloud to help you remember the connections between academic disciplines. Access the CourseMate via www.cengagebrain.com/shop/ISBN/1439083908 to listen to the iAudio summary for this chapter.

 Read/Write: Find a book that extends the ideas presented in this chapter. Select a passage that impresses you from the book to share with your classmates.

 Kinesthetic: Go on a "field trip" to the Career Center on your campus. Collect resources you find there and bring them to class or access the CourseMate via www.cengagebrain.com/shop/ISBN/1439083908 to watch the FOCUS TV episode for this chapter and answer the questions.

(from top to bottom) Marcela Barsse/MarsBars/iStockphoto.com; Johanna Goodyear/Dreamstime.com; Nadezda Firsova/iStockphoto.com; Pascal Genest/iStockphoto.com

step 3 INSIGHT *Now* What Do You Think?

At the beginning of this chapter, Ethan Cole, a confused and discouraged student, faced a challenge. Now after reading this chapter, would you respond differently to any of the questions you answered about the "FOCUS Challenge Case"? Using what you learned in the chapter, write a paragraph ending to Ethan's case study. What are some of the possible outcomes for Ethan?

step 4 ACTION Your Plans for Change

1. Where are you when it comes to choosing a major or career? If you haven't decided yet, what specific information from this chapter will you use? If you've already decided, had you already taken these suggestions into account? Will you change any of your plans?

2. Do you know someone working in a career field that is disillusioned or disappointed with the choice he or she made? How will you know your decision is a wise one? What can you do to make sure?

What did you Learn?

On a scale of 1 to 5, answer these questions now that you've completed this chapter.

1 = not very/not much/very little/low   5 = very/a lot/very much/high

How much do you know *now*?

Now rate your current level of knowledge about topics covered in this chapter.

Connections between disciplines

1 2 3 4 5

Majors

1 2 3 4 5

Careers

1 2 3 4 5

SWOT analysis

1 2 3 4 5

How useful might the information in this chapter be to you?

How much do you think this information might affect your college success?

1 2 3 4 5

How much do you think this information might affect your career success after college?

1 2 3 4 5

How long did it actually take you to complete this chapter (both the reading and writing tasks)?

_____ Hour(s) _____ Minutes

  Challenge Yourself Online Quiz. To find out how much you've learned, access the CourseMate via www.cengagebrain.com/shop/ISBN/1439083908 to take the Challenge Yourself Online Quiz.

Compare these answers with your answers from the "Readiness Check" at the beginning of this chapter. How might the gaps between what you thought before starting the chapter and what you now think affect how you approach the next chapter?

13 chapter

Creating Your Future

You're About to Discover...

✓ How to launch a career
✓ How to write a résumé and interview successfully
✓ What to consider if you're thinking of continuing your education
✓ How to put what you learned in college to good use

© Larry Harwood Photography. Property of Cengage Learning.

READINESS CHECK

What do you **Know?**

Before beginning this chapter, take a moment to answer these questions. Your answers will help you assess how ready you are to focus.

1 = not very/not much/very little/low   5 = very/a lot/very much/high

How much do you *already* know?

Rate your current level of knowledge about topics covered in this chapter.

Launching a career

      1 2 3 4 5

Writing a résumé

      1 2 3 4 5

Continuing your education

      1 2 3 4 5

Knowing what employers really want

      1 2 3 4 5

How motivated are you to learn *more*?

In general, how motivated are you to learn the material in this chapter?

      1 2 3 4 5

How much do you think this information might affect your college success?

      1 2 3 4 5

How much do you think this information might affect your career success after college?

      1 2 3 4 5

How ready are you to read *now*?

How ready are you to focus on this chapter—physically, intellectually, and emotionally? Which of these three areas is most challenging for you right now? Circle a number to represent it.

      1 2 3 4 5

If any of your answers is below a 3, consider addressing the issue before reading. Then, read the chapter carefully, while looking for ways to improve your focus.

Finally, how long do you think it will take you to complete this chapter? If you start and stop, keep track of the overall time.

_____ Hour(s) _____ Minutes

Anthony Lopez

Anthony Lopez was average in nearly every sense of the word. He played T-ball as a kid, but not particularly well. He didn't like school much, but he went when he felt like it. He didn't have many friends except for a few kids that lived in the eight city blocks that made up his neighborhood. He was even sandwiched between two older brothers and two younger sisters. His brothers were successful—one was an attorney and the other a doctor. Somehow, deep inside himself, Anthony knew that measuring up would be hard for him. Maybe that's why he decided to make his mark in his own way.

You could say that Anthony's kid sister, Gina, was his closest friend. Even though she was four years younger, the two of them would pal around the neighborhood. They could laugh over absolutely anything, and their specialty was pulling pranks on all the other neighborhood kids. For a while, the two of them were inseparable. Whenever you saw Gina, you knew that Anthony was close by.

But as Anthony got older, things changed. The trouble started in middle school. His Mom, who worked more than one job to keep the family afloat, was worried that he was getting in with the wrong crowd. But Anthony wasn't worried. His friends knew where to get cigarettes and alcohol—even drugs. When he was with them, he imagined the other kids looked up to him and his tough-guy friends. By the time high school rolled around, Anthony already had a record. Eventually, he dropped out, left home, and basically lived on the streets. When he needed money, he snatched a purse or wallet. He lost contact with his family, and there seemed to be no turning back. Drugs were a way of life for him, and he began sinking deeper and deeper into a life that most people predicted wouldn't turn out well.

Criminal Search- County

Name: Lopez, Anthony   **DOB:** 7-10-1989   **SSN:** XXX-XX-XXXX

RESULT: RECORD FOUND

STATE/COUNTY: VERIFIED INFORMATION

Case #:   T3-13145
Filing Date: 8-18-08

But that was then, and this was now. Anthony's life probably would have been headed in the wrong direction entirely, if it hadn't been for several wakeup calls, including seeing his little sister, Gina, on the street one day. He tried to talk with her, but she was so high that she didn't even recognize him. Anthony saw that she was repeating his worst mistakes, which troubled him deeply. The stark realization that he might be ruining her life in addition to his own shocked him back into reality.

Now Anthony is part of an inner-city youth organization for kids like him. The group's leader, Nicky Russo, had once been a gang member himself. He reached out to Anthony, and Anthony responded. Anthony was on a mission to find Gina and get her into the group. Anthony's life was changing, and his life's goal was becoming clear: to help other people like him. He decided to earn his GED and enroll in the best college he could find to earn an associate's degree in social services. And that's exactly what he did.

As he sat in his favorite class, Urban Social Issues, Anthony realized that he had made the right choice. So much of what he heard his instructor lecturing about had been a part of his own past. As he got deeper into the associate's program, Anthony learned that an associate's degree in social services was a general degree that prepared graduates for many types of jobs. But what if he wanted to be an actual social worker? He learned that the need for social workers was very high, working with young children to older adults. He was taking classes like Racial, Ethnic, and Minority Groups and Sociology of the Family.

Even though the classes were hard, it wasn't long before Anthony was totally engrossed, and he knew he wanted to continue his education. With an associate's degree in social services, he could certainly work more knowledgeably alongside Nicky in the inner city. But what if he continued in a four-year program for a bachelor's degree in sociology? What if he wanted to earn a master's degree in social work to specialize and become a school or hospital social worker? What if he wanted to conduct research and teach, like his college instructors? What would getting a Ph.D. require, and should he even be thinking that far ahead? A million questions were forming in his mind.

What did the future hold for Anthony? Right now, he couldn't answer that question. But he did know that his future would be different from the future he might have had without college. What had always been true about Anthony was now true in the best possible sense: Anthony would make his mark.

Scholastic Studio 10/Index Stock Imagery / PhotoLibrary

Sociology Program Comparison

	Bachelor's Degree
Ethnic Relations	
City in a Global Society	
Societal Change and Development	
Environmental Sociology	
Global Sociology	
Sociological Analysis	
Classical Theories of Society	
Contemporary Theories of Society	
Sociological Field Methods	
Gender and Society	
Global Sociology	
Quantitative Methods	
Regression and Multivariate Data Analysis	
Policy Issues in Education	
Economics of Educational Policy	
Public Policy	
Demographic Analysis	
Evaluation of Educational Programs	
Race and Class in American Cities	
Masters Thesis Project	
Qualitative Research	
Sociological Analysis	

© Cengage Learning

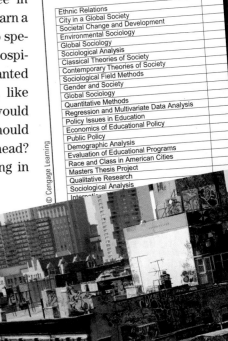

Philip Lange, 2010. Used under license from Shutterstock.com.

© Cengage Learning

SOCIOLOGY
ASSOCIATE OF ARTS DEGREE

The AA degree with an emphasis in Sociology is designed to provide a better understanding of how humans act and interact in social settings. The program offered provides an excellent foundation for students seeking to continue their education in Sociology, either pursuing a Bachelor's or Master's degree.

First Semester	
ENGL 101 English Composition I	3
SOC 101 Introduction to Sociology	3
Science Elective	3
Humanities Elective	3
Total Credits	12

© Cengage Learning

Sociology Program Course Comparison

	Bachelor's Degree	Master's Degree	Doctoral Degree
Ethnic Relations			
City in a Global Society			
Societal Change and Development			
Environmental Sociology			
Global Sociology			

1. Do you have anything in common with Anthony? If so, how are you managing the situation so that you can be successful?

2. Anthony appears to be headed toward a life of service. Do you know anyone like him who has turned his or her life around? Describe the situation.

3. What are the pros and cons of continuing his education beyond an associate's degree?

4. In your view, should he continue his education beyond a two-year degree? Why or why not?

What's the Next Step?

You've done it. You've nearly finished your first term of college. Perhaps at this point, you're even jumping ahead to when you finish all of your courses. Then what? Yogi Berra, the baseball giant, is known for having a way with words. His advice was, "When you come to a fork in the road, take it." *Which one?* you ask. Precisely! (Yogi Berra is said to have been giving directions to his New Jersey home, and both streets worked equally well.)

After you achieve your college goals—whether you're taking a few targeted classes for a particular reason or earning a certificate, an associate's degree, or bachelor's degree—you'll come to a fork in the road. Should you take the fork leading toward pursuing a particular career right away or the fork leading toward continuing your education? This chapter won't answer the question *for* you, but it will give you some things to think about. Just as was the case with Yogi Berra's famous advice, both forks in *your* road will lead you toward the same thing: *your* future. What you decide to do and when you decide to do it will be up to you.

When you come to a fork in the road, take it.

Yogi Berra, baseball player and manager

ibusca/iStockphoto.com

The huge printing presses of a major Chicago newspaper began malfunctioning on the Saturday before Christmas, putting all the revenue for advertising that was to appear in the Sunday paper in jeopardy. None of the technicians could track down the problem. Finally, a frantic call was made to the retired printer who had worked with these presses for over forty years. "We'll pay anything; just come in and fix them," he was told.

When he arrived, he walked around for a few minutes, surveying the presses; then he approached one of the control panels and opened it. He removed a dime from his pocket, turned a screw ¼ of a turn, and said, "The presses will now work correctly." After being profusely thanked, he was told to submit a bill for his work.

The bill arrived a few days later, for $10,000.00! Not wanting to pay such a huge amount for so little work, the printer was told to please itemize his charges, with the hope that he would reduce the amount once he had to identify his services. The revised bill arrived: $1.00 for turning the screw; $9,999.00 for knowing which screw to turn.

(Anonymous)

So what does it take? After forty years on the job, the retired printer knew many things, including one little-known but critical piece of knowledge—which screw to turn. But perhaps you're just starting out, and experience is something you don't have yet. No matter where *you* are on your journey, how will *you* achieve life and career success?

Mel Levine, author of *Ready or Not, Here Life Comes*, says, "We are in the midst of an epidemic of work-life unreadiness because an alarming number of emerging adults are unable to find a good fit between their minds and their career directions....Because they are not finding their way, they may feel as if they are going nowhere and have nowhere to go."[1]

How can anyone have nowhere to go with more than 12,000 different occupations or careers to choose from with 8,000 alternative job titles—for a total of over 20,000 options?[2] Some students, like Ethan, start college and become overwhelmed. Sometime during the first year, or possibly later, they take a step back and announce in so many words, "There are too many choices. I refuse to choose at all."[3]

Here's another tough issue many college graduates face when entering the world of work. Many of them

have had boring jobs thus far in life. They don't want to climb the ladder of success. They'd like to skip the bottom and start somewhere closer to the top rung. But every job involves some element of grunt work, even those at the top. No job is round-the-clock fun, and in every new job, eventually the honeymoon is over, and the tough challenges begin. The simple truth is this: building a career takes time, persistence, dedication, and focus. Seemingly overnight successes like J. K. Rowling of *Harry Potter* fame are rare; steady progress toward a goal is the norm.[4]

So what does it take to launch your career successfully? You'll need to focus your I's on four things: Inner direction, Interpretation, Instrumentation, and Interaction—the four I's of career-life readiness. Here's what they mean.[5]

- **Inner direction.** You've lived with yourself for some time now, but how well do you know yourself? Can you honestly and accurately judge your potential? Are you well suited for your major and career destinations? You must first understand the inner you before you can direct it toward a career that fits.

- **Interpretation.** On the job there's more required than repeating back what the boss has told you. You must interpret the information and apply it in your own way, which will demonstrate whether you do (or don't) understand what you're doing.

- **Instrumentation.** In your career, you'll need a toolkit filled with abilities, like high-level thinking, brainstorming, problem solving, decision-making and creativity skills, and developing both hard (technical) and soft (interpersonal) skills. And not only must you know how to use each of these tools, but you'll need to know when and why.

- **Interaction.** Business (or any profession) isn't just about facts and figures. It's about people and relationships—not products, not machines, not words in a report. While these things are important, too, chances are that people will be what help you build your career. Without people to buy, sell, trade, or produce, there is no business.

These four I's are keys to your future. The more you focus your I's, the better prepared you'll be for the challenges ahead.

Launching a Career: Plan Your Work and Work Your Plan

EXERCISE 13.1

Career Auction

Assume you have $100,000 to spend on the following items. In a few minutes, your instructor will begin a real-live auction, putting one item at a time up for auction. Before the auction begins, budget your money in the first column. You may select as many items as you wish to bid on, but you may not place all your money on any single item. As the group auction proceeds, fill in the appropriate amounts that are actually spent by members of the class for each item.

	BUDGETED AMOUNT	WINNING BID
1. Becoming the CEO of a leading Fortune 500 company	_____	_____
2. Being a top earner in your career field	_____	_____
3. Being the number-one expert in your profession	_____	_____
4. Having good friends on the job	_____	_____
5. Being your own boss	_____	_____
6. Creating a good balance between productive work and a happy family life	_____	_____
7. Having opportunities for travel and adventure in your job	_____	_____
8. Doing work you find fully satisfying	_____	_____
9. Working in a beautiful setting	_____	_____
10. Being a lifelong learner so that your career can develop and change over time	_____	_____

Let's assume, for now, that you decide to go straight into your chosen career field after college. You've been focused all along, earned your degree, and now you're ready to find a job that fits your new skills, your personality—*you*! "Fit" is the key word in that last sentence. Where you choose to work and who you work with will be critical factors in your job satisfaction.

The two questions posed early in this book resurface now: "Who are you?" and "What do you want?" Working your way through *FOCUS*, you have learned more about who you are (although this is a lifelong quest). In this final chapter, we'll deal with "What do you want?" The answer to that question can be just as important.

What do you really want from a career? What's important to you? Even though your views may change over time, it's important to start thinking about them now. In Exercise 13.1, item 4, "Having good friends on the job," may be a top priority now, but item 5, "Being your own boss," may be more appealing a few years down the road, after you have some additional work experience under your belt. Maybe you already prepared for a career once, but something has changed. The field you entered has transformed over time, so that you need to retool. Or a career that attracted you earlier turned out to be much less engaging than you expected. Or your family has grown and you need a career that brings in more resources. You may be older than the students sitting around you, but you deserve the same educational opportunities. Interestingly, according to research, the most important factor in job satisfaction isn't any of the ten items above. The number one contributor to job satisfaction, statistically speaking, is the quality of your relationship with your boss.[6] Here are some suggestions to help you launch the career you're aiming for.

> I always wanted to be somebody, but I should have been more specific.

Lily Tomlin, comedian

Looking for a Job? Create a Job Search Plan

It's smart to come up with a plan before you start searching for specific jobs. Your job search plan should be a list of what you want to do and how you can get it done. Start with a job-related career goal that will help focus your job hunt.

> **Think about the skills and experiences you have and the types of jobs that match.** You might try using one of the many "Skills Profilers" on the web to identify your skills and find matching jobs. If needed, update your job goals with what you learn about your skills and matching occupations.

> **Think about what you will need when you find jobs you want to apply for.** Will they ask you to fill out a job application? Have that information ready. Will they ask for a résumé, cover letter, and references? Create or update your résumé and cover letters to highlight what that employer is looking for. Be specific. If the job advertisement emphasizes that creativity is important, note that in your cover letter for that particular job. Ask previous professors or supervisors if they're willing to serve as references.

> **Learn about the employers you want to work for.** Try networking with people in the field for information about employers. You will need to contact each potential employer to see if they are hiring.

> **Identify good places to look for jobs.** Many job search websites have "Employer Locators" that you can search by occupation and location.

> **Keep track of your money and your credit rating.** Budgeting while job searching will help you to organize and prioritize your life while in transition. And be sure your credit rating is healthy—many employers run credit checks as part of the hiring process.

Looking for work is a full-time job in itself. Create a job search schedule as a part of your overall plan. You'll feel more accomplished, more confident, and will likely get hired faster if you'll follow a weekly action plan. If you're employed, you might find it difficult to look for another job, but it's still possible. You'll need to use your lunch break to make phone calls and do the rest of your searching in the evening and on weekends. Consider this sample schedule with time management tips for your job search:

Day 1

> **Review and update your résumé and cover letter.**
>
> **Check the print and online versions of local and national publications and job search websites for job openings.** Apply (and send résumés) via e-mail and the Web to as many jobs as possible to get yourself motivated.

Day 2

> **Set your alarm each morning.** Don't make a habit of sleeping in or you will be groggy for job interviews and will have a difficult time adjusting to your new schedule when you do start a new job.
>
> **Check your phone messages and e-mail and respond to employers right away.**
>
> **Make a list of your networking contacts with addresses and phone numbers.** You'll learn more about networking in this chapter.
>
> **Choose five to seven people to use as references.** Ask each person if they would be a professional reference for you and give them an updated copy of your résumé.
>
> **Create a job search worksheet to keep track of which jobs you apply for at which companies.** Leave a space to make notes on your follow ups.

Day 3

> **Follow up on the résumés sent on Day 1.**
>
> **Check newspapers and websites for new job openings.** Apply to at least 5 more jobs.
>
> **Find five people who are also job searching (even if they are not in your field) to create a "support group."**
>
> **Look up professional organizations, list-serves, and websites in your field.** Sign up for free e-mails from the groups and get a list of their upcoming events.
>
> **Stay organized.** Create a space in your house for your job search that is near the computer and the phone.

> **Check your phone messages and e-mail.** Immediately follow up with employers.

> **Stay active, stay alert.** Take breaks and clear your head.

Day 4

> **Get local.** Walk or drive around your neighborhood. Note every business that could use your skills. Be creative and think broadly of ways you could fit in with a company.

> **Get out of the house.** Pick a secondary place to job search like the library, or one of the thousands of "One-Stop Career Centers" in communities around the country. If you're not sure how to find one near you, check a website like http://www.servicelocator.org/.

> **Stay informed.** Watch the news, read the business section of the newspaper. Pay attention to local and world events.

> **Follow up with the jobs you applied for on Day 2.** Check to make sure they received your résumé.

> **Apply to at least five more jobs.**

> **Spend time with people you enjoy.** Take your mind off your job search and reconnect with other important things in your life.

Day 5

> **Identify five people whom you'd like to interview for information on specific jobs or occupations.** Learn, connect, and network in these informational interviews.

> **Think long term.** Expect to be job searching for one to four months, depending on the type of job you are looking for. Make a budget for the next few months.

> **Use or increase your professional skills while job searching.** Sign up with temp agencies for short-term jobs in your field. Volunteer for a nonprofit agency or school in a position that uses your professional and technical skills. Even if you don't get paid, it will look great on your résumé and you can use these new clients as references.

> **Make a plan of action for next week's job search.**

> **Take a few days off.** The less stressed you are, the more positive you will be during job interviews.

Remember to ask for help. At any time during your job search, don't be embarrassed or afraid to ask the people around you or a career counselor for new ideas on how to find work. Find resources and assistance for your job search—you're not in this alone.[7]

Try on a Career for Size

If all your jobs thus far have been just that—*jobs*—to help you pay the bills, how do you know what you want in a *career*? A career is different from a job. It's a profession you've chosen and prepared for. Perhaps you've had more than a string of jobs, and your career is well underway, but now you'd like to go in a different direction. Or perhaps you haven't launched your career yet. Exactly how *do* you launch a new career? You have to start somewhere, so perhaps you'd search online or through actual newspaper want ads. There are plenty of career exploration websites online. Check out these career mega websites to explore some options:

> Careerbuilder.com
> Monster.com
> The Occupational Outlook Handbook (www.bls.gov/oco/)
> Americasjobexchange.com
> Career-Journal.com
> Jobcentral.com
> USAJobs.gov
> TrueCareers.com
> AllJobSearch.com
> NowHiring.com[8]

You can Google and surf to your heart's content.

But you may be likely to read something like this: "Opening in . . . (anything). Experience required." Isn't that the way it always goes? You have to *have* experience in order to get a job that will *give* you experience. This problem is one many people face. Sure, you have experience. It's just not the right kind. Perhaps you've bagged fries, mowed yards, bussed tables, and chauffeured pizzas up to this point. If that's not the kind of experience the posted opening is looking for, how do you get the right kind? Or perhaps you're in school to switch career fields. You have experience, but it won't help you go in a different direction. The process of job-hunting includes many different steps. Here are some things for you to consider doing during your time in college. One important suggestion is to try a job on for size. Take a look at the three possibilities described in Figure 13.1.

These experiences help you in three ways. First, they allow you to test a potential career field. The actual day-to-day work may be exactly what you expected, or not. They show you whether that particular career field is one you'd really be interested in. *I had no idea this field was so cutthroat, hectic, dull . . . exciting, stimulating, invigorating. . . .* A thumbs-down can be just as informative as a thumbs-up. At least you can remove one option from your list. Second, internships, co-ops, and service-learning opportunities give you experience to list on your résumé. And third, they help you make connections with others in the field, and sometimes they even lead to employment.

Eric Robert/SYGMA/CORBIS

It is not what we get but who we become, what we contribute . . . that gives meaning to our lives.

Anthony Robbins, motivational speaker and author

	Description: What is a . . . ?	What kind of experience do I get?	Why would I want to do it?	How do I get involved?
Internships	An internship is an opportunity for you to work alongside a professional in a career field of interest to you, and to learn from him or her.	Your supervisor will mentor you, and you'll get a clearer picture of what the career field is like.	Some majors will require you to complete an internship as a part of your program, for licensure or certification, for example.	Internships may be offered through your academic major department, or through a central office on campus, or sometimes you can pursue one on your own through the Internet or personal connections.
Co-op Program	Co-op programs allow you to take classes and then apply what you've learned on the job, either after or while you take classes.	You may take classes for a term and then work full-time for a term. You can test a career field.	A potential employer can get a sense of your potential, and you can gain practical experience to put on your résumé.	Your advisor will be able to tell you if your program has co-op opportunities.
Service-Learning	Some classes contain service-learning experiences in which you volunteer your time.	A service-learning component built right into the syllabus can give you valuable, practical experience.	The emphasis is on hands-on learning and connecting what you're learning in class with what you're experiencing out of class. If you take a class on aging, for example, you may work with a senior citizen at an assisted living facility to apply what you're learning in class.	If you're particularly interested in hands-on learning, ask your advisor to recommend classes with service-learning components that will benefit you.

The key to successful trial experiences such as internships is the relationship between you and your sponsor in the host organization. If you're not being given enough to do, or not allowed to test your skills in a particular area, speak up. The answer may be put in terms of company policy, or you're "not quite ready for prime time." Nevertheless, you must communicate about these kinds of important issues. No one can read your mind! As you work toward launching your career, keep up with the latest information. Read up on résumé writing and interviewing, networking, hot career fields, and the latest employment trends. Use the information in this chapter to pique your interest, and search further on your own.

FIGURE 13.1

Three Ways to Try a Job on for Size

Group Résumé[9]

Your instructor will provide a sheet of newsprint and several markers per team of three to four students. Your job is to work on the floor, desktops, or somewhere with sufficient space to create a group résumé, highlighting all the characteristics you bring with you as a group that can help you succeed in college. Your combined group qualifications may look like this:

Qualifications:

- 27 combined years of work experience
- background in four different industries
- familiarity with Word, PowerPoint, Photoshop, and Excel
- proven research skills
- eagerness to learn
- well-developed time management skills
- interest in networking with others

After each team has completed the task, hang the newsprint sheets on the walls to create a gallery and present your group résumé to the rest of the class.

Build a Portfolio of Your Best Work

Even though it feels good to progress through your degree plan, and move on from one course to another, it's important to keep a record of each class. A potential employer may want to know exactly what you learned in Principles of Web Design, so that she can tell if what you learned matches the way her company does things. An interviewer may ask you about the course you were most successful in. You don't want to stammer and say, "Uh, let me get back to you on that . . ." You want to sound knowledgeable. Build a portfolio of your best work. Your college may have a formal way to help you do that through a course management system like Blackboard or an online electronic portfolio requirement, for example. If not, begin compiling a portfolio of your own. Keep copies of your best papers or other assignments and write a summary of how each assignment relates to your career goals. If a prospective employer asks you about your writing skills, you can produce a paper on the spot. Or if you bring a laptop with you to an interview, you can access your best PowerPoint presentation, or show a website you designed yourself.

> " **Don't follow your dreams; chase them.** "
>
> *Attributed to Richard Dumb*

MichaelSvoboda/iStockphoto.com

Network, Network, Network!

The old saying is partially true: "It's not *what* you know, it's *who* you know." Who you know *is* important, but what you know is important, too. Another version of the saying, which is more accurate, goes like this: "It's not who you know, it's who you know knows." If you're a Facebook or MySpace addict, put these skills to work as you start to launch your career. Online sites help you "hook up" professionally with people who can help you, like LinkedIn (www.linkedin.com), where you can build an online network of contacts, contacts of your contacts, and so forth. In minutes, you can find thousands of people who know people who work in the industry you're interested in. According to the site, you can connect, stay informed about your contacts and industry, and find the people and knowledge you need to achieve your goals. And of course, instead or in addition, you can network with real people in person, too. Ask people you know about who they know that works in your career field, contact these people, meet for coffee, for example, and pursue networking the old-fashioned (but highly effective) way.[10]

Write the Right Résumé

In today's competitive world, when literally hundreds of people may be applying for one choice position, how should a résumé be written? Can a résumé be solid, but not stuffy? Professional, but still personal? Thorough, but brief? Actually, there's more than one way to write a résumé, depending on how much experience you have in the career field you'd like to work in.

> "To dare is to lose one's footing momentarily. To not dare is to lose oneself.

Søren Kierkegaard, Danish philosopher and theologian (1813–1855)

> **Skills Approach:** If your work experience has little to do with the career field you'd like to enter, but you've learned important skills you could transfer to your new job, use a *skills* approach, as shown in Marcus Brown's résumé.

> **Chronological Approach:** If you have a work history that's relevant, use a chronological approach (that details job by job, what you've done), as shown in Jennifer Ortega's résumé.

chronological arranging information in time order beginning with the most recent job

Take a look and see if you can detect the differences between these two applicants' résumés. Assume they earned the same degree and are applying for the same job.

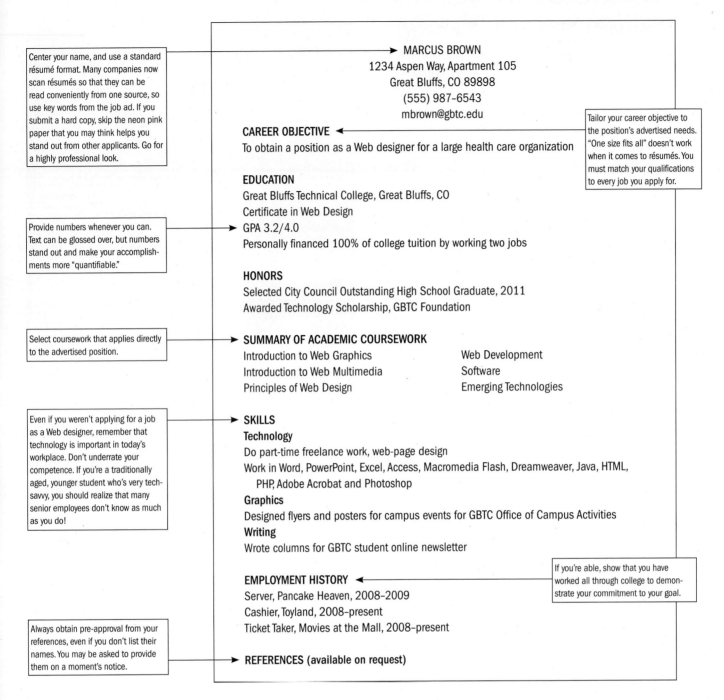

MARCUS BROWN
1234 Aspen Way, Apartment 105
Great Bluffs, CO 89898
(555) 987-6543
mbrown@gbtc.edu

CAREER OBJECTIVE
To obtain a position as a Web designer for a large health care organization

EDUCATION
Great Bluffs Technical College, Great Bluffs, CO
Certificate in Web Design
GPA 3.2/4.0
Personally financed 100% of college tuition by working two jobs

HONORS
Selected City Council Outstanding High School Graduate, 2011
Awarded Technology Scholarship, GBTC Foundation

SUMMARY OF ACADEMIC COURSEWORK
Introduction to Web Graphics   Web Development
Introduction to Web Multimedia   Software
Principles of Web Design   Emerging Technologies

SKILLS
Technology
Do part-time freelance work, web-page design
Work in Word, PowerPoint, Excel, Access, Macromedia Flash, Dreamweaver, Java, HTML,
    PHP, Adobe Acrobat and Photoshop
Graphics
Designed flyers and posters for campus events for GBTC Office of Campus Activities
Writing
Wrote columns for GBTC student online newsletter

EMPLOYMENT HISTORY
Server, Pancake Heaven, 2008–2009
Cashier, Toyland, 2008–present
Ticket Taker, Movies at the Mall, 2008–present

REFERENCES (available on request)

Annotation boxes:

Center your name, and use a standard résumé format. Many companies now scan résumés so that they can be read conveniently from one source, so use key words from the job ad. If you submit a hard copy, skip the neon pink paper that you may think helps you stand out from other applicants. Go for a highly professional look.

Tailor your career objective to the position's advertised needs. "One size fits all" doesn't work when it comes to résumés. You must match your qualifications to every job you apply for.

Provide numbers whenever you can. Text can be glossed over, but numbers stand out and make your accomplishments more "quantifiable."

Select coursework that applies directly to the advertised position.

Even if you weren't applying for a job as a Web designer, remember that technology is important in today's workplace. Don't underrate your competence. If you're a traditionally aged, younger student who's very tech-savvy, you should realize that many senior employees don't know as much as you do!

If you're able, show that you have worked all through college to demonstrate your commitment to your goal.

Always obtain pre-approval from your references, even if you don't list their names. You may be asked to provide them on a moment's notice.

It's likely that Marcus Brown is a traditionally aged college student. Notice that he has little experience in the field he'd like to work in after getting his certificate in Web Design. Contrast his résumé with the following one, where Jennifer Ortega has considerable experience working in the IT field. Rather than using a skills approach, her résumé uses a chronological approach that shows everything she's done that's related to the job she's applying for.

You may automatically assume that Jennifer has the advantage over Marcus, but the health care company with the opening may be looking for fresh, new talent, and Marcus should capitalize on his web design freelance work or get an actual internship with a professional web designer. Everyone has to start somewhere. Do your best with whichever approach fits you. Finally, remember that you can hire a professional to write a résumé for you, but if you read up on résumé writing and follow the suggestions here, you can do just fine on your own. Hiring

JENNIFER ORTEGA
789 Breckenridge Court, Apartment C
Great Bluffs, CO 89898
(555) 333-9999
jortega@gbtc.edu

CAREER OBJECTIVE
To obtain a position as a Web Designer in a large health care organization

> Jennifer has had several jobs in the IT field. On her résumé, she lists what she did in each one that might be useful in the job she wants.

EMPLOYMENT HISTORY
2009–present   Technology Helpdesk Manager, Central College
· Developed new phone answering system that increased the unit's responsiveness by 50%
· Oversaw a staff of 10 student technology experts
· Installed software and made troubleshooting visits to approximately 15 faculty offices
   per week

> Numbers are important and memorable! Notice how they stand out.

2008–2009   IT Supervisor, Great Bluffs School District 1
· Coordinated software maintenance in 12 elementary school administrative offices
· Managed a team of 8 technology employees
· Installed financial software to improve budget management at the K-6 level
2004–2008   Sales staff member, Tech 4 U, Great Bluffs, Colorado
· Earned Salesperson of the Quarter Award, Jan–Mar, 2008
· Recognized with Sales and Service Award, June 2008
· Initiated store display rearrangement

> Notice that Jennifer gives specific dates and has listed a variety of things to discuss with an interviewer.

EDUCATION
Great Bluffs Technical College, Great Bluffs, CO
Certificate in Web Design
GPA 3.2/4.0
Personally financed 100% of college tuition

HONORS
Selected student representative to GBTC faculty government
Earned a place on the GBTC Dean's Honor Role each term

SUMMARY OF ACADEMIC COURSEWORK

Introduction to Web Graphics	Web Development
Introduction to Web Multimedia	Software
Principles of Web Design	Emerging Technologies

SKILLS
Technology
Do part-time freelance work, web-page design
Work in Word, PowerPoint, Excel, Access, Macromedia Flash, Dreamweaver, Java, HTML, PHP,
   Adobe Acrobat and Photoshop
Graphics
Design brochures for local health care organizations as a freelancer:
   Forest Hills Rehabilitation Center, Mercy Hospital, and Sunnydale Senior Center
Writing
Write brochure content after consulting with management at these organizations

> Notice that Jennifer starts each phrase with a verb to emphasize action, and that all verbs are in the same tense (past or present).

REFERENCES (available on request)

a professional or going through an employment agency can be helpful, but they can also be expensive propositions. And if they promise you the moon ("You'll have a new job at the starting salary of your dreams in just one week!"), be wary.

Write the Right Cover Letter, Too

Your cover letter should be written specifically for each job you seek—don't just send a form letter to every potential employer. Effective cover letters are addressed to a person, not a position or "to whom it may concern"—you should research the company and find out who you'll be writing to. Then explain the reasons for your interest in the specific organization and identify your most relevant skills or experiences (remember, relevance is determined by the employer's self-interest). If the job description identifies "creativity" as a requirement, make sure you include examples of your creative work. Then express a high level of interest and knowledge about the position.

You may write an application letter for a job you're interested in; a prospecting letter asking about possible job openings; or a networking letter which asks for information and help in your search. Here's a sample opening paragraph for each:

> **Application Letter.** Please accept my application for the (named) position you posted on (name of source). I am confident that my background and skills will prove to be an effective match for your needs. I am anxious to speak with you about the position and our respective goals.

> **Prospecting Letter.** I recently read in (named) Trade Publication that your organization was awarded the (named) Federal Grant for (name of effort). Since I will be graduating from (name of your college) in May, I am anxious to continue my own (name of work) full-time. I would like to discuss the work I have done and how it complements your projects.

> **Networking Letter.** I am most interested in talking with you about the field of (area of interest) to learn more about typical entry-level positions, recommended preparation, and necessary qualifications.[11]

EXERCISE 13.3

Cover Letter Critique

When you submit a résumé, you should send a well-written cover letter along with it. Take a look at the following cover letter from Marcus Brown and critique it. What has he done right, and what has he done wrong? After finding the mistakes Marcus made, rewrite this letter to bring to class or submit to your instructor.

15 September

To Whom It May Concenr,

I'd like to apply for your opening at Anderson-Wallace Healthcare Industries. I have heard a lot about your company and it sounds great. A friend of mine works there, and he said his starting salary was unbelieveable. What exactly do you do at your company? He's told me a few things, but I'm eager to learn more!

As you can see from my résumé, I don't have much experience. But I have just earned my web design certificate from GBTC, and I did pretty well. I want to start my career at a great company like yours.

I hope to hear from you soon.

Warmly,

Marcus Brown

Interview at Your Best

By now, you have probably already been interviewed several times to get a job. But when you're ready to launch your career, you'll be facing interviews for the new job you really want, the one you prepared for by earning a certificate or degree. Often interviewers aren't particularly skilled at asking questions. They haven't been trained on how to interview prospective employees, so they just ask whatever questions come to them. And often, interviewees don't quite know what they're doing either. Of course, you should always be honest, but there are various ways to communicate the same information. Telling an interviewer you "like to work alone" sounds antisocial. But if you say you "like to really focus on what you're doing without distractions," you show dedication to your work ethic. You also need to be aware of real pitfalls to avoid. See what you think of these suggestions.

1. **Play up the positive, and downplay the negative.** A trap question interviewers sometimes ask is, "What's your worst fault?" While you may be tempted to say the first thing that comes to mind, that could be a big mistake. "Umm . . . sleeping too much! I really like to sleep in. Sometimes I sleep half the day away." Not good. But some faults you could identify might actually be seen as strengths: "I have a little too much nervous energy. I'm always on the go. I like to stay busy."

2. **Stay focused.** "Tell me about yourself" is a common question interviewers ask. How much time do you have? Most of us like to talk about ourselves, but it's important to stay on track. Think possible questions through in advance, and construct some hypothetical answers. Keep your answers job-focused: what your long-term career goals are, how this job can help you prepare, what you liked about your last job. You don't need to go into your family background or your personal problems. And it's always a bad idea to bash a previous job or former boss. The interviewer may worry that you'll bring whatever didn't work there with you to this new job.

3. **Don't just give answers, get some.** A job interview is like a first date. Find out what you need to know. If the job is one you're interested in long-term, ask questions such as these three key ones:

   > **What does this company value?** Listen to the answer. Hard work? New ideas? Communication skills? The answer will tell you about the personality of the company.

   > **What's a typical day like for you?** Ask the interviewer. An answer such as "I get up at 5:00 a.m., get here at 6:30 a.m., and go home around 7:00 p.m.—and then I do paperwork all evening" tells you something. This may—or may not—be the job or the company for you.

   > **What happened to the last person in this job?** If you find out he was promoted, that's one thing. But if you learn he was fired or quit, see if you can find out why. Maybe he had job performance problems, or maybe this is an impossible job that no one could do well. Listen to the interviewer. She may be looking for an opportunity to tell you things she thinks are important, too.

4. **Watch for questions that seem to come out of left field.** Some companies like to get creative with their interviewing. Microsoft, for example, is known for asking problem-solving questions, such as "If you could remove any of the fifty states, which would it be? Be prepared to give specific reasons why you chose the state you did." There is no right or wrong answer, although some answers are better than others. ("We should just nuke state X. I had a bad experience there once" would probably concern some people, and naming Washington state, where Microsoft is located, might be a bad choice.) The interviewer just wants to hear how you can think critically and give reasons for your answers.[12] Remember: Today's interviewers are looking for more than technical skills; they're looking for critical thinking skills, problem-solving skills, and creativity.[13]

5. **Don't start off with salary questions.** Make sure the first question out of your mouth isn't, "So tell me about the salary, again? Any way to notch that up a bit?" The last thing you want to do is give the interviewer the idea you're in it for the money. Of course, you are, but not just for that. More importantly, in every job you have, you'll gain experience and knowledge that will always better prepare you for every job that will be a part of your long-term career. Don't start negotiating a salary until you've actually been offered a job.

6. **Negotiate wisely.** If the interviewer asks you to name a salary figure, be careful. Saying "I could probably live on $30,000," when the actual figure the interviewer is authorized to start with is $38,000, has just given the employer the option to lower the salary based on your expectations. A good rule of thumb is: Never name a number. It's always best to ask the interviewer what the salary range for the job is. It's also good to research the salaries of similar jobs, and it's even better to have another job offer you're considering, so that you have choices. Otherwise, you're not negotiating, you're begging.[14]

7. **Know what you're dealing with.** One of the easiest ways to blow a job interview is by doing nothing. Candidates who don't do their homework usually don't pass an interview. If the interviewer asks "So what do you know about the company?" and you reply "Oh, not much, but I'm a fast learner," you'll be perceived to care very little about the outcome of the interview. Go online or read up about the place you'd like to work. Your knowledge, and therefore your interest, will show. And it goes without saying (although here it is, anyway) that you should arrive early, dress professionally, overprepare, and send a follow-up thank-you note or e-mail.[15]

Continuing Your Education

Like Anthony Lopez, perhaps you're exploring the idea of continuing your education. Typically, the more education you get, the more money you can make, the more you can do, and the more responsibility you have. Figure 13.2 summarizes both earnings and unemployment rates by educational level achieved, but the decision to continue is yours and yours alone. You know yourself and your interests best.

By the end of the "FOCUS Challenge Case," Anthony was considering four alternatives: an associate's degree, a bachelor's degree, a master's degree, and a Ph.D. Each level of these four educational paths has distinct differences he needs to know about. Anthony seems to have "found his bliss," and his heart is in the work. He is convinced that being a social worker is the right career field for him. He is motivated, engaged in what he's learning, and looking forward to a career of service. But at what level? Figure 13.3 lists some basic considerations for Anthony. Can you compare his choices to ones you may be considering?

If Anthony thinks he may wish to take the first step beyond getting his associate's degree, he must begin planning now. If his college does offer four-year degrees and he decides to continue there, his choice is relatively easy. If he must transfer to another institution to complete his bachelor's degree, however, he may experience what's called "transfer shock." Courses can be taught differently, classes can be larger, and in a class with several hundred students, the atmosphere can seem more impersonal. According to research, math and science courses, in particular, may seem (and be) harder.[16] The campus itself may have a very different feel to it, and transfer students can feel lost and isolated, which can hurt their academic performance. Anthony must work closely with his college advisor and an advisor at the school where he plans to transfer, to make sure his credits are transferable. His goal should be to make the process as seamless as possible by visiting the new campus now and talking with advisors and professors there. Take control of the situation: Ask for help, if you need it, and get involved in campus life.[17]

FIGURE 13.2

Education Pays

Source: Bureau of Labor Statistics. (2009, December). Available at http://www.bls.gov/emp/ep_chart_001.htm.

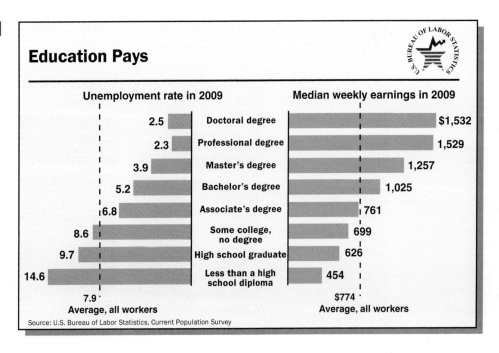

The important thing for Anthony—and for you—is to determine what you really want. Many different educational and career paths exist. Don't feel pressure from others to continue your education if you know that decision isn't right for you—or isn't right for you *now*. Think about your goals in life, what you want to achieve, and what kind of work you would find most fulfilling, and then decide which educational level is right for you.

FIGURE 13.3

An Educational Career Path[18]

	Associate's Degree in Social (Human) Services	Bachelor's Degree in Sociology (or a related field)	Master's of Social Work (MSW)	Ph.D. in Sociology (or Doctorate of Social Work)
Average Time to Complete:	2 years	4–5 years	2 years beyond a bachelor's degree	3–4 years beyond a master's degree
Average Number of Required Courses:	Approximately 20	Approximately 40	10 courses and 900 hours of supervised field experience or internship	10 (plus dissertation)
Type of Work:	Social Service Assistant or Aide, work with social workers, pharmacists, psychologists, etc. Varying levels of responsibility. Help people in need.	Social Worker (although an MSW is increasingly required), help clients cope with disabilities (like substance abuse or homelessness). Work in schools, public health agencies, hospitals, etc. and visit clients in their homes.	Social Worker clinical work, supervise other social workers, manage case loads. Must pass state licensure exam. May wish to go into private practice at least part-time. May specialize in such areas as • Child, family, or schools • Medical and public health • Mental health and substance abuse	Professor, High-level administrator, researcher. May teach at the college or university level, conduct research, or run a health-care or non-profit organization, for example.
Future Demand:	Much higher than average. Expected growth of 34 percent between 2006 and 2016.	Favorable (varies by type of specialization).	Favorable, much faster than average (varies by type of specialization).	Generally good for faculty positions (although varies by type of specialization and preference for full- or part-time work).
Median Salary:	$27,280 (as of May, 2008)	$42,402 (as of May, 2008)	$45,790 and higher (as of May, 2008)	$58,830 (for all full-time college professors as of May, 2008)

Circling the Right Career[19]

Different people are motivated by different types of careers. Think of motivation as three overlapping circles with one circle labeled "Service," one labeled "Power," and one labeled "Money." Anthony Lopez is choosing a career that focuses primarily on service. Power and money are not particularly important to him, it seems. Think of six different careers (several of which you may be considering) and place them on the chart wherever you think they belong. Start with careers that you think belong primarily in one circle, and then brainstorm some careers that overlap into two (money and power, for example). Can you think of any careers that contain elements of all three circles? Then compare notes with your classmates. Where would you put the career you think you would find most fulfilling?

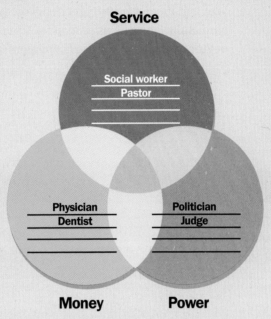

How **FULL** is your plate?

> **Time is the quality of nature that keeps events from happening all at once. Lately it doesn't seem to be working.**
> —ANONYMOUS

Your time management skills are something a prospective employer will be interested in. An interviewer may ask you: "How good are you at juggling many things at once?" or "This is a fast-paced company. Are you willing to work overtime?" It seems that most jobs today require a significant—sometimes frantic—investment of your time and energy. When requests are coming at you from all sides on the job, how will you fare? Can you prioritize?

Hemera Technologies/PhotoObjects.net/Jupiter Images

TRY IT!

At the beginning of each day, decide on three things that must get done, no matter what. Check back at the end of the day to see how successful you've been. If you're a stay-at-home mom, it may be preparing three nutritious meals for your kids. If you're in the workforce, it may be making continual progress on a big project with a deadline. When everything seems to be happening at once, you have to decide which of those things are most important.

Put What You've Learned to Good Use: Twelve Things Employers Hope You Will Learn in College

You must motivate yourself EVERY DAY!

Matthew Stasior, motivational speaker

Regardless of which fork in the road you choose—launching a career or continuing your education—college teaches many lessons, and they're not all about the subject matter in your classes. Many of the important lessons are about broader life skills. Throughout the course we've emphasized some traits that are important to your success both in college and in your career. Let's review this set of twelve things employers care about, regardless of exactly which college courses you've taken or degree you've worked on. Employers want you to:

1. **Be Noticeable.** Start strong. When you show up for an advisor appointment, a first class, or a job interview, you want to create a positive first impression.

2. **Be Observant.** Learn the rules of the game. In school—and throughout your life—you'll be learning what's sometimes called "The Hidden Curriculum." Understand the culture of the organization you work for.

3. **Be Hard-Working.** Exhibit a work ethic. In college, you're at your best when you demonstrate your work ethic. The same will be true in your career.

4. **Be Disciplined.** Manage your time, your money, and yourself. College is about self-responsibility. In many ways, your ability to manage time and money will affect your personal and professional future.

5. **Be Analytical.** Prove you're a problem solver. While taking your college classes, you learn problem-solving skills. On the job, everyone values the person who comes up with a workable solution when others are stumped.

6. **Be Resourceful.** Know how to gather information and use it. In college, you're asked to develop your research skills. On the job you'll use these skills as you consider specific challenges, anticipate possible problems, and develop proposals that take both your research and your analysis into account.

7. **Be Clear.** Speak and write well. Your college career may put more emphasis on these skills than any others. We learn in the competitive world of business that poor speaking, writing, and listening skills will lead people to take their business elsewhere. When you communicate effectively and professionally, you help your organization succeed—and that helps you succeed!

8. **Be Skilled.** Understand that numbers count. Unfortunately, math often gets a bad rap. Many people approach math classes in college fearfully, when actually the ability to work with numbers is one key to success in the world of work. People who know how to use numbers on the job are highly sought after.

9. **Be Knowledgeable.** Study up. In college, you are encouraged to learn deeply, not just memorize facts. Transfer this principle to the workplace. On the job, learn the ins and outs of your industry. All other things being equal, when there's a promotion coming up, the person who has shown a pattern of "studying up" the organization will be the person most often promoted.

10. **Be Remarkable.** Go for extra credit. In some of your courses, your instructors may give extra credit. You could be allowed to do something extra, beyond the requirements on the syllabus, to raise your grade. But what's extra credit in terms of your career? On the job, you earn "extra credit" when you develop and use abilities that stand out.

11. **Be Personable.** Polish your people skills. Your college instructors may assign group projects in your classes to help you learn teamwork skills. Good teamwork skills are key to a successful career in any area! People can be difficult to work with, yet people are the way work gets done. So treating your colleagues with respect, with civility, and with openness is one of the cornerstones to professional success.

12. **Be Reliable.** Do what you say you'll do. When you say you'll do something, do it on time and with real quality. This character trait, reliability, is a cornerstone of professional achievement and recognition. When your colleagues and supervisors learn that they can trust you to do what you say you'll do, you become recognized—and rewarded—as a valuable member of the team.

What Ifs

Life is full of "what ifs?" isn't it? What if you had dated someone else? What if you took the other job? What if things were different?

What If College Isn't Right for You?

What if you decide, after a term or two, that college isn't right for you? Perhaps your heart just isn't in it, and neither is your head. If so, know that you aren't alone. That realization comes to many students. The important question to ask yourself is whether you're really making the right decision, not just getting discouraged if college seems too challenging. Remember that "College is a team sport," and use all of the campus resources available to you before you abandon your efforts. But something other than college may also be the right decision for you—right now at this particular point in your life.

Every adversity, every failure, every heartache carries with it the seed of an equal or greater benefit.

Napoleon Hill, author, Keys to Success:
The 17 Principles of Personal Achievement
(1883–1970)

Improve Your Grade
Online Flashcards
Glossary

ONLINE **TechKnow**

This course is almost over, but the online skills and practices you're developing will carry over into other courses, and even into your jobs during and after college. Carry-over skills—later online work. Almost any career field, you'll be able to use the skills and habits you've formed while taking courses online.

- **Organization and time management**
- **Working ahead**
- **General communication skills**
- **E-mail skills**
- **Information technology skills**
- **Online teamwork**

Here are some cautionary tips on using technology in the workplace—rules that extend those you'll find in your college coursework.

- **Downloading some programs may be prohibited.**
- **Understand that your company has the right to monitor your use of e-mail.** Violating company policies can have serious consequences.
- **Learn your company's policies on the use of electronic devices at work.**
- **Beware of a false sense of security in sending e-mails.** Ask yourself if you would mind if your message was sent to the world. Remember you have no control over where your message goes after you click send.
- **Certain websites can be off-limits.** Let your IT department know right away if you accidentally encounter one of these.
- **Some companies prohibit personal use of office technology.** You may have to use a personal e-mail address for such purposes.
- **You may want to limit your personal use of the Internet to breaks, lunch hours, or time at home.**[20]

What If You Can't Finish a Degree Now?

Even though you have dreams and goals, sometimes "life happens." A turn of events changes everything, a new job consumes all of your time and energy, or someone needs you. Don't feel like a failure if that happens. Take time off, regroup, and come back when you can. Going to college expands your thinking and gives you a whole new take on life. Beyond a certificate or diploma, the learning that takes place in college changes you forever—and it's worth the investment in your future.

My, How You've Grown! Goodbye and Good Luck!

Remember Aunt Ruth (or whatever her name was)? Every time she visited when you were a kid, she remarked about how much you'd grown. Or when you went to visit her, she'd measure you and mark a notch on the wall to compare your height now to the one from last year's visit. She loved watching you grow, and the fact that she noticed made you feel special.

There's no doubt about it. In this first term of college, you have grown. You have gained new perspectives, new insights, and new ways of thinking about things. Like Aunt Ruth, others may notice. If those close to you are threatened by these changes, reassure them that your newfound knowledge hasn't made you think less of them. Remember: "You should have education enough so that you won't have to look up to people; and then more education so that you will be wise enough not to look down on people." If they are proud of you and your accomplishments, and have supported you along the way, thank them!

The important thing is to keep learning and never stop. Continuing to learn—whether in college or in life—is what will determine who you are and what you will become. Learn new things, update your goals, and reinvent yourself. This book, and the course for which you're reading it, have begun that process. Now the rest is up to you!

> People succeed in as many ways as there are people. Some can be completely fulfilled with destinations that are much closer to home and more comfortable. But if you long to keep going, then I hope you are able to follow my lead to the places I have gone. To within a whisper of your own personal perfection. To places that are sweeter because you worked so hard to arrive there. To places at the very edge of your dreams.

Michael Johnson, American sprinter

VARK Activity

Complete the activity recommended for your preferred VARK learning style and bring it to class (or follow your instructor's instructions).

Visual: Create a flowchart that shows long-term planning for how you want your life to go over the next ten years. For example:

Complete degree in → Launch career in → Get entry-level position as → Get promoted to → Continue on for degree in → Complete degree by

_____ _____ _____ _____ _____ _____

Aural: Interview someone in your intended career field or access the CourseMate via www.cengagebrain.com/shop/ISBN/1439083908 to listen to the iAudio summary for this chapter. Be prepared to report back to class or e-mail your instructor the results.

Read/Write: Write up a paragraph for a possible item 11 for the section of the chapter called "Ten Things Employers Hope You Will Learn in College." Read your contribution to the class.

Kinesthetic: Identify a YouTube video that summarizes a lesson you learned from reading this chapter. Why did you choose it, and what is the lesson you learned?

(from top to bottom) Marcela Barsse/MarsBars/iStockphoto.com; Johanna Goodyear/Dreamstime.com; Nadezda Firsova/iStockphoto.com; Pascal Genest/iStockphoto.com

step 3 INSIGHT *Now* What Do You Think?

At the beginning of this chapter, Anthony Lopez faced a series of challenges as a new college student. Now after learning from this chapter, would you respond differently to any of the questions you answered about the "FOCUS Challenge Case"? Using what you learned in the chapter, write a paragraph ending to Anthony's case study. What are some of the possible outcomes for Anthony?

step 4 ACTION Your Plans for Change

1. Identify one new thing you learned in reading this chapter. Why did you select the one you've selected? How will it affect what you do in your college classes?

2. How will this chapter change how you approach your future, no matter which fork of the road you choose as a next step? What will be most challenging for you?

3. How do you plan to increase your skills in college so that you can be more successful in your next step?

REALITY CHECK | What did you **Learn?**

On a scale of 1 to 5, answer these questions now that you've completed this chapter.

1 = not very/not much/very little/low   5 = very/a lot/very much/high

How much do you know *now*?

Now rate your current level of knowledge about topics covered in this chapter.

Launching a career

    1 2 3 4 5

Writing a résumé

    1 2 3 4 5

Continuing your education

    1 2 3 4 5

Knowing what employers really want

    1 2 3 4 5

How useful might the information in this chapter be to you?

How much do you think this information might affect your college success?

    1 2 3 4 5

How much do you think this information might affect your career success after college?

    1 2 3 4 5

How long did it actually take you to complete this chapter (both the reading and writing tasks)?

    _____ Hour(s) _____ Minutes

 Challenge Yourself Online Quiz. To find out how much you've learned, access the CourseMate via www.cengagebrain.com/shop/ISBN/1439083908 to take the Challenge Yourself Online Quiz.

Compare these answers with your answers from the "Readiness Check" at the beginning of this chapter. How might the gaps between what you thought before starting the chapter and what you now think affect how you approach your next term of college?

FOCUS EXIT INTERVIEW

Although you have not quite completed your first term as a college student, we're interested in your reactions to college so far: how you have spent your time, what challenges you've experienced, and your general views about what college has been like. Please answer thoughtfully.

INFORMATION ABOUT YOU

Name _____

Student Number _____ **Course/Section** _____

Instructor _____

Gender _____ **Age** _____

INFORMATION ABOUT YOUR COLLEGE EXPERIENCE

1. **How did you find you learned best in college? (Check all that apply.)**

   ____ by looking at charts, maps, graphs   ____ by reading books

   ____ by looking at color-coded information   ____ by writing papers

   ____ by looking at symbols and graphics   ____ by taking notes

   ____ by listening to instructors' lectures   ____ by going on field trips

   ____ by listening to other students during an in-class discussion   ____ by engaging in activities

   ____ by talking about course content with friends or roommates   ____ by actually doing things

2. **For each of the following pairs of descriptors, which set sounds most like you based on what you've learned about yourself this term? (Please choose between the two options on each line and place a checkmark by your choice.)**

   ____ Extraverted and outgoing   or   ____ Introverted and quiet

   ____ Detail-oriented and practical   or   ____ Big-picture and future-oriented

   ____ Rational and truthful   or   ____ People-oriented and tactful

   ____ Organized and self-disciplined   or   ____ Spontaneous and flexible

3. *FOCUS* **is about 13 different aspects of college life. Which did you find most interesting personally? Which contained information that you found to be most challenging to apply in your own life? (Check all that apply.)**

Most interested in	Most challenging to apply to myself		Most interested in	Most challenging to apply to myself	
____	____	Getting the right start	____	____	Engaging, listening, and note-taking in class
____	____	Building dreams, setting goals	____	____	Developing your memory
____	____	Learning to learn	____	____	Reading and studying
____	____	Managing time, energy, and money	____	____	Taking tests
____	____	Thinking critically and creatively	____	____	Building relationships, valuing diversity
____	____	Developing technology, research, and information literacy skills	____	____	Assessing your major and career
			____	____	Creating your future

4. **Which one of your classes was most challenging this term and why?**

   Which class? (course title *or* department and course number) _____

   Why?_____

   Did you succeed in this class? ____ yes ____ no

   Somewhat (please explain): _____

5. **How many total hours per week did you spend outside of class studying for your college courses this term?**

____ 0-5	____ 16-20	____ 31-35
____ 6-10	____ 21-25	____ 36-40
____ 11-15	____ 26-30	____ 40+

6. **Which of the following on-campus resources did you use once or more this term? (Please check all that apply.)**

____ library

____ campus learning centers (whatever is available on your campus, such as a Writing Center, Math Learning Center, etc.)

____ computer labs

____ the Student Success Center or New Student Center, if one is available

____ the Counseling Center, if one is available

____ instructors' office hours for individual meetings/conferences/help

____ student clubs or organizations

____ none

7. **For the following sets of opposite descriptive phrases, please put a checkmark on the line between the two that best represents your response.**

My first term of college:

challenged me academically	____ ____ ____ ____ ____	was easy
was very different from high school	____ ____ ____ ____ ____	was a lot like high school
was very different from previous college	____ ____ ____ ____ ____	was a lot like previous college
was exciting	____ ____ ____ ____ ____	was dull
was interesting	____ ____ ____ ____ ____	was uninteresting
motivated me to continue	____ ____ ____ ____ ____	discouraged me
was fun	____ ____ ____ ____ ____	was boring
helped me feel a part of this campus	____ ____ ____ ____ ____	made me feel alienated

8. **Please mark your *top three areas of concern* relating to your first term of college by placing 1, 2, and 3 next to the items you choose.**

____ I did not fit in.

____ I did have difficulty making friends.

____ I was not academically successful.

____ My performance disappointed my family.

____ My personal life interfered with my studies.

____ My studies interfered with my personal life.

____ I had financial difficulties.

____ My job(s) interfered with my studies.

____ My studies interfered with my job.

____ My social life interfered with my studies.

____ My studies interfered with my social life.

____ My instructors did not care about me as an individual.

____ I may not finish my degree.

____ I did not manage my time well.

____ I was bored in my classes.

____ I felt intimidated by my instructors.

____ I was overwhelmed by all I had to do.

____ other (please explain) _____

9. **Have you changed your thinking about selecting a major since entering college? Broadly speaking, now which area do you expect to major in?**

____ A bachelor's degree in _____ .

____ An associate's degree in _____ .

____ A certificate in _____ .

____ Other (please explain) _____

10. **How certain are you now of a chosen major (1 = totally sure, 5 = totally unsure)** ____

11. **How certain are you now that you will complete your degree or certificate? (1 = totally sure, 5 = totally unsure)** ____

12. **How certain are you now that you will complete your degree or certificate at this school? (1 = totally sure, 5 = totally unsure)** ____

13. **How certain are you now of your intended career choice? (1 = totally sure, 5 = totally unsure)** ____

14. **How certain are you now about whether you'll transfer to another school? (1 = totally sure, 5 = totally unsure)** ____

15. **What will your grade point average to be at the end of your first term of college?**

____ A+   ____ B+   ____ C+   ____ D or lower

____ A   ____ B   ____ C

____ A−   ____ B−   ____ C−

16. **Which of the following sources of information about college turned out to be most accurate? (Mark your top three information sources with 1, 2, and 3.)**

____ TV and movies

____ friends/family who have already gone to college

____ discussions with teachers/counselors in high school

____ information I received from colleges in the mail

____ talks with my family

____ talks with my friends who are also now starting college

____ the Internet

____ other (please explain) _____

17. **How confident are you in yourself in each of the following areas now? (1 = very confident, 5 = not at all confident)**

____ overall academic ability

____ mathematical skills

____ leadership ability

____ reading skills

____ public speaking skills

____ study skills

____ technology skills

____ physical well being

____ writing skills

____ social skills

____ emotional well being

____ teamwork skills

18. **Why did you decide to go to college? Now that you've experienced your first term of college, how would you respond? (Check all that apply)**

____ Because I want to build a better life for myself.

____ Because I want to build a better life for my family.

____ Because I want to be very well off financially in the future.

____ Because I need a college education to achieve my goals.

____ Because my friends were going to college.

____ Because my family encouraged me to go.

____ Because it was expected of me.

____ Because of active duty military or VA assistance.

____ Because I want to continue learning.

____ Because the career I am pursuing requires a degree.

____ Because I was unsure of what I might do instead.

____ other (please explain) _____

19. **Looking ahead, how satisfied do you expect to be with your decision to attend this school?**

____ very satisfied   ____ somewhat dissatisfied

____ satisfied   ____ very dissatisfied

____ not sure

20. **Did you achieve the outcomes you were hoping to achieve at the beginning of this term? Why or why not?** _____

21. **What was the biggest difference between what you thought college would be like and what it was actually like for you?** _____

APPENDIX

Additional Time Monitors

7:00 a.m. _____	3:00 _____	11:00 _____
7:30 _____	3:30 _____	11:30 _____
8:00 _____	4:00 _____	12:00 a.m. _____
8:30 _____	4:30 _____	12:30 _____
9:00 _____	5:00 _____	1:00 _____
9:30 _____	5:30 _____	1:30 _____
10:00 _____	6:00 _____	2:00 _____
10:30 _____	6:30 _____	2:30 _____
11:00 _____	7:00 _____	3:00 _____
11:30 _____	7:30 _____	3:30 _____
12:00 p.m. _____	8:00 _____	4:00 _____
12:30 _____	8:30 _____	4:30 _____
1:00 _____	9:00 _____	5:00 _____
1:30 _____	9:30 _____	5:30 _____
2:00 _____	10:00 _____	6:00 _____
2:30 _____	10:30 _____	6:30 _____

7:00 a.m. _____	3:00 _____	11:00 _____
7:30 _____	3:30 _____	11:30 _____
8:00 _____	4:00 _____	12:00 a.m. _____
8:30 _____	4:30 _____	12:30 _____
9:00 _____	5:00 _____	1:00 _____
9:30 _____	5:30 _____	1:30 _____
10:00 _____	6:00 _____	2:00 _____
10:30 _____	6:30 _____	2:30 _____
11:00 _____	7:00 _____	3:00 _____
11:30 _____	7:30 _____	3:30 _____
12:00 p.m. _____	8:00 _____	4:00 _____
12:30 _____	8:30 _____	4:30 _____
1:00 _____	9:00 _____	5:00 _____
1:30 _____	9:30 _____	5:30 _____
2:00 _____	10:00 _____	6:00 _____
2:30 _____	10:30 _____	6:30 _____

7:00 a.m. _____	3:00 _____	11:00 _____
7:30 _____	3:30 _____	11:30 _____
8:00 _____	4:00 _____	12:00 a.m. _____
8:30 _____	4:30 _____	12:30 _____
9:00 _____	5:00 _____	1:00 _____
9:30 _____	5:30 _____	1:30 _____
10:00 _____	6:00 _____	2:00 _____
10:30 _____	6:30 _____	2:30 _____
11:00 _____	7:00 _____	3:00 _____
11:30 _____	7:30 _____	3:30 _____
12:00 p.m. _____	8:00 _____	4:00 _____
12:30 _____	8:30 _____	4:30 _____
1:00 _____	9:00 _____	5:00 _____
1:30 _____	9:30 _____	5:30 _____
2:00 _____	10:00 _____	6:00 _____
2:30 _____	10:30 _____	6:30 _____

7:00 a.m. _____	3:00 _____	11:00 _____
7:30 _____	3:30 _____	11:30 _____
8:00 _____	4:00 _____	12:00 a.m. _____
8:30 _____	4:30 _____	12:30 _____
9:00 _____	5:00 _____	1:00 _____
9:30 _____	5:30 _____	1:30 _____
10:00 _____	6:00 _____	2:00 _____
10:30 _____	6:30 _____	2:30 _____
11:00 _____	7:00 _____	3:00 _____
11:30 _____	7:30 _____	3:30 _____
12:00 p.m. _____	8:00 _____	4:00 _____
12:30 _____	8:30 _____	4:30 _____
1:00 _____	9:00 _____	5:00 _____
1:30 _____	9:30 _____	5:30 _____
2:00 _____	10:00 _____	6:00 _____
2:30 _____	10:30 _____	6:30 _____

NOTES

CHAPTER 1

1. See http://www.degreetutor.com/library/distance-vs-local/taking-online-courses;http://www.distance-education.org/Articles/Who-Takes-Online-Classes--Not-Just-College-Students-50.html;http://chronicle.com/article/For-Profit-Colleges-Change/64012/.

2. Balderrama, A. (2009, May 1). The ten best jobs requiring two-year degrees. Available at http://www.careerbuilder.com/Article/CB-1366-Job-Search-10-Best-Jobs-Requiring-Two-Year-Degrees/?ArticleID=1366&cbRecursionCnt=1&cbsid=960a4ed9fa914960bc395ac15340 70d9-322921368-w0-6&ns_siteid=ns_us_g_percentage_of_jobs_re_.

3. Crosby, O. (2002–2003, Winter). Associate degree: Two years to a career or jump start to a bachelor's degree. *Occupational Outlook Quarterly*, 2–13. Available at http://www.bls.gov/opub/ooq/2002/winter/art01.pdf.

4. What's the Difference between an Associate Degree and a Certificate? *Brookhaven College*. Available at http://www.brookhavencollege.edu/studentsvcs/counseling/faq.aspx#q18.

5. Certificate program vs. associate's degree—What's the difference? *Top Colleges Blog*. Available at http://www.top-colleges.com/blog/2007/04/11/certificate-program-vs-associates-degree/.

6. (2007, January/February). Different paths for different majors. Datanotes: *Achieving the Dream*. Available at http://www.achievingthedream.org/_pdfs/datanotes/datanotes-janfeb-2007.pdf.

7. Marchand, A. (2010, 29 March). 6 strategies can help entering community-college students succeed. *The Chronicle of Higher Education*. Available at http://chronicle.com/article/6-Strategies-Can-Help-Entering/64871.

8. Hart Research Associates. (2010, January 20). *Raising the bar: Employers' views on college learning in the wake of the economic downturn*. Available at http://www.aacu.org/leap/documents/2009_Employer Survey.pdf.

9. Shoenberg, R. (2005). *Why do I have to take this course? A student guide to making smart educational choices*. Association of American Colleges and Universities. Washington, DC: AAC&U.

10. Kocel, K. C. (2008, March 12). Advising first-generation college students for continued success. *The Mentor: An Academic Advising Journal*. Available at http://www.psu.edu/dus/mentor/080312kk.htm; Knight, T. M. (2000, May 17). Planting the seeds of success: Advising college students with disabilities. *The Mentor: An Academic Advising Journal*. Available at http://psu.edu/dus/mentor/000517tk.htm.

11. The challenges of remedial education: Views of 3 presidents (2006, October 27). *The Chronicle of Higher Education*. Available at http://chronicle.com/article/The-Challenges-of-Remedial/32361/.

12. (2006, September/October). Developmental education and student success. *Datanotes: Achieving the Dream*. Available at http://www.achievingthedream.org/_pdfs/DataNotes/DataNotes-SeptOct-2006.pdf.

13. Crews, D. M., & Aragon. S. R. (2004). Influence of a community college developmental education writing course on academic performance. *Community College Review, 32*(2), 1–18.

14. Dweck, C. S. (2006). *Mindset: The new psychology of success*. New York: Random House, 104–105.

15. Employment Projections—2008–2018 Summary. Available at http://www.bls.gov/news.release/ecopro.nr0.htm.

16. Rampell, C. (2009, July 13). Preparing today's workers or tomorrow's jobs. *The New York Times*. Available at http://economix.blogs.nytimes.com/2009/07/13/preparing-todays-workers-for-tomorrows-jobs/.

17. (2006, July). Fact Sheet. Community Colleges: Challenges and Benefits. *Achieving the Dream*. Available at http://www.lee.edu/atd/pdf/FS-ChallengeBenefit.pdf.

18. (2005, July). Fact Sheet: Characteristics and challenges of community college. *Achieving the Dream*. Available at http://www.diverseeducation.com/artman/publish/article_6422.shtml.

19. Omara-Otunnu, E. (2006, July 24). Conference examines transition from high school to college. University of Connecticut *Advance*. Available at http://advance.uconn.edu/2006/060724/06072407.htm.

20. Pascarella, E. T., Pierson, C. T., Wolniak, G. C., & Terenzini, P. T. (2004). First-generation college students: Additional evidence on college experiences and outcomes. *Journal of Higher Education, 75*(3), 249–284.

21. Tyler, M. D., Johns, K Y. (2009). From First-Generation College Student to First Lady. *Diverse Issues in Higher Education Psychology, 25*(25). Available at http://diverseeducation.com/article/12184/.

22. Based on Lynch, M. M. (2004). *Learning online: A guide to success in the virtual classroom*. New York: Routledge Falmer, 18.

23. Bal, F. T., Zhang, S., & Tachlyama, G. T. (2008). Effects of a self-regulated learning course on the academic performance and graduation rate of college students in an academic support program. *Journal of College Reading and Learning, 39*(1), 54–73; O'Gara, L., Karp, M. M., & Hughes, K. L. (2009). Student success courses in the community college: An exploratory study. *Community College Review, 36*(3), 195–218.

CHAPTER 2

1. Multi-tasking adversely affects brain's learning, UCLA psychologists report. (2006, July 26). *ScienceDaily*. Available: http://www.sciencedaily.com/releases/2006/07/060726083302.htm; Hamilton, J. (2008, October 9). Multitasking teens may be muddling their brains. *NPR Morning Edition*. Available at http://www.npr.org/templates/story/story.php?storyId=95524385; Gorlick, A. (2009, August 24). Media multitaskers pay mental price, Stanford study shows. *Stanford University News*. Available at http://news.stanford.edu/news/2009/august24/multitask-research-study-082409.html; Tugend, A. (2008, October 24). Multitasking can make you ... lose ...um ... focus. *The New York Times*. Available at http://www.nytimes.com/2008/10/25/business/yourmoney/25shortcuts.html; Pennebaker, R. (2009, August 30). The mediocre multitasker. *The New York Times*. Available at http://www.nytimes.com/2009/08/30/weekinreview/30pennebaker.html; Glenn, D. (2010, February 28). Divided attention. *The Chronicle of Higher Education*. Available at http://chronicle.com/article/Scholars-Turn-Their-Attention/63746/.

2. Spielberg finally to graduate. (2002, May 15). BBC News. Available at http://news.bbc.co.uk/2/hi/entertainment/1988770.stm.

3. Staley, C. (2003). *50 ways to leave your lectern*, "Spending Time," 54.

4. Davis, J. R. (1993). *Better teaching, more learning*. Phoenix, AZ: Oryx Press.

5. French, B. F., & Oakes, W. (2003). Measuring academic intrinsic motivation in the first year of college: Reliability and validity evidence for a new instrument. *Journal of the First-Year Experience, 15*(1), 83–102; French, B. F. Executive summary of instruments utilized with system-wide first-year seminars. Policy Center on the First Year of College.; French, B. F., Immerkus, J. C., & Oakes, W. C. (2005). An examination of indicators of engineering students' success and persistence. *Journal of Engineering Education, 94*(4), 419–425.

6. Based on DuVivier, R. (2009). *100% online student success*. Clifton Park, NY: Delmar Cengage Learning, 12.

7. Based on Harrell, K. (2003). *Attitude is everything: 10 life-changing steps to turning attitude into action*. New York: HarperBusiness.

8. Dweck, C. S. (2000). *Self-theories: Their role in motivation, personality, and development.* New York: Psychology Press, 1.

9. Berglas, S. & Jones, E. E. (1978). Drug choice as a self-handicapping strategy in response to noncontingent success. *Journal of Personality and Social Psychology, 36,* 405–417; Jones, E. E. & Berglas, S. (1978). Control of attributions about the self through self-handicapping strategies: The appeal of alcohol and the role of underachievement. *Personality and Social Psychology Bulletin, 4,* 200–206; Dweck, C. S. (2006). *Mindset: The new psychology of success.* New York: Random House.

10. Dweck, C. S. (2000). *Self-theories: Their role in motivation, personality, and development.* New York: Psychology Press; Dweck, *Mindset.*

11. Robins, R. W., & Pals, J. (2002). Implicit self-theories of ability in the academic domain: A test of Dweck's model. *Self and Identity, 1,* 313–336.

12. Mangels, J. A., Butterfield, B., Lamb, J., Good, C. D., & Dweck, C. S. (2006). Why do beliefs about intelligence influence learning success? A social cognitive neuroscience model. *Social Cognitive and Affective Neuroscience, 1*(2), 75–86.

13. Bauer, A. R., Grant, H., & Dweck, C. S. (2006). *Personal goals predict the level and impact of dysphoria.* Unpublished manuscript.

Chapter 3

1. Leamnson, R. (1999). *Thinking about teaching and learning: Developing habits of learning with first year college and university students.* Sterling, VA: Stylus.

2. Caine, R. N., & Caine, G. (1994). *Making connections: Teaching and the human brain.* Menlo Park, CA: Addison Wesley.

3. Shuster, W. G. (2001). Less stress? Yes! *Jewelers' Circular Keystone, 172*(2), 98.

4. Jozefowicz, C. (2004, June). Sweating makes you smart. *Psychology Today,* 56–58.

5. Csikszentmihalyi, M. (2006). *Flow: The psychology of optimal experience.* New York: Academic Internet Publishers; Csikszentmihalyi, M. (1997). *Creativity: Flow and the psychology of discovery and invention.* New York: Harper Perennial; Gross, R. (1999). *Peak learning.* New York: Tarcher.

6. Caine & Caine, *Making connections*; Jensen, E. (2000). *Different brains, different learners.* San Diego: The Brain Store.

7. Brandt, R. (1998). *Powerful learning.* Alexandria, VA: Association for Supervision and Curriculum Development, p. 29.

8. Campbell, B. (1992). Multiple intelligences in action. *Childhood Education, 68*(4), 197–201; Gardner, H., & Hatch, T. (1989). Multiple intelligences go to school: Educational implications of the theory of multiple intelligences. *Educational Researcher, 18*(8), 4–9; Gardner, H. (1983). *Frames of Mind: The Theory of Multiple Intelligences.* New York: Basic Books.

9. Armstrong, T. (2000). *MI and cognitive skills.* Available at http://www.ascd.org/publications/books/100041/chapters/MI_and_Cognitive_Skills.aspx.

10. Law of Supply and Demand. Wikipedia. Available at http://en.wikipedia.org/wiki/Supply_and_demand.

11. Davis, B. (1993). *Tools for teaching.* San Francisco: Jossey-Bass, p. 185.

12. Fleming, N. D. (1995). I'm different; not dumb: Modes of presentation (VARK) in the tertiary classroom. In A. Zeimer (Ed.), *Research and Development in Higher Education, Proceedings of the 1995 Annual Conference of the Higher Education and Research Development Society of Austral-asia (HERDSA), HERDSA, 18,* 308–313; Fleming, N. D., & Mills, C. (1992). Not another inventory, rather a catalyst for reflection. *To Improve the Academy, 11,* 137–149. Available at http://www.ntlf.com/html/lib/suppmat/74fleming.htm.

13. Fleming, I'm different; not dumb.

14. Fleming, N. D. (2005). *Teaching and learning styles: VARK strategies.* Christchurch, NZ: Microfilm Limited.

15. Based on DiTiberio, J. K., & Hammer, A. L. (1993). *Introduction to type in college.* Palo Alto, CA: Consulting Psychologists Press.

Chapter 4

1. Austin, C. (2010). Go with the flow: Fresh ideas for managing time. *Prezi.com.* Available at http://prezi.com/7gypurup9uke/go-with-the-flow/.

2. Eade, D. M. (1998). Energy and success: Time management. *Clinician News,* July/August. Available at http://www.adv-leadership-grp.com/articles/energy.htm.

3. Loehr, J., & Schwartz, T. (2003). *The power of full engagement: Managing energy, not time, is the key to high performance and personal renewal.* New York: Free Press

4. Bittel, L. R. (1991). *Right on time! The complete guide for time-pressured managers.* New York: McGraw-Hill, p. 16.

5. DeMaio, S. (2009). The art of the self-imposed deadline. *Harvard Business Review.* Available at http://blogs.hbr.org/demaio/2009/03/the-art-of-the-selfimposed-dea.html.

6. Bittel, Right on time! p. 16.

7. Astin, A. W., Astin, H. S., Lindholm, J. A., & Bryant, A. N. (2005). *The spiritual life of college students: A national study of college students' search for meaning and purpose.* Los Angeles: Higher Education Research Institute, UCLA; http://spirituality.ucla.edu/; Crosby, J. (2010, April 4). College students struggle with religion and spirituality. *Cape Cod Times.* Available at http://www.capecodonline.com/apps/pbcs.dll/article?AID=/20100404/LIFE/4040307/-1/NEWSMAP.

8. Loehr, The power of full engagement.

9. Nathan, R. (2005). *My freshman year: What a professor learned by becoming a student.* Ithaca, NY: Cornell University Press.

10. Based on Covey, S. R., Merrill, A. R., & Merrill, R. R. (1996). *First things first: To live, to love, to learn, to leave a legacy.* New York: Free Press, 37.

11. Fortino, M. (2001). *E-mergency.* Groveland, CA: Omni Publishing.

12. Hobbs, C. R. (1987). *Time power.* New York: Harper & Row, pp. 9–10.

13. Based on Berglas, S. (2004, June). Chronic time abuse. *Harvard Business Review,* 90–92.

14. Solomon, L. J., & Rothblum, E. D. (1984). Academic procrastination: Frequency and cognitive-behavioral correlates. *Journal of Counseling Psychology, 31,* 503–509.

15. Hoover, E. (2005, December 9). Tomorrow I love ya! *The Chronicle of Higher Education, 52*(16), A30–32.

16. Ferrari, J. R., McCown, W. G., & Johnson, J. (2002). *Procrastination and task avoidance: Theory, research, and treatment.* New York: Springer Publishing.

17. Hoover, Tomorrow I love ya!.

18. Sandholtz, K., Derr, B., Buckner, K., & Carlson, D. (2002). *Beyond juggling: Rebalancing your busy life.* San Francisco: Berrett-Koehler Publishers.

19. Adapted from Sandholtz et al., *Beyond juggling.*

20. Farrell, E. F. (2005, February 4). More students plan to work to help pay for college. *The Chronicle of Higher Education, 51*(22), A1. Available online at http://chronicle.com/weekly/ v51i22/22a00101.htm.

21. McFaddon, L (2009, August 20). 8 major benefits of new credit card law. *Bankrate.com.* Available at http://www.bankrate.com/finance/credit-cards/8-major-benefits-of-new-credit-card-law-1.aspx.

22. Norvilitis, J. M., & Santa Maria, P. (2002). Credit card debt on college campuses: Causes, consequences, and solutions. *College Student Journal, 36*(3), 356–364.

23. Choosing a credit card. The Federal Reserve Board. Available at http://www.federalreserve.gov/pubs/shop/default.htm.

24. Muller, K. *New credit card laws (2009) and students.ezine@articles.com*. Available at http://ezinearticles.com/?New-Credit-Card-Laws-(2009)-And-Students&id=2410035; Miranda. (2009, May 21). Credit CARD Act of 2009: How it affects you. Personaldividends.com. Available at http://personaldividends.com/money/miranda/credit-card-act-of-2009-how-it-affects-you.

25. Kantrowitz, M. (2007). *FAQs about financial aid. FinAid: The Smart Student Guide to Financial Aid*. Available at http://www.finaid.org/questions/faq.html.

CHAPTER 5

1. Halx, M. D., & Reybold, E. (2005). A pedagogy of force: Faculty perspective of critical thinking capacity in undergraduate students. *The Journal of General Education, 54*(4), 293–315.

2. Walkner, P., & Finney, N. (1999). Skill development and critical thinking in higher education. *Teaching in Higher Education, 4*(4), 531–548.

3. Diestler, S. (2001). *Becoming a critical thinker: A user friendly manual*. Upper Saddle River, NJ: Prentice Hall.

4. Perry, J. (1995–2008). *Procrastination and perfectionism*. Philosophy Talk @Stanford. Available at http://www.structuredprocrastination.com/light/perfectionism.php

5. Falcione, P. A. (1998). *Critical thinking: What it is and why it counts*. Millbrae, CA: California Academic Press.

6. Twale, D., & Sanders, C. S. (1999). Impact of non-classroom experiences on critical thinking ability. *NASPA Journal, 36*(2), 133–146.

7. Thomas, C., & Smoot, G. (1994, February/March). Critical thinking: A vital work skill. *Trust for Educational Leadership, 23*, 34–38.

8. Kaplan-Leiserson, E. (2004). Workforce of tomorrow: How can we prepare all youth for future work success? *Training & Development, 58*(4), 12–14. 13. Based in part on Brookfield, S. D. (1987). *Developing critical thinkers: Challenging adults to explore alternative ways of thinking and acting*. San Francisco: Jossey-Bass.

9. Van den Brink-Budgen, R. (2000). *Critical thinking for students*. (3rd ed.). Oxford: How to Books; Ruggiero, V. R. (2001). *Becoming a critical thinker*. (4th ed.). Boston: Houghton Mifflin.

10. Blakey, E., & Spence, S. (1990). Developing metacognition. ERIC Clearinghouse on Information Resources, Syracuse NY. Available at http://www.vtaide.com/png/ERIC/Metacognition.htm.

11. Florida, R. (2002). *The rise of the creative class: And how it's transforming work, leisure, community and everyday life*. New York: Basic Books, xii.

12. Sternberg. R. J. (2004). Teaching college students that creativity is a decision. *Guidance & Counseling, 19*(4), 196–200.

13. Rowe, A. J. (2004). *Creative intelligences: discovering the innovative potential in ourselves and others*. Upper Saddle, NJ: Pearson Education, pp. 3–6, 34.

14. Michalko, M. (2001). *Cracking creativity: The secrets of creative genius*. Berkeley, CA: Ten Speed Press.

15. Pink, D. (2006). *A whole new mind*. New York: Riverhead Books, 1.

16. Adapted from Adler, R., & Proctor, R. F. II (2011). *Looking out/Looking in*. (13th ed.) New York: Holt, Rinehart, and Winston, 110–116.

17. Douglas, J. H. (1977). The genius of everyman (2): Learning creativity. *Science News, 111*(8), 284–288.

18. Harris, R. (1998). Introduction to creative thinking. VirtualSalt. Available at http://www.virtualsalt.com/crebook1.htm.

19. Eby, D. Creativity and flow psychology. Talent Development Resources. Available at http://talentdevelop.com/articles/Page8.html.

CHAPTER 6

1. Guess, A. (2007, September 17). Students' 'Evolving' use of technology. Inside Higher Ed. Available at http://www.insidehighered.com/layout/set/print/news/2007/09/17/it; (2007, September). Key findings: The ECAR study of undergraduate students and information technology, 2007. Educause. Available at http://net.educause.edu/ir/library/pdf/ERS0706/ekf0706.pdf; Smith, S. D., Salalway, G., & Caruso, J. B. (2009, October). *Key findings: The ECAR study of undergraduate students and information technology, 2009*. Educause. Available at http://net.educause.edu/ir/library/pdf/EKF/EKF0906.pdf.

2. Roach, R. (2004). Survey unveils high-tech ownership profile of American college students. *Black Issues in Higher Education, 21*(16), 37.

3. Jones, S., & Madden, M. (2002, September 15). The Internet goes to college: How students are living in the future with today's technology. Pew Internet. Available at http://www.pewinternet.org/PPF/r/71/report_display.asp.

4. Internet World Stats. Available at http://www.internetworldstats.com/stats.htm.

5. Billout, G. (2008, July/August). Is Google making us stupid? *The Atlantic.com*. Available http://www.theatlantic.com/magazine/print/2008/07/is-google-making-us-stupid/6868/.

6. (2010, June). Social insecurity. *Consumer Reports: Best and worst computers*, 24–27.

7. Holson, L. M. (2010, May 8). Tell-all generation learns to keep things offline. *The New York Times*. Available at http://www.nytimes.com/2010/05/09/fashion/09privacy.html.

8. Cohen, C. (2009, April 23). 5 clues that you are addicted to Facebook. *CNN News*. Available at http://www.cnn.com/2009/HEALTH/04/23/ep.facebook.addict/index.html.

9. Facebook addiction is needless, yet compelling. *The Volante Online*. Available at http://media.www.volanteonline.com/media/storage/paper468/news/2005/10/05/Opinion/Facebook.Addiction.Is.Needless.Yet.Compelling-1008873.shtml.

10. Greenfield, D. N. (1999). *Virtual addiction*. Oakland, CA: New Harbinger Publications; Yair, E., & Hamburger, A. (2005). *The social net*. Oxford: Oxford University Press; Young, K. S. (1998). *Caught in the net*. New York: John Wiley.

11. (2010, June). Social insecurity. *Consumer Reports: Best and worst computers*, 24–27.

12. Kelly, W. E., Kelly, K. E. & Clanton, R. C. (2001). The relationship between sleep length and grade-point average among college students. *College Student Journal, 35*(1), 84–86; Stein, R. (2005, October 9). Scientists find out what losing sleep does to a body. *The Washington Post*. Available at http://www.washingtonpost.com/wp-dyn/content/article/2005/10/08/AR2005100801405.html; Frisinger, C. (2009, October 24). Not getting enough sleep is more serious than you think. *The News Argus*. Available at http://www.thenewsargus.com/2.5246/not-getting-enough-sleep-is-more-serious-than-you-might-think-1.799912.

13. Guess, A. (2007, September 17). Students' 'Evolving' use of technology. *Inside Higher Ed*. Available at http://www.insidehighered.com/layout/set/print/news/2007/09/17/it; Caruso, J. B., & Salaway, G. (2007, September). Key findings: The ECAR study of undergraduate students and

information technology, 2007. *Educause.* Available at http://net.edu cause.edu/ir/library/pdf/ERS0706/ekf0706.pdf.

14. http://compnetworking.about.com/od/dns_domainnamesystem/a/ domain-name-tld.htm; http://lists.econsultant.com/top-10-domain -name-extensions.html; http://webfoot.com/advice/email.domain.php.

15. Sullivan, D. (2007, March 28). Major search engines and directories. SeachEngineWatch.com. Available at http://searchenginewatch.com/ showPage.html?page=2156221; (2008). Recommended search engines. UC Berkeley Library. Regents of the University of California. Available at http://www.lib.berkeley.edu/TeachingLib/Guides/Internet/Search Engines.html.

16. Caruso, J. B., & Salaway, G. (2007, September). Key findings: The ECAR study of undergraduate students and information technology, 2007. *Educause.* Available at http://net.educause.edu/ir/library/pdf/ERS0706/ ekf0706.pdf.

17. Trunk, P. (2008, July/August). Show me the blog. *Wild Blue Yonder,* 44.

18. Caruso, J. B., & Salaway, G. (2007, September). Key findings: The ECAR study of undergraduate students and information technology, 2007. *Educause.* Available at http://net.educause.edu/ir/library/pdf/ERS0706/ ekf0706.pdf.

19. Jaschik, S. (2008, April 7). Distance ed continues rapid growth at community colleges. *Inside Higher Ed.* Available at http://www.inside highered.com/news/2008/04/07/distance.

20. Bollet, R. M., & Fallon, S. (2002). Personalizing e-learning. *Educational Media International, 39*(1), 39–45; Thompson, G. (2001–2002); Online student induction package. Available at http://oes.online.tafesa.edu.au/ support/induct/conn.htm.

21. (1998). What is research? Available at http://danroh89.wordpress.com/ 2010/01/19/research-methodology-2—reading-1/. *Practical Research* by P. D. Leedy and J. D. Ormrod.

22. Fitzgerald, M. A. (2004). Making the leap from high school to college. *Knowledge Quest, 32*(4), 19–24; Ehrmann, S. (2004). *Beyond computer literacy: Implications of technology for the content of a college education.* Liberal Education. Available at http://www.aacu.org/liberaleducation/ le-fa04/le-fa04feature1.cfm; Thacker, P. (2006, November 15). Are college students techno idiots? *Inside Higher Ed.* Available at http://www. insidehighered.com/news/2006/11/15/infolit.

23. Ableson, H. Ledeen, K., & Lewis, H. (2008). *Blown to bits: your life, liberty, and happiness after the digital explosion.* Boston, MA: Pearson Education, Inc.

24. Thacker, P. (2006, November 15). Are college students techno idiots? *Inside Higher Ed.* Available at http://www.insidehighered.com/ news/2006/11/15/infolit.

25. Ibid.

26. De Vos, I. (1988, October). Getting started: How expert writers do it. *Training & Development Journal,* 18–19.

27. Bean, J. C. (1996). *Engaging ideas: The professor's guide to integrating writing, critical thinking and active learning in the classroom.* San Francisco: Jossey-Bass.

28. Based on Wood, G. (2004, April 9). Academic original sin: Plagiarism, the Internet, and librarians. *The Journal of Academic Librarianship, 30*(3), 237–242.

CHAPTER 7

1. Burchfield, C. M., & Sappington, J. (2000). Compliance with required reading assignments. *Teaching of Psychology, 27*(1), 58–60; Hobson, E.

H. (2004). *Getting students to read: Fourteen tips.* IDEA Paper No. 40, Manhattan, KS: Kansas State University, Center for Faculty Evaluation and Development; Maleki, R. B., & Heerman, C. E. (1992). *Improving student reading.* IDEA Paper No. 26, Manhattan, KS: Kansas State University, *Center for Faculty Evaluation and Development.* Most Idea Center papers available at http://www.idea.ksu.edu/.

2. Marburger, D. R. (2001). Absenteeism and undergraduate exam performance. *Journal of Economic Education, (32)*, 99–109; Romer, D. 1993. Do students go to class? Should they? *Journal of Economic Perspectives* 7 (Summer), 167–74.

3. Perkins, K. K., & Wieman, C. E. (2005). The surprising impact of seat location on student performance. *The Physics Teacher, 43*(1), 30–33. Available at http://scitation.aip.org/journals/doc/PHTEAH-ft/vol_43/iss_1/30_1.html.

4. Armbruster, B. B. (2000). Taking notes from lectures. In R. F. Flippo & D. C. Caverly (Eds.), *Handbook of college reading and study strategy research.* Mahwah, NJ: Erlbaum, pp. 175–199.

5. Hughes, C. A., & Suritsky, S. K. (1993). Notetaking skills and strategies for students with learning disabilities. *Preventing School Failure, 38*(1).

6. Staley, C. C., & Staley R. S. (1992). *Communicating in business and the professions.* Mahwah, NJ: Erlbaum, 229–236.

7. Kiewra, K. A., Mayer, R. E., Christensen, M., Kim, S., & Risch, N. (1991). Effects of repetition on recall and note-taking: Strategies for learning from lectures. *Journal of Educational Psychology, 83,* 120–123.

8. Brock, R. (2005, October 28). Lectures on the go. *The Chronicle of Higher Education, 52*(10), A39–42; French, D. P. (2006). iPods: Informative or invasive? *Journal of College Science Teaching, 36*(1), 58–59; Hallett, V. (2005, October 17). Teaching with tech. *U.S. News & World Report, 139*(14), 54–58; *The Horizon Report.* (2006). Stanford, CA: The New Media Consortium.

9. Adapted from Mackie, V., & Bair, B. Tips for improving listening skills; *International Student and Scholar Services.* University of Illinois at Urbana–Champaign. Available at http://isss.illinois.edu/students/ englang.shtml#listen.

10. Based on Staley, C. (2003). *50 ways to leave your lectern.* Belmont, CA: Wadsworth, 80–81.

11. Adapted from *Effective listening skills. Elmhurst College Learning Center.* Available at http://www.elmhurst.edu/library/learningcenter/ Listening/listening_behaviors_survey.htm.

12. Palmatier, R. A., & Bennett, J. M. (1974). Note-taking habits of college students. *Journal of Reading, 18,* 215–218; Dunkel, P., & Davy, S. (1989). The heuristic of lecture notetaking: Perceptions of American and international students regarding the value and practices of notetaking. *English for Specific Purposes, 8,* 33–50.

13. Armbruster, *Handbook of college reading and study strategy research.*

14. Van Meter, P., Yokoi, L., & Pressley, M. (1994). College students' theory of note-taking derived from their perceptions of note-taking *Journal of Educational Psychology, 86,* 323–338.

15. Davis, M., & Hult, R. (1997). Effects of writing summaries as a generative learning activity during note taking. *Teaching of Psychology 24*(1), 47–49; Boyle, J. R., & Weishaar, M. (2001). The effects of strategic notetaking on the recall and comprehension of lecture information for high school students with learning disabilities. *Learning Disabilities Research & Practice 16*(3); Kiewra, K. A. (2002). How classroom teachers can help students learn and teach them how to learn. *Theory into Practice 41*(2), 71–81; Kiewra, How classroom teachers can help students learn and teach them how to learn; Aiken, E. G., Thomas, G. S., & Shennum, W. A. (1975). Memory for a lecture: Effects of notes, lecture rate and informational density. *Journal of Educational Psychology, 67,* 439–444; Hughes, C. A., & Suritsky, S. K. (1994). Note-taking skills of

university students with and without learning disabilities. *Journal of Learning Disabilities, 27,* 20–24.

16. Bonner, J. M., & Holliday, W. G. (2006). How college science students engage in note-taking strategies. *Journal of Research in Science Teaching, 43*(8), 786–818.

17. Pauk, W. (2000). *How to study in college.* Boston: Houghton Mifflin.

18. Montis, K. K. (2007). Guided notes: An interactive method of success in secondary and college mathematics classrooms. *Focus on learning problems in mathematics, 29*(3), 55–68.

19. Pardini, E. A., Domizi, D. P., Forbes, D. A., & Pettis, G. V. (2005). Parallel note-taking: A strategy for effective use of Webnotes. *Journal of College Reading and Learning, 35*(2), 38–55. Available at http://www.biology .wustl.edu/pardini/TeachingMaterials/JCRL_spring2005_pardini.pdf.

20. Glenn, D. (2009, May 1). Close the book. Recall. Write it down. *The Chronicle of Higher Education.* Available at http://chronicle.com/ article/Close-the-Book-Recall-Write/31819.

21. De Simone, C. (2007). Applications of concept mapping. *College Teaching, 55*(1), 33–36.

22. Kiewra, How classroom teachers can help students learn and teach them how to learn.

23. Porte, L. K. (2001). Cut and paste 101. *Teaching Exceptional Children, 34*(2), 14–20.

24. Craik, F. I. M., & Watkins, M. J. (1973). The role of rehearsal in short-term memory. *Journal of Verbal Learning and Verbal Behavior, 12,* 599–607.

25. Adapted from Staley, *50 Ways to Leave Your Lectern,* 116.

26. For a list of the top ten online note-taking tools, see Ningthoujam, P. Top ten online note taking applications. Available at http://mashable .com/2008/08/19/online-note-taking applications/.

CHAPTER 8

1. Bolla, K. I., Lindgren, K. N., Bonaccorsy, C., & Bleecker, M. L. (1991). Memory complaints in older adults: Fact or fiction? *Archives of Neurology, 48,* 61–64.

2. Higbee, K. L. (2004). What aspects of their memories do college students most want to improve? *College Student Journal, 38*(4), 552–556.

3. Higbee, K. L. (1988). *Your memory: How it works and how to improve it* (2nd ed.). New York: Prentice Hall.

4. Ibid.

5. Nairine, J. S. (2006). *Psychology: The adaptive mind.* Belmont, CA: Wadsworth/Thomson Learning.

6. Klingberg et al., Computerized training of working memory in children with ADHD.

7. Nairine, *Psychology.*

8. Miller, G. A. (1956). The magical number seven plus or minus two: Some limits on our capacity for processing information. *Psychological Review, 63,* 81–97.

9. Narayanan, K. *The neurological scratchpad: what is working memory?* (2004, July 7). Brain Connection.com. Available at http://brain connection.postitscience.com/topics/?main=fa/working-memory; Kerry, S. (1999–2002). *Memory and retention time.* Education Reform. net. Available at http://www.education-reform.net/memory.htm; Goodhead, J. (1999). The difference between short-term and long-term memory [On-line].

10. Rozakis, L. (2003). *Test-taking strategies and study skills for the utterly confused.* New York: McGraw Hill; Meyers, J. N. (2000). *The secrets of taking any test.* New York: Learning Express; Ehren, B. J. Mnemonic devices. Available at http://www.athens.edu/academymodules/a304/

support/xpages/a304b0_20600.html; Lloyd, G. (1998–2004). *Study skills: Memorize with mnemonics.* Available at http://www.back2 college.com/memorize.htm.

11. Willingham, D. T. (2004). Practice makes perfect—but only if you practice beyond the point of perfection. *American Educator.* Available at http:// archive.aft.org/pubs-reports/american_educator/spring2004/cogsci.html.

12. Tigner, R. B. (1999). Putting memory research to good use: Hints from cognitive psychology. *College Teaching, 47*(4), 149–152.

13. Murdock, B. B., Jr. (1960). The distinctiveness of stimuli. *Psychological Reports, 67,* 16–31; Neath, I. (1993). Distinctiveness and serial position effects in recognition. *Memory & Cognition, 21,* 689–698.

14. Cahill, L. (2003). Similar neural mechanisms for emotion-induced memory impairment and enhancement. *Proceedings of the National Academy of Sciences, 100*(23), 13123–13124. Available at http://www .pnas.org/cgi/content/full/100/23/13123.

15. Dingfelder, S. F. (2005). Feelings' sway over memory. *Monitor on Psychology, 26*(8). Available at APA Online at http://www.apa.org/monitor/ sep05/feelings.html.

16. Noice, H., & Noice, T. (2006). What studies of actors and acting can tell us about memory and cognitive functioning. *Current Directions in Psychological Science, 15*(1), 14–18.

17. Higbee, *Your memory.*

18. Higbee, *Your memory.*

19. Bean, J. (1996). *Engaging ideas.* San Francisco: Jossey-Bass.

20. Higbee, *Your memory.*

21. Caine, R. N., & Caine, G. (1997). *Education on the edge of possibility.* Alexandria, VA: Association for Supervision and Curriculum Development.

22. Berk, R. A. (2002). *Humor as an instructional defibrillator.* Sterling, VA: Stylus; Berk, R. A. (2003). *Professors are from Mars®, students are from Snickers®.* Sterling, VA: Stylus.

23. Schacter, D. L. (2001). *The seven sins of memory: How the mind forgets and remembers.* Boston: Houghton Mifflin; Murray, B. (2003). The seven sins of memory. *Monitor on Psychology.* Available at APA Online at http://www.apa.org/monitor/oct03/sins.html.

24. Tagg, J. (2004, March-April). Why learn? What we may really be teaching students. *About Campus,* 2–10; Marton, F., & Säljö, R. On qualitative differences in learning: I-Outcome and process. (1976). *British Journal of Educational Psychology, 46,* 4–11.

CHAPTER 9

1. Rogers, M. (2007, March-April). Is reading obsolete? *The Futurist,* 26–27; Waters, L. (2007, February 9). Time for reading. *The Chronicle of Higher Education, 53*(23), 1B6.

2. Caverly, D. C., Nicholson, S. A., & Radcliffe, R. (2004). The effectiveness of strategic reading instruction for college developmental readers. *Journal of College Reading and Learning, 35*(1), 25–49; Simpson, M. L., & Nist, S. L. (1997). Perspectives on learning history: A case study. *Journal of Literacy Research, 29*(3), 363–395.

3. Colarusso, K. (2000). Using a faculty survey of college-level reading and writing requirements to revise developmental reading and writing objectives. Kellogg Institute final report, practicum 1999 (ERIC Document Reproduction Service No. ED448823)

4. Bean, J. C. (1996). *Engaging ideas: The professor's guide to integrating writing, critical thinking, and active learning in the classroom.* San Francisco: Jossey-Bass; Wood, N. V. (1997). College reading instruction as reflected by current reading textbooks. *Journal of College Reading and Learning, 27*(3). 79–95.

5. Saumell, L., Hughes, M. T., & Lopate, K. (1999). Under-prepared college students' perceptions of reading: Are their perceptions different than other students? *Journal of College Reading and Learning, 29*(2), 123–125.

6. Smith, B. D. (2006). *Breaking through college reading.* New York: Pearson Education, Inc., 351.

7. Paulson, E. J. (2006). Self-selected reading for enjoyment as a college developmental reading approach. *Journal of College Reading and Learning, 36*(2), 51–58.

8. Buzan, T. (1983). *Use both sides of your brain.* New York: E. P. Dutton.

9. Ibid.

10. Sternberg, R. J. (1987). Teaching intelligence: The application of cognitive psychology to the improvement of intellectual skills. In J. B. Baron & R. J. Sternberg (Eds.), *Teaching thinking skills: Theory and practice.* New York: Freeman, 182–218.

11. Based on Bean, *Engaging ideas.*

12. Glenn, D. (2009, May 1). Close the book. Recall. Write it down. *The Chronicle of Higher Education.* Available at http://chronicle.com/free/v55/i34/34a00101.htm.

13. English language. Wikipedia. Available at http://en.wikipedia.org/wiki/English_language.

14. The sounds of English and the International Phonetic Alphabet. Antimoon.com. Available at http://www.antimoon.com/how/pronunc-soundsipa.htm.

15. Al-Jarf, R. S. (2002). *Effect of online learning on struggling ESL college writers.* San Antonio, TX: National Educational Computing Conference. Available at http://scholar.google.com/scholar?hl=en&lr=lang_en&q=cache:nUFnaTizpjgJ:dwc.hct.ac.ae/elearning/Research/Saudi ResearchESL.pdf+ESL+college+success+recommendations.

16. Tessler, L. G. (1997). *How college students with learning disabilities can advocate for themselves.* LD OnLine. Available at http://www.ldonline.org/article/6136.

17. Mangrum, C. T., & Strichart, S. S. (Eds.) (1997). *Peterson's guide to colleges with programs for students with learning disabilities.* Princeton, NJ: Peterson's Guide.

18. Strichart, S. S., & Mangrum, C. T. II. (2002). *Teaching learning strategies and study skills to students with learning disabilities, attention deficit disorder, or special needs.* (3rd ed) Boston: Allyn and Bacon; Learning Disabilities Online. Available at http://ldonline.org; Sousa, D. A. (2001). How the special needs brain learns. Thousand Oaks, CA: Corwin Press.

19. Soldner, L. B. (1997). Self-assessment and the reflective reader. *Journal of College Reading and Learning, 28*(1), 5–11.

20. VanBlerkom, M. L., & VanBlerkom, D. L. (2004). Self-monitoring strategies used by developmental and non-developmental college students. *Journal of College Reading and Learning, 34*(2), 42–50.

21. Melchenbaum, D., Burland, S., Gruson, L., & Cameron, R. (1985). Metacognitive assessment. In S. Yussen (Ed.), *The growth of reflection in children.* Orlando, FL: Academic Press, 5.

22. Hall, C. W. (2001). A measure of executive processing skills in college students. *College Student Journal, 35*(3), 442–450; Taylor, S. (1999). Better learning through better thinking: Developing students' metacognitive abilities. *Journal of College Reading and Learning, 30*(1), 34–45.

23. Learning to learn. Study Guides and Strategies. Available at http://www.studygs.net/metacognition.htm.

24. Simpson, M. L. (1994/1995). Talk throughs: A strategy for encouraging active learning across the content areas. *Journal of Reading, 38*(4), 296–304.

25. How Air Traffic Control Works. Available at http://travel.howstuffworks.com/air-traffic-control.htm.

26. Glenn, D. (2010, February 7). How students can improve by studying themselves. *The Chronicle of Higher Education.* Available at http://chronicle.com/article/Struggling-Students-Can/64004/?sid=pm&utm_source=pm&utm_medium=en.

27. Elias, M. (2004, April 5). Frequent TV watching shortens kids' attention spans. *USA Today.* Available at http://www.usatoday.com/news/health/2004-04-05-tv-kids-attention-usat_x.htm.

28. Bol, L., Warkentin, R. W., Nunnery, J. A., & O'Connell, A. A. (1999). College students' study activities and their relationship to study context, reference course, and achievement. *College Student Journal, 33*(4). 608–622.

29. When students study makes a difference too. (2005, November). *Recruitment & Retention.*

30. Trainin, G., & Swanson, H. L. (2005). Cognition, meta-cognition, and achievement of college students with learning disabilities. *Learning Disability Quarterly, 28*, 261–272.

31. Cramming bites. Study Skills for College. Available at http://www.bmb.psu.edu/courses/psu16/troyan/studyskills/cramming.htm; Final exams and cramming. Eastern Illinois University. Available at http://www.eiu.edu/~lrnasst/finals.htm.

32. Meyers, D. (2001). *Psychology* (6th ed.). New York: Worth Publishers.

33. Based on "10 tips to retain more of what you read online." http://vandelaydesign.com/blog/blogging/10-tips-to-retain-more-of-what-you-read-online/; Agger, M. "Lazy eyes: How we read online." http://www.slate.com/id/2193552/.

CHAPTER 10

1. Petress, K. (2004). What do college examinations accomplish? *College Student Journal, 38*(4), 521–522.

2. Coren, S. (1996). *Sleep thieves.* New York: Free Press.

3. Grant, K. B. (2003, September 4). Popping pills and taking tests. *The Ithacan Online.* Available at http://www.ithaca.edu/ithacan/articles/0309/04/news/2popping_pill.htm.

4. Segerstrom, S. C., & Miller, G. E. (2004). Psychological stress and the human immune system: A meta-analytic study of 30 years of inquiry. *Psychological Bulletin, 130*(4), 601–630. Available at http://www.apa.org/pubs/journals/releases/bul-1304601.pdf; (2004, July 4). Stress affects immunity in ways related to stress type and duration, as shown by nearly 300 studies. *APA Press Release.* Available at http://www.apa.org/news/press/releases/2004/07/stress-immune.aspx.

5. Brinthaupt, T. M., & Shin, C. M. (2001). The relationship of academic cramming to flow experience. *College Student Journal, 35*(3), 457–472.

6. Tigner, R. B. (1999). Putting memory research to good use: Hints from cognitive psychology. *Journal of College Teaching, 47(4),* 149–152.

7. Small, G. (2002). *The memory bible.* New York: Hyperion.

8. Counseling and Career Services. (2004). Do you have test anxiety? *Glendale Community College.* Available at http://www.gc.maricopa.edu/ccs/test.html.

9. Tozoglu, D., Tozoglu, M. D., Gurses, A., & Dogar, C. (2004). The students' perceptions: Essay versus multiple-choice type exams. *Journal of Baltic Science Education, 2*(6), 52–59.

10. Schutz, P. A., & Davis, H. A. (2000). Emotions and self-regulation during test taking. *Educational Psychologist, 35*(4), 243–256.

11. Coren, *Sleep thieves.*

12. Perina, K. (2002). Sum of all fears. *Psychology Today.* Available at http://www.psychologytoday.com/articles/pto-20021108-000001.html.

13. Perry, A. B. (2004). Decreasing math anxiety in college students. *College Student Journal, 38*(2), 321–324.

14. Perry, Decreasing math anxiety in college students.

15. Jonides, J., Lacey, S. C., & Nee, D. E. (2005). Processes of working memory in mind and brain. *Current Directions in Psychological Science, 14*(1), 2–5.

16. Ashcraft, M. H., & Kirk, E. P. (2001). The relationships among working memory, math anxiety, and performance. *Journal of Experimental Psychology: General, 130*(2), 224–237.

17. Beilock, S. L., Kulp, C. A., Holt, L. E., & Carr, T. H. (2004). More on the fragility of performance: Choking under pressure in mathematical problem solving. *Journal of Experimental Psychology: General, 133*(4), 584–600.

18. Mundell, Test pressure toughest on smartest.

19. Arem, C. (2003). *Conquering math anxiety,* second edition. Belmont, CA: Brooks/Cole.

20. Glenn, D. (2010, February 7). How students can improve by studying themselves. *The Chronicle of Higher Education.* Available at http://chronicle.com/article/Struggling-Students-Can-Imp/64004/.

21. Firmin, M., Hwang, C., Copella, M., & Clark, S. (2004). Learned helplessness: The effect of failure on test-taking. *Education, 124*(4), 688–693.

22. Heidenberg, A. J., & Layne, B. H. (2000). Answer changing: A conditional argument. *College Student Journal, 34*(3), 440–451.

23. See http://news.bbc.co.uk/2/hi/uk_news/scotland/glasgow_and_west/4755297.stm.

24. Based on Barrett, S. (2009) *Power up: A practical student's guide to online learning.* Upper Saddle River, NJ: Pearson, 82.; and DuVivier, R. (2009) 100% online student success. Clifton Park, NY: Delmar Cengage Learning, 120.

25. Preparing for tests and exams. (2007). York University. Available at http://www.yorku.ca/cdc/lsp.skillbuilding/exams.html#Multiple.

26. Taking exams. Brockport High School. Available at http://www.frontiernet.net/~jlkeefer/takgexm.html. Adapted from Penn State University; On taking exams. University of New Mexico. Available at http://www.unm.edu/~quadl/college_learning/taking_exams.html; Lawrence, J. (2006). Tips for taking examinations. Lawrence Lab Homepage. Available at http://cobamide2.bio.pitt.edu/testtips.htm; The multiple choice exam. (2003). Counselling Services, University of Victoria. Available at http://www.coun.uvic.ca/learning/exams/multiple-choice.html; General strategies for taking essay tests. GWired. Available at http://gwired.gwu.edu/counsel/asc/index.gw/Site_ID/46/Page_ID/14565/; Test taking tips: Guidelines for answering multiple-choice questions. Arizona State University. Available at http://neuer101.asu.edu/additionaltestingtips.htm; Landsberger, J. (2007). True/false tests. Study Guides and Strategies. Available at http://www.studygs.net/tsttak2.htm; Landsberger, J. (2007). Multiple choice tests. Study Guides and Strategies. Available at http://www.studygs.net/tsttak3.htm; Landsberger, J. (2007). The essay exam. Study Guides and Strategies. Available at http://www.studygs.net/tsttak4.htm; Landsberger, J. (2007). Short answer tests. Study Guides and Strategies. Available at http://www.studygs.net/tsttak5.htm; Landsberger, J. (2007). Open book tests. Study Guides and Strategies. Available at http://www.studygs.net/tsttak7.htm; Rozakis, L. (2003). *Test-taking strategies and study skills for the utterly confused.* New York: McGraw-Hill; Meyers, J. N. (2000). *The secrets of taking any test.* New York: Learning Express; Robinson, A. (1993). *What smart students know.* New York: Crown Trade Paperbacks.

27. Plagiarism.org. Available at http://www.plagiarism.org/facts.html; A cheating crisis in America's schools. (2007, 29 April). ABC News. Available at http://abcnews.go.com/Primetime/story?id=132376&page=1.

28. Young, J. R. (2010, March 28). High tech cheating on homework abounds. *The Chronicle of Higher Education.* Available at http://chronicle.com/article/High-Tech-Cheating-on-Homew/64857/.

29. Caught cheating. (2004, April 29). *Primetime Live,* ABC News Transcript. Interview of college students by Charles Gibson; Zernike, K. (2002, November 2). With student cheating on the rise, more colleges are turning to honor codes. *The New York Times,* Q10, column 1, National Desk; Warren, R. (2003, October 20). Cheating: An easy way to cheat yourself. The Voyager via U-Wire. University Wire (www.uwire.com); Thomson, S. C. (2004, February 13). Heyboer, K. (2003, August 23). Nearly half of college students say Internet plagiarism isn't cheating. *The Star-Ledger* Newark, NJ.

CHAPTER 11

1. Some situation topics suggested at Hay Group Transforming Learning EI Quiz. *Haygroup.com.* Available at http://www.haygroup.com/leadershipandtalentondemand/Demos/EI_Quiz.aspx.

2. Gardner, H. (1993). *Multiple intelligences: The theory in practice.* New York: Basic Books; Checkley, K. (1997). The first seven . . . and the eighth: A conversation with Howard Gardner. Expanded Academic ASAP (online database). Original Publication: *Education,* 116.

3. Parker, J. D. A., Duffy, J. M., Wood, L. M., Bond, B. J., & Hogan, M. J. (2005). Academic achievement and emotional intelligence: Predicting the successful transition from high school to university. *Journal of the First Year Experience & Students in Transition 17*(1), 67–78; Schutte, N. S., & Malouff, J. (2002). Incorporating emotional skills content in a college transition course enhances student retention. *Journal of the First Year Experience & Students in Transition 14*(1), 7–21.

4. EQ-i:S™ Post Secondary, Multi-Health Systems, Inc. North Tonawanda, NY. Available at http://www.mhs.com. Used with permission.

5. Turning lemons into lemonade: Hardiness helps people turn stressful circumstances into opportunities. (2003, December 22). *Psychology Matters.* Available at *APA Online* at http://www.apa.org/research/action/lemon.aspx; Marano, H. E. (2003). The art of resilience. *Psychology Today.* Available at http://www.psychologytoday.com/articles/pto-20030527-000009.html; Fischman, J. (1987). Getting tough: Can people learn to have disease-resistant personalities? *Psychology Today, 21,* 26–28; Friborg, O., Barlaug, D., Martinussen, M., Rosenvinge, J. H., & Hjemdal, O. (2005). Resilience in relation to personality and intelligence. *International Journal of Methods in Psychiatric Research, 14*(1), 29–42; Schulman, P. (1995). Explanatory style and achievement in school and work. In G. M. Buchanan & M. E. P. Seligman (Eds.), *Explanatory style* (pp. 159–171). Hillsdale, NJ: Lawrence Erlbaum; American Psychological Association. (1997). Learned optimism yields health benefits. *Discovery Health.* Available at http://health.discovery.com/centers/mental/articles/optimism/optimism.html.

6. Cherniss, C. (2000). *Emotional Intelligence: What it is and why it matters.* Paper presented at the Annual Meeting of the Society for Industrial and Organizational Psychology, New Orleans, LA. Available at http://www.eiconsortium.org/research/what_is_emotional_intelligence.htm.

7. Ibid.

8. Goleman, D. (2002, June 16). Could you be a leader? *Parade Magazine,* 4–6.

9. Boyatzis, R. E., Cowan, S. S., & Kolb, D. A. (1995). *Innovations in professional education: Steps on a journey from teaching to learning.* San Francisco: Jossey-Bass.

10. Saxbe, D. (2004, November/December). The socially savvy. *Psychology Today.* Available at http://www.psychologytoday.com/articles/pto-3636.html.

11. Kelly, W. E. (2003). Worry content associated with decreased sleep length among college students: Sleep deprivation leads to increased worrying. *College Student Journal, 37,* 93–95.

12. Cramer, D. (2004). Satisfaction with a romantic relationship, depression, support and conflict. *Psychology and Psychotherapy: Theory, Research and Practice, 77*(4), 449–461.

13. Ibid.

14. Fisher, H. (2004). *Why we love.* New York: Henry Holt.

15. Beach, S. R. H., & Tesser, A. (1988). Love in marriage; a cognitive account. In R. J. Sternberg & M. L. Barnes (Eds.), *The Psychology of Love.* 330–355 New Haven, CT: Yale University Press; Hatfield, E., & Walster, G. W. (1978). *A new look at love.* Lanham, MD: University Press of America.

16. Rath, T., & Clifton, D. O. (2004). *How full is your bucket?* New York: Gallup Press.

17. Parker-Pope, T. (2009, April 20). What are friends for? A longer life. *The New York Times.* Available at http://www.nytimes.com/2009/04/21/health/21well.html?_r=1; Ybarra, O., Burnstein, E., Winkielman, P., Keller, M. C., Manis, M. Chan, E., & Rodriguez, J. (2008). Mental exercising through simple socializing: Social interaction promotes general cognitive functioning. *Personality and Social Psychology Bulletin, 34,* 248–259.

18. Knox, D., Schacht, C., & Zusman, M. E. (1999, March). Love relationships among college students. *College Student Journal, 33*(1), 149–154. Available at http://findarticles.com/p/articles/mi_m0FCR/is_1_33/ai_62894068/.

19. Schwartz, P. (2003, May–June). Love is not all you need. *Psychology Today.* Available at http://www.psychologytoday.com/articles/200302/love-is-not-all-you-need.

20. Bach, G. R., & Goldberg, H. (1974). *Creative aggression: The art of assertive living.* Garden City, NJ: Doubleday; Bach, G. R. & Wyden, P. (1972). *The intimate enemy: How to fight fair in love and marriage.* New York: Avon; Bach, G. R., Deutsch, R. M., (1985). *Stop! You're driving me crazy.* New York: Berkley Publishing Group; Tucker-Ladd, C. E. (1996–2006); *Driving each other crazy.* Psychological self-help. Available at http://psychologicalselfhelp.org/Chapter9/chap9_90.html.

21. Fisher, *Why we love.*

22. Fisher, R., & Brown, S. (1988). *Getting together: Building a relationship that gets to yes.* Boston: Houghton Mifflin, xi.

23. Wilmot, W. W., & Hocker, J. L. (2010). *Interpersonal conflict* (8th ed.). New York: McGraw Hill.

24. Based in part on Marano, H. (2002). Relationship rules. *Psychology Today.* Available at http://www.psychologytoday.com/articles/200410/relationship-rules.

25. Dakss, B. (2006, March 3). Study: Bad relationships bad for heart. *CBS News.* Available at http://www.cbsnews.com/stories/2006/03/03/early show/contributors/emilysenay/main1364889.shtml. (2005, December 5). Unhappy marriage: bad for your health. *WebMD.* Available at http://www.webmd.com/sexrelationships/news/20051205/unhappy-marriage-bad-for-your-health. Based on Keicolt-Glaser, J. (2005). *Archives of general psychiatry, 62,* 1377–1384.

26. Dusselier, L., Dunn, B., Wang, Y., Shelley, M. C., & Whalen, D. F. (2005). Personal, health, academic, and environmental predictors of stress for residence hall students. *Journal of American College Health, 54*(1), 15–24; Hardigg, V., & Nobile, C. (1995). Living with a stranger. *U.S. News & World Report, 119*(12), 90–91. Available at http://www.usnews.com/usnews/edu/articles/950925/archive_032964_print.htm; Nankin, J. (2005). Rules for roomies. *Careers & Colleges, 25*(4), 29.

27. Thomas, K. (1977). Conflict and conflict management. In M. D. Dunnette (Ed.), *Handbook of industrial and organizational psychology,* 889–935 Chicago: Rand McNally; Kilmann, R., & Thomas, K. W. (1975). Interpersonal conflict handling behavior as reflections of Jungian personality dimensions. *Psychological Reports, 37,* 971–980;

Rahim, M., & Magner, N. R. (1995). Confirmatory factor analysis of the styles of handling interpersonal conflict: First-order factor model and its invariance across groups. *Journal of Applied Psychology, 80,* 122–132; Wilmot, W. W., & Hocker, J. L. (2001). *Interpersonal conflict* (6th ed.). New York: McGraw Hill. Kilmann, R. H., and K. W. Thomas. (1977). Developing a Forced Choice Measure of Conflict-Handling Behavior: The MODE Instrument, *Educational and psychological measurement, 37*(2), 309–325.

28. Miller, G. R., & Steinberg, M. (1975). *Between people: A new analysis of interpersonal communication.* Chicago: Science Research Associates.

29. Staley, C. (2003). *50 Ways to Leave Your Lectern,* Belmont, CA: Wadsworth, 32.

30. Fulbeck, K. (2010). *Mixed: Portraits of multiracial kids.* San Francisco: Chronicle Books.

31. *Race, the power of an illusion.* PBS. California Newsreel. Available at http://www.pbs.org/race/000_General/000_00-Home.htm.

32. Based on "Sorting People" activity at http://www.pbs.org/race/002_SortingPeople/002_00-home.htm.

33. Wyer, K. (2007). Today's college freshmen have family income 60% above national average, UCLA survey reveals. *UCLA News.* Available at http://www.heri.ucla.edu/PDFs/PR_TRENDS_40YR.pdf.

34. Humphrey, D., & Davenport, A. (2004, Summer/Fall). What really matters in college: How students view and value liberal education. *Liberal Education.* Excerpt: Diversity and civic engagement outcomes ranked among least important. Available at http://www.diversityweb.org/Digest/vol9no1/humphreys.cfm.

35. Laird, T. F. (2005). College students' experiences with diversity and their effects on academic self-confidence, social agency, and disposition toward critical thinking. *Research in Higher Education, 46*(4), 365–387.

36. Bucher, R. D. (2004). *Diversity consciousness: Opening our minds to people, cultures, and opportunities* (2nd ed.). Upper Saddle River, NJ: Pearson Education.

37. Moore, D. G. (2003, November 14). Toward a single definition of college. *The Chronicle of Higher Education, 50*(12), B7; Diversity defines new generation of college students. (2009, June 18). *The Chronicle of Higher Education.* Available at http://www.phoenix.edu/colleges_divisions/office-of-the-president/articles/diversity-defines-new-generation-college-students.html.

38. Pusser, B., Breneman, D. W., Gansneder, B. M., Kohl, K. J., Levin, J. S., Milam, J. H., & Turner, S. E. (2007). *Returning to learning: Adults' success in college is key to America's future.* Lumina Foundation. Available at http://www.luminafoundation.org/publications/ReturntolearningApril2007.pdf.

39. Gomstyn, A. (2003, October 17). Minority enrollment in colleges more than doubled in past 20 years, study finds. *The Chronicle of Higher Education, 50*(8), A25; Schmidt, P. (2003, 28 November). Academe's Hispanic future. *The Chronicle of Higher Education, 50*(14), A8.

40. Jaschik, S. (2007, November 28). Growth and consolidation of minority enrollments. *Inside Higher Ed.* Available at http://www.insidehighered.com/news/2007/11/28/minority.

41. Staley, C. (2003). *50 ways to leave your lectern.* Belmont, CA: Wadsworth, 67. Based on Defining "Diversity." (1995). In B. Pike & C. Busse, *101 games for trainers* (p. 11). Minneapolis: Lakewood Books.

42. Carnes, M. C. (2005). Inciting speech. *Change, 37*(2), 6–11.

43. Based on Nilsen, L. B. (1998). The circles of awareness. *Teaching at Its Best.* Bolton, MA: Anker Publishing; Bucher, R. D. (2008). *Building cultural intelligence: Nine megaskills.* Upper Saddle River, NJ: Pearson.

44. Lyons, P. (2005, April 15). The truth about teaching about racism. *The Chronicle of Higher Education, 51*(32), B5.

45. Epstein, G. (2005, June 5) More women advance, but sexism persists. *College Journal from the Wall Street Journal*. Women CEOs. CNNMoney.com. Available at http://money.cnn.com/magazines/fortune/fortune500/2008/womenceos/.

46. Wessel, D. (2003, September 9). Race still a factor in hiring decisions. *College Journal from the Wall Street Journal*. Available at http://usearch.mnscu.edu/news/fw/fw4522FutureWork.html.

47. Beilke, J. R., & Yssel, N. (1999). The chilly climate for students with disabilities in higher education. *College Student Journal, 33*(3), 364–372.

48. Parker, P. N. (2006, March–April). Sustained dialogue: How students are changing their own racial climate. *About Campus, 11*(1), 17–23.

49. Gortmaker, V. J., & Brown, R. D. (2006). Out of the college closet: Differences in perceptions and experiences among out and closeted lesbian and gay students. *College Student Journal, 40*(3), 606–619.

50. Incidences and Statistics. (2005). *Hate crime statistics 2005*. Department of Justice, Uniform Crime Reporting Program. Available at http://www.fbi.gov/ucr/hc2005/incidentsoffenses.htm; *FBI Hate Crime Statistics*. Available at http://www.fbi.gov/ucr/hc2007/table_01.htm.

51. Based on Earley, P. C., & Mosakowski, E. (2004, October). Cultural intelligence. *Harvard Business Review*, 143.

52. Earley, P. C., & Mosakowski, E. (2004, October). Cultural intelligence. *Harvard Business Review*, 139–146; Early, C. P., Ang, S., & Tan, J. (2006) CQ: *Developing Cultural Intelligence at Work*. Stanford, CA: Stanford University Press; Osborn, T. N., (2006). *"CQ": Another aspect of emotional intelligence*. Available at http://www.teaminternational.net/resources/docs/cultural%20intelligence.pdf.

53. Earley, P. C., & Mosakowski, E. (2004, October). Cultural intelligence. *Harvard Business Review*, 139–146.

54. Bucher, R. D. (2004). *Diversity consciousness: Opening our minds to people, cultures, and opportunities* (2nd ed.). Upper Saddle River, NJ: Pearson Education.

55. Dwyer, T., & Flannigan, K. (2001). Web globalization: Write once, Deploy worldwide. Available amazon.com; see http://www.internetworldstats.com/stats.htm.

56. Based on Barrett, S. (2009) *Power up: A practical student's guide to online learning*. Upper Saddle River, NJ: Pearson, 34.

57. http://www.compact.org/.

58. Zlotkowski, E. (1999). Pedagogy and engagement. In R. G. Bringle, R. Games, & E. A. Malloy (Eds.). (1999). *Colleges and Universities as Citizens* (pp. 96–120). Needham Heights, MA: Allyn & Bacon.

59. Honnet, E. P., & Poulsen, S. J. (1989). *Principles of good practice for combining service and learning: A Wingspread special report*. Racine, WI: The Johnson Foundation. Available at http://servicelearning.org/filemanager/download/Principles_of_Good_Practice_for_Combining_Service_and_Learning.pdf.

60. Eyler, J., Giles, Jr., D. E., & Schmiede, A. (1996). *A practitioner's guide to reflection in service learning: Student voices and reflections*. Nashville, TN: Vanderbilt University Press.

CHAPTER 12

1. Gregory, M. (2003, September 12). A liberal education is not a luxury. *The Chronicle of Higher Education, 50*(3), B16.

2. Staley, R. S., II. (2003). In C. Staley, *50 ways to leave your lectern*. Belmont, CA: Wadsworth, 70–74.

3. Farrell, E. F. (2006, December 12). Freshmen put high value on how well college prepares them for a profession, survey finds. *The Chronicle of Higher Education*. Farrell, E. F. (2007, January 5). Report says freshmen put career prep first. *The Chronicle of Higher Education, 53*(18), A32. Available at http://chronicle.com/article/Report-Says-Freshmen-Put-Ca/19260/; Bok, D. (2010, January 31). College and the well-lived life. *The Chronicle of Higher Education*. Available at http://chronicle.com/article/Collegethe-Well-Lived-/63789/; Bok, D. (2010, January 31). College and the well-lived life. *The Chronicle of Higher Education*. Available at http://chronicle.com/article/Collegethe-Well-Lived-/63789/.

4. Associated Press (2007, January 22). Polls say wealth important to youth. WBZTV.com. Available at http://wbztv.com/national/wealth.youth.money.2.277926.html; Schwartz, B. (2004, January 23). The tyranny of choice. *The Chronicle of Higher Education, 50*(20), B6.

5. Koeppel, D. (2004, December 5). Choosing a college major: For love or for the money? *The New York Times*, section 10, p. 1, column 4. Available at http://www.nytimes.com/2004/12/05/jobs/05jmar.html?ex=1259989200&en=51dcc14fa52a65e7&ei=5090&partner=rssuserland; Dunham, K. J. (2004, March 2). No ivory tower: College students focus on career. *Wall Street Journal* (Eastern Edition), pp. B1, B8. Available at http://online.wsj.com/article/SB107818521697943524.html.

6. Based in part on Gordon, V. N., & Sears, S. J. (2004). *Selecting a college major: Exploration and decision making, 5th edition*. Upper Saddle River, NJ: Pearson Education.

7. Based on Hansen, R. S., & Hansen, K. *Using a SWOT analysis in your career planning*. Quintessential Careers. Available at http://www.quintcareers.com/SWOT_Analysis.html.

8. Rowh, M. (2003, February-March). Choosing a major. *Career World, 31*(5), 21–23.

9. Ezarik, M. M. (2007, April-May). A major decision. *Career World, 35*(6), 20–22.

10. To read more about these and other fast-growing occupations, go to http://education.yahoo.net/articles/6_fast-growing_careers.htm; or http://www.careerexplorer.net/ten-hottest-careers.asp?affiliateid=4085&type=&adgroup=&kw=&acctid=&ovkey=&SearchEngine=&Keyword=&AffiliateSite=&SubAffiliateID=&TrackingCode=.

11. Rask & Bailey, Are faculty role models?

12. Based on Staley, *50 ways to leave your lectern*, p. 82.

CHAPTER 13

1. Levine, M. (2005). *Ready or not, here life comes*. New York: Simon & Schuster, p. 4; Levine, M.(2005, February 18). College graduates aren't ready for the real world. *The Chronicle of Higher Education, 51*(24), B11.

2. *Dictionary of occupational titles*. (1991). Washington, DC: Bureau of Labor Statistics. Or see O*Net Online (Occupational Information Network) at http://online.onetcenter.org/find/.

3. Based on Schwartz, The tyranny of choice.

4. See J. K. Rowling Biography at http://www.biography.com/search/article.jsp?aid=9465815&page=2&search=.

5. Levine, *Ready or not, here life comes*.

6. Goldhaber, G. M. (1986). *Organizational communication* (4th ed.). Dubuque, IA: Wm. C. Brown, 236. In Staley, R. S., II, & Staley, C. C. (1992). *Communicating in business and the professions: The inside word*. Belmont, CA: Wadsworth.

7. Adapted from http://www.sc.edu/career/Pdf/jobsearchplan.pdf; and http://www.acinet.org/explore/View.aspx?pageID=20.

8. See Top Job Search Websites at http://wwwcareeroverview.com/job-search.html.

9. Staley, *50 ways to leave your lectern*, 33. Based on "Group Resume." (1995). In M. Silberman, *101 ways to make training active*. Johannesburg: Pfeiffer, 49–50.

10. McConnon, A. (2007, September 7). innetworks: Social networking is graduating—and hitting the job market. *BusinessWeek*, IN 4, IN 6.

11. Adapted from http://jobsearch.about.com/od/resumes/a/coverlet.htm.

12. *Job interviews get creative*. (2003, August 22). NPR. Available at http://www.npr.org/templates/story/story.php?storyId=1405340.

13. Vance, E. (2007, February 2). College graduates lack key skills, report says. *The Chronicle of Higher Education, 53*(22), A30.

14. Ashler, D. (2004). *How to get any job with any major*. Berkeley, CA: Ten Speed Press.

15. Pollak, L. (2007). *Getting from college to career*. New York: HarperCollins.

16. Cedja, B. D., Kaylor, A. J., & Rewey, K. L. (1998). Transfer shock in an academic discipline: The relationship between students' majors and their academic performance. *Community College Review, 26*(3), 1–13.

17. Conde, C. Absorbing the shock: Dealing with the transition between schools. CollegeView. Available at http://www.collegeview.com/articles/CV/application/absorbing.html; Thurmond, K. Transfer shock: Why is a term forty years old still relevant? National Academic Advising Association (NACADA). Available at http://www.nacada.ksu.edu/clearinghouse/AdvisingIssues/Transfer-Shock.htm; Rhine, T. J., Milligan, D. M., & Nelson, L. R. (2000). Alleviating transfer shock: Creating an environment for more successful transfer students. *Community College Journal of Research and Practice, 24*, 443–452.

18. Occupational Outlook Handbook, 2008-2009. Available at http://www.bls.gov/oco/ocos059.htm and http://www.bls.gov/oco/ocos060.htm.

19. Idea from Wallace, P. C. (2005). *Life 101*. New York: iUniverse, Inc., 3.

20. Adapted from Jobweb's "General Rules for Using Technology in the Workplace" at http://www.jobweb.org/studentarticles.aspx?id=2353.

Index